Praise for *Dark Ages America*

"It is usual in sad reports like Professor Berman's to stop abruptly the litany of what has gone wrong and then declare, hand on heart, that once the people have been informed of what is happening, the truth will set them free and a quarter-billion candles will be lit and the darkness will flee in the presence of so much spontaneous light. But Berman is much too serious for the easy platitude. Instead he tells us that those who might have struck at least a match can no longer do so because shared information about our situation is meager to nonexistent. . . . Mr. Berman spares us the happy ending, as, apparently, has history."

—Gore Vidal, "President Jonah," Truthdig.com

"A resounding . . . indictment of all that is wrong with American culture, from arrogance to xenophobia and all points between. . . . Berman fires with both barrels at a culture that, he argues, is rapidly slipping into "second- or third-rate status" as an international power. . . . There's no room for comfort in Berman's critique: If he's right, we're doomed. Hope he's wrong, then, but by all means consider his provocative argument."

—*Kirkus Reviews*

"Berman has put together the most comprehensive critique of how far out on the precipice we stand that I have yet seen. The repeal of Bretton Woods and ensuing devastation of the world economy by finance capitalism play out like Gibbon's great work on Rome. He is relentless in his analysis—and we ignore what he writes at our peril. Maybe it is too late to turn back, but Berman's book draws on commentaries left and right to instruct us on surviving the fall."

—Lloyd Gardner, research professor of history at Rutgers University

"Morris Berman makes a compelling case, at once learned, passionate, and sensible, that the United States is a civilization in crisis, and that it may well lack the ability to face it. Bringing his deep knowledge of social and cultural history to bear, Berman shows that the "shadow" side of America that has always come with America's promise of individualism and reliance on the market and technology—a pervasive deficit of empathy and caring for others and for the public good—has profound implications for its decline as a nation as well as its reckless militarism abroad. Anyone who wants unsparing truth rather than comforting nostrums must read *Dark Ages America*."

—Gareth Porter, author of *Perils of Dominance: Imbalance of Power and the Road to War in Vietnam*

"Drawing heavily on Enlightenment values, modern sociology, and just plain common sense, Morris Berman dissects contemporary American culture with the skill of a heart surgeon. He argues that out-of-control individualism, consumerism, and faith in technology have left Americans vulnerable to both internal corrosion and international attack. *Dark Ages America* is essential reading for anyone grappling with our current set of political, social, and economic dilemmas."

—Ferenc Morton Szasz, Regents Professor of History, University of New Mexico

Also by Morris Berman

The Twilight of American Culture

Social Change and Scientific Organization

TRILOGY ON HUMAN CONSCIOUSNESS
The Reenchantment of the World

Coming to Our Senses:
Body and Spirit in the Hidden History of the West

Wandering God:
A Study in Nomadic Spirituality

Dark Ages America

The Final Phase of Empire

Morris Berman

W. W. NORTON & COMPANY

NEW YORK   LONDON

Excerpt from "Shine, Perishing Republic" by Robinson Jeffers, from *Selected Poetry of Robinson Jeffers*, copyright © 1934 by Robinson Jeffers and renewed 1962 by Donnan Jeffers and Garth Jeffers. Used by permission of Random House, Inc. Excerpt from "Waiting for the Barbarians" by C. P. Cavafy, translated by Edmund Keeley and Philip Sherrard, from *C. P. Cavafy: Collected Poems*, copyright © 1975 by Edmund Keeley and Philip Sherrard. Reprinted by permission of Princeton University Press. Excerpt from "America, America" by Saadi Youssef, translated from the Arabic by Khaled Mattawa, from *Without an Alphabet, Without a Face*; English translation copyright © 2002 by Khaled Mattawa. Reprinted with the permission of Gray Wolf Press, Saint Paul, Minnesota. Excerpt from "Waking Early Sunday Morning" by Robert Lowell, from *Collected Poems* by Robert Lowell, copyright © 2003 by Harriet Lowell and Sheridan Lowell. Reprinted by permission of Farrar, Straus and Giroux, LLC.

For information about permission to reproduce selections from this book, write to Permissions, W. W. Norton & Company, Inc., 500 Fifth Avenue, New York, NY 10110

Manufacturing by R. R. Donnelley, Bloomsburg
Book design by Lovedog Studio
Production manager: Julia Druskin

Library of Congress Cataloging-in-Publication Data

Berman, Morris, 1944–
Dark ages America : the final phase of empire / Morris Berman.
p. cm.
Includes bibliographical references and index.
ISBN 0-393-05866-2 (hardcover)
1. United States—Civilization—1970– 2. United States—Social conditions—1980–
3. United States—Politics and government—2001– 4. United States—Foreign relations
—2001– 5. United States—Economic conditions—2001– I. Title.
E169.12.B3937 2006
973.931—dc22

2005030773

ISBN 978-0-393-32977-3 pbk.

W. W. Norton & Company, Inc., 500 Fifth Avenue, New York, N.Y. 10110
www.wwnorton.com

W. W. Norton & Company Ltd., Castle House, 75/76 Wells Street, London W1T 3QT

1 2 3 4 5 6 7 8 9 0

[We are coming to] a twenty-first-century crisis in America's informal empire, an empire based on the projection of military power to every corner of the world and on the use of American capital and markets to force global economic integration on our terms, at whatever costs to others. . . . What form our imperial crisis is likely to take years or even decades from now is, of course, impossible to know. But history indicates that, sooner or later, empires do reach such moments, and it seems reasonable to assume that we will not miraculously escape that fate.

—Chalmers Johnson,
Blowback: The Costs and Consequences
of American Empire (2000)

Contents

Acknowledgments

I WAS HELPED BY so many people in the course of writing this book that it would be difficult to list them all, but those who were especially generous in terms of suggestions, discussion, or bibliography include James Allsup, Anthony Arnove, Loren Edizel, Robert Fishman, Sarah Frueh, John Henry, Paul Krugman, Leon Hadar, Todd LaPorte, Jochen Leibig, Alex Marshall, Noel Pugach, Gresham Riley, Sylvia Scherr, John Trotter, and Peter Werres. I particularly wish to thank Candice Fuhrman for her continuing moral support, as well as her willingness to act as a substantive editor on the manuscript. A better agent, no author could ever have. Robert Weil, my editor at Norton, has also been a very important ally on this journey, helping me to reorganize and rethink the text in ways that improved it immensely. I also wish to thank Trent Duffy, my copy editor, for his meticulous work, and for saving me from making a number of embarrassing errors. I am additionally grateful to Peter Boltz for taking the time and trouble to read through the entire manuscript and provide me with essential feedback. Kelly Gerling and Ferenc Szasz have been enormously kind and helpful colleagues, supplying numerous references and hashing out ideas with me as the book took shape. Finally, I owe a great debt to the sociology department at the Catholic University of America, where I have been a visiting professor since 2003, and I am especially grateful to Sandra Hanson, who was kind enough to extend the invitation. As is always the case, no one is responsible for the contents of this work other than myself, but I do wish to say thank you to the friends and colleagues who helped make it a reality.

Dark Ages America

Introduction

THE OMINOUS TITLE *Dark Ages America* will very likely be incomprehensible to most of my fellow Americans, especially to those who reelected George W. Bush in 2004. Indeed, for the majority, there appears to be little doubt that America is at the zenith of its military power, capable of shaking up the world as it sees fit and charged with the mission of bringing the light of democracy to the darkest corners of the globe. Does it make sense, they will undoubtedly ask, to talk of a new Dark Age, when American power extends so far and wide?

Yet for some members of this society, the title might not be so far-fetched. For them, the future appears potentially treacherous; they believe that it is not at all clear where we are going as a civilization, or whether we can throw any light on other people, much less on ourselves. These individuals have become quite jittery, or even despondent, about America's terminal decadence. For them, the downward spiral of our culture and the exponential, even cultlike growth of forces that threaten our long-standing secular and humanistic values are causes for increasing alarm. For this segment of the population, then, the title *Dark Ages America* is not likely to be as anomalous as it might first sound.

Of course, it does seem like a gross exaggeration to equate the present (and in my view, final) phase of American history with the Dark or Middle Ages, but I am not trying to be dramatic here. Empires, and civilizations, rise and fall, and they go through a series of stages in the process. We were already in our twilight phase when Ronald Reagan, with all the insight of an ostrich, declared it to be "morning in America"; twenty-odd years later, under the "boy emperor" George W. Bush (as Chalmers Johnson refers to him), we have entered the Dark Ages in earnest, pursuing a short-sighted path that can only accelerate our decline. For what we are now seeing are the obvious characteristics of the West after the fall of Rome: the triumph of religion over reason; the atrophy of education and critical thinking; the integration of religion, the state, and the apparatus of torture—a troika that was for Voltaire the central horror of the pre-Enlightenment world; and the political and economic marginalization of our culture. Of course, the Dark Ages were not uniformly monochromatic, as recent scholarship has demonstrated; but then, neither is present-day America. The point is that in both cases "dark" is the operative word.

To understand what we mean by the term, we need to look, historically, at what constituted the light. In his famous essay of 1784, "What Is Enlightenment?," the German philosopher Immanuel Kant wrote, "Enlightenment is man's release from his self-incurred tutelage," which he defined as his "inability to make use of his understanding without direction from another." *Sapere aude!*, cried Kant; "have the courage to use your own reason!—that is the motto of enlightenment."

These are fabulous words, and the ideals they embody inspired the Founding Fathers and the American Constitution. Commenting on Kant's call to reason, the Israeli historian Shmuel Feiner writes:

> The explosive nature of this brief definition lies in its sweeping criticism of the "old" world, in which man, out of pessimism and passivity, allows the existing order to dictate his life and those possessing religious and spiritual authority to determine for him what is truth. In contrast, the enlightened man is an autonomous, rational, and skeptical person, who has the power to free himself of the shackles of the past and authority, and to pave new and better ways for himself and for all humanity.[1]

My question for the reader is this: in all seriousness, which direction do you believe the United States is going in, at this point in time? My guess is that most of you will recognize this as a no-brainer; but to address the issue in greater depth, it might be instructive to consider the extent to which the four post–Roman Empire characteristics of the West apply to our present situation.

The Triumph of Religion over Reason

With the reelection of George W. Bush, and the prospect of long-term Republican hegemony over American politics, it seems likely that American civilization is now transitioning from the twilight phase I wrote about several years ago in *The Twilight of American Culture* to an actual dark age. Indeed, the British historian Charles Freeman published an extended discussion of this transition as it occurred during the late Roman Empire, the title of which could serve as a capsule summary of our current president: *The Closing of the Western Mind.* Mr. Bush, God knows, is no Augustine; but Freeman points to the latter as the epitome of a more general process that was under way in the fourth century: namely, "the gradual subjection of reason to faith and authority." This is what we are seeing today, and it is a process that no society can undergo and still remain free. Yet it is a process of which administration officials, along with much of the American population, are aggressively proud. Interviewing a number of policy advisers and people who had known or been close to Mr. Bush at one time, journalist Ron Suskind discovered a consensus among them: they felt the president—along with his evangelical base—believes he is on a mission from God and that faith trumps empirical evidence. "A writ of infallibility . . . guides the inner life of the White House," writes Suskind. Thus a senior adviser to Bush said that the White House regards people like Suskind as living in "the reality-based community"—i.e., among people who "believe that solutions emerge from your judicious study of discernible reality." But, he went on, "that's not the way the world really works anymore. We're an empire now, and when we act, we create our own reality."[2]

It sounds heroic, in a baroque kind of way. But as the eminent philosopher Karl Popper argued, falsifiability—running the risk of empirical refutation—is the touchstone not only of perceptual accuracy but also of freedom, and even of meaningful discourse itself. Revealed "truth" and faith-generated "reality" are not open to this criterion, which is one reason that Mr. Bush seems to be incapable of acknowledging a mistake. They also make democracy impossible, because they close down discussion; this is why they have typically been the centerpiece of authoritarian regimes (rule by divine right, in one form or another). It is also the case that if a nation is unable to perceive reality correctly, and persists in operating on the basis of faith-based delusions, its ability to hold its own in the world is pretty much foreclosed.

And so, where are we now? Early in 2005 the *New York Times* reported that increasingly, across the nation, secondary school teachers were leaving the subject of evolution out of the curriculum because they'd get in trouble with their principal if he or she found out they were teaching it. Even when evolution is listed in the curriculum, it may not make it into the classroom. Many administrators discourage teachers from discussing it, and teachers often avoid the topic out of fear of protests from fundamentalist parents. Add to this the pervasive hostility toward science on the part of the current administration (e.g., stem cell research), and we get a clear picture of the Enlightenment being steadily rolled back.[3]

Religion also shows up in the current American tendency to explain world events (in particular, terrorist attacks) as part of a cosmic conflict between Good and Evil, rather than in terms of political processes. This is hardly limited to the White House. Manichaeanism rules across the United States. According to a poll taken by *Time* magazine—can this really be correct?—59 percent of Americans believe that John's apocalyptic prophecies in the Book of Revelation will be fulfilled, and nearly all of these believe that the faithful will be taken up into heaven in the "Rapture" (the latter discussed in Thessalonians). According to the Book of Revelation, God is going to punish the nonbelievers with various plagues, after which Christ will return to earth—with a sword in his mouth—for the final showdown between Good and Evil (the battle of Armageddon).[4]

The vengeful quality of the apocalyptic vision comes across quite clearly in the *Left Behind* series by Tim LaHaye (one of the founders of the Moral Majority) and Jerry Jenkins, which had, by early 2003, sold more than 62 million copies. One in eight Americans reads these books, and they are a favorite with American soldiers in Iraq. The Book of Revelation is pretty much the road map for the novels, and the worldview is reassuringly black-and-white, with "good" triumphing in the end. At the end of the series, Jews who have persisted in their faith are consigned to the Everlasting Fire, along with Catholics, Muslims, Hindus, and devotees of other "aberrant religions." Seas turn to blood; locusts torment the unbelievers; and 200 million demonic horsemen wipe out a third of the planet—a kind of cosmic ethnic cleansing, as it were. It doesn't get much darker than this.

Finally, we shouldn't be surprised at the antipathy toward democracy displayed by the Bush administration, a fact that has been reported on, in various manifestations, numerous times. As already noted, fundamentalism and democracy are completely antithetical. The opposite of the Enlightenment, of course, is tribalism, groupthink; and more and more, this is the direction in which the United States is going. Thus Mr. Bush's first official response to his reelection was to create a cabinet of completely uniform voices, as David Gergen, who has been an adviser to four presidents, pointed out—"closing down dissent and centralizing power in a few hands." In the world of groupthink, loyalty is everything; and it was also this kind of tribalism, I believe, that got Bush reelected. We are moving, or so it seems, toward a one-party system, a kind of presidential dictatorship, one that is fundamentally theocratic in nature.

Nor does one see much by way of grassroots objection to this trend. American hatred of freedom, for example, shows up quite clearly in the statistics of public attitudes toward the Bill of Rights. Anthony Lewis, who worked as a columnist for the *New York Times* for thirty-two years, observes that what has happened in the wake of 9/11 is not just the threatening of the rights of a few detainees, but the undermining of the very foundation of democracy. Detention without trial, denial of access to attorneys, years of interrogation in isolation—these are all now standard American practice, and most Americans don't care. Nor did they care about the revelation, in July 2004 (reported in *Newsweek*), that for several months the White House and the Department of Justice had been discussing the feasibility of canceling the upcoming presidential election in the event of a possible terrorist attack, which would have been a first in American history. In a "State of the First Amendment Survey" conducted by the University of Connecticut in 2003, 34 percent of Americans polled said the First Amendment "goes too far"; 46 percent said there was too much freedom of the press; 28 percent felt that newspapers should not be able to publish articles without prior approval of the government; 31 percent wanted public protest of a war to be outlawed during that war; and 50 percent thought the government should have the right to infringe on the religious freedom of "certain religious groups" in the name of the war on terror. Quite honestly, we may be only one more terrorist attack away from a police state.[5]

The Breakdown of Education and Critical Thinking

Increasingly, the evidence piles up that intellectually speaking, this nation is very obviously "living in the dark." What is one to make of the fact (reported in the *New York Times* early in 2005) that a number of school districts around the country are now making sobriety tests a regular feature of the school day? Or that millions of American adults are ignorant of the most elementary facts, such as the identity of our enemy in World War II? Or that more often than not, our children graduate from university not knowing the difference between an argument and an assertion, are unable to reason clearly, and don't really know what evidence is? One listens to a radio interview with a travel agent in Arizona who relates how numerous customers ask him questions such as whether it would be cheaper to take the train to Hawaii rather than the plane; or one reads that 11 percent of young adults can't find the United States on a world map, and that only 13 percent of them can locate Iraq. It turns out that only 12 percent of Americans own a passport, that more than 50 percent were (prior to the fall of the Berlin Wall) unaware that Germany had been split into eastern and western sectors in the aftermath of World War II, and that 45 percent believe that space aliens have visited the earth. As in the Middle Ages, when most individuals got their understanding of the world from a mass source—i.e., the Church—most Americans get their "understanding" from another mass source: television. Political and historical "analysis," on this basis, typically amounts to a few slogans they picked up the day before from broadcast news or even from a late-night comedy show. No surprise, then, that on the eve of the 2004 presidential election, 42 percent believed Saddam Hussein was involved in the September 11 attacks, and 32 percent believed that he had personally planned them.[6]

And what does it mean when this level of ignorance, and (amazingly enough) an actual pride in such ignorance, finally inhabits the White House? As Los Angeles journalist John Powers writes in his book *Sore Winners*, Mr. Bush is in fact a mirror of the nation. We can see his fractured image, writes Powers, reflected in the wildly popular dog-eat-dog reality shows, the frenzy over *The Passion of the Christ*, the celebration of consumerism as self-expression, and the general climate of fear. Bush rules over a "polarized culture of unreality," and it is this culture that created him and gave him his power. Personally, he is a bit eerie, a kind of hologram created by Dick Cheney and Karl Rove, and sold to the American people as a "concocted persona." He takes "obvious pleasure in announcing violence," writes Powers, and is "possessed of a need for order that borders on rage." Yet this robotic behavior has proven to be quite effective in an American context. The lack of intellectual suppleness or curiosity, the distaste for ambiguity, are tailor-made for this particular audience. Once again, both the population and the president can simplistically relate to the world, medieval style, as a battleground between the forces of Good and Evil. Ignorant of historical context, and conditioned by the media to "think" in terms of sound bites and slogans, the American public comes to regard Bush's Manichaeanism and simple-minded view of the world as "sturdy common sense." "If George W. Bush vanished tomorrow," Powers concludes, "everything genuinely awful about this presidency would still be in place. . . . Bush World is not simply the emanation of one sore winner. It's a collection of ideas, values, symbols, and policies."[7]

Legalization of Torture

More than anything else, I suppose, torture evokes the culture of the Dark and Middle Ages. We associate these eras with barbarism, with "cruel and unusual punishment," and use phrases such as "medieval torture chamber" to characterize them. As we observed, nothing, for Voltaire, was more representative of pre-Enlightenment regimes. What, then, are the implications of Abu Ghraib, which, along with Afghanistan and Guantánamo Bay, constitutes only "part of an American gulag," as Al Gore candidly put it? Just to understand the larger picture, for a moment: not only are we supporting governments that routinely practice torture, but in the wake of 9/11 we began transferring suspected terrorists to Saudi Arabia, Egypt, Syria, and Morocco to do our dirty work for us, which includes hanging prisoners from the ceiling, subjecting them to electric shocks, forcing objects up their rectums, tearing their fingernails out, and fracturing their spines. It seemed, though, as time went on, that we were willing to be pretty brutal ourselves. Since Abu Ghraib, there have been periodic revelations in the press about American-led torture being worse, and more widespread, than previously thought. Articles began appearing with headlines such as "The U.S. Military Archipelago," or "Secret World of U.S. Interrogation." Phrases used in these unflinching reports include "worldwide constellation of detention centers," "elaborate CIA and military infrastructure," and "global detention system run by the Pentagon."[8]

In fact, writes Mark Danner, the author of *Torture and Truth*, America has been transformed "from a country that condemned torture and forbade its use to one that practices torture routinely." Americans began torturing prisoners after 9/11 and never really stopped. For example, the near drowning of suspects, or "water-boarding," a technique long used in Latin American dictatorships, is now common to us. Yet there was no outcry over any of this, and the few congressional hearings that took place were "distinguished by their lack of seriousness." And what should we make of the post-2004 election outcome of all this, that Alberto Gonzales, the man who wrote the legal briefs justifying the use of torture, is now, in Orwellian fashion, head of the Department of Justice? Add to this the substantial evidence that many of these practices are a standard feature of the domestic prison system, and our return to the Dark Ages would seem to be complete.[9]

Marginalization of the United States on the World Stage

Would you believe it if I were to tell you that the U.S. infant mortality rate is among the highest for developed democracies, and that the World Health Organization rates our health care system as thirty-seventh best in the world, well behind that of Saudi Arabia (which came in as twenty-sixth)? That the American legal system, at one time the world standard, is now regarded by many other nations as outmoded and provincial, or even barbaric, given our use of the death penalty? That we have lost our edge in science to Europe, that our annual trade deficit (half a trillion dollars) reveals a nation that is industrially weak, and that the U.S. economy is being kept afloat by huge foreign loans ($4 billion a day during 2003)? What do you think will happen when America's creditors decide to pull the plug, or when OPEC members begin selling oil in euros instead of dollars? The *Boston Globe* actually compared our habit of borrowing against the future to that of ancient Rome, and an International Monetary Fund report of 2004 concluded that the United States was "careening toward insolvency." Meanwhile, while America is spending hundreds of billions of dollars on phony wars, the money is piling up in Europe and Asia, and in 2003 China finally supplanted the United States as the number one destination for worldwide foreign investment, with France weighing in as number two. Almost any of our domestic economic problems, writes the *Washington Post*, "is a greater threat to the economy than virtually any imaginable form of terrorism." And in response, we do nothing about it.[10]

Rome in the late-empire period is the obvious point of comparison here, and it is important to remember that it did not so much fall as fall away. As it became socially and economically nonviable, as its military was finally strained to the breaking point by what has been called "imperial overstretch," Rome simply became irrelevant on the world stage. Power eventually flowed to the Eastern (Byzantine) Empire, and the revival of Europe, when it began in the eleventh century, occurred elsewhere, to the north. As for the United States, all that awaits it on the domestic front is bankruptcy and popular disaffection; internationally speaking, we'll be looking at second- or third-rate status by 2040, if not before. History is no longer on our side; time is passing us by, and the star of other nations is rising as ours is sinking into semidarkness.

IF ALL of this has been under way since the 1960s or 1970s, it is clear that 9/11 constituted some kind of coup de grâce. In the wake of that event, civil liberties were severely compromised, the already huge gap between rich and poor was rendered even more extreme, and we began to behave like a rogue nation, acting as a law unto ourselves. Our whole posture has been one of dealing with symptoms, crushing external manifestations; sophisticated analyses of the underlying *causes* of terrorism— let alone of how we might address these—have a hard time becoming part of our public dialogue ("they hate freedom" or "they are jealous of us" doesn't exactly qualify as sophisticated). So 9/11 has entered our national mythology as a day on which the United States, a decent and well-meaning nation, was attacked by crazed fanatics hell-bent on destroying its way of life. All indications are that this is how it will be remembered—at least by Americans. It will definitely *not* become the day on which we began to reflect on our *own* fanaticism, on how *we* were living, and on how historically, we had treated the peoples of the Third World. In fact, it is not likely that such a day of self-examination will ever come to pass. It will, in short, serve the very blindness that brought it on, and that is doing us in. Whatever the outcome of the war on terrorism, or its war on us, one could argue that the terrorists are already winning, in that they have managed to push us further along the downward trajectory we were already on.

So the question remains, What kind of a future does the United States really have? Not a bright one, quite obviously. If "morning in America" was little more than a joke when Reagan uttered it in 1981, it is a total delusion today. I see no way of avoiding the conclusion that the four developments that I have just outlined constitute a new Dark Age. Of course, there are differences as well: we are not literally living in A.D. 600, and I don't wish to stretch the metaphor too far. Nevertheless, it would be a mistake to believe that it was more evocative than real. A stretch, maybe, but hardly off-base as a description of America's present and near future situation. If the past is any guide at all here, we can pretty much predict that over the course of the next thirty or forty years the only alternative solutions we shall pursue will be at best cosmetic, and will, in the long run, amount to very little.

This leaves one final question, at least in an American context: Why bother to write this book? If we have no way of saving ourselves, what's the point? This is where the goats and sheep part company, in my opinion. Americans have been raised on Walt Disney and Ralph Waldo Emerson; they take optimism in with their mother's milk. Nor is this all bad, of course: optimism can be a very good thing if the situation truly warrants it. But there are no levers of social change today. The Democratic party is politically and intellectually bankrupt, the "greens" are minuscule this side of the Atlantic, and claims for the existence of dynamic grassroots movements or some putative "radical middle" are without any basis in fact. But as many non-Americans, as well as a small percentage of Americans, know, there is value in the truth for its own sake, not just because it may possibly be put to some utilitarian or optimistic purpose. The truth is no less true because it is depressing, and to ignore or suppress it because it may not make one happy is the behavior of fools. This book was written for those individuals, American or not, who are more interested in reality than illusion, more committed to understanding America as it is than in being comforted by a fantasy of what it is, or of what it might supposedly become. And if this is depressing on one level, it may prove to be exciting on another. For the story of the trajectory of American civilization, from Plymouth Rock to Dead-End Iraq, is a fascinating one. If the reader is willing to view this "from the outside," as it were—

which is to say, dispassionately—the adventure can be a liberating one; or so I believe. Americans, after all, are not trained to think historically or sociologically, to understand that their culture is but one among many, and thus to be able to grasp it objectively, as a whole. But without this "X-ray" ability, there can be no freedom at all: one is just sleepwalking through life, taking a mass myth for reality. And ignorance is *not* bliss; it's always better to leave Plato's cave, or so it seems to me. So if I am not able to offer the reader any upbeat message, I'm nevertheless hoping to offer him or her a kind of slow-motion "aha!" experience: "Oh, so *that's* why . . ." There are, in short, readers who find reality—whether "good" or "bad"—finally more fulfilling than fairy tales, and it is to this audience that *Dark Ages America* is addressed.

～ 1 ～

Liquid
Modernity

Western culture is changing already into a symbol system
unprecedented in its plasticity and absorptive capacity.
Nothing much can oppose it really, and it welcomes all
criticism, for, in a sense, it stands for nothing.

—Philip Rieff, *The Triumph of the Therapeutic*

Rome did not fall because her armies weakened but
because Romans forgot what being a Roman meant.... O
Dream-America, was civilization's quest to end in obesity
and trivia ...?

—Salman Rushdie, *Fury*

THERE IS A SAYING that comes from the medieval science of alchemy:
as above, so below. In other words, what happens in the larger world—the
macrocosm—influences, and is reflected by, what happens in the fine
details of everyday life: the microcosm. Global process, local fallout: that is
the theme of the first two chapters of this book.

The macrocosm, of course, is globalization, the economic integration
of the world along the lines of a laissez-faire market economy. It was the
trendy word of the 1990s, and the popular conception of it is of something completely new. Yet the liberalization (i.e., deregulation, or the
removal of controls) of financial markets on an international scale is actu-

ally a nineteenth-century phenomenon, one that lasted through the 1920s. After the crash of '29, it was in abeyance for a while, and the Bretton Woods Agreement of 1944 institutionalized a system geared toward full employment and the maintenance of a social safety net for society's less fortunate—the so-called welfare or interventionist state. It did this by establishing fixed but flexible exchange rates among world currencies, which were pegged to the U.S. dollar, while the dollar, for its part, was pegged to gold. It also set limits on international capital mobility, so that large-scale speculative capital flows would not threaten any member nation's economy. In a word, Bretton Woods saved capitalism by making it more human. For various reasons, however, the agreement was abandoned by Richard Nixon in 1971, and by 1973 huge amounts of capital began moving upward from the poor and the middle class to the rich and the superrich. By 1995, 1 percent of the American population owned 47 percent of the nation's wealth; by 1998, the 400 richest individuals in the world had as much wealth as the bottom half of the world's population (more than 3 billion people). It is not for nothing that some commentators have called the repeal of Bretton Woods one of the most pivotal events of the postwar period, equal in significance to the collapse of the Soviet Union.[1]

Equally important to the globalization process is the factor of technological innovation—especially in microelectronics, telecommunications, and eventually microprocessors—that was concomitant with these economic changes. Thus Will Hutton and Anthony Giddens define globalization more broadly as "the interaction of extraordinary technological innovation combined with world-wide reach driven by a global capitalism."[2] However, it is more the way modern technology is inherently structured, rather than any specific new technologies, that has been crucial for the globalization process. I am referring here to an "internal" development—namely, the increasing separation of the inner workings of technological devices from their function as commodities. (For example, most of us have no idea how central heating systems—let alone transistors or computers—work, whereas we certainly know how wood-burning stoves work.) This development underlay the shift from the craft tradition to modern technology that has been building since the early years of the Industrial Revolution and that began to take off quite dramatically in the 1960s. The result of this, combined with the unchecked flow of speculative capital, is a dramatic change in our way of life, not the least of which is the frenzied acceleration of time itself. (We are more removed from the world of the 1950s than we care to imagine.) The way of life characterized by this change is perhaps best captured by the phrase "liquid modernity."

Liquid Modernity is the title of a book by the Polish-British sociologist Zygmunt Bauman, who defines it as the condition of a society that lacks a clear sense of orientation, or the kind of stability that derives from a long-standing tradition or set of norms. In Will Hutton's version of it, it is a situation in which all of life is lived in "a permanent state of contingency." It is the social and cultural face of globalization, the ideational and emotional counterpart of the New Economy. America has been the cutting edge of this way of life, a society characterized by speed, fluidity, and transience—obsessive change, in short. Being modern in this context means having an identity that is always shifting, always "under construction." In effect, says Bauman, it is like living a life of musical chairs. The problem is that this fluidity is not a choice we are free to make. Despite the unifying patriotic rhetoric that permeates the United States, on some level Americans are not really fooled: at bottom, each person knows he or she must continually "reinvent themselves," which is to say, go it alone. America is the ultimate anticommunity.[3]

Of course, we didn't get to this peculiar state of affairs overnight. The notion that each person is free to choose his or her own destiny was the ideal of a New World that was rejecting the social chains of the old one. As the British writer Ian Buruma puts it, "the promise of freedom in America is precisely to be liberated from the past." Not for Americans the suffocating restrictions of class, history, religion, and tradition, but rather the absolute weightlessness of choice. This remains the lure of America for many traditional cultures, or at least for many individuals in those cultures: the world of limitless possibilities. The irony for Americans, however, is that in the fullness of time, the limitless possibilities and the absolute weightlessness of choice became as suffocating as the social restrictions of the Old World. American citizens cannot choose *not* to participate in the utterly fluid, high-pressure society that the United States has become. Liquid modernity is, in short, quite rigid: a world of compulsive self-determination. But since it is norms that make life possible, when normlessness becomes the norm, the social order turns into a hall of mirrors. This way of life, says Bauman, may prove to be the greatest discontinuity in human history.[4]

Work

The consequences of liquid modernity show up in many areas of American life, including, notably, the realm of work. It is, after all, the arena in which most of us spend most of our waking hours, and the impact of globalization here is going to be especially telling. What do we find? Within a single generation, almost everything has changed. A young American with moderate education, says Bauman, can expect to change jobs at least eleven times during his or her lifetime. The modern place of employment, he adds, typically feels like a "camping site." Fleeting forms of association are more useful than long-term connections. The main source of profits are ideas, not material objects, and so everything seems ephemeral. Workers know they are disposable, so see no point in developing any commitment to jobs, workmates, or even to the tasks they perform. Everything seems to be ever new, endlessly produced, consumed, and discarded. Globalization means greater competition, intercommunal (and, often, intracommunal) enmity. The most functional work attitude in such a context is one of cynicism.[5]

While it is of course possible to dismiss this description as the jaded evaluation of a disaffected European cultural critic, that really won't wash. Similar descriptions (sans sociological analysis, for the most part) can be found, among other places, in the *Wall Street Journal*. Thus reporter Clare Ansberry describes the "just-in-time" labor force that has to make it "in an ever-more-fluid economy." In Cleveland, for example, the Lincoln Electric Company shifted salaried workers to hourly clerical jobs. A & R Welding of Atlanta maintains a cluster of welders to work out of state, when needed. In South Carolina, the Nestlé Corporation has created an in-house roster of part-time workers "who stick by the telephone to hear if they should report on a given day to assemble frozen chicken dinners." Flexibility, writes Ansberry, can be a euphemism for less pay (and fewer benefits) and largely random work arrangements, but workers really have no choice: it's that or nothing. The New Economy takes no prisoners.[6]

A dramatic case study of the new work ethic is provided by computer programmer Ellen Ullman in her memoir, *Close to the Machine*. This new ethic, she says, is one in which all of life is about "positioning." Projects and human connections bubble up and collapse with dizzying speed; everyone is running his or her own little virtual company in which skills aren't cumulative and everyone is disposable. There is constant talk of "teamwork," but it is a phony courtesy, part of the workplace "process." In reality, says Ullman, we are all "creatures swimming alone in puddles of time." Her description of the people she meets along the way is that of nonpersons, people who say and do all the right things but who seem to be completely empty. And all of this, she concludes, is very likely everyone's future:

> We wander from job to job, and now it's hard for anyone to stay put anymore. Our job commitments are contractual, contingent, impermanent, and this model of insecure life is spreading outward from us. . . . We programmers are the world's canaries. We spend our time in front of monitors; now look up at any office building, look into living-room windows at night: so many people sitting alone in front of monitors. We lead machine-centered lives; now everyone's life is full of automated tellers, portable phones, pagers, keyboards, mice. We live in a contest of the fittest, where the most knowledgeable and skillful win and the rest are discarded; and this is the working life that waits for everybody. . . . Where we go the world is following.[7]

An equally disturbing portrait is provided by the American sociologist Richard Sennett in *The Corrosion of Character*. What is now absent from our lives, he writes, is a sense of narrative coherence. The way we have to live in order to survive in the New Economy has set our inner lives adrift. One can no longer deploy a single set of skills through the course of a working life; in fact, the fastest-growing sector of the American labor force is that of temporary job agencies. The domination of consumer demand has now created a "strategy of permanent innovation." Skill, craftsmanship, and commitment are dysfunctional in a world in which, according to Bill Gates, one should "position oneself in a network of possibilities." Such a world, however, might well be regarded as a form of dementia.

In the course of his research, Sennett went back to a bakery in Boston that he had studied twenty-five years previously. The place was now entirely computer run, a streamlined, high-tech, "flexible" workplace. There was no contact with the bread itself; the workers just monitored the process via on-screen icons. Bread had become virtual. The "bakers" had no hands-on knowledge at all; they didn't actually know how to bake bread. The resulting attitude, the pervasive psychology of this place, was one of detached irony. In a world characterized by constant change and fluidity, nothing is or can be taken very seriously.

As one might expect, in a society such as this, failure becomes a normal prospect, a regular event, even in the lives of the middle classes. Few can make it in this new winner-take-all market, and in fact the so-called prosperity of the 1990s was, as many economic observers have pointed out, a prosperity only for the upper 20 percent of the population. But as Sennett notes, the failure here is more than just financial; rather, it is a "failure to make one's life cohere, failure to realize something precious in oneself, failure to live rather than merely exist." That's because the short-term, flexible regime of the New Economy precludes making a narrative out of one's labors. The whole system, says Sennett, radiates indifference. He ends his book with these words: "a regime which provides human beings no deep reasons to care about one another [or, one might add, about their work] cannot long preserve its legitimacy." What we can actually do about it, of course, is an entirely different matter.[8]

As a final commentary on the nature of work in the New Economy, we have the astute analysis of Robert Reich, who was secretary of labor during the first Clinton administration. He too points out that everything is now in overdrive: the New Economy is at work 24–7. In 2000, he notes, the average American couple worked seven more weeks than they did in 1990, and the average American now puts in 350 hours per year more than his or her European counterpart. In addition, there are fewer steady jobs now; less and less pay is derived from regular salaries. We have to worker harder and longer, and under much greater stress. One is either on the fast track or out of the loop, and this has created a frenzy to be in the "winners' circle." Our lives, notes Reich, are frantic; people are constantly on call via cell phones, beepers, faxes, voice mail, e-mail and the like, which now "break into our lives like burglars," destroying any vestige of private life. The brain, he writes, is like "a sentry on continuous alert." Our personal lives are, not surprisingly, often a shambles. The new work arrangements have meant the erosion of families, the fragmenting of communities, and threats to our integrity. Parents spend far less time with their children than they did three decades ago; friends, spouses, a deeper meaning in life—all that is hurriedly shoved aside. Everything gets telescoped down to Me, as the primacy of self-loyalty becomes a necessary survival strategy—what marketing guru Tom Peters approv-

ingly calls "The Brand Called You." But "The Brand Called You," says
Reich, is quite pernicious; it is the psychology of a world in which people
are endlessly selling themselves, promoting themselves. The macrocosm
of the larger world and the microcosm of everyday life have collapsed
into each other, in short. "We are the economy," Reich concludes; "the
economy is us."[9]

On the grassroots level of people's working lives, this merger of our
identities with the economy is surely one of the most destructive aspects
of the new globalized world order. This destructiveness permeates health
care and the media, urban life and community, the lives of children and
the (discarded) norms of courtesy and civility—the list goes on and on.
Yet floating above all this, as Thomas Frank documents in *One Market
Under God,* is a halo of corporate propaganda designed to celebrate this
way of life as nothing less than salvation. The Italian political theorist
Antonio Gramsci pointed out long ago that if you capture people's
minds, their hands will follow. He called this "hegemony," the symbolic
level of the dominant culture that convinces people—the evidence of
their lives notwithstanding—that this is the best of all possible worlds.[10]
Before we go on to review the impact of globalization on other aspects of
our lives, then, it will be useful to have a look at how the insanity of the
frenzied work life is given a positive spin by those most in position to
benefit from it: those who, like Bill Gates, know how to successfully
"position themselves in a network of possibilities," and who in fact
believe that this is a fabulous thing to do.

The ideology of the frantic life, argues Frank, is the mystique of the
market, the notion that markets "are where we are most fully human . . .
[the place] where we show that we have a soul." By the time the 1990s
rolled around, if not a decade earlier, many Americans had fallen victim to
a kind of "market populism," the belief that financial markets were more
democratic in nature than democratically elected governments. These
ideas, writes Frank, "became canonical, solidified into a new orthodoxy
that anathemized all alternative ways of understanding democracy, history, and the rest of the world." While millions of workers got laid off
and then rehired as temps by their former employers (now without
health and pension benefits), economists such as Lester Thurow wrote
odes to riches, raving about the wealthy as being the real winners in life,
and labeling everyone else "second rate." *New York Times* columnist

Thomas Friedman praised globalization as an agent of freedom, citing things such as the availability of more TV channels as evidence. His motto for this version of democracy was "one dollar, one vote," which is actually the description of a plutocracy. In the wake of the Seattle protests of 1999, newspapers across the country treated free trade as something akin to humanitarian work. A huge army of pundits called the nineties a glorious age of humanity, an age of "rebellion." All of this spin on how hip business was had a great cultural impact, really dating from the beginning of the Reagan presidency. The equation of the market with freedom got enacted into public policy and permitted a huge upward transfer of wealth, which was somehow regarded as an an expression of popular will. All of this was a bogus populism, in Frank's words, "rosy fantasies of the People and their Dow." Even Lester Thurow acknowledged that 86 percent of the market advances of 1995–99 went to the wealthiest 10 percent of the population.[11]

Much of this was given a "spiritual" spin, revealing (for those who cared to look) what the real religion of this country is. Books such as *God Wants You to Be Rich* and *Jesus, CEO* became best sellers. Thomas Friedman claimed that the things celebrated by management theory were the very things that pleased the Almighty. Business consultant Peter Senge proclaimed that business advice was "a way of attuning oneself to the cosmic rhythms of the universe" and laced his works with Sufi tales and quotes from the *Bhagavad Gita*. Bookstores were flooded with texts filled with "astrologies of creativity," absurd syllogisms, chaos and complexity theory, phony narratives, meaningless diagrams and the like. ("Market" is sometimes even capitalized in these books.) Senge told his readers that the hallmark of a good corporation was its "spiritual foundation," and that part of the "sacred" relationship between it and its workers was the abolition of contracts. Instead, he said, workers should have nonbinding "covenants," which would "reflect unity and grace and poise." Other managerial books talked about the corporate soul and the inherent goodness of the market, using words such as "telos" and "spirit." On the back cover of *Orbiting the Giant Hairball*, the author, Gordon MacKenzie, is referred to as a "corporate holy man."

In typical New Age style, all of this was wedded to notions of "empowering the individual" and (supposed) grassroots democracy. So pervasive was this way of thinking, says Frank, that laid-off workers left the parking lots of their former employers in an orderly fashion, excited about their impending careers as "free agents." While the management gurus glorified "teamwork" and "interactive styles," top managers saw their salaries rise in direct proportion to the number of employees they could fire. A headline on the front page of the *International Herald Tribune* said it all: "Rise in Joblessness Delights U.S. Markets."[12] All of this was good, according to the popular New Age/business literature, because it supposedly enabled workers to escape from corporate conformity and "realize their full humanity." Stable employment would no longer be necessary, went the argument, because workers were now too cool for that sort of thing. Meanwhile, real wages declined; workers were much worse off in the 1990s than they had been in the 1960s or 1970s. In actual practice, management talk of "empowerment" and "participation" was typically followed by intensification of management demands and/or massive layoffs. Underneath all the spiritual and populist rhetoric, says Frank, lay an ideology of not democracy, but insanity. What was being praised in this avalanche of silly (and widely respected) literature was a "panorama of destruction and waste."

Writing in the late nineties, Frank predicted that "we will look back at this long summer of corporate love and wonder how it was that we ever came to believe this stuff." He may be right; in the wake of the dot-com collapse, the subsequent recession, and the barrage of revelations of corporate fraud that surfaced in 2002, following Enron in 2001 (WorldCom, Global Crossing, Merck, Freddie Mac, Adelphia, AOL, Sunbeam, Qwest, Tyco, ImClone, Bristol-Myers Squibb . . .), one would think that the ecstatic ideology of corporate greed would seem to be a horribly bad joke, if not a species of lunacy. Personally, I'm not so sure. Globalization is our destiny; it is, in effect, the late phase of capitalism. We did not evolve to this place by accident, and short of massive civilizational breakdown, there seems to be no way to alter this trajectory—not even slightly. And since we now swim in it as a total environment, ideological or religious justifications of it are not going to be easily discarded or seen through. If people's heads are filled with anything at all, it should be obvious that it's more likely to be the ideas of, say, the American Enterprise Institute than those of obscure cultural critics such as Zygmunt Bauman.

I stumbled across a striking example of the pervasiveness of this upbeat, pro-business thinking a few years ago, when I was on a flight from Zurich to Washington, D.C., and sat next to a Swiss woman who was working for an international communications firm based in the United States. She enthusiastically described how "her" firm regularly held retreats, at which they did leadership training, focusing on "teamwork" and "nonhierarchy." The company also supplied its employees with tons of precisely the sort of management books that Thomas Frank ridicules. The woman told me how terrific this education was: you learned to work cooperatively with others, respect different opinions, and so forth. Then she said, "But most of the world seems to have opposite values, ones of cruelty and violence. I just don't understand why people behave that way."

This woman seemed like a very kind, intelligent person; she basically wanted to be successful at her job, marry, and have children (so she told me). All well and good; most people want these things, I imagine. But what is typical here, and also disturbing, is the problem of not making connections. What these supposedly "responsive" corporations are frequently doing—inadvertently or not—is creating the conditions for the very violence this woman rightly deplores. Unless people start making these connections, absolutely nothing is going to change; and they aren't going to start making these connections. For every copy of *One Market Under God* sold, it is a good bet that a huge number of copies of management books such as *Who Moved My Cheese?*, or some equivalent nonsense, get sold. In the absence of broad structural awareness, alternatives to a world characterized by liquid modernity don't have much of a chance.

It is also the case that the absence of such alternatives in our consciousness is an inherent feature of this world. In such a context, anything truly different, and certainly anything truly creative, has to swim against an enormous tide of commercial garbage. As Robert Reich points out, the life of the mind is now "subject to the same underlying dynamic that is affecting the rest of the economy." When everything is reduced to marketing, he writes, "the only legitimate measure of worth seems to be what is desired." Professional integrity starts to evaporate, because livelihoods now depend on popularity. As a result, few writers will try to say something daring or disturbing; few will do research that has no commercial value. So what we get now are "little slivers of artistic defiance" that exert no influence whatever on the larger culture. As Zygmunt Bauman hauntingly puts it, "In the case of an ailing social order, the absence of an adequate diagnosis . . . is a crucial, perhaps decisive, part of the disease."[13]

To find such a diagnosis, it is sometimes necessary to look in unexpected places, such as MIT physicist Alan Lightman's novel of a few years ago, entitled (appropriately enough) *The Diagnosis*. As in the case of the novels of Don DeLillo (*White Noise, Underworld*, etc.), it is a brilliant example of fiction being truer than fact; for all intents and purposes, it really *is* fact.

The book opens with corporate executive Bill Chalmers riding Boston's "T" to work, perfectly on schedule, having slotted his time to the minute. He is not exactly sure what his company does; its declared purpose is to "transfer information," and its motto is "the maximum information in the minimum time." His current project is the preparation of a report on TEM, or "Total Efficiency Management." He looks around him, noticing how his fellow riders' faces are "waxy and yellow beneath the underground fluorescent bulbs." His cell phone rings; two men nearby immediately reach into their briefcases. Bill checks his voice mail every twenty minutes; someone calls him, and is then interrupted by call waiting. He looks up: a digital sign in the subway has an ad from some company promising the buyer that he can now get stock quotations on his pager, every minute ("Work wherever, whenever"). Everyone around him is on a cell phone, or plugged into a Walkman, or dictating into a tape recorder, or typing on a laptop. His assistant speaks to him periodically on his cell phone in a "high-voltage, caffeine voice." At a later point on his journey, he watches a young mother feeding her baby Diet Coke, and two octagenarians with long white hair and canes arguing about something while eating Egg McMuffins.

In the midst of this, Bill cascades into a nervous breakdown. First he can't recall where he is supposed to get off; then he can't remember his name. Finally, he takes his clothes off. When the police board the train, they find him curled up on the floor in a fetal position, clutching his cell phone to his bare chest. Bill does recover from the breakdown and amnesia, but slowly his entire body goes numb, and none of the doctors can come up with the obvious diagnosis: no sane person can live this way.

Eventually confined to a wheelchair, Bill is taken to a shopping mall by his son, who leaves his father for a moment while he goes to look for something. Bill takes in the sight of two-hundred-plus stores "stacked together like toy blocks"; watches everyone rushing through the doors to buy at Ralph Lauren, Ann Taylor, Banana Republic, Liz Claiborne, Enzo Angiolini; sees the ocean of exercise machines and cameras, microwaves, blenders, computers and calculators, digital alarm clocks, bedsheets and towels, CD players, robot swimming-pool cleaners, humidifiers, rugs and carpets, virtual-reality helmets, skis and ice skates, televisions and stereos, cosmetics, jogger clips measuring speed and calories burned, correct-posture dog feeders, lamps and pens and end tables, spray paint, automobile accessories. It was all here. Bill could sense the frantic urge to stay current, the eagerness to buy and consume, the sobs of desire caught by the churning bodies and the spastic blasts of automobiles moving through the gray, teeming swamp.

By the end of the story, Bill is blind, and his body has shriveled up. The book is courageous and honest; it offers no hope for Bill, nor for America. This is the diagnosis: there is simply no way out of this way of life short of a total breakdown of it, because there is no way that it can transform itself. It just doesn't have the will, the resources, or even the self-awareness to do so. What happens to Bill has effectively happened to the United States, which is awash, as one reviewer wrote, in "information overload, unimaginable prosperity [for a tiny handful] and spiritual bankruptcy." The United States, like Bill, has no real purpose anymore; it is just running for the sake of running.[14]

Many other countries are, of course, aware that America is running on empty; some hope to avoid the same fate. A few years ago, thirty-three Italian towns banded together to protect their human-paced way of life from America's turbocharged economic model. Todi, Asti, Orvieto, Positano—these and other medieval jewels have prohibited McDonald's and Starbucks from setting up franchises within their city limits. Some have enacted strict limits on electromagnetic emissions from mobile phone towers; others have banned car alarms and garish neon signs. The Italians sit in the piazzas, linger over lunch. "Only stupid people run," says Todi archivist Giorgio Comez. The organization, Città Lente (Slow Cities), refuses to accept the notion that "a life with time for nothing but work represents progress." Americans tend to consider such attitudes quaint, but (ironically enough) the ones who do go abroad typically go to places such as these on their holidays, never imagining that perhaps this is what a healthy life ought to consist of in general, not just on vacations.[15]

What, in any case, are the alternatives? What happens to towns that do not resist the market-driven way of life? I saw the answer to that first-hand in April 2002, when I stayed with friends who live in a tiny French village across the border from Geneva. It is picturesque, classically beautiful, and essentially ruined. Most of the men gather in the local café-bar at 11 A.M.; they are farmers, and unemployed. Globalization had undercut their ability to sell local produce (lettuce and zucchini, in particular). The stores are empty or boarded up; ten kilometers away, a large shopping mall, complete with McDonald's, attracts customers for miles around. Teenagers wander around town all day, talking on cell phones. The majority of the townspeople voted for the extreme right-wing candidate, Jean-Marie Le Pen, in that spring's elections; he is the understandable outlet for their frustration over unemployment and the collapse of their culture. Racist or not, he speaks to and for these people, who see that globalization is destroying their way of life. Indeed, the only other alternative to this situation, outside of Città Lente–style resistance, is a kind of eerie co-optation, such as one finds in so many of the villages of Provence, which are now living fossils, filled with boutiques sporting Visa stickers in shop windows. Neither alternative is a happy one, it seems to me.

The fact is that liquid modernity has a strongly addictive quality to it: its participants are often convinced that death is actually life. In "The Numbing of the American Mind," Thomas de Zengotita points out that it constitutes "a vast goo of meaningless stimulation." Stress, he writes, has become for most Americans

> how reality feels. People addicted to busyness, people who don't just use their cell phones in public but display in every nuance of cell-phone deportment their sense of throbbing connectedness to Something Important—these people would suffocate like fish on a dock if they were cut off from the Flow of Events they have conspired with their fellows to create. To these plugged-in players, the rest of us look like zombies, coasting on fumes. For them, the feeling of being busy *is* the feeling of being alive.[16]

One has to ask, of course, exactly who "the rest of us" is. Increasingly, there are fewer and fewer Americans who don't fit his description, and it is spreading to the rest of the world as well. It's an extremely self-destructive path, to be sure, but as more of the world gets pulled in this direction, it becomes more and more difficult to recognize it as a path to nowhere.

Media

One American institution that has been particularly susceptible to the influence of globalization and the market-driven mentality is the public media, a development closely documented by the American sociologist Todd Gitlin in his book *Media Unlimited*. It is not merely that we now have a whole host of new media technologies, but that during the last twenty years the saturation of our lives by the media has attained astronomical levels. Spending large amounts of time with communications machinery, says Gitlin, is what most of us now do. The average American child, for example, lives in a house with 2.9 TVs, 1.8 VCRs, 3.1 radios, 2.6 tape players, 2.1 CD players, and 1 computer. Forty-two percent of American homes are "constant TV households," meaning the set is on most of the time. The average American watches it about four hours per day, and it now consumes 40 percent of his or her free time. There are, of course, lots of different media, but underneath them all, observes Gitlin, is a unity at work—a torrent of sounds and images, a constant wraparound collage in which we are immersed and that moves at a relentless pace. It is liquid modernity reduced to a buzz, the buzz of the inconsequential. This, says Gitlin, is the media's essence.[17]

The connection of all this to the globalization phenomenon is more subtle than one might imagine, although—amazingly enough—it was discerned as early as 1900 by the German sociologist Georg Simmel. In *The Philosophy of Money*, Simmel writes that the more money moves to the center of our lives, the more cynical we become about higher values. This, he continues, generates a culture of sensation, a longing for speed and excitement, because natural excitement is increasingly absent. One hundred years later, we live in a din of hip-hop car stereos, dial tones, airplane noise, Walkmans, air conditioners, Muzak, and so on. The world, says Gitlin, has become an "electronic multiplex," and as we move through it we are literally drowned in a "corporate-produced pastiche." The intensity of this pastiche increases year by year. Television programs of twenty-five years ago seem sluggish to us now, and if we look back fifty years we see that in terms of action, movies were much slower, and that magazine articles were much longer and more complex. Since, as Simmel observes, the point of all this is speed and sensation, we should not be surprised that the content is largely banal. In the case of action films, for example, the goal is to deliver an adrenaline rush, so directors aim for the lowest common vocabulary. Sound bites from presidential candidates aired on television newscasts shrank in length from an average of 42.3 seconds in 1968 to 7.8 seconds in 2000. A survey of the top ten best-selling novels taken from the *New York Times* between 1936 and 2001 shows a drop of 43 percent in sentence length and of 32 percent in number of punctuation marks per sentence. The shortening of attention span that goes with all of this, writes Gitlin, leads to an emphasis on stereotypes. TV and movies have to have easily recognizable types for fidgety (and increasingly, simpleminded) audiences to pay attention to. Hence, the steady dumbing down of American culture, as life becomes more formulaic. As Neal Shapiro, former executive producer of NBC's *Dateline*, told prospective producers pitching projects to him, "It's gotta be high school."

And so it is. As Gitlin points out, in such a situation, democracy is reduced to a sideshow: "The ceaseless quest for disposable feeling and pleasure hollows out public life altogether." In addition, American popular culture makes the whole notion of right and wrong seem ridiculous, and so replaces democracy with a safe, comfortable nihilism. Even beyond that, we can see the political aspect of the media in the massive data accumulated by Harvard sociologist Robert Putnam in *Bowling Alone* (more on this later), showing the evaporation of interest groups, neighborhood alliances, and all forms of civic life—the very stuff of democracy. In brief, the life of the mind has been drowned in a huge consumerist fantasy.[18]

A further consequence of the new media supersaturation has been the privatization—and hence destruction—of public space. By 2003, nearly 73 percent of American adults owned cell phones, and these people move around in "mobile bubbles." Most of them treat public space as an extension of their living rooms or offices; that they are disturbing the private space of those around them barely crosses their minds. Indeed, I've even witnessed people talking on cell phones as they walk through the Metropolitan Museum of Art in New York, totally oblivious of the notion that there might be something wrong with this behavior (the concept of "the commons" is virtually nonexistent in the United States). Worse, it is behavior that the Met and other such institutions tacitly condone; they're "in business," after all. The result? It is now almost impossible to find peace and quiet on a train or bus or subway or street corner or even in a restaurant or art gallery; and if you politely ask a cell phone user to take the conversation elsewhere, he or she typically tells you to go to hell (just try it, as an experiment). "I'm the only one that counts" is the reigning (infantile) ideology. But there is apparently more in store for us. In his book *What Will Be*, Michael Dertouzos describes a projected "Bodynet" that will let us walk down the street embedded in a cocoon of digital information, such that we shall be able to do research, talk with the office, play video games, etc., without any handheld device. (Many people in our culture are essentially there already.) The sensory world will fall away, replaced by a self-created existence, a virtual world we personally design. "Long live science!" as Aldous Huxley commented in 1937 regarding a similar projection.[19]

The narcissism of all this is breathtaking, but in truth the new media technologies merely enable the elaboration of a narcissism that runs deep in the American psyche, an infantilism that is a trademark of American culture. And in that, says Gitlin, lies its attraction for other cultures as well. It is one of the things that gives contemporary American culture its unbounded nature. French media scholar Daniel Dayan maintains that European and traditional cultures have a superego, whereas American culture does not. But the market for entertainment is mostly a market for the id, and that constitutes its enormous attractive force. When the youth of Iran, for example, want to express their rebellion against a repressive, religious government, they do so by flirting with the symbols of American culture: jeans, Coca-Cola, MTV, and the "empire of informality." Some of this is, of course, good; even Islamic fanatics get the blues. But it is broader than this. A poll taken by Zogby International in 2002 revealed widespread Muslim approval of American consumer products, movies, and television programs—as high as 75 percent in Iran, for example. Even those battered by American power are nevertheless seduced by the American culture industry, by what has been called "soft power." "The way of life with the greatest allure," Gitlin muses, "turns out to be this globalizing civilization of saturation and speed." Nor is there any way of stopping it, he concludes, short of its total breakdown. Of course, one could reasonably argue that a world remade in the image of Walt Disney, and driven by an increasingly sophisticated communications technology, *is* the total breakdown of civilization.[20]

Children

If mass-market culture is driven by infantile needs and impulses, we also need to explore what such a world is doing *to* our children. Concomitant with the "turbo-capitalism" of the 1990s came a host of reports on the state of the union's children and teens. I confess I have lost a good many of the references here because of the increasing density of this material: by the late nineties, a week didn't go by that I did not hear, see, or read a report on the subject. "Latchkey" kids, broken homes, hundreds of thousands of children being bullied or attacked in school, or being terrified that this would happen to them, the increase (by 100 percent) of teen depression during the last fifteen years of the twentieth century—etc., etc. By the year 2000, 25 percent of U.S. teens were involved with weapons; 70 percent admitted cheating on tests in school; more than 15 percent had shown up for class drunk; and five million children—including three-year-olds—were regularly left at home alone to care for themselves. On 29 February 2000 Kayla Rolland, age six, was shot dead by another six-year-old, Chico Owens, in Flint, Michigan; less than two weeks later, the boy's adopted father began negotiating with publishing and PR firms about getting a deal for a book or movie on the event. Soon after, President Clinton appeared on the *Today* show, arguing for a child-trigger-lock law, legislation that had been blocked by the National Rifle Association (did anyone notice how bizarre it was that a society should be discussing the *need* for such a law?). On 25 June 2001, National Public Radio reported the results of a survey that indicated that one out of three parents feared their children would be bullied in school, and one out of four feared they might get shot. Meanwhile, in Miami, the police are now using stun guns on children in elementary school (preparation for prison, I suppose).[21]

But it gets worse (almost). An estimated six million American children have been diagnosed with attention-deficit–hyperactivity disorder (ADHD), including perhaps two hundred thousand between the ages of two and four. One million children now receive Ritalin (methylphenidate) every day in school; other drugs in the "behavioral" tool kit include Prozac and Pamelar (antidepressants), Risperdal (an antipsychotic), and Adderall, now the most prescribed stimulant in the country. In 2002, the Food and Drug Administration approved the use of Prozac for children as young as seven years of age, and in general there was a spike in the use of antidepressant medication for the five-and-under crowd during 1999–2004. All in all, the use of antidepressants among American children grew three- to tenfold between 1987 and 1996, and there was a further 50 percent increase in such prescriptions from 1998 to 2002. In fact, children in the United States now receive four times as many psychiatric drugs as children in all other countries of the world combined. Meanwhile, depression, anxiety, and behavioral disorders are skyrocketing. What we probably need is a drug called Reject-It-All. Unfortunately, the majority opinion seems to be "repress symptoms, no problem." The minority opinion, which points to the obvious—"overcrowded schools, stressed-out parents with little time for the children and a society . . . that is intolerant of anything but success"—can barely get a hearing in a culture characterized by frenzy and denial. But when the use of psychoactive drugs triples among two to four-year-old Medicaid patients between 1991 and 1995, the causes are likely to be sociological, not chemical.[22]

What might those causes be? To get a closer look, we need to examine the larger economic picture—in particular, the relationship of the corporate world to the world of childhood, and the way that that relationship shapes children's perceptions. Perhaps the most obvious entry point into this relationship is the world of toys, with which children spend large amounts of time (when they aren't watching TV). In *Kids' Stuff: Toys and the Changing World of American Childhood*, Gary Cross charts the evolution of American toys during the twentieth century, showing that the frantic, contingent character of contemporary life that we have seen operating in the areas of work and the media are fully operative in the lives of our children as well. One thing that emerges from his study is how the "themes" of the toys have changed over time, along with parental relations to children with respect to those toys. The old-style toys, says Cross—the ones that can perhaps still be found in upscale stores and hobby shops—conveyed messages of continuity between parent and child. The new toys don't do this. Whereas the old toys were about real-life situations—dolls that expressed notions of motherhood, for example, to which both mothers and daughters could relate—the new ones simulate activities from movies and television. Playthings, in other words, used to teach the young the values and customs of their culture; they were "part of a society that had a clear vision of the future." The new ones, by contrast, are the product of a simplistic vision, that of a corporate marketing strategy that has no particular interest in child rearing per se but a very great interest in sales, turnover, and profit.

As a result, parents have become onlookers in their children's playtime activity, not active participants in it. The Barbie doll of the sixties, for example, was what the little girl's mother was not: a fashion model with a large wardrobe, who required a host of clothing and accessories. "Barbie play," writes Cross, "was an education in consumption." Mattel, the manufacturer of Barbie, succeeded in persuading little girls to "trade in" their Barbies for the "new look" the next year. Some adults undoubtedly found their child voluntarily parting with a "loved doll" disturbing. This is a major break in a deep pattern of attachment, well-known in the psychological literature; violating it is a surefire recipe for neurosis. But the little girls saw it as just doing what their parents did: trading in last year's Chevy for the next year's new, "exciting" model. Even as early as the 1930s, says Cross, toys were becoming "play props of a parentless and ahistoric world." He continues, "The old view that children should learn from the past and prepare for the future is inevitably subverted in a consumer culture where memory and hope get lost in the blur of perpetual change. The toy industry exploits these trends, but it did not create them." All of this leaves children with few models of past or future. Boys, he writes, get a "magical pseudo-technology of violent conflict"; girls get models of female caring (if at all) that are not grounded in reality.[23]

Cross' second point, about the sheer volume of toy sales, and the frenetic quality of the whole marketing and consumption process, overlaps with the first. Retail sales rose from $4.2 billion in 1978 to $17.5 billion in 1993, and this latter figure excludes nearly $4 billion spent on video games. By 2002, toy sales had risen to $30.6 billion.[24] The new industrial pattern, says Cross, reflects the general American commitment to open-ended markets and constant change. Again, this is tied to the issue of subject matter, because what is spiking those sales is the fact that toys are typically inspired by characters in the mass media. This trend was launched by Walt Disney in 1937, when *Snow White and the Seven Dwarfs* got linked to toys that precipitated a "merchandizing frenzy." The strategy that now dominates children's culture is the Disney-style coordination of licensed goods and movie fantasy, generating a "commercial festival." By the 1950s, Cross writes, "the marketing techniques that were used to promote the accumulation of goods among adults also cultivated the children's market." When the *Mickey Mouse Club* aired on TV in 1955, it created a craze for Mousketeer memorabilia. Mattel purchased a huge number of commercials on the show, and its sales skyrocketed.

By the 1980s, toys had become part of what Cross terms a "vast inter-connected industry that creates novel fantasies for profit." Toy giants began to carve out the market and consolidate, such that the majority of sales started coming through Toys "R" Us, Wal-Mart, Kmart, and Target. The central technique was now the managed fad, the creation of a sus-tained demand for toys linked to movies, cartoons, TV programs, and the like. In 1983, $221 million was spent on toy ads; in 1993, $790 million. Movies such as *The Lion King* and *Pocahontas* generate a continuous buy-ing season. The result is that children now live in an "ethos of fantasy consumerism." Modern American childhood, says Cross, is for the most part an education in shopping.

The corporate propaganda for making this happen is (again) part of the strategy of saturation; this is now a "casual" feature of the media environ-ment. A TV ad for McDonald's, for example, has a family eating together at the golden arches, with the children playing with some robotic objects as a voice-over happily intones (to upbeat, Disney-like music), "A family interacting over Robo-Chi toys"—or some such thing. This is, in effect, the breakdown of the traditional American family and its redefinition or repackaging along corporate lines. Not dinner at home and conversation around the table—being human, in short—but a load of cholesterol at a fast-food joint while the kids play with androids. Not the deep attachment to a loved object, but psychological indifference to *any* object.[25]

Not that some parents are unaware of what's going on, or the dangers it poses; the problem is what any of us can do about it. In 1999, Gary Ruskin published a very disturbing article on the subject in *Mothering* magazine called "Why They Whine: How Corporations Prey on Our Children." Noting that "today we increasingly see kids through an eco-nomic lens," Ruskin assembles a cast of characers who are literally scary—they see this development as positive, if not actually wonderful. Thus James McNeal, a professor of marketing at Texas A & M, enthuses over the new view of regarding children as "economic resources to be mined," adding that advertising that targets elementary schoolchildren "works very effectively in the sense of implanting brand names in their minds...." One marketer actually refers to children as "consumer cadets," in whom "the consumer embryo begins to develop in the first year of existence" (apparently some research shows that one-year-olds are capable of "brand associations"). Thus Mike Searles, former president of Kids "R" Us, said of advertising aimed at children: "If you own this child at an early age, you can own this child for years to come." Similarly, Wayne Chilicki of General Mills boasts that the firm's operating model is one of cradle to grave: "We believe in getting them early and having them for life." Another marketing researcher Ruskin quotes states the idea about as baldly as possible: "Imagine a child sitting in the middle of a large circle of train tracks. Tracks, like the tentacles of an octopus, radiate to the child from the outside circle of tracks. The child can be reached from every angle. This is how the marketing world is connected to the child's world."[26]

Specific examples of this corporate intrusion into our children's minds include Channel One, a marketing company that broadcasts ten minutes of news to eight million children in twelve thousand schools across the United States. The problems are that this ten-minute "news" broadcast includes two minutes of commercials, and the children *have* to be there— they are a captive audience. Thus Joel Babbitt, former president of Channel One, points out that "the biggest selling point to advertisers" lies in "forcing kids to watch two minutes of commercials." The atmosphere of the school, he comments, is an advertiser's dream. Then there is ZapMe!, a company that, like Channel One, offers free equipment to schools—in this case, computers and Internet browsers. In return, it advertises online and also collects data on what the children are interested in, supplying this information to advertisers and marketers.

The upshot of all this is that school is turned into a venue for corporate and consumerist indoctrination—with the blessing of many schools and probably most of society. "The ads," writes Ruskin, "teach kids that buying is good and will make them happy. They teach that the solution to life's problems lies not in good values, hard work, or education, but in materialism and the purchasing of more and more things." What they get, he adds, is "a worldview in which products are the means and ends of life." Or as George Will recently put it, "schools are becoming case studies in the commodification of *everything*."[27] The results are all around us, of course. If this corporate supersaturation becomes our children's daily fare, then they grow up into adults for whom such a world appears perfectly natural. There is then no place else to go, no place not completely defined by a corporate mindscape.

It's a chilling thought, of course, and the theme (as a general metaphor) of that classic film *Invasion of the Body Snatchers*. An updated version of this can be found in *The Matrix*, which is a brilliant elaboration of the same psychosocial configuration. In this film, the world has been devastated by a war between humans and robots, and the victorious robots then attach their defeated enemies to computers, which make them (the humans) think that they are normal beings living in a normal world. Their experiences cannot tell them how the world "really" is because there is no external reference point, no way of escaping the charmed circle of their robotic existence (*The Truman Show*, starring Jim Carrey, plays on this theme as well, very effectively). That is to say, if you are raised in or live in the world of corporately engineered definition of reality, you are not going to be able to think thoughts outside of that matrix. No other life or awareness is possible in such a situation because nothing can be thought or imagined without using the mental constructs of Disney, Channel One, etc. In *The Mouse That Roared*, his study of the Disney corporation, Henry Giroux puts it this way:

> How children learn and what they learn, in a society in which power is increasingly held by megacorporations, raises serious concerns about what noncommodified public spheres exist to safeguard children from the ravages of a market logic that provides neither a context for moral considerations nor a language for defending vital social institutions and policies as a public good.[28]

As one reviewer of the book remarked, ad campaigns aimed at children "teach market consumption as the essence of a person's identity." The end result is the absence of "any social space that is not dominated by ever more intrusive corporate marketing. . . ." This, I predict, is going to be the situation Americans increasingly find themselves in as the twenty-first century "progresses." What else might one expect? A programmed embryo is inevitably going to turn into a programmed adult.

Community

What kind of communities will such adults want to live in? Historically, community certainly existed in this nation of immigrants, but the highly centrifugal nature of American capitalism, along with the ethos of competition and "rugged individualism," often made it hard to maintain, even before the modern era of globalization. Today, there isn't much of it left. Notions of community support and civic obligation are pretty feeble in the United States, forming, as journalist Alex Marshall puts it, "a thin, tepid brew." We live, he says, "in one of the loneliest societies on earth," or as Will Hutton poignantly sums it up, "a market society makes strangers of us all."[29]

In fact, as globalization accelerated and the economy shifted into high gear, the last vestiges of community in America were effectively snuffed out. As we shall see, the data on this are so grim as to defy the imagination. Writers such as Barbara Ehrenreich, Alan Ehrenhalt, and Robert Putnam have documented the destruction of our social fabric in painstaking detail. What follows is merely my own summation of the general obituary, with some personal observations thrown in.

I live in a large condominium in Washington, D.C. When I first moved in, several years ago, I was startled by the fact that at least half the time, people did not respond when I said hello in the elevator or laundry room. They could be male or female, old or young—it made no difference. They would simply not look up, or would just look away. I also discovered that it was common for residents to cross paths in the lobby and barely nod to each other. Was I living on a different planet? My own experience was that hotels were friendlier than this. If I were a Martian sociologist observing this behavior, I would have no way of decoding it; it seems almost barbaric.

My general impressions were reinforced late in 2001, when I ran across a small (and badly written) notice entitled "Welcome Your New Neighbor" in the condominium newsletter. "There has been a lot of turnover with owners this summer," it read. "If you see a new face, stop them with a welcome to the building and introduce yourself. This is a good habit to do for keeping safety in mind." In the worldview of the then superintendent, the primary purpose of being friendly was utilitarian—to prevent crime, or possibly terrorism. The notion that one might be friendly for its own sake, out of basic human sociability, apparently never entered her mind.

By 2004, I was more or less inured to this behavior, but I also got to know two residents who had lived in the place for twenty or more years. The first told me that when she originally moved in, the building had a spirit of camaraderie to it; the people were openly friendly. Slowly, she said, the mood changed; over the last decade, other residents began to react to her hello on the elevator with a kind of hostility. She thought of moving frequently, she said. The second long-term resident I talked with confirmed my experience of elevator and laundry room, as well as the observations of the first resident: at some point during the last decade, she said, it became a distinctly antisocial place.

Resident No. 2 also told me a story about someone who had lived in the building a few years back and who suddenly disappeared. "Barbara," for some odd reason, was being threatened and verbally abused by her neighbor across the hall. She did go to the police and get a restraining order, but as her neighbor lived less than twenty feet away, and was apparently a bit crazy, it didn't do much good. She then got the superintendent to write her neighbor, which also didn't work. Finally, she was physically assaulted by the woman, and appealed to the condo board for help. They responded by saying, "it's your problem, we don't want to get involved." "Good luck with it," they told her. So they did nothing, and for her own safety Barbara finally had to sell her unit and move away.

It's not merely that these vignettes reflect how callous much of American life is; what is so striking is that this behavior is largely unconscious, not *perceived* as callous by those engaging in it. After all, it's the cultural ethos. Why should *we* care if someone is threatening you? (for example); what's it to *us*? This is, quite simply, the norm. As the sociologist Philip Slater remarked many years ago, most Americans are living in a psychological slum.

Of course, not all American cities fall into this category; Washington is probably the worst of the lot, as Harry Truman observed when he famously remarked that if you wanted a friend in this town, you'd best be advised to get yourself a dog. I find New York and Philadelphia immensely friendly, for example, and many towns in the Midwest are as well (at least superficially). In Washington, however, one confronts "iron in the soul" on a daily basis. Store clerks typically don't say hello to their customers; they don't even bother to make eye contact. The interaction is purely commercial, and the sullen, subliminal message is Go Away. (The same is true for most government agencies, both federal and the local District ones.) In response to a question I had about telephone answering machines, a Radio Shack clerk shrugged his shoulders and mumbled (sans eye contact), "I just sell the stuff; I don' know nothin' about it." As I said, this is pretty much the norm.

One of my "favorite" Washington stories involves a friend of mine—I'll call her Jane—who went sailing on Chesapeake Bay as part of a singles event that was posted on the Web. It was a very small group, and about two hours into the afternoon one of the other women accidentally let go of the rope that held one of the sails taut. It whiplashed out, and as luck would have it, coiled around Jane's leg, raising a long, blistering welt and inflicting what proved to be a third-degree burn. Jane was knocked flat, and went completely white; a very slight, petite woman, she could have lost her leg. Somebody, at least, cared enough to bring her an ice pack, but that was the extent of the group's concern. Instead of heading for shore, and getting her to an ER, they mixed another pitcher of margaritas and socialized among themselves as Jane lay stretched out on the deck. When the boat docked two hours later, they wished her "luck" with her injury. Jane was left to drive herself to the hospital (a full hour away). Somebody in the group subsequently did send her a fruit basket; not a single person followed up the incident with a phone call to inquire how she was doing.

Finally, at the far end of this spectrum (as though the above were not bad enough) is an incident that occurred here in early 2003, in which a man was shot at a gas station and those present had no reaction. The store videotape shows these witnesses not fearful, but completely indifferent, as the body lay bleeding on the pavement. One man actually drove up, inserted the gas pump into his tank, briefly looked over at the body, finished pumping gas, paid for the purchase, and drove off. Nor is this restricted to Washington: Louis Mizell, a security consultant who maintains a forty-thousand-category database on crimes in the United States, reports that similar episodes of "depraved indifference," as he calls them, have occurred across the country.[30]

Depraved, yes; but by whose standards? If a whole society behaves this way, can it still be said to be depraved? The anthropologist Colin Turnbull believed this to be the case when he studied a tribe in Uganda known as the Ik, which had been reduced to a condition of savage self-interest due to economic hardship. Turnbull describes, for example, how, when someone in the tribe died, neighbors (as well as children and siblings) would fight over the person's few belongings and abandon the corpse. Turnbull comments that in this system of mutual exploitation, affection and trust were actually dysfunctional. "Does that sound so very different from our own society?" he asks at the end of the book. "Almost any kind of

exploitation and degradation of others, impoverishment and ruin, is justified [in our society] in terms of an expanding economy and the consequent confinement of the world's riches in the pockets of the few." These
words were written in 1972; one can only wonder what Turnbull would
have thought of American life thirty-plus years later, were he still alive.[31]

It is difficult for any culture to view itself objectively, which is why I
find it important to travel, to live abroad (occasionally), and to talk with
foreigners living in the United States. At one point I struck up a conversation with a Croatian man about my age, who suddenly, and very unexpectedly, unburdened himself. Americans care only about their individual
lives, he said; there is no genuine friendliness here, no community, and no
consideration of the less fortunate. While Canada and most European
countries provide health care and some sort of social safety net, the United
States is cruel; the motto seems to be "succeed or be damned." Women
react to a friendly hello as though one were a potential rapist, and men see
everything in terms of competition. "When I was living in Europe," he
went on, "America appeared to me as the land of opportunity. That proved
to be true, in many ways; but socially the place is a disaster."

Shortly after, I was talking with a young man from the Ivory Coast
who had been living in the United States for three years, and who works
as a barista at Starbucks. The clients, he told me, are rude as a matter of
course; they bark their orders while talking on cell phones. American
culture seems to consist of nothing more than money and television, and
nobody gives anybody else a break. "If you can survive here," he told me,
"you can survive anywhere; but who would want to live under such conditions? I intend to return to the Côte d'Ivoire, where I plan to take care
of kids." While I much prefer living here to his war-torn homeland, I did,
nevertheless, see his point.

Two months later, I was getting needled by my acupuncturist, a Bel-
gian woman who has lived here for more than a decade. "Eventually," she
said, as she inserted a needle at point Spleen 6, "I'll have to go back.
Washingtonians are friendly only if they think you might be able to
advance their careers. I can't imagine growing old here, living in a nursing home, with the other patients being willing to talk to me only if I
give them my Jell-O."

Again, one might argue that Washington is an extreme case: nowhere
else in the United States are power and ambition so highly regarded and
humane values so inconsequential. Still, I was struck by an incident in

Seattle a few years back in which a woman threatened to jump from a bridge during rush hour, and drivers got out of their cars and encouraged her to do it. (She finally decided to take their advice.) And Madison, Wisconsin, doesn't prove to be much better. In his autobiography, *Who Am I?*, Yi-Fu Tuan, who was teaching geography at the University of Wisconsin in the eighties, recounts the events of a Saturday when he was working in his campus office. Suddenly he felt ill, so he decided to go home; by the time he was at his apartment, he was experiencing a lot of pressure in his chest. He was unable to reach his doctor; a standby physician told him that it might be a heart attack, and that he should get over to the ER, but not drive himself. Tuan called a colleague, who turned down the request; he couldn't drive him to the hospital, he said, because he had a previous engagement(!). Tuan finally did find someone to drive him to the ER, and it turned out that he didn't have a heart attack; but his reaction regarding his colleague's refusal to help—"I had taken for granted that in a life-threatening situation I could certainly count on the help of someone I had gone to lunches and dinners with"—was one of complete shock. Later, he mentioned the incident to another friend, who half persuaded him that his colleague's behavior was reasonable, and that Tuan was being neurotic about it(!).[32] (I subsequently wrote Professor Tuan a letter, telling him that it was America that was neurotic, not he.)

I'll talk about the statistical evidence for these impressions in a moment; for now, I wish to point out that there are increasingly frequent commentaries in the popular media that take this feature of contemporary American life for granted. Editorializing in *The New Yorker*, for example, Louis Menand points out that the dominant social attitude in this country is "Other people do not exist." He goes on:

> The family that spreads out its towels in front of yours acts as though there were nothing but empty beach where you are sitting. Cars bunch up along the highway, maneuvering in and out of each other's lanes, without their drivers ever making eye contact. People chatter away on their cell phones in front of strangers as if they were alone in their kitchens. Americans now behave in public places the way New Yorkers have always behaved in the subway: they carefully keep one inch of space between themselves and all adjacent bodies, and stare blankly into the middle distance. If someone spoke to them, they would jump out of their shoes.

Welcome, concludes Menand, to "the new Gesellschaft, where monads circulate in a culture of total disconnection. . . ."[33]

In a similar vein, we might also consider the final episode of *Seinfeld*, in which Jerry and the gang are arrested by a policeman in a small town in Massachusetts that has passed a Good Samaritan law, requiring citizens to come to the aid of others in distress. When Jerry phones Kramer's attorney (a Johnnie Cochran look-alike), to explain the situation to him, the lawyer exclaims indignantly, "You don't have to help *anybody*! That's what this country's all about!" As the popular saying goes, he got that one right.

Television, of course, reveals this all the time. The reason shows such as *Seinfeld* or *Friends* were so popular is that they depicted community situations—i.e., ones in which people hang out together on a daily basis and have a shared history. The irony of millions of isolated Americans sitting home alone and vicariously participating in a group experience that they themselves will never have, *because* they will never have it, hardly needs comment—although it has, in fact, evoked a fair amount of same. Thus David Blum, writing in the *Washington Post*, observes that the "together-forever spirit" of such shows is "TV's ace in the hole. . . . Honest, truth-baring relationships . . . have formed the basis of a medium that has, since the '50s, distracted us successfully from our real lives." What makes these shows intoxicating, he goes on, is the bonding, the psychic connection the TV neighbors have with one another. But we prefer not to run the risk of reality, of getting hurt, and as a result very few of us have "a neighbor whose private thoughts we truly share." The unpleasant truth of middle-class American life, he concludes, is that "most of us don't talk to our neighbors about anything except the weather."[34]

As far as romantic relationships go, the possibility that we have reached an all-time low in that department was captured by the wildly popular HBO show *Sex and the City* (especially in its first few years), in which four hip New York women regard men with utter contempt and go from one lover to the next, casually chewing them up, spitting them out, and then wondering why they (the women) are sad and lonely. Is this really an exaggeration? Surely, it is only the New Economy manifested in our "love" life. In that regard, I was particularly amused and depressed (they seem to go together these days) by an interview that Public Radio International aired on 17 July 2001 with a woman named Courtney from Cape Elizabeth, Maine, who had started a "relationship breakup business." For a fee, Courtney will call or write your significant other on your behalf and tell him or her that the relationship is over. She describes this as a service for people "who don't have the courage to do it themselves." Apparently, she's doing a brisk trade.

Along the same lines, we might consider Rachel Greenwald's book *Find a Husband After Thirty-five Using What I Learned at Harvard Business School*, in which the author encourages women to create a "personal brand" (for instance, "architect, charming, international"), test it out on focus groups, and then send it out into the "market." As sociologist Arlie Russell Hochschild points out (in *The Commercialization of Intimate Life*), we have replaced the therapeutic model of human relations with one drawn from business-management theory. Greenwald never says what sort of husband might be acquired by these techniques; she counsels only that "a key marketing goal is to sell your product to as many customer segments as possible."[35] Ah, love!

Another important aspect of the breakdown of community life in America is the erosion of civility. Articles in the *New York Times Magazine* and *The New Republic* have commented, for example, on how Americans have started relying on the courts as a substitute for sitting down with one another and working out their differences in a civil manner. In fact, between 1960 and 1997 the number of lawsuits brought annually tripled, and since 1970 the legal profession has grown three times faster than the economy. Writing in the *Washington Post* a few years ago, George Will observed how normal rudeness and incivility have become in American life, and called for a "unified field theory of contemporary vulgarity." And Nancy Ann Jeffrey, commenting on America's epidemic of rudeness in the *Wall Street Journal*, suggested that it may be the "dark side of the New Economy."[36]

Jeffrey was, of course, closer to the mark than she may have realized. The New Economy has created a Hobbesian world, one of all against all (Dick Cheney's psyche writ large, one might say). In what other context would we expect to find "reality" shows on TV, such as *Survivor*, in which screwing the other person is the name of the game, and which millions find vastly entertaining? On ABC's *Nightline* of 13 June 2001, Ted Koppel speculated that the reason for the immense popularity of shows such as these is that our civilization has broken down ("civilization" obviously has "civility" at its root), and in such a context Americans delight in watching people betray one another (the mental equivalent of gladiatorial combat in ancient Rome, perhaps, although that was obviously a lot more straightforward). On another "reality" show, participants get paid $50,000 for letting themselves get bitten by swarms of rats. Asked by Koppel to comment on the condition of contemporary American civilization, novelist Kurt Vonnegut Jr. replied: "What makes you think we *have* a civilization? There is nothing *precious* here," he went on. "We have only *pockets* of civilization. What is *national* civilization is garbage." "Do you have a final word for the American public?" Koppel asked Vonnegut at the end of the program. "Yes," said the latter; "go watch a symphony orchestra." To which Koppel sarcastically replied, "Oh, yeah, that'll attract millions."

One of the most thoughtful studies of the whole subject is *Civility* by Yale law professor Stephen Carter, who believes that loss of national purpose is at least partly responsible for the breakdown of civility. "As we watch the collapse of civility in America," he writes, " . . . everybody seems to be wondering why Americans treat each other so shabbily." A market-driven society, he goes on to say, exists only to satisfy individual desire; we spend all our time acquiring things because we lack alternative sources of meaning. The result is that we no longer see ourselves on a common journey. By the early seventies, America had "none of the social glue that makes a people a people." Sometimes a single statistic says it all: in 1997, according to Carter, a poll by the National Association of Secondary School Principals revealed that 89 percent of grade school teachers and principals reported regularly facing abusive language from students.[37] Clearly, this is not the America of the 1950s.

Or of the sixties. Given the incidents in my Washington apartment building, I was especially moved by one particular vignette in Carter's book, in which he describes his family's 1966 move into a house on Macomb Street, which is just a few blocks from where I live. Carter relates how, to welcome the new folks on the block, the neighbor from across the street came over with a plate of sandwiches. Thirty-three years later, during Christmas 1999, I brought a plate of cookies to my neighbor across the hall, who reacted with nervousness and embarrassment. I knew her casually, had spoken to her a few times during the year; as a result, I wanted to make a friendly, 1966-type gesture. It proved to be an awkward moment; apparently, she didn't know how to react. We stood in her foyer, each of us ritually eating a cookie, after which I left. Her discomfort was palpable; I wouldn't be surprised if she threw the remaining cookies away. But the story doesn't end there. About eighteen months later, she got cancer, and when she returned from the hospital spent a month in her apartment, recuperating. (I learned about it only months later.) I'm sure she had friends who came by—at least, I hope so—but I have no idea as to who from the building came by to look in on her. I imagine, no one. On whose door could she knock? What "neighbor" could she ask to sit with her? As Carter puts it, the condition for most of us in America now is that "we drag ourselves through endless unfriendly days." One can only wonder what the cumulative effect of all this alienation, this anger and depression and muted violence, must be. (Consider Abu Ghraib, for example.)

This shift from neighborliness to suspicion and isolation took only a few decades to achieve, as Alan Ehrenhalt documents for Chicago during the period 1955–95 in his sensitive and disturbing study, *The Lost City*. As the author himself admits, nostalgia has its limits; few Americans would wish to return to the era of segregated water fountains. Yet there is no avoiding the recommendation anyone who lived through the fifties would make about this book: read it and weep. For most of American history, says Ehrenhalt, we had clear geographical communities, real neighborhoods that defined identity and activity. People need these sorts of anchors. But today, only a house is a community (and that's if you're lucky)—which is to say that we *have* no community. Even the suburbs of the fifties had it, with dance parties and conga lines and weekend volleyball. (Try even *suggesting* such activities today!) People spent their summer evenings in front of the stoop talking to their neighbors.[38] Now they stay inside, in air-conditioned apartments, alone, hooked on the remote.

During the fifties, Ehrenhalt continues, relationship took precedence over the profit motive. We had a society in which market forces challenged traditional values, whereas today we have a society in which market forces have triumphed over those values. Thus, for instance, what we can expect at banks and shops is rudeness and impersonality. People who have done business with their bank for twenty years have to show their ID to a teller who has been there for two weeks and who will be gone as soon as she gets a better offer. The ATM is friendlier; most people prefer to use it. Writing in the *Washington Post*, Sally Pfoutz recalls how, when she bought a house in Arlington, Virginia, in the 1980s, people would eat on tray tables outside in warm weather, or congregate at someone's house for a marathon card game. "The spirit of the neighborhood," she writes, "was defined by laughter, children calling, dogs barking hello to other

dogs and so many birds. . . ." Twenty years later, with Reaganomics and
Clinton's globalization having done their work, it is a different world. All
of that earlier energy evaporated; people no longer evince any interest in
the community. "Now," she admits, "I don't even want to put letters in
the mail to my neighbors. I may know whom they are voting for because
they choose to display a sign in their yard, but I don't know if they're still
employed or if they've recently had a death in the family. In fact, I don't
know anything personal about them."[39]

It is easy, of course, to argue that America has always been a nation in
rebellion against stifling communities, or that Western civilization itself,
from the Renaissance and Reformation onward, has been about the rise
of individualism and impersonality. One hears this sort of analysis from
time to time. The problem, says Ehrenhalt, is that these explanations don't
really work; they ignore the dramatic and tangible differences that have
occurred during the last forty or fifty years. Even the contemporary dis-
respect for leadership and the cynicism about politics are unparalleled in
American history. The world of the fifties, as noted earlier, is far more
removed from our own world than people realize. Yet most Americans
are aware that community has disappeared, that their schools are not better, their streets not safer, that local government and business are less
responsive than they were just a few short decades ago. Not exactly a
pretty picture.

All of this falls into the category of the erosion of what has been called
"social capital," the connections among individuals that are based on rec-
iprocity and trust. What it really amounts to is the informal "institution-
alization" of the Golden Rule: I'll do this thing for you without any
expectation of return, but in the general expectation that someone else in
the community will do something for me later on. The decline of this
informal understanding, the erosion of social capital, was carefully documented in 2000 by Robert Putnam in his detailed study, *Bowling Alone.*[40]
His database is, in fact, enormous, drawing on surveys such as the DDB
Needham Life Style, Roper Social and Political Trends, and the General
Social Survey. These data reveal that during the last third of the twentieth
century all forms of social capital fell off precipitously, something Putnam
regards as a threat to American civic health. Americans have, he says,
become dramatically disconnected from family, friends, neighbors, and
social structures; this has happened in every walk of life, and across all sections of the population, irrespective of gender, race, class, and educational

background. Tens of thousands of community groups disappeared from 1973 to 1994; more than one-third of our social infrastructure vanished during that time. Church groups, union membership, dinners at home with friends, bridge clubs—all have been decimated. By 1993, the number of Americans who attended even one public meeting on town or school affairs during the previous year was down 40 percent from what it had been twenty years before that time. Social capital, says Putnam, also includes things such as nodding to a jogger we might see on our daily route, and studies show that even casual friendliness of this sort has steeply declined—something that can have a very powerful effect on the overall quality of a community. In the midseventies, Americans entertained friends at home an average of fourteen to fifteen times per year; by the late nineties, that figure had dropped 45 percent. Spending social evenings with neighbors declined by a third between 1974 and 1998; getting together to play cards dropped 50 percent from 1981 to 1999. Between 1985 and 1999, there was a 30 percent decline in the readiness of Americans to make new friends. By 1993, 63 percent stated that most people couldn't be trusted, whereas in 1964 77 percent of people interviewed said that most people *could* be trusted. Decline in social trust, Putnam notes, has been especially steep among the young. From 1990 to 1996, violent aggressive driving shot up 50 percent. And so on. The social cost of all this is quite severe, because it has been demonstrated that communities with high levels of social capital are much better equipped to deal with poverty, unemployment, drugs, and crime; their general vibrancy and political effectiveness are much greater.

Putnam wants to believe that America is not sunk, that it can reverse this trajectory, which bespeaks a very sad nation indeed. But he is forced to admit that for the foreseeable future, the erosion of social capital can only deepen. Thus, as possible causes of this massive destruction of community, he cites in particular the impact of television, which has privatized American lives, and also changes of scale in the American economy. The corner grocery store was replaced by the huge commercial supermarket, and community-based enterprises by multinational outlets. Shopping malls are now America's most distinctive public space, and mall culture is about being in the presence of others, but not in their company. All of this undermined the *physical* basis for civic engagement. The point is that the rebuilding of social capital cannot occur in a context in which power, money, celebrity and the like have become the key values of the dominant culture—those which, as a kind of mass pathology, most Americans seem to be caught up in; and that ethos, which is the ethos of globalization and late-capitalist corporate hegemony, is going to be with us for most of this century.

Putnam's observation that we have destroyed the physical basis of community is a crucial one, because it is an obvious factor in the disintegration of community life. Although there is a large literature on the subject, I want to confine my focus for now to Bettina Drew's *Crossing the Expendable Landscape*, the result of a driving tour that she made around the United States in the late 1990s, and her reflections on what has happened to the American landscape since the 1980s. Perhaps the most obvious feature is one we have already alluded to: shopping malls, which have replaced the downtowns of many American cities. "Much of the American landscape," she writes, "had been turned into a kind of endless commercial"—roads dotted with chain-food outlets and gas stations and quick-stop marts. Alternatively, we have walled-off communities and isolated corporate headquarters, which give off a sanitary, impersonal feeling. Our landscapes, she writes, reveal "a nation ruled by economic forces with little vision beyond the dollar." In Stamford, Connecticut, for example, corporate buildings are divorced from the street, with no sidewalk access; the downtown area is a mall, filled with chain stores, and staffed by "young hourly workers with no future or ties there."

One city after another shows the same pattern. Towns to the east of Kansas City, which in 1900 had been filled with all kinds of stores and shops, are now dried up, cluttered with abandoned façades, and on their outskirts are Wal-Marts, gas stations, and fast-food restaurants. The underground walkways in Dallas, writes Drew, "will never be the site of political demonstrations, homeless people, begging, or other signs of social unrest or injustice, and musicians, oddballs, marginal artists, and the other colorful bit players of an open society have also been excised by a strange surgery that gives the illusion of a clean and prosperous public life." Instead, the desire seems to be for a "seamless consumer culture without past, poverty, or idiosyncrasy," and the citizen is now seen as "nothing more than a consumer or a child to be entertained." The classic suburb discourages strolling, mingling with neighbors; as historian Kenneth Jackson put it, "there are few places as desolate and lonely as a suburban street on a hot afternoon."[41]

The architectural historian Vincent Scully once remarked that a society will build what it values.[42] What, then, does our society value? In his recent documentary *Domestic Violence*, Frederick Wiseman gives us a visual answer to this question in the opening scenes of the film, where he first shows us the gleaming glass office buildings of Tampa, Florida, and then, says film critic David Denby,

> retreats to cruddy-looking stores and strip malls along the highways leading out of the city, and from there to broken-down neighborhoods of tract homes and mangy gardens. It's America at its most incoherent, where collections of workers and shoppers live without much community, and people fall through the cracks.[43]

What we see in Bettina Drew's description of the America of the New Economy or in Wiseman's pictorial representation of it is the physical embodiment of the globalization process, of a society dominated by the values and concerns of the market. Ultimately, community is about tolerance and relationship, about human connection. These intangibles of life, which in fact *make* it life, are now very much in abeyance. Alan Lightman's haunting image of a naked man curled up on the subway in a fetal position, clutching his cell phone, is something of an icon of how we now live.

How did things come to such a pass? How did the United States arrive at the point that money, power, speed, and mindless entertainment came to be the defining characteristics of American civilization? We have identified these changes with roughly the last forty years, and so the question inevitably arises: What happened during that time to reduce the country to a cultural and emotional wasteland? Enough discussion of effects, then; time to have a look at the causes.

~ 2 ~

Economy, Technology

To allow the market mechanism to be sole director of the fate of human beings and their natural environment . . . would result in the demolition of society.

—Karl Polanyi, *The Great Transformation*

The most important consequence of [the rule of technology] is that, in a fundamental way, the whole society runs off track.

—Langdon Winner, *Autonomous Technology*

WE HAVE, THEN, LOOKED at the effects of globalization—what I have called the microcosm, or the (unhappy) details of our daily lives—at some length. What we need to do now is examine the macrocosm, in particular the factors that have been driving this process. To do this we need to pick up the thread of the discussion with which we began the last chapter: the liberalization of financial markets, especially as achieved through the repeal of the Bretton Woods Agreement, and the concomitant acceleration of the pace of technological innovation. As the above epigraphs indicate, there are (inter alia) two guaranteed ways of ruining a society—namely, letting the market "be the sole director of the fate of human beings," and allowing technology to permeate every aspect of our lives. In the United States, both of these developments have converged, creating a huge chasm between rich and poor and pushing us over the edge into a kind of antisociety, the leading features of which I discussed in chapter 1. While these developments have been widely hailed as the dawn of a golden age, the likelihood is that they actually amount to a death knell, the beginning of the end of the American empire. Political scientist George Modelski, in *Long Cycles in World Politics* (1987), dated the onset of the decline of American hegemony to 1971–75, specifically linking the former date to the repeal of the Bretton Woods Agreement; but this was definitely a minority view. The dominant public voice has been one of insistent celebration, most especially during the 1990s, which brings to mind the astute observation of the British historian Arnold Toynbee, that it is precisely in the declining phase of a civilization that it beats the drum of self-congratulation most fiercely.[1]

In the discussion that follows, I am going to review the nature of the Bretton Woods Agreement and the significance of its repeal for the process of globalization, and then turn to the role modern technology has played in this drama as well. In terms of the first topic, I need the reader to bear with me as I attempt to summarize sixty years of economic history. In order to make it easier, however, let me state my arguments in advance:

✦ Bretton Woods was a protective measure, and a very successful one, both in terms of economic productivity and social equality. It underwrote the welfare state.

✦ Its repeal in 1971 set the stage for a "predatory" economy, both at home and abroad. The floating exchange rates that resulted stimulated the growth of finance (i.e., speculative and investment) capitalism, which in turn led to a huge gap between rich and poor, as well as to a "Wall Street–Treasury Department" complex that had a powerful (and baleful) impact on American domestic and foreign policy.

✦ These policies, which have eroded democracy and led to a much more aggressive foreign policy, have destabilized the American empire both at home and abroad. The repeal of Bretton Woods, in short, is a major factor in our decline.

Economy

Much of the thinking that led up to the Bretton Woods Agreement was shaped by the man who could arguably be called the last century's greatest economist, John Maynard Keynes. His *General Theory of Employment, Interest, and Money* (1936), which was, in effect, a nonrevolutionary alternative to Marxism, had an enormous impact on the postwar international economic order, wherein Western governments committed themselves to maintaining a high level of employment. Keynes' worldview, in fact, was so unusual that it is amazing that he was listened to at all, let alone chosen to be Great Britain's chief negotiator at the Bretton Woods conference. Truth be told, Keynes' writings and economic advice had been ignored for years. However, with the onset of the Depression and the trauma of the Second World War, the phenomenon of a purely laissez-faire (unregulated) economy had lost much of its intrinsic appeal. Western governments were more open to notions of state intervention and planned (but not Soviet-style) economies, and in that context Keynesian ideas began to find an audience. In this sense, the "era" of Bretton Woods was an unusual one, and both Barry Eichengreen (in *Globalizing Capital*) and Herman Schwartz (in *States Versus Markets*) regard it as an anomaly. To put this another way, in the late phase of capitalist development the relentless pressure for markets leads to imperialism, or what we now euphemistically call globalization. This process is the norm (in a laissez-faire economy), and in that sense Bretton Woods can be viewed as an odd interruption, a rare moment of sanity in which social protection prevailed over the logic of the market. Keynes' own position was clear: "to suppose," he wrote, "that there exists some smoothly functioning automatic mechanism of adjustment which preserves equilibrium if we only trust to methods of laissez-faire is a doctrinaire delusion which disregards the lessons of historical experience without having behind it the support of sound theory."[2]

Keynes' fundamental insight was that the economy, at root, was psychological in nature. Given the fact that the future is completely uncertain, he said, the function of money is essentially to provide a hedge against insecurity—basically, a strategy for calming the nerves. He regarded market fluctuations as irrational, the product of "herd" behavior (great waves of optimism and pessimism that were not grounded in empirical reality), and declared at one point that love of money was a form of mental illness. So shrewd was Keynes regarding the operation of the stock market, however, that—unlike most of today's economists—he became wealthy from his own theories. Yet Keynes had little interest in economic growth for its own sake; it was for him only a means of creating a civilized way of life. Money should serve humanity, in short, not the other way around.[3]

It was only in the hothouse atmosphere of 1944, then, that such an outlook could have a chance of being taken seriously, let alone get incorporated into the agreement that was signed at the United Nations Monetary and Financial Conference at the Mount Washington Hotel in Bretton Woods, New Hampshire, on July 22. The Bretton Woods Agreement created a system of more or less fixed exchange rates (the so-called adjustable peg) among world currencies, and placed controls on international capital mobility. It also established the International Monetary Fund (IMF) and the World Bank. The objective was to create a favorable environment for trade and investment while allowing countries to pursue full employment and social welfare policies. The articles were in part a reaction to the interwar period, which saw the collapse of the gold standard and the Depression. According to David Felix, professor emeritus at Washington University, the lessons of the interwar period were two:

1. Floating exchange rates, such as existed in the 1930s, invited huge capital flows that destabilized commodity prices and foreign trade. Currencies left free to fluctuate led to speculation that played havoc with exchange rates.
2. However, restoration of multilateral trade and investment required a system of convertible exchange rates that was flexible (unlike the gold standard).[4]

To accomplish this, the IMF would oversee compliance with Bretton Woods obligations and also provide emergency financing to members in temporary difficulty. Member countries would be allowed to approach full convertibility of their currency gradually, to maintain permanent capital controls, and to make small (under 10 percent) changes in their fixed exchange rate with IMF approval. The Bretton Woods perspective was one of protection and human welfare; it gave primacy to full employment and social welfare programs over currency and trade liberalization.[5]

So the Bretton Woods Agreement pegged the dollar to gold, and all other currencies to the dollar. The United States could not adjust its own exchange rates with other currencies; it could only adjust the value of the dollar with respect to gold. As for other countries, their job was to maintain their chosen exchange rate with the dollar. Hence the value of every currency was tied to the value of the dollar, and the United States guaranteed that it would convert dollars to gold on demand. America thus provided other countries with an anti-inflationary anchor, which was sound Keynesian economics. In other words, in the 1920s and 1930s, currencies had floated against each other, which created massive speculative flows and was disastrous. Keynes' idea, in contrast, was to return to a modified gold standard that would constitute a managed exchange-rate system. It was part of Keynes' genius, in short, to create a balancing act between capitalism and socialism, and this was what the Bretton Woods Agreement was roughly designed to do.[6]

To state this all in another way: at Bretton Woods, the United States established what is sometimes called an "embedded liberal order," which endorsed restrictive economic practices, ones required to defend the autonomy of the new interventionist welfare state. Such an order is thus only partly liberal ("liberal" in this sense refers to laissez-faire economics, not to left-wing politics), because of the use of capital controls (e.g., fixed exchange rates). The belief was that only capital controls could prevent the welfare state from being undermined by large speculative international ("abnormal") flows of capital. In the spirit of Keynes, finance was to be the servant of economic and practical goals, not the master.[7]

During the time leading up to Bretton Woods, in fact, Keynes argued that it was not just "abnormal" capital flows (i.e., ones motivated purely by speculation) that were the problem, but also "normal" flows responding to interest rate differentials between countries. Both he and Harry Dexter White, the American negotiator, felt that the only way to prevent problems in these areas was to give individual states the right to control capital movements. This would be accomplished by the monitoring of these movements and by cooperation among countries in enforcing one another's regulations. The New York banking establishment, of course, was opposed to this, as it would remove what had been a lucrative business for them in the 1930s: receiving capital flight from Europe. So while Keynes and White argued that controls on the investment behavior of a wealthy minority were essential for a government's political autonomy, the bankers argued that any government intervention was coercive and totalitarian. For the most part, however, Keynes and White prevailed, since the capital (both moral and financial) of the New York banking establishment was shot.[8]

What was the result? Proponents of financial liberalization argue that the post–Bretton Woods period, when capital controls were lifted, was the period of greater prosperity, and that this action led to an improvement in the global economy. Close comparison of the two eras, however, shows pretty clearly that the quarter century between the signing of the agreeement was the true "golden age." The volume of trade between America and the rest of the world, for example, rose nearly sevenfold from 1944 to 1974, while investment increased fivefold, and the median American wage rose 80 percent between 1947 and 1974. Significantly, wages did not rise at all between 1974 and 2001, and it was only after Bretton Woods was abandoned that a slowdown of per capita GDP growth began to affect both the developing and the industrial nations. Thus David Felix writes, "No period of comparable length, past or present, comes close to the high output and productivity growth rates, low sustained unemployment, and distributional equity of the Bretton Woods era." How in the world, then, did Bretton Woods get dumped? Why abolish something that was so successful?[9]

This is a complicated story, but if, as Lenin once said, the key question of politics is Who does what to whom?, then it becomes clear that issues of power and vested interests are the overriding ones in this case. Not that we need a Lenin to tell us this. In *Bank Restructuring: Lessons from the 1980s,* Andrew Sheng writes that under a globalized regime—that is, a world of free capital flows—the burden of economic losses from financial crises falls on those who cannot escape the system. Loss distribution, in short, is a political matter.[10]

So let's see if we can't untangle the story of the Bretton Woods repeal. On one level, of course, there may be nothing to explain. If Karl Polanyi's "great transformation" is globalization itself, the subjugation of all of economic life to an international market economy, and Bretton Woods was a brief interregnum in this relentless process, then we would expect that with the revival of the economy in the postwar period the dynamic of unchecked greed would reassert itself, until eventually it would become business as usual. In this sense, Richard Nixon's decision to torpedo the agreement in 1971 was the *result* of globalization, sweeping this "odd aberration" out of the way. Hence the first factor in the repeal was the pressure of late-capitalism for markets, including the desire of a small, wealthy class to profit from speculation in currency. Two other factors were public inflationary spending during the Johnson administration, especially for the Vietnam war (which continued under Nixon), and a major ideological shift that was taking place in the country, from the idea of a welfare interventionist state back to notions of unrestrained economic growth.[11]

To deal with the first factor first, then: with postwar economic recovery came the emergence of a large amount of highly mobile international capital. In such a context it became difficult to operate a system of quasi-fixed exchange rates; even minor changes in existing rates by a country could subject it to massive capital outflows, as speculators tried to profit from slight differences in currency values. As trade and investment flows grew, the United States wanted to prevent capital from leaking out of the country, and to depreciate the dollar so as to give its manufacturers the advantage in world markets. Under Bretton Woods rules, however, America was not allowed to devalue the dollar; so it simply abandoned the agreement. Appearing on national television on 15 August 1971, President Nixon announced his decision to devalue the dollar by 10 percent and to make it inconvertible into gold. What then followed, of course, was the dramatic rise of other currencies—in particular, the yen and the Deutschmark—against the dollar, thus threatening the ability of Japan, Germany, and a number of other countries to export goods to the United States (the purchase of which would become prohibitively expensive for Americans). Rather than suffer domestic recessions as a result, these countries floated their currencies against the dollar—that is, they allowed their value to be determined by the market. So floating rates replaced fixed rates, and by 1973 the Bretton Woods Agreement was effectively dead.[12]

How could America do this? The fact is that the cooperative structure of Bretton Woods was de jure; the de facto reality was an asymmetry between the United States and everybody else, and this had existed from the very beginning. America, which was the only country with the power to break the Bretton Woods rules, had been fairly benevolent in the postwar era, during the period of gradual European recovery. Due to its growing deficits, however, by the time the 1960s rolled around it adopted a more self-centered, even predatory, foreign economic policy. Basically, the United States was in a position to force other countries to pay for its weakness in the arena of trade by using the hegemonic power it had in the arena of finance; so that is what it did. As Will Hutton puts it in *The World We're In*, the Bretton Woods repeal "laid down the essential tramlines of American foreign economic policy for the next thirty years . . . the international economic order was to be built unilaterally around American interests."[13]

To the noneconomist (such as myself), these developments sound like no big deal: restrictions were lifted so that the different currencies were free to determine one another's value (exchange rate) on the market. But the fact is that this move represented a momentous alteration in the structure of the entire global economy. The move to floating exchange rates, whereby the dollar and other currencies could be converted into one another at the prevailing market rate, introduced enormous instability into international trading systems and strongly stimulated the growth of finance capitalism (making money from currency speculation, trade in stocks and bonds, loans to companies and governments, etc., as opposed to making it from the manufacture and sale of products). Finance capitalism means making money by manipulating money—this had prevailed in the nineteenth century and down to the (inevitable) crash of 1929. It aggravates problems of equilibrium within and among capitalist economies in order to profit from discrepancies. The return to finance capitalism resulted in the Wall Street–Treasury Department complex, which continues to make a tiny handful of people extremely wealthy, but which contributes very little to the global economy. By the middle of 2002, 90 percent of the money circulating around the world every day had nothing to do with the exchange of goods and services. Roughly $1.82 trillion was then changing places daily for purely speculative reasons (the figure is undoubtedly larger now). It was, in fact, from 1973 on that money in the United States began its steady, and ultimately torrential, migration from the poor and the middle class to the rich and the super-rich.[14] (We shall return to these issues below.)

The second factor leading to the repeal of Bretton Woods was the dramatic rise in public spending from about 1964 on. It couldn't have come at a worse time. Although ultimately worth it, the financing of the Great Society programs was very expensive. Add to this an expense that was definitely *not* worth it—the war in Vietnam—and you have an extremely inflationary situation on your hands. In particular, the rising military spending made the American role as the world's anti-inflationary anchor very difficult to maintain. Expenditures for Vietnam led to the economy's overheating during 1966–69, and this expansion fueled the first factor—i.e., the large-scale capital flows and the pressure for markets. In this context, the postwar Keynesian order began to look like a mistake, for by the early seventies inflation had accelerated way beyond the expectations of Keynesian analysts. (A more reasonable conclusion might have been that our involvement in Vietnam was an immoral and misguided venture that we should never have gotten into in the first place, but it was a lot easier to blame Keynes than Robert McNamara.) This in turn fed the third factor, a shift away from Keynesian economics and toward the "neoliberal" position of market ideology, although the latter had been building for some time.[15]

The ideological shift I am referring to came to be called Reaganomics in the 1980s—market fundamentalism, or the ideology of unrestrained growth. This theory posits that the wealth at the top will eventually "trickle down" to the less fortunate. This has always been a lie; very little, in fact, ever manages to trickle down. But to those at the top, who stand to profit from these neoliberal policies, it is a philosophy with enormous appeal. Ironically enough, the classic text of this school appeared the same year that Bretton Woods was signed. *The Road to Serfdom* was a strange, Manichaean manifesto penned by the Austrian economist Friedrich von Hayek, who regarded any type of state intervention, or economic planning, as a step toward totalitarianism. Only an unregulated laissez-faire economy, he believed, could guarantee political freedom, and for Hayek it had something of a divine status. (Margaret Thatcher declared his book to be her bible.) It was not for nothing that Keynes once referred to Hayek's theory as "one of the most frightful muddles I have ever read."[16]

Hayek's campaign to defeat Keynesianism began in 1947, when he organized the first meeting of what would be called the Mont Pelerin Society, bringing together a host of neoliberal thinkers, such as Milton Friedman, in a private forum committed to championing their cause. The society met almost every year in different countries under Hayek's leadership; its avowed enemy was any regulation of the market, such as was represented by Bretton Woods. It developed an international intellectual network, dedicated to promoting the neoliberal notions that a pure laissez-faire economy would create more personal freedom and that floating exchange rates were the only way to go. Not surprisingly, it attracted a new coalition that favored these ideas: representatives of multinational industrial firms, officials of private financial institutions, central banks, financial ministries, and the like—figures such as George Shultz and William Simon, both of whom were to later become secretary of the treasury under Nixon, and Paul Volcker, eventually chairman of

the Federal Reserve System. These and other officials rejected the principles of Bretton Woods, arguing that capital controls were contrary to
individual liberty and constituted a kind of police power exercised by the
state. Welfare and social safety nets were anathema to this group; its only
interest was in unrestrained growth. Think tanks such as the American
Enterprise Institute also served to raise the profile of these ideas, ideas
that ultimately prevailed.[17]

WHAT WERE the consequences of Nixon's decision to abandon the
Bretton Woods agreement? I have already described a good bit of that in
chapter 1, but let me be specific in terms of the economic fallout. The
first and most obvious consequence was the erratic movement of
exchange rates and the correspondingly volatile movement of speculative
capital flows. Keynes had warned of this possibility as far back as 1941,
stating that without controls on capital movements, "loose funds may
sweep around the world, disorganizing all steady business." After 1973
this happened with a vengeance. The new floating exchange environment created a world in which the weak got weaker, and the strong,
stronger. Vicious circles of disequilibrium afflicted countries pursuing
expansionary policies. When zealous currency traders suddenly lost con-
fidence in a particular country, the value of its currency plummeted
overnight. During the last decade, in particular, we have seen a series of
economic crises: the Mexican meltdown of 1994–95, the Asian financial
crisis of 1997–98, Brazil and Russia in 1998, Argentina in 2000,
Venezuela in 2002, and so on. All of these countries bought into the
promises of neoliberalism and were ruined or severely damaged by it as a
result. The reason for this is that unrestrained laissez-faire is a euphemism
for anarchy. As political commentator Robert Kuttner points out, financial flows are different from product (trade) flows; they are not self-regu-
latory, and the post–Bretton Woods system "has no defense against
destabilizing fads." By the late 1990s, in fact, capital flows were one hundred times as great as trade flows, and as we have already indicated, most
of these capital flows are not about "real" economic activities. Rather,
they are purely speculative, the attempt to profit from guesswork as to
how exchange rates will move. So we now have the "herd" behavior
Keynes warned about, sudden surges of short-term capital that can overwhelm even a large Third World country. It is a very small constituency

that benefits from this state of affairs, which is one of continued instability and volatility.[18]

The second result of the abolition of Bretton Woods has been massive social inequality, on both a worldwide and a domestic scale. To take the American situation first: for a capitalist country, America proved to be remarkably egalitarian for a good portion of its history. The rise in inequality over the nineteenth century was dramatically reversed after World War II by the Bretton Woods Agreement, and by 1968 income distribution was not more unequal than it had been in 1776. This all changed after 1971. Data from the Congressional Budget Office show that from 1973 to 2000, the average real income of the bottom 90 percent of American taxpayers fell by 7 percent, while the income of the top 1 percent rose 148 percent, and of the top 0.1 percent rose 343 percent—and this is excluding capital gains. By 1998, the average pay received by CEOs was 419 times that of the average worker, and in that same year Bill Gates was worth more than 45 percent of the entire population of the country combined. Between 1990 and 2000 the compensation awarded to the head of Citicorp (now Citigroup) rose 12,444 percent, while that of the average schoolteacher in New York City went up 20 percent. During the same decade, the wealthiest 1 percent made over 40 percent of all the stock market gains, and by 1999 this group (2.7 million people) had as much after taxes as the bottom 100 million Americans. Meanwhile, 15 percent of the population lives below the (officially defined) poverty level, 5.5 million are in the criminal justice system, and as of 2002, more than 2 million are in prison—the highest per capita rate of incarceration in the world, 1 per 143. The homeless population jumped 13 percent in 2001; nearly thirty thousand homeless people sleep in city shelters every night in New York City, while many states provide no legal rights to shelter and just let these people sleep on the street. Reviewing Kevin Phillips' book *Wealth and Democracy* in the *Washington Post*, Thomas Ferguson writes: "The United States today increasingly resembles a banana republic, in which Amazon-like rivers of money flood the political system to perpetuate and extend a typically Latin American style of income distribution." And since the early 1970s, according to Phillips, indicators of general health and social well-being stagnated or declined as the wealth of the rich skyrocketed.[19]

Even then, the figures for poverty in America may be worse than they seem, because the official poverty level is calculated by an archaic formula from the early 1960s, one based on food; it does not take subsequent inflation in housing costs into account. In *Hardships in America*, Washington's Economic Policy Institute reports that by the late 1990s, 29 percent of families with one or two adults and one to three children below twelve years of age fell below basic family budget levels for their communities. In 1996 nearly 30 percent of families with incomes below twice the poverty line faced "critical hardship" (defined as no food, housing, or medical care), and over 72 percent had at least one "serious hardship" (for example, unpaid rent payments or reliance on an ER for medical care). Over 40 percent of this group is chronically worried about food. Nor does being employed make that much of a difference: "The rate of serious hardships experienced in families below 200% of [the old] poverty [line] is virtually identical across families with and without a worker."[20]

The grimness of these statistics was lived out, as an experiment, by Barbara Ehrenreich in 1998, when she went "underground" for three months and worked as a waitress, hotel maid, cleaning woman, nursing home aid, and Wal-Mart sales clerk. Ehrenreich wanted to see if, on minimum wage, she could match income to expenses, as the poor attempt to do every day (almost 30 percent of the work force earns $8 an hour or less). It was a "prosperity" year, supposedly, and she had some significant advantages as well: a car, good health, no dependent children, white skin, an education. So this was a best-case scenario. Housing, she discovered, was the crucial issue: most of her fellow waitresses in Key West lived in flophouses, sharing with a roommate, or in vans, trailers, or motels. You can't save money by cooking in such situations, unfortunately, and the slightest medical expense knocks you for a loop. Also, since the pay actually amounted to about $5.15 an hour, she quickly had to find a second job—housekeeping, at $6.10 an hour. Working for a Wal-Mart in St. Paul, Minnesota, Ehrenreich was finally defeated, having to spend $500 the first three weeks while receiving nearly nothing in income, because the company holds back your first week's pay. (She never did find an apartment or affordable motel in St. Paul.) Ehrenreich observes that her coworkers showed all the signs of poverty: crooked yellow teeth, inadequate footwear, a hopeless look. Other industrial nations, she reflects at the end of her book, compensate for low wages with health insurance, subsidized child care and housing, public transportation and the like. The United States leaves its citizens to fend for themselves, and as a result, a lot of the daily situations of the working class are emergency ones: faintness from not having enough to eat, for example, or injuries that are too expensive to treat. Companies such as Wal-Mart, she remarks, often promote the notion that the firm is a "family," but the reality of the situation is obviously something else (Wal-Mart's reputation for exploiting workers is legendary). "You'd need a lot stronger word than *dysfunctional*," she writes, "to describe a family where a few people get to eat at the table while the rest ... lick up the drippings from the floor: *psychotic* would be closer to the mark."[21]

And it continues to get worse. As soon as he was inaugurated in 2001, George W. Bush began pushing for a tax cut that would give 40 percent of the benefits to the richest 1 percent of the taxpayers, and less than 1 percent of the benefits to the bottom 20 percent. Passed that May, the tax bill created an even greater upward redistribution of wealth and income than was already in place. It conferred a monthly stipend of at least $50,000 on the four hundred richest Americans, while the bottom 20 percent got, on average, $5.40. The poorest 10 percent got less than nothing, because the meager public services on which they relied were going to be cut or reduced. Finally, in the wake of September 11, the "economic stimulus package" passed in the House of Representatives on October 24 earmarked more than $140 billion in tax cuts for wealthy individuals and corporations, in addition to retroactive benefits that would pay back some of the taxes levied on corporations over the previous fifteen years(!). The Senate, for its part, suggested a tax-cut package that would cost $220 billion over three years, more than half of which would go to the top 1 percent of the population, and 6 percent of which would go to the bottom 60 percent. Political columnist Mark Shields commented that he had never before heard of "going into a war cutting taxes [and] rewarding the richest in society at a time of sacrifice."[22]

The data for 2001–3, reported by the U.S. Census Bureau, make this trend quite clear. During that time, the U.S. government spent $400 billion on tax cuts, most of which went to the wealthy, while 4.3 million more Americans fell below the federal poverty line (unrealistically set at $18,600 for a family of four). The total number living in poverty (thus defined) as of 2003 was nearly 36 million people, or 12.5 percent of the total population (note that it had actually been worse—12.7 percent—under the Clinton administration, in 1998). Adjusting for inflation, the federal minimum wage of $5.15 an hour was actually 30 percent less than it had been in 1968. The number of Americans without health insurance grew from 2000 to 2003 by 5.2 million to 45 million, or 15.6 percent of the population. Meanwhile, the proposed federal budget for fiscal year 2005 (as of this writing) is $2.4 trillion, which includes a 7 percent increase in military spending, a 10 percent increase in domestic security spending, and a mere 0.5 percent increase in spending for a vast array of domestic programs. The projections for 2009 are that child care assistance could be cut for as many as 365,000 children, while those individuals earning $1 million or more per year will receive an annual $155,000 in tax cuts. These cuts, if made permanent, will cost the government nearly $1 trillion over the next ten years.[23]

The combined result of tax cuts, recession, and a plunging stock market was reported on the front page of the *Wall Street Journal* early in 2002: "As Budget Deficits Loom, Many Promises, Programs, Could Suffer." Social Security is now vulnerable, the *Journal* reports, and "the government won't do much to help the elderly or the uninsured with mounting health-care costs." Yet the *Journal* is not without its (unconscious) irony: right next to this article was one entitled "The Civilizing Effect of the Market." Yes, how civil all this is; it brings to mind a famous remark made by Louis Brandeis over one hundred years ago: "We can have a democratic society or we can have the concentration of great wealth in the hands of the few. We cannot have both." But the situation, of course, is absolutely clear: with the collapse of Bretton Woods, and the subsequent globalization that got unleashed, "we" have made our decision—and it wasn't for democracy.[24]

If America doesn't treat its own underclass compassionately and democratically, what might we expect its treatment of the Third World to be like? I am anticipating some of the argument of chapter 3 here, because American foreign policy is at least partly driven by its economic policy, and this warrants an extended discussion. But it may be useful to say a few words about it here. As already noted, by 1998 the richest four hundred people on the planet had as much wealth as the bottom half of the population, and 3 billion people live on less than two dollars a day. During the past fifteen to twenty years more than one hundred developing countries suffered failures in growth and living standards that were more severe than anything suffered by the industrial nations during the Depression, and between 1987 and 1993 the number of people with incomes of less than one dollar per day increased by 100 million, to 1.3 billion people. In more than one hundred countries, per capita income is lower today than it was fifteen years ago, and nearly 1.6 billion people live in worse conditions than they did in the early 1980s. In 1998, emerging markets represented 7 percent of the capital value of world markets, but constituted 85 percent of the world's population. A U.N. report of 2003 found that nearly one-sixth of the world's population lived in slums, and predicted that the figure would rise to one-third by 2033; and it specifically held globalization, neoliberal economics, the IMF, and the World Trade Organization responsible for this. "To date," editorialized the *International Herald Tribune* in 2003, "globalization remains a flawed game whose rules have been fixed by rich nations."[25]

One of the best discussions of these developments is that of economist Robert Blecker in his 1999 book *Taming Global Finance*. Noting that volatile flows of speculative capital have fueled currency crises, stock market collapses, and financial panics, Blecker comments that the response of the U.S. government and the IMF is to blame the victims "while insisting that they accept more of the same types of policies that have led to their current predicament." In fact, international capital flows tend to reinforce both the upswings and the downswings of the business cycle. In developing countries the peaks are sharper, and so are the troughs. The IMF, created at Bretton Woods to avoid another depression, "mutated into its antithesis" (says Robert Kuttner) after 1971. The Fund is now the main advocate of what is known as the "Washington consensus," the neoliberal model of a global, integrated economy based on the free flow of capital, and conducted on American terms. Contrary to the intentions of its original founders, the IMF has long been led by economists who push liberalization onto countries that lack the internal institutions necessary for managing the resulting capital inflows. It and the World Bank are largely creatures of the U.S. Treasury Department and Wall Street financial interests. IMF assistance to countries in crisis is now dependent on stringent reforms intended to promote the neoliberal agenda. The result of all this is that those countries' economies frequently get severely damaged, if not actually wrecked.[26]

An even more searing indictment of the IMF can be found in Joseph Stiglitz's masterful study, *Globalization and Its Discontents*. Stiglitz, a Nobel laureate who teaches economics at Columbia University, cannot easily be dismissed, since he writes from the vantage point of an insider. He was chairman of President Clinton's Council of Economic Advisers and senior vice president and chief economist at the World Bank. In a detailed, case-by-case analysis, Stiglitz repeatedly castigates the IMF as destructive and dogmatic, a major source of Third World misery. In country after country, the IMF prescribed "solutions" based on market fundamentalism that took no account of what effect these actions would have on people. Its neoliberal policies often led to hunger and riots; the few benefits that did accrue usually went to the rich. Upper-echelon IMF personnel (for instance, Robert Rubin and Stanley Fischer) typically come from the private sector (Goldman Sachs, Citigroup), have little concern for the environment, democracy, or social justice, and basically act as representatives of the American financial community. They cut fuel and food subsidies to the Third World and insist on cutbacks in health expenditures, while Prada, Benetton, and Ralph Lauren come in for the benefit of the few urban rich, and vast numbers of rural poor wind up worse off than before. From the top floors of luxury hotels, he says, the IMF directors impose policies that destroy people's lives and don't think twice about it. "Globalization," concludes Stiglitz, "seems to replace the old dictatorships of national elites with new dictatorships of international finance."[27] (Meanwhile, back in the United States, we sit around asking ourselves, "Why do they hate us?" Duh!)

To Manfred Steger, a specialist in globalization, there is no doubt that neoliberalism, or the Washington consensus as it was developed during the Reagan administration and after, has a civilizational bias. The whole thing, he says, was really a gigantic repackaging of classical laissez-faire economics, now labeled the New Economy. But the "metanarrative," as it is sometimes called—that is, the story underneath the story—is essentially one of "modernization," which casts Western countries (read: the United States and the United Kingdom) as "the privileged vanguard of an evolutionary process that applies to all nations." (And make no mistake about it: the so-called war on terror has the hidden agenda of trying to get Islamic civilization to accept the value structure of Western modernity—an agenda that a dissenting advisory panel within the Pentagon was, by late 2004, calling a "strategic mistake.") Globalization, adds historian and former CIA analyst Chalmers Johnson, is "a kind of intellectual sedative that lulls and distracts its Third World victims while rich countries cripple them, ensuring that they will never be able to challenge the imperial powers."[28]

A vivid illustration of all this can be found in Stephanie Black's 2001 documentary on Jamaica, *Life and Debt*, in which it becomes clear that loans made to the country by the IMF and the Inter-American Bank resulted in lower productivity, higher debt, and greater poverty. The loans had a crucial rider: they required the abolition of tariffs. So Jamaica was forced to compete in the open globalized market, which they could not do because foreign goods, coming in at lower prices, overwhelmed the country. (As Stiglitz testifies, this happened to many other developing nations as well.) As a result, the native economy was ruined. Crime went up; in one sobering scene in the film we see attack dogs being trained in what has suddenly became a flourishing industry.

Of course, the American middle and upper classes know little or nothing of this; they just go to Jamaica, sip rum by the pool, and listen to all the groovy music. The contrast here is the theme of a remarkable play by Wallace Shawn entitled *The Fever*, in which a person (the gender is never specified; I'll use feminine pronouns) who always takes her holiday in a Third World country wakes up in her hotel room sick. As "the fever" takes her over, she begins to figure out the connection between her way of life and the existence of Third World poverty. The illness, in fact, becomes a metaphor for this grotesque social inequality that is really the sickness of an entire planet. She realizes that the cup of coffee she is drinking (Jamaica Blue Mountain?) "contains the history of the peasants who picked the beans, how some of them fainted in the heat of the sun, some were beaten, some were kicked." It's all interwoven, she finally realizes: "we cannot escape our connection to the poor." In order to be free of the fever, the horrible truth of our situation has to be confronted head-on—in particular, the fact that a way of life based on such social inequality cannot be justified. "The life I live," she says to herself,

> is irredeemably corrupt. . . . Standing naked beside the beggar—there's no difference between her and me except a difference in luck. I don't actually deserve to have a thousand times more than the beggar has. I don't deserve to have two crusts of bread more.
>
> And then, this too: My friends and I were never well meaning and kind. The sadists were not compassionate scholars, trying to do their best for humanity. The burning of fields, the burning of children, were not misguided attempts to do good. Cowards who sit in lecture halls or the halls of state denouncing the crimes of the revolutionaries are not as admirable as the farmers and nuns who ran so swiftly into the wind, who ran silently into death. The ones I killed were not the worst people in all those places; in fact, they were the best. . . .

The chambermaid's condition is not temporary. A life sentence has been passed on her: she's to clean for me and to sleep in filth. Not, she's to clean for me today, and I'm to clean for her tomorrow, or I'm to clean for her next year. Not, she's to sleep in filth tonight, and I'm to sleep in filth tomorrow night, or some other night. No. The sentence says that *she* will serve, and then on the next day *she* will serve, and then *she* will, and *she* will, right up until her death.[29]

Is there no way of reversing this situation, or at least mitigating it? The problem is that countries who don't get on the globalization bandwagon get left behind; and developing countries get left behind whether they get on the bandwagon or not. The fever of wealth, consumption, and power is threatening to engulf the entire planet, and as in the case of contagion it is hard to keep it from spreading. The post–Bretton Woods dynamic is captured very well by Hans-Peter Martin and Harald Schumann in their book *The Global Trap:*

> The more dependent countries become on the good will of investors, the more ruthless must governments be in favouring the already privileged minority who have sizable financial assets. Their interests are always the same: low inflation, stable external value of the currency, and minimum taxation of their investment income. . . . The financial short-circuit between different countries forces them into a competition to lower taxes, to reduce public expenditure, and to renounce the aim of social equality—a competition which brings nothing other than a global redistribution from those at the bottom to those at the top. Rewards go to whoever creates the best conditions for big capital, while sanctions loom for any government that obstructs this law of the jungle.[30]

"The law of the jungle" is, in fact, the regime we've been living under for the past thirty-plus years.

Technology

The story of globalization, of course, is not entirely an economic one. Certain developments in technology have managed to play a pivotal role, ones that require close examination. These developments have been building for more than two hundred years, and go to the heart of the disintegration of our civilization, as described earlier. They also shape, or "condition," the economy in powerful ways, and thus may be more fundamental to the globalization process than the economic developments described above.

The most insightful inquiry into the relationship between technology and the way we live today, at least that I am aware of, is *Technology and the Character of Contemporary Life* (1984), by the American philosopher Albert Borgmann. Borgmann's analysis makes it possible to see that much of globalization, as well as the condition we have labeled liquid modernity, is the result of an internal logic of technological development that reached its highest point (thus far) in the last few decades of the twentieth century. In this sense, his approach is a corrective to the common perception of technology as being neutral, a tool, a force for good or evil that can be managed or directed by political or economic institutions. The reality, Borgmann argues, is actually very different: modern technology, he says (stress on the word "modern"), provides a "characteristic and constraining pattern to the entire fabric of our lives." This pattern shapes politics and economics, not the reverse. Borgmann calls this pattern the "device paradigm."[31]

Consider, for example, a stereo system providing music, as opposed to a group of friends who gather at someone's home to play music together. What is going on in each case? The first situation involves a kind of abstraction or concealment. Looking at a record or a CD, I have no way of knowing what kind of music it contains, nor do the speakers resemble the human voice or the strings of a violin. From the technology itself, I don't know the musicians and may not be able to identify the instruments employed; the character of the apparatus on which the hearing of music rests is inaccessible to me. And this, in a nutshell, is the device paradigm: the separation of the commodity (in this case, music) from the machinery that produces it. What I get is abstraction: "mere" commodity.

The opposite of this is what Borgmann calls a "focal practice" or focal thing. A focal practice—for instance, when friends gather to play their musical instruments—is one that centers and illuminates our lives. In this case, the machinery is not separated from the product; it is fully present and embodies a long tradition of craft, method, and musical literature. As a group activity, as an engagement of body and mind, a focal practice does not separate means and ends. It is fully "whole," and thus makes *us* whole. This arrangement, in fact, characterizes a good deal of premodern culture. With the device paradigm, on the other hand, the world is transformed in a radical way.

Let us take heat as a second example. For most of the nineteenth century, across much of America, if you wanted your house to be warm in the winter you had to do certain things: cut down a tree, saw and split logs, haul and stack wood, and finally burn the wood in a stove. Here, says Borgmann, we see the difference between a focal thing and a device. A thing is inseparable from its context; and it provides more than one commodity. Few of us today, of course, would welcome the labor involved in this process, and we appreciate the fact that central heating now renders this work unnecessary. But let's not kid ourselves: this technological comfort comes with heavy cultural costs. The wood-burning stove furnished more than just warmth; it was also a focus, a hearth. It gathered the family, gave the home its center. It required different tasks from each member of the family, and its use marked the seasons. It had an important sensuous dimension as well: the smell of the smoke, for example, or the perspiration you felt on the body as you sawed the wood. It also involved skill—"intensive and refined world engagement"—and this skill was bound up with social interaction. Focal practices such as these molded the person, gave him or her character. They embodied a whole way of life.

Now consider central heating. It supplies mere warmth—and "mere" is the operative word here, because central heating relieves us of all the other elements, now seen as a drag, a bunch of oppressive chores. The machinery is completely concealed; beyond occasionally adjusting a thermostat, we are separated from the process and, in fact, completely in the dark about it. It makes no demands on our skill or attention. What we get is a commodity (heat) that is totally "anonymous"; there is no social engagement involved. Similarly, if you go to a gym and exercise in front of a video, as opposed to running outdoors, there is no engagement with the natural world. And this is the crucial shift from the pretechnological era (when *premodern* technologies were used) to the technological one: "the presence of things is replaced with the availability of commodities." Devices, writes Borgmann, "dissolve the coherent and engaging character of the pretechnological world of things." The historical pattern, in other words, is the destruction of focal things and the reconstitution of them as devices. As this process became pervasive in our society, it increasingly emptied it out, creating a way of life that lacks a center.[32]

It is for this reason that the common view of the continuity of technology is a mistake. Yes, man has been a tool user since the Paleolithic era, and no, technology did not suddenly arise with the invention of central heating. But such a view misses the point that the discontinuities are much greater than the continuities. The tools and technologies of traditional cultures are never "mere" means; they are always woven into the context of human ends. *Modern* technology (say, post-1800), based as it is on the device paradigm, introduced a radical new force into society, one that has restructured it from the ground up. A similar rupture can be posited for the last fifty or sixty years. This is another reason that we are so utterly removed from the world of the 1950s. Walt Disney cartoons are not derivatives of cave paintings at Lascaux, and the Internet is not some logical or historical extension of the Talmud.[33]

Still, one might argue that Borgmann is romanticizing the pretechnological era. After all, much of the life of peasant, premodern cultures boiled down to hardship, drudgery, and boredom, and modern technology eliminated a lot of that misery. Personally, I prefer central heating to a wood-burning stove; it provides me with the time to sit at home in cozy comfort and write books on the joys of the premodern age. But how is it, asks Borgmann, that the initial feats of liberation achieved by technology, which made life easier for millions, evolved into the procurement of frivolous comfort ("Jog in the privacy of your own home," etc.)? We need to make a distinction between two kinds of burdens: those of hunger, disease, and backbreaking labor, and those that are ennobling, that are exacted by the demands of community and the standards of human excellence. Our problem is that we seek relief from all burdens whatsoever—we want an anodyne for every discomfort—and the result is that we have neither community nor excellence. Fast-food outlets may make life more convenient; they also contribute to the nationwide epidemic of obesity as well as the disintegration of the family, and they make life a lot more empty. Focal things and practices require discipline and commitment; devices, which are mostly forms of short-lived entertainment, require neither. As the twentieth century finally played out, technology freed us up for more technology; it became its own goal. Commodities and their consumption constitute the ultimate purpose of the technological enterprise, and ultimately, of our lives. This is the real force of the device paradigm, over the last forty years in particular, and the emergence of liquid modernity as a condition of those lives would have been impossible without it.[34]

What, then, *is* the good life? To sketch this out, Borgmann draws on central elements of the classical and Judeo-Christian traditions. Four features, it would seem, characterize the "person of excellence," in this account:[35]

1. He or she is a world citizen—that is, someone who knows a fair amount about the world (science and history, in particular).
2. He or she seeks both physical valor and intellectual refinement ("*mens sana in corpore sano*").
3. He or she is accomplished in music and versed in the arts.
4. He or she is charitable—i.e., aware that real strength lies not in material force, but in the power to give, forgive, help, and heal.

Now let's consider our current situation. Does it match up to this ideal?

The reader will probably not be too shocked to learn that it doesn't even come close, and that it is much worse now than when Borgmann was writing his book. All of the things he cites—that our command of science is weak, and participation in politics minimal; that we tolerate grave social injustice; that most of us are overweight and out of shape; that a huge fraction of the American adult population is functionally illiterate; that there is a vast gap between rich and poor; that our politics is strident and bellicose—have gotten appreciably worse in the last twenty years. If, for example, we consult John Robinson's 1977 study, *How Americans Use Time*, we learn that what Borgmann calls focal practices are almost unknown among the American population. On an average daily basis, five minutes are spent on reading books (of any kind), six minutes on active sports, two minutes on outdoor activities, one minute on making music, thirty seconds on theater and concerts, and less than thirty seconds on artwork or museum visits. That was the average individual profile of nearly thirty years ago, and things have greatly deteriorated in the interim (as cited in chapter 1, for example, the average American watches TV four hours a day). Quite obviously, we are not a nation devoted to the pursuit of excellence, as defined by the classical and Judeo-Christian traditions; even from a contemporary European perspective, we are something of a joke. The overwhelming majority of Americans are simply not interested in the life of the mind, and in a participatory sense not terribly interested in the life of the body. What else is left?

One might also ask what kind of happiness modern technology actually provides. A number of studies have demonstrated that beyond a level of minimal material comfort, people in advanced technological societies are no happier than those living in less developed ones. In fact, the degeneration of things to commodities, which finally entails making instant gratification the purpose of life, has its logical conclusion in drugs or the direct stimulation of the brain (pure commodity). A person living in this way—and if we put compulsion around food, alcohol, tobacco, television, sex, shopping, and spectator sports on the list, we've probably targeted 95 percent of the American population—is at the extreme opposite end of the spectrum from the person of excellence described above.

How did we fall so low? How did the device paradigm, internal to modern technology, manage to expand to the point that it eviscerated practically everything of quality in the United States? Part of the answer, oddly enough, can be located in the liberal democratic tradition itself (here I am using "liberal" in the political, rather than the economic, sense), which contains within it a latent moral vacuum, one that proved to have explosive potential. This issue came to light in one of the most famous analyses of that tradition ever penned, Isaiah Berlin's *Two Concepts of Liberty*, which he delivered as an inaugural lecture at Oxford in 1958.[36] Basically, Berlin distinguished between "negative freedom," or freedom *from*, and "positive freedom," or freedom *to*. Negative freedom means I can do whatever I want so long as it doesn't interfere with the rights of others. This concept lies at the heart of liberal democratic politics; it deals with people at the level of what they say they want. (If they want central heating or fourteen shades of lip gloss, let them have it; it's their right.) Positive freedom is altogether different; it holds that political power can and should be used to free human beings so that they can realize their hidden potential. This notion, said Berlin, which goes back to Rousseau and the Romantics, holds that people are free only when they can realize their innermost natures, their "true" purpose. (They may *think* they want lip gloss, but authentic life can't possibly be about lip gloss.)

Using communism as the worst-case scenario, Berlin spent most of the lecture (and in fact, most of his life) focusing on the downside of positive freedom, which is certainly real. All utopian political schemes shade into their totalitarian opposite, he said, because of the arrogance inherent in the position that I know better than someone else what his "true" desires are, his hidden potential is, and am willing to coerce him into living the way he "ought" to live. If he cries (to borrow a line from Janis Joplin) "Oh Lord! Won't you buy me a Mercedes-Benz!" well, that's false consciousness, and it needs to be corrected. The most vicious tyrannies, as history has shown, have been erected on the foundation of the theme that people are alienated from their true natures and have to have their consciousness raised so they can live the lives they were "meant" to live.

So far, so good; I'm not a big fan of enforced self-realization myself. The problem is that Berlin neglected to examine the downside of *negative* freedom, which renders his analysis lopsided. His lecture made clear what liberal democracy was against, but not what it was for; nor did he clarify why negative freedom should have priority over all other political values. Negative freedom is essentially a position of absence; it corresponds perfectly to the laissez-faire economy, and might be said to be an apology for it. Berlin's insight was into the human susceptibility to utopias that promised release from the burden of moral choice, but that is exactly what a laissez-faire economy and the device paradigm do. The Canadian philosopher John Ralston Saul pegs this perfectly in a recent essay, "The Collapse of Globalism," in which he points out that in the psychic vacuum generated by the fall of the USSR, globalization got elevated to the level of transcendent vision, redemption, and "the answer to every one of our problems." And of *course* this was utopian in nature. "At the core of every ideology lies the worship of a bright future," observes Saul. This is exactly why the reaction to the antiglobalization demonstrations in Seattle in 1999 and those that followed evoked such rage among the world's elites, with Tony Blair calling the protesters "anti-democratic hooligans," Thomas Friedman referring to them as "flat-earth advocates," and Silvio Berlusconi (a vein throbbing in his neck) denouncing them as "Talibanized hordes."[37]

The truth is that we never really have negative freedom, when you think about it. Something always moves in to fill the vacuum created by such a philosophical position, and in our case that something has been (modern) technology and the commodity universe. Freedom is hardly the absence of all traditional structures; that would be anarchy. And this is precisely where the ideal of self-realization—for example, the classical/Judeo-Christian definition of excellence—comes into play, for the just society remains incomplete without an explicit definition of the good life. In pretechnological society, this was (ideally) lived as a lifelong commitment. In the world of the modern technological order, one winds up worshiping the colors of Benetton.

More to the point, the entire globalized economy has the form of the device paradigm, because following Adam Smith, it presupposes a hidden machinery, the "invisible hand" of individual self-interest operating in the market and sorting things out all by itself. In this sense, what some critics of globalization are doing is daring to challenge market fundamentalism by examining the hidden machinery behind it. Joseph Stiglitz, for example, was able to show that the invisible-hand theory applies only under certain very restricted conditions (and very badly, it turns out, in the case of the developing countries).[38] But normally, light does not get shined on the hidden machinery; instead, we are dazzled by the visible commodity. Things didn't start out this way, of course; America began as an embodiment of the Enlightenment tradition, and the four features of excellence described above were hardly alien concepts to our colonial and postcolonial forebears. Under the advance of the device paradigm, however, we became a very different country. We retain the rhetoric of liberal democracy, but in concrete terms this supposed democracy gets enacted as the commodity culture, in which freedom of choice really means Wendy's versus Burger King. Real politics has evaporated in this country. As Will Hutton puts it, we have "only a shrivelled conception of the public realm." Or in Michael Sandel's terminology (*Democracy's Discontent*), the United States is now little more than a "procedural republic." The same could be said of Rome, even before Caesar's time.[39]

Similarly, Daniel Boorstin, the former Librarian of Congress, once described advertising as the "rhetoric of democracy." Ultimate existential questions get answered by the culture of every society, advertently or not—they all define "meaning" for members of the culture—and if this is not done explicitly and deliberately, such as happens in traditional cultures, then a hidden agenda emerges and fills the gap. Much of what America worships, and how it prays, can be seen any weekend at a large suburban shopping mall. This is now our "public space," and it is obviously not very public.[40]

It is for these reasons that it is very difficult to criticize contemporary socioeconomic arrangements or even find a vocabulary to voice that criticism. Commodities are sharply defined and easily measured: for example, the number of McDonald's franchises in Iowa, or the number of Big Macs sold during the past twelve months. Focal practices, on the other hand, engage us in so many subtle and contextual ways that they cannot be captured by quantification. How does one measure the value of a family meal? A hike in the wilderness? One can talk about the value of these things only through testimony and appeal, and it often comes off as arrogant. In a land of people who have little interest in, or even awareness of, the tradition of excellence described above, how could an appeal to such things come off as anything else? What chance does such an alternative voice have when, for example, gas-saving hybrid cars are often ridiculed for being "virtuous"? In an upside-down world, *all* quality is going to be viewed as elitist.[41]

For Marx, of course, the crucial distinction was between the worker/consumer and the corporations, with the latter doing their best to screw the former. This goes on all the time; we didn't really need the corporate scandals of 2001–02 to tell us that. But is it really the case that CEOs' interests are opposed to the rest of the population? Not at all, when you think about it; the privileges of the ruling class are exercised in consonance with popular goals. Rich and poor both want the same things, and in this way commodities and the device paradigm are the stabilizing factors of technological societies. Social inequality favors the advancement of the reign of technology, in other words, because it presents a ladder of what can be attained through that technology. This results in an equilibrium that can be maintained only by the production of more and more commodities. The less affluent must be able, at least in theory, to catch up with the more affluent. Hence politics remains without substance, a realm from which the crucial dimensions of life, the core values, are excluded.[42]

Who, then, can criticize this situation? Who has the right to speak out (and what difference would it make)? In the aftermath of Isaiah Berlin's inaugural lecture, the American diplomat George Kennan wrote to ask whether Berlin thought that the American electorate of "this sprawling, careless country before me—this 175 million people stumbling thoughtlessly into self-indulgence, bad habits, decadence and political apathy" could really be trusted with negative freedom. Why *not*, he asked Berlin, have an elite that suggests to this mass of people how they might best use their freedom? Berlin's reply was never recorded, but we do know what he thought of directing the masses "for their own good," and he would have undoubtedly referred Kennan to Juvenal's famous remark about who was going to guard the guardians. Of course, suggesting is not directing, and it certainly isn't coercion; nor does self-realization necessarily lead to totalitarianism. But leaving the question of arrogance or elitism aside (which may be a red herring anyway), how could this possibly work?[43]

The truth is that things are so far gone now that we don't even have a public language for the focal position, for the life of craft and commitment, for the long-lost world of civic responsibility. The classical notion of virtue began to lose ground with the eclipse of the Federalists in the 1790s; eventually, what we were left with was pure self-interest, supposedly channeled into the greater good via the pressure of market forces (see chapter 7). How can I explain to the man sitting at the next table, mindlessly yakking away on his cell phone, and making it impossible for me to have a quiet moment with a friend at this restaurant, that he is privatizing public space and thereby destroying it? Should I give him a crash course in the device paradigm, or perhaps hand him a copy of Borgmann's book and ask him to phone me (preferably on his land line) when he's finished reading it so we can sit down and discuss it together? It's all a catch-22, because as long as the goal of our society is to advance the standard of living, no alternatives to the technological paradigm are possible. Quite obviously, I would come off as some kind of fanatic. It makes no sense to become a "focal saint," preaching to those trapped in the so-called choices of the unregulated market that they should do something different. In a situation in which the economy itself has become a device, such an approach is not likely to get much of a hearing; nor does there seem to be anything anyone can do to change it. In the last analysis, there is no way of making more than a hortatory case for excellence or the good life.[44]

It remains only to comment on how the device paradigm and globalization so neatly meshed and reinforced each other in the closing decades of the twentieth century, and where we may be headed as a result. My own impression is that it was at some point in the late 1960s that the device paradigm attained a kind of critical mass, and that innovative technology—especially in microelectronics and telecommunications—really hit its stride. As already noted, these developments roughly coincided with the repeal of Bretton Woods, for both they, and it, greatly accelerated the process of market liberalization, throwing the consumer society into high gear. The next quantum leap, according to the Spanish sociologist

Manuel Castells, was the microprocessor revolution, which allowed quasi-instantaneous worldwide trading and led to even greater financial globalization, beginning in the late eighties (this was, for example, a key factor in the crash of October 1987). Advanced mathematical models, made operational by means of powerful new computer systems in which information transmitted from around the world was constantly adjusted, assisted greatly in the explosive growth of financial markets. In 1995, for example, investments made by mutual funds, pension funds, and institutional investors in general amounted to $20 trillion in the United States, which represented a tenfold increase since 1985. Online transactions and computer-based information systems allow for movements of capital between currencies and countries in a matter of seconds. The result, says Castells, is that we may have

> created an Automaton, at the core of our economies, decisively conditioning our lives. Humankind's nightmare of seeing our machines taking control of our world seems on the edge of becoming reality—not in the form of robots . . . but as an electronically based system of financial transactions. The system overwhelms controls and regulations put in place by governments, international institutions and private financial firms. . . . Its logic is not controlled by any individual capitalist or corporation—nor, for that matter, by any public institution.

This Automaton, he goes on to say, is not the market, and does not follow market rules. It is much larger, and its elements combine in ways that are increasingly unpredictable—as Keynes told us years ago. Technology just makes the whole thing more volatile, and more unassailable.[45]

Nor is that likely to be the worst of it. If all of our socioeconomic, political, and cultural life is falling in line with the device paradigm, there is no reason that our personal and psychological life shouldn't follow suit—as Aldous Huxley in effect predicted in *Brave New World*. Following that gloomy vision, Francis Fukuyama, in *Our Posthuman Future*, outlines the logical end point of the whole process: human beings as devices. We are, he points out, halfway there already. The world of cloning, electronic implants, and Prozac-for-all is already on the horizon; nobody will get hurt in this soft totalitarian society because—at least from a quaint, focal point of view—there will be nothing that is recognizably human, and so nobody to *be* hurt. As in *The Matrix*, there may be no counterpoint to the technological order—now completely meshed with culture and the economy—because there may no longer be any "focal saints" to preach otherwise. No one will have to be compelled to do anything, because all of us will have been seduced by this way of life ("positive" freedom!).[46]

All of this is perhaps the biotechnological version of human relations described by Zygmunt Bauman, Ellen Ullman, and even Rachel Greenwald, in which people become living embodiments of the device paradigm, marketing themselves as commodities, whether at work or in "love," while the inner "machinery" (if it even exists anymore) is hidden from them and from everybody else. This description applies equally to the gurus and spiritual leaders who loudly and publicly condemn the soullessness of modern technological society and who market themselves or their teachings as alternatives to it. This has not made, and will not make, the slightest difference for the globalization process and serves only to demonstrate that, within the technological order itself, rebellion can merely copy the format of the device paradigm and thereby extend it ("commodify your dissent," as Thomas Frank puts it). Real alternatives will have to come from a more "muscular" place than a New Age pulpit.

And that muscular place, I predict, will prove to be history itself. Arthur Koestler, that veteran cold warrior (*Darkness at Noon*), did not mince his words regarding the United States any more than he did about the USSR: a "civilization in a cul de sac," he wrote, also calling America a "contactless society" populated by automatons. The United States, he continued, is like Rome in the later stages of the Empire: "a similarly soulless, politically corrupt, everybody-for-himself civilization."[47] It seems clear enough that when you put money (or commodities) at the center of a culture, you finally don't *have* a culture. Indeed, the Germans have a word to describe this type of situation: *sinnentleert* ("devoid of meaning"). America can strut and puff all it wants, but on some level, all of us know this (it struts and puffs *because* it is empty). After all, Rome may have *looked* invincible in, say, A.D. 300, but history proved otherwise.

I PROMISED to talk about global process and local fallout in chapters 1 and 2; I hope I have been at least moderately successful in that attempt. The society I described in the previous chapter, in which lives are overwhelmed by (often meaningless) work, existence is trivialized and supersaturated by the media, children are indoctrinated with corporate consumerist ideology, and communities are destroyed by technologies of isolation and privatization—such a society could not have arisen without the forces of globalization, both economic and technological, which have turned everything into competition and commodity. As above, so below: what happened in the macrocosm finally made its way into the details of our daily lives, and how we live those lives in turn strengthens those larger forces. With this synergy at work, everything is disintegrated: human bonds, work, romantic partnerships, communities. Such things are seen only, says Zygmunt Bauman, as items meant to be consumed: "the new loneliness of body and community," he writes, "is the result of a wide set of seminal changes subsumed under the rubric of liquid modernity." Or as Christopher Clausen of Pennsylvania State University recently put it, "no inherited identity or way of life makes more than minimal demands on the vast majority of the population." The loss of culture that we have experienced, Clausen says, has left America with a "mass individualism. . . . No wonder fundamentalists of every kind see us as a moral threat."[48]

Which brings us back to September 11, and the so-called attack on civilization. Was it really that? Is America really the standard bearer of a genuine civilization that it was, say, only sixty years ago? The choice of targets, after all, was highly symbolic: not, say, the Jefferson Memorial or Columbia University, which once did represent American civilization, but rather the World Trade Center and the Pentagon, the symbols of American financial and military power—what we have become. America sees the rest of the world as one big happy market to be exploited, and, if we are going to be completely candid about it, to be ruled or controlled. But how does the rest of the world see *America*, and what has America done to create that perception? There are undoubtedly many reasons for the 9/11 attacks, but the fear that the American technocultural wasteland will, via U.S. foreign and economic policy, overwhelm the Islamic nations surely has to be high on the list.

I am no fan of fundamentalist regimes, or even of religion at all, if the truth be told; and if that were the only answer available, I would have to conclude that the remedy was much, much worse than the disease. Traditional or "tribal" cultures are typically repressive, hierarchical, and claustrophobic; the way they treat women (just for starters) says enough, as far as I am concerned. But they do have one thing that we seem to lack: a spiritual center, a mode of guidance (focal practice) that is deeper than the world of commodities and the device paradigm. The choice is hopefully not going to be between the Taliban and Enron; faced with that "clash of civilizations," the still sane among us might contemplate colonizing the moon (assuming we can get there before Halliburton does). But the question of the relationship between the secular and the tribal is, some might argue, the issue of our time, and one that has become—inevitably—an integral part of U.S. foreign policy. If we hope to learn something from the events of 9/11, this might be a good place to start.

~ 3 ~

The Home and the World

The East is to be opened and transformed whether we will it or not; the standards of the West are to be imposed on it; nations and peoples which have stood still the centuries through . . . [will be] made part of the universal world of commerce and of ideas.

—Woodrow Wilson, 1901,
in defense of the annexation of the Philippines

WE NEED TO HAVE a look, then, at the secular-tribal dichotomy, and how the tensions it embodies constitute a—or perhaps even *the*—crucial element in the unfolding drama of the twenty-first century. Before we can do that, however, I would like to give the reader a brief outline of the major arguments of the foreign policy section of this book (chapters 3–6). In very basic terms, these are as follows:

✦ U.S. foreign policy has finally landed the country in a huge mess, one that is both self-destructive and—sad to say—largely of America's own making.

✦ This policy is closely tied to the nation's domestic policies, and both in turn are integrally related to life "on the ground"—that is, to the values and daily behavior of American citizens.

✦ The Bush Doctrine of 2002, announcing the right of preemptive military strike, and America's de facto intention to rule the world, is not entirely new, but it does mark the transition from a twilight phase in American history (characterized, for example, by our involvement in Vietnam) to an actual Dark Age.

✦ 9/11 was a wake-up call that was not understood and that went unheeded. It was America's last chance to try to pull away from (or, at least, decelerate) a downward trajectory, a chance that was completely blown. A scenario of steady decline is probably all that is left to us at this point; we will not get another chance.

That said, let me now turn to the larger cultural backdrop.

Secular versus Tribal

What Isaiah Berlin called negative freedom is a freedom that was hard won, in the West, through the great bourgeois revolutions of the seventeenth and eighteenth centuries. It is essentially the freedom to be left alone. Societies without this type of freedom tend to be tribal (or organic) in nature, heavily dominated by custom and tradition. In those cultures, the separation of church and state—a mainstay of secular democracy—is usually absent. Thus both Israel and Iran are torn by internal strife along the secular-tribal spectrum, as are Turkey and—as must be obvious in the wake of the 2004 presidential election—the United States. In fact, many American evangelicals probably have more in common with the citizens of Damascus than they do, say, with many of the inhabitants of New York or Los Angeles (something they would not, I am sure, be terribly happy to hear, especially given the profound anti-Muslim feeling among many right-wing Christians).

The crucial point here is that for any given society, there is a price to be paid at either end of the spectrum. Consider the following vignette, which appears in the book *Earthwalk* by the American sociologist Philip Slater. Slater received a letter from a Moroccan graduate student, describing his attempt to conduct a sociological survey over the phone in the town in Morocco where he was then living. He was using a public phone, which meant (at that time) having to go through an operator. Instead of putting through the student's calls, however, the operator insisted on having a discussion regarding the nature and purpose of the survey. What then ensued was an argument over the value and methodol-

ogy of the entire project. It ultimately took the student three days before
he was able to place his calls.[1]

From a "secular" point of view, this is pretty strange. In fact, the student
wrote Slater that what he had most objected to while he was living in the
West—the quality of *anesthésie*, as he put it, or being oblivious of other
human beings—"is in fact what allows you to be efficient there." The
absence of this quality, he went on, "leaves you completely immersed in
an environment you can't control because you are so emotionally
involved [in it]."[2] This reminds me of the remark a Palestinian friend living in the United States once made, that although she generally regarded
Americans as a species of robots, she was nevertheless equally annoyed by
her extended family, who expected to be constantly informed of the
slightest thing she did or said. "It's pretty claustrophobic," she told me;
"you feel like you can hardly breathe." This is, in fact, quite characteristic
of tribal or traditional cultures, where relationships are primary and individual achievement is secondary. One is not free, in those cultures, to treat
the social environment impersonally, whereas in the United States that
seems to be the requirement for survival.

Of course, I may be overdrawing the contrast here; no culture today is
purely tribal or purely secular. Still, the archetypes do exist in people's
minds, and do operate across the cultures of the world to varying degrees.
One of the best portrayals of these polar opposites occurs in the novels of
Thomas Pynchon, especially *V.* and *Gravity's Rainbow*, in which the literary structure resembles a funnel. The narratives begin with a completely
anomic, open-ended, scientific world, in which everything that happens
is random and nothing has any relationship to anything else. The first two
hundred pages or so are extremely difficult to read; they depict a totally
anarchic and meaningless world. But just at the point that the reader can't
take it anymore, and he or she is ready to throw in the towel, Pynchon
begins to reveal that all of these random people, objects, and events are
actually part of a web of hidden connections. As he draws the net tighter
and tighter, the relief initially felt by the reader—that of being out of the
anomic world—turns into a claustrophobia of the kind described by my
Palestinian friend: there is nowhere to hide. By the end of the story, the
reader is faced with two horrendous, and totally opposite, paranoias: the
open end of the funnel, the world of *anesthésie*, where (as in my apartment
building) you could basically drop dead and nobody would notice; and
the contracted end of the funnel, in which you don't have a moment's

privacy, and where everything you do is everybody else's business. Which would *you* choose?

This dichotomy reflects two profoundly different ways of being in the world, one characterized by no meaning, and the other characterized by "too much" meaning. The relevance of this to the present conflict between "the West and the rest," as some scholars have put it—and certainly, between the West and Islam—should be obvious, as I shall elaborate on below. First, however, let's examine the ideas of the sociologist who put this whole subject on the map, the French scholar Emile Durkheim. Durkheim held that every society was held together by a *conscience collective*, a "system of beliefs and sentiments" that the members of any given society had in common, and that defined the nature of their mutual relations. Remove this, said Durkheim, replace it with the pure pursuit of self-interest, and a society would quickly collapse into a Hobbesian state of every man for himself. This, to my mind, is largely what we have in the United States today, and Islamic religious leaders have not been shy about pointing this out.

However, that is hardly the end of the story. As noted, it is possible for the *conscience collective* to be *too* intense, a condition that anthropologists refer to as "hypercoherence," and which—as my Palestinian friend pointed out—has a serious downside. To examine how the essential elements of a culture are internalized by individuals as part of their personalities, Durkheim focused on, of all things, suicide. He proposed that there are two fundamental types of suicide, "altruistic" and "egotistic." In the former case, the individual is so pressured to conform that he feels he has no identity of his own. In the egotistic situation, on the other hand, the individual feels a constant pressure to stand out, achieve, be apart from the collectivity. Enough intensity in either direction, said Durkheim, and certain individuals will decide to pack it in.

Durkheim also posited a third category, "anomic" suicide, which he said arose when society was turned upside down, when rules and conventions collapsed and individuals felt themselves to be in crisis. Ironically enough, this state of affairs might be descriptive of both Islam *and* the West. America is disintegrating, in part, because it is living in a moral vacuum. The Islamic nations are in crisis, in part, because they are simultaneously attracted to and repelled by that moral vacuum (Iran is an obvious example of this). My point is that if there *is* a "clash of civilizations" going on in the world today, as the conventional wisdom has it, one aspect of that is the larger archetypal drama posited by Slater, Pynchon, and Durkheim: is life going to be tribal in nature, or is it going to be secular? Jihad or McWorld, as political scientist Benjamin Barber has put it? This is part of what was involved in the events of September 11.[3]

Barber elaborated on this dichotomy in a talk he gave at the University of Maryland thirteen days after the attack on the World Trade Center. There is no way, he remarked, that this attack can be dismissed as the work of a few crazies, because the terrorists swim in a sea of popular support. Millions of Muslims cheered the event, some openly, others silently. The truth is that for them, the American international economic order is a great disorder. It renders the majority of them poor, and it tramples on their values. Hence, Barber subsequently stated in an interview in the *Washington Post*, the impulse behind jihad is nothing less than "a holy struggle against something that is seen as evil." A large percentage of Muslims and Arabs view TV programs such as *Dynasty* or *The Simpsons* as part of a Western plot to destroy their religious values; they "feel they are being colonized by Nike and McDonald's and by the garbage" of the American media. Should we be so surprised that they applaud our deaths?[4]

Perhaps one of the most lyrical descriptions of tribal culture, at least as it exists within Islam, is Muhammad Asad's *The Road to Mecca*. Asad's birth name was Leopold Weiss; he was an Austrian Jewish journalist who converted to Islam. The book suffers (greatly) from a tendency to romanticize his newfound faith, as is often the case with converts, but it does manage to capture the quality of tribal consciousness that is largely absent in the West. Riding in a sea of Bedouins during a *hadj* to Mecca, Asad felt himself part of a large brotherhood, no longer a stranger in the world. The word "Islam," after all, means "surrender"; and this, the author says, was something he was never able to do in a Western context, in which one is supposed to grasp life, to "master" it. Faustian cultures such as those of the West never experience a moment's peace. Their adoration of progress, says Asad, is but "a pseudo-faith devised by people who had lost all inner strength" and now believed that economic success would save them. Whereas the Bedouin world is one of tribal solidarity and cooperation, the Western world is one of unacknowledged spiritual despair. The danger for Islam, he goes on, is that it might fall under the sway of this deluded notion of progress, and that as a result the souls of Muslims will shrivel up and die.[5]

This concern—that the cultural impact of the West, the power of its economic and technological juggernaut, will seduce the Muslim world and thereby destroy its spiritual integrity—is a key anxiety for that world and one that goes back a long way. A crucial aspect of that anxiety is the Western separation of church and state, a separation that is anathema to Islamic societies. As the British scholar of religion Karen Armstrong explains it, the Koran gives Muslims a historical mission, that of building a just community (*ummah*) in accordance with the will of Allah. As a result, politics is the stuff of religion itself—a sacrament, if you will, and the arena that enables God to function in the world. Islam is thus regarded by its followers as the sacralization of history.[6] (It's quite eerie how similar much of this is to the beliefs of many Americans, if "Christianity" is substituted for "Islam.")

From a Muslim perspective then, the modern West is inevitably going to appear godless and shallow, a danger to those who regard politics as an expression of the divine. This is a theme that has been repeated down through the years by numerous Muslim leaders and thinkers, because they regard Western notions of material progress as inimical to the fabric of any society. It is hardly the product of 9/11. Thus the Indian poet and philosopher Sir Muhammad Iqbal (1876–1938) wrote that the secular individualism of the West separated the notion of the personality from God, making it potentially demonic. The outcome, he said, is clear: the West will eventually destroy itself. In *Persian Psalms* (1927) he wrote: "Europe's hordes with flame and fire / Desolate the world entire." (None of this, it must be added, has been helped by the fact that secularization—one thinks of Atatürk in Turkey, Nasser in Egypt, or Pahlavi in Iran—often consisted in brutal repression of the devout, including torture.) Even things such as the veil (chador), which is seen in the West as oppressive of women, can, says Armstrong, also be seen as a critique of modernity. For the wearing of the veil is a rejection of the Western obsession with sex and the flaunting of the body in public, in favor of modesty and the notion that sexuality is and should be sacred. It is a question of which end of the telescope one is looking through.[7]

It is easy, in other words, to get on the bandwagon of Thomas Friedman and Princeton historian Bernard Lewis (they seemed to be everywhere after 9/11), shake our fingers at the Islamic nations, and self-righteously urge them to do some soul searching, discover "what went wrong" with their culture. As Middle Eastern specialist Kenneth

Pollack points out, when Americans asked in the wake of September 11 "Why do they hate us?," they didn't really want an answer. The question was purely rhetorical; what Americans wanted was an explanation that would justify their anger, their demand for revenge, and Lewis' timely best seller *What Went Wrong?* neatly stepped into the void. It told Americans, who probably lead the field in introspection avoidance, that that wouldn't be necessary: Muslims were blaming us for the decay of their own civilization when the problem really lay with *them*.[8]

But is that—can that be—the end of the story? Kishore Mahbubani, who served as Singapore's permanent representative to the United Nations and deputy secretary of foreign affairs, points out that between 1960 and 1995 violent crime in the United States increased 560 percent, single-mother births went up 419 percent, and divorce rates and numbers of children living in single-parent homes both climbed by 300 percent. This, he says, is "massive social decay. Many a society shudders at the prospect of this happening on its shores." ("If the family is unstable, the society is unstable," I once heard an Iranian ayatollah say in an interview on the PBS television program *Frontline*. Kind of hard to argue with.) Or to take the even more obvious example of the two world wars and the horrors of the twentieth century, we might reasonably ask, "What went wrong with *the West*?" In his review of *What Went Wrong?* Robert Irwin tosses the ball back into Lewis' court:

> It is the Americans and Europeans who should ask themselves what has gone wrong with the West, where superior technology and wealth go hand in hand with arrogance, oppression, corruption, pornography, loose sexual morals, rising street crime and the leisured pursuit of trivia. As for the Middle East, most of its problems arise from continued Western intervention in the region.

Or as the Egyptian writer Sayyid Qutb—dubbed "the intellectual grandfather to Osama bin Laden" by the *New York Times*—once put it in a postcard he mailed from New York, "If all the world became America it would be the disaster of humanity." We might have reservations about some of these statements, of course (can one imagine if the whole world became Egypt, which later tortured Qutb very badly?), but the point remains that there is more than one way to look at this issue.[9]

This raises the question as to whether Islam and the West are inherently at odds. Certainly, many thinkers on both sides of the divide believe this to be the case, because the things they point to are variations on the secular-versus-tribal theme we have been discussing. If Islamic readers of this book would register no surprise at the extent of American spiritual poverty, as documented earlier, it is also the case that Western scholars and journalists would be quick to point out that closed, tribal cultures are not exactly big on individual rights and freedom of thought, and that historically speaking, many of these cultures have been slave-owning. They might additionally remind us that Muslim societies in general do not offer their people the rule of secular law, nor are they big on economic development or active civil participation; and those that come closest to this model (Turkey, Malaysia) have often done so via a brutally enforced secularism. Clearly, there are arguments to be made on both sides, but it is possible that both camps would agree on this: the two civilizations clash fundamentally; there is no common ground.[10]

To give Bernard Lewis his due, he explored this issue very perceptively in his 1993 article "Islam and Liberal Democracy." There is, of course, no compatibility between liberal democracy and Islamic fundamentalism; that much, says Lewis, is perfectly clear. To the fundamentalists (or Islamists, as they are often called—advocates of fundamentalist Islamic political rule), all foreign ideologies are evil. Their goal is a holy war (jihad) against apostates and infidels, and a return to pristine Islamic roots. So they and their Western enemies would agree that their worldviews and purposes are dramatically opposed.

However, Lewis goes on, "Islamic fundamentalism is just one stream among many." Historically, its influence has waxed and waned, and it has often been suppressed by the ruling establishment. It hardly represents all of Islam. The real question then is whether liberal democracy is compatible with Islam itself, with a mainstream that is far less doctrinaire. But even here we find a key difference. Europe and the United States, after all, have a dual heritage—Judeo-Christian religion and ethics, Greco-Roman statecraft and law—that is really not part of the Islamic tradition, fundamentalist or otherwise. Roman law had the notion of the legal person, or corporate entity, that could enter into contracts and obligations and act as plaintiff or defendant in legal proceedings. This principle made possible the effective functioning of representative assemblies—of government as such. And it is precisely this type of assembly, or corporate entity—Roman senate, Jewish Sanhedrin, parliament of many nations within Christendom—that was absent from the Islamic world. Thus, writes Lewis, "almost all aspects of Muslim government have an intensely personal character. . . . The Islamic state was in principle a theocracy. . . ." Without legislative or corporate bodies, there was no need for representation or collective decision. "Not surprisingly," he concludes, "the history of the Islamic states is one of almost unrelieved autocracy." This is, in short, a tribal and intensely personal world, not a secular and contractual one.[11]

Although the theological details need not concern us here, the Scottish scholar Malise Ruthven, in *A Fury for God*, deepens this analysis by arguing that the key forms of modernity—the business corporation and the modern nation-state—developed out of doctrines that are basic to Christianity. Attempts to export capitalism and parliamentary democracy to the Islamic world have not, as a result, been successful. This world certainly had a golden age, a period of cultural flowering that lasted for centuries, but it did not undergo the sort of psychic reorientation that was inherent in the Renaissance, the Reformation, and the Scientific and Industrial Revolutions. The Roman Catholic doctrine of the *corpus mysticum*, secularized as the corporation or institution that transcended an individual's life span, was integral to these developments. Thus eternity was programmed into these "bodies," and as a result, they operate in a way that is nonteleological. The raison d'être of capitalism and technology is expansion *for its own sake*; science, after all, is about procedures, not values. These "cellular structures," says Ruthven, are now multiplying across the globe—like a cancer, many in the Third World would say. For millions of Arabs and Muslims, this universe of abstract systems, this world of Western freedom and individualism, constitutes the soullessness of modernity. The attack on the World Trade Center, in this interpretation, was not so much an attack on the United States, but on modernity—secular, nontribal modernity—itself.[12]

Again, it really is a question of where one's values lie. To take an example closer to home: in October 2002 I was doing a lecture tour in Mexico, and began by flying from Mexico City to Mazatlán, where the first conference was being held. I arrived at the Mexico City airport with two Mexican friends, and after checking our luggage and getting our boarding passes we went to the food court to have breakfast. Coffee and muffins in hand, we began to look for a place to sit; all the tables were taken. We finally asked two businessmen in their forties, who were sitting at a table and busily working together on a project, if we could sit down. "*Sí, sí, naturalmente.*" They immediately put their work aside, we all introduced ourselves and shook hands, and then we made polite conversation for the next fifteen minutes. The message was clear: people (not to mention courtesy) come first; work comes second.

As a gringo witnessing this ritual, I was astounded. I hadn't been in Mexico since 1989, and I guess I forgot how different the ethos was. In a comparable situation in the United States, the American counterparts to these two men would have looked up briefly, grunted, and then returned to their work. No introductions or small talk would have taken place; when they—or we—departed, there might have been at most a brief nod (probably not). Now an American might point to the fact that 50 percent of the Mexican people live in poverty, that the economy is always shaky, and that much of this may even be due to the *mañana* work ethic and the fact that businessmen "waste time" on pleasantries. That's certainly one way of looking at it. The Mexican perspective, however, would be to regard these busy, important people as rude, crude, and graceless. As a California migrant worker once remarked to his family, on a return visit south of the border over the Christmas holiday, "The gringos don't like to be reminded that they are corpses."

Shift now to the Middle East, and the reaction, the contempt, is much more severe. It is probably not an accident that Mohammed Atta, who coordinated the attack on the World Trade Center, wrote his thesis on the Islamic city, on the fabric of tradition that one finds in the marketplaces of Aleppo. Here, he wrote, in the labyrinth of *souks*, the open booths of small merchants, one finds real human interaction—courtesy, dignity, and charm—as a matter of course, in contrast to the cold, dismissive attitudes of checkout persons in the West. As Malise Ruthven puts it, Western social interactions are crude and formulaic:

> The "Have a nice day" of the waiter or cabin steward conveys no sense of the real hospitality, esteem and affection one experiences as a guest in the Middle East. . . . The visitor to Cairo's crowded Gamaliyya district does not experience the indifference accorded the foreigner in London or Manhattan.[13]

Similarly, V. S. Naipaul relates the American experiences of his guide in Jakarta, a nineteen-year-old college student who had spent a year in Arizona on scholarship. One morning the student asked his next-door neighbor, as a matter of courtesy and friendliness (as he would do in Indonesia), what he was going to do that day. "That's *my* business," the American replied brusquely. On another occasion the student went to the house of a friend, for no particular reason except to visit. The boy's mother stared at him for a moment and then said, "What do you want?"[14]

We may cluck our tongues at these real-life examples, and note how shabby such behavior is . . . except that we, all of us, do it (or some variant of it) on a regular basis and think nothing of it. This is daily fare for us, in the United States. In *The Broken Covenant*, Robert Bellah suggests that there is something sad and karmic about all this: "our material success is our punishment, in terms of what that success has done to the natural environment, our social fabric, and our personal lives."[15] This comment could be our collective obituary.

And yet, if the shadow side of secular capitalist culture is glaring, the darkness of tribal cultures is as well. Thus Naipaul points out that Hamid Ali's *Combined Set of Islamic Laws*, published in Pakistan in 1979, lays out the penalties for theft (amputation of the right hand), illicit sex (death by stoning), and a huge number of offenses that are punished by whipping. Amnesty International's 1997 report on Saudi Arabia consists of a thick dossier on secret trials, flogging, amputation, abuse of women, and institutionalized torture. Pretty much the same thing prevails for the Muslim population of Nigeria, where *sharia*—Islamic justice—metes out barbaric sentences. Iran, Sudan, Afghanistan under the Taliban . . . it's all pretty depressing. Where there is no separation of church and state, where "tribal" interconnectedness leaves people with no place to hide, this kind of brutality is often the norm, and no amount of courtesy in the *souks* of Aleppo can make it okay.[16]

There is also the question of whether the secular-versus-tribal clash is philosophical as well as social and political. Many students of Muslim culture have remarked on the heavy Islamic opposition to critical analysis (especially when applied to religion) and to the philosophical basis of modern science. Is this opposition inherent to Islam? The civilization had a marvelous period of scientific achievement from the eighth to the twelfth centuries, during most of which time the intellectual culture of Europe amounted to very little by comparison. It also served as the (or a) midwife of modern Western science, preserving and translating many of the classic works of Greek thought, whose reintroduction into mainstream European culture started the ferment leading up to the Scientific Revolution. As one scholar puts it, "much of what we value as a distinctly Western intellectual tradition derives from Muslim thinkers and from their stewardship of the inquisitive spirit of Greek science and philosophy. . . ."[17] Nevertheless, Islamic science did not, to my knowledge, ever manage to cross over to the "Galilean revolution," that unique combination of mathematics and experiment that finally led European thinkers to separate fact from value—to break with religion as the arbiter of truth. Even at its apogee, Islamic science reconciled the demands of reason with those of faith, whereas Galileo and (most of) his intellectual descendants insisted on a strict separation of the two. This separation is something many critics have seen as a *weakness* of Western science, responsible for the anomie of modern life. Again, it depends on your point of view: Reason, or revelation? Secular allegiances, or tribal ones? Separation of church and state, or theocracy? We keep coming back to the same dichotomy.

The point is that Western science is based on doubt, experiment, and measurement, and the truth is regarded as unfolding and provisional; whereas in tribal cultures, the truth is typically regarded as revealed—God-given and final. Group solidarity always trumps skeptical questioning or the search for the truth. And whatever prevailed in the past, there can be no doubting the severe antisecular and anti-intellectual bias of contemporary Muslim thought and politics (much like the Bush administration, ironically enough). Present-day Islamic civilization seems to display little interest in challenging received wisdom. Scholars are persecuted in the Muslim world and frequently chased out. Egypt put one scholar in a cage(!) for conducting a survey, and the Egyptian in the street applauds this.[18] In 1994 an attempt was made on the life of novelist and Nobel laureate Naguib Mahfouz for trying to bring some secular fresh air into Egyptian culture. Another secular writer, Farag Foda, was assassinated in 1992 with the apparent approval (or, as some have charged, connivance) of some of the leading scholars of Al-Azhar University in Egypt, the foremost academy of Sunni Islam. In 2003, Abbas Abdi, an Iranian reform strategist, was sentenced to seven years in prison for publishing a poll showing that three out of four Iranians favored talks with Washington.[19]

It would seem to be the case that the one thing most offensive to millions of Muslims is the attempt to view the Koran in historical and secular terms. Whereas the application of critical and historical analysis to the

Bible began in Europe nearly two hundred years ago, modern Islamic scholarship will have none of it (Christian fundamentalists feel the same way). As a consequence, says Aziz Al-Azmeh in *Islams and Modernities*, Islamic politics is based on passion and a denial of reality. Critical thinking is regarded as "reactionary." Those who attempt to examine the Muslim canon from a rational point of view get vilified, and there has been a systematic attempt within Islam to stop intellectuals from accumulating social and historical knowledge. Thus in 2002, an Iranian history professor and war veteran, Hashem Aghajari, was sentenced to death for asking why clerics were the only ones authorized to interpret the Koran (under student protests and international pressure, this got commuted to five years in jail). Perhaps the most notorious case of this sort in recent years is that of the Cairo University professor Nasr abu Zeid, who had the temerity to apply the techniques of literary criticism to the Koran and to suggest that it was a book that needed to be seen in historical context. The result was an accusation of apostasy; a *fatwa* issued by Osama bin Laden's associate Ayman al-Zawahiri; and Zeid's decision to flee the country (he now lives in Holland). "What did I do?" he said in an interview with the *Chronicle of Higher Education*. "I was trying to . . . teach the Egyptian people how to think."[20]

The fact is that thought, in Zeid's sense of the term (or in the modern Western sense), is not welcome in much of the Islamic world. Even Muhammad Asad, the Austrian convert, concedes this, noting that Islam stopped producing great thinkers several centuries ago, that Islamic scholars have been content to repeat what others have written, and that the whole Muslim world is sunk in intellectual sterility. After the twelfth century, he says, the intellect gave way to obscurantism, and this scholastic petrifaction, he asserts, lies at the heart of the social and political sterility of the Muslim world.[21]

In the end, it comes down to a question of balance. Critical thought for its own sake—like capitalistic expansion or technological innovation—has the potential to erode the foundations of any society. In the end, argued Nietzsche, all rationality can do is bite its own tail. As Albert Borgmann points out, science and technology cannot bind people together, and taken to their logical conclusion they make community and tribal feeling impossible (a sad and alienated world of people addicted to cell phones and laptops should be evidence enough). The other side of the coin, however—pure tribalism—finally issues out into a suffocating world, one no less nihilistic than a purely secular one. Where to draw the line? Islam and the West not only clash with each other, they also mirror one another quite faithfully. Thomas Pynchon revisited, one might say.

On the one side, then, faith over reason, and the community over the individual; on the other, the notion that the whole world is and should be little more than one big supermarket. However, it is no longer quite so stark as this; there are in fact a lot of crossovers. The *souks* of Aleppo are now probably selling jeans from the Gap; evangelical Christians in the Midwest hold bible study meetings in Starbucks, and their fundamentalism now stretches right up to a White House that has made its bias for faith over reason quite clear. In France, a Tunisian-born entrepreneur is doing a vigorous trade in "Mecca-Cola," encouraging his millions of customers to "buy Muslim" (the label on the bottle reads, "Don't drink stupid, drink committed"). As already noted, a 2002 poll taken by Zogby International found that Muslims in the Arab world hate American politics and love American culture—especially American movies and TV shows. Iranian youth in huge numbers find the reigning Islamic orthodoxy repellent and are, as one American reporter notes, "more interested in checking their e-mail than in dying for Islam." And while modernization has brought all of the familiar evils along with it—prostitution, drug addiction, and widespread alienation—89 percent of Iranians say they want reform or radical change, and a great many of them favor a separation of church and state.[22]

There are, then, some qualifications that have to be made to the strict secular-versus-tribal dichotomy that I've outlined, since Westerners, Asians, and Arabs all participate in a modernity that is now worldwide. This is what Benjamin Barber calls "soft power." And yet, as Barber points out, globalization is reinforcing the fragmenting tendencies of jihad that it seeks to overcome. There still remains, says Malise Ruthven, a clash of civilizations, no matter how much Western goods have penetrated the Near and Far East. The Islamic nations regard the West as having a pagan culture of celebrity, hedonism, commercialism, and instant gratification. Millions upon millions of Muslims would undoubtedly agree with the sentiment expressed a few years ago by a Pakistani scholar, that Michael Jackson and Madonna are (even more so now) "torchbearers of American society . . . that are destroying humanity. They are ruining the lives of thousands of Muslims and leading them to destruction, away from their religion, ethics and morality."[23]

• • •

THE PHRASE "clash of civilizations" was made current by Harvard University's Samuel Huntington, first in an article published in *Foreign Affairs* in 1993, and a few years later in a lengthy monograph. Basically, Huntington's thesis is that in the twenty-first century, conflicts that occur on the world's stage will not be primarily ideological or economic, but cultural, specifically civilizational. The world, he says, consists of seven or eight major civilizations—Western, Confucian, Japanese, Islamic, Hindu, Slavic-Orthodox, Latin American, and possibly African—and as the differences among these are very old, these civilizational distinctions are more fundamental than other types of distinctions. As groups come into conflict over cultural fault lines, Huntington concludes, the major question will thus be one of identity: not "Which side are you on?," but rather "What are you?"[24]

As one might imagine, the argument has been sharply criticized, especially in the Muslim world (although, ironically enough, the fundamentalists would agree with it and even celebrate it), where it is seen as a self-fulfilling prophecy and a possible justification for inevitable and possibly unending conflict between Islam and the West.[25] After all, if the differences between civilizations are essentialist—matters of identity—then there really isn't much that can be done to build bridges between the conflicting parties. In this regard, it is instructive to note that Huntington's work overlaps in important ways with the work of Bernard Lewis, who in fact coined the phrase "clash of civilizations" in his 1990 article "The Roots of Muslim Rage." Those roots, according to Lewis, go right back to the seventh century, when Islam first arose. The rage of Islam is directed against "the millennial enemy," writes Lewis, viz. Christendom, and "draws its strength from ancient beliefs and loyalties." The rise of European colonialism during the last three centuries is thus, in his view, merely the latest episode in an age-old conflict. In the wake of 9/11, Lewis returned to the theme of this supposed thirteen-hundred-year-old antagonism, claiming that for "Osama bin Laden, 2001 marks the resumption of the war for the religious dominance of the world that began in the seventh century."[26]

In the same vein, Huntington argues that the "Western-Islamic fault line" goes back to this early period, and that Islam is the ancient enemy of our own Judeo-Christian heritage. Western notions of individualism, free

markets, and separation of church and state, he asserts, have little resonance in Islamic cultures. Islamic society, he continues, is inherently intolerant; even in the past, "Muslim countries have [had] problems with
non-Muslim minorities comparable to those which non-Muslim countries have with Muslim minorities."[27]

Since I agree with Huntington to some extent, it might be useful to clarify the varieties (or degrees) of essentialism we are talking about. The crucial issue seems to be this: one can espouse a "clash" theory without taking
the whole thing back to the seventh century. Profound conflicts don't have
to be about "ancient beliefs and loyalties"; they can be four or five decades
old (or less). I shall deal with the more recent causes of the "clash" below;
for now, consider the essentialist arguments already presented:

1. The West champions individual freedom over relationship, or group
   (tribal) loyalty; Islam does the reverse.
2. The West, at least theoretically, separates church and state; Islam does
   not.
3. The West developed the notion of the "corporate body," the senate or
   representative assembly; Islam did not.
4. The West, in a secularization of the Catholic *corpus mysticum*, eventually developed the idea of the corporation that lies at the heart of
   capitalism; Islam did not.
5. Western science has the notions of the fact-value distinction, genuine
   critical analysis, and provisional truth; Islam keeps reason subordinate
   to faith.

These do, of course, seem pretty essentialist—except that only item 3
is older than four or five hundred years. All of the other items, which are
really variations on the secular-versus-tribal theme, arose in the West relatively recently, in the early modern period. While it was these things that
enabled the West to "pull away" from other cultures, and eventually dominate the globe, we have to remember that until around 1600 or so, we
did not possess those features (leaving aside certain aspects of item 5 that
the Greeks were already onto). Down to the Renaissance, the Christian
West was a religious society, more tribal than secular. In terms of actual
practice, in fact, it can probably be said that the crucial shift from organic
to secular occurred with the Enlightenment or Industrial Revolution—
i.e., going back only about 250 years. While I believe that these differ-

ences are great, and fully real, it doesn't make them "genetic," somehow inherent to Islam versus the West; and it can also be argued that even the differences that arose with the Enlightenment served more as a backdrop to the explosive East-West conflicts of the last few decades than as genuinely causal factors. They set the stage, in other words, and act as a kind of "baseboard" that Muslim rage can plug into when something contemporary arises. However, they may not be as powerful or ever present as Lewis and Huntington make them out to be.

A major problem with Huntington's argument is that it contains a number of internal contradictions. He writes, for example, that through "the IMF and other international economic institutions, the West promotes its economic interests and imposes on other nations the economic policies it thinks appropriate." It uses its military and economic resources, he continues, "to run the world in ways that will maintain Western predominance, protect Western interests and promote Western political and economic values." Western intervention in the affairs of other civilizations, he concludes, is "probably the single most dangerous source of instability and potential global conflict in a multicivilizational world."[28]

True enough . . . but then why appeal to the seventh century? Occam's razor would suggest that this contemporary situation of aggressive American economic and military imperialism is explanation enough. Or at least, if I were an Arab living in the Middle East, I wouldn't need the history of the Crusades or the lost glory of Saladin to make me resentful of the United States, even though these might echo in my historical memory. And if one really feels the need to rely on the past, the last 250 years—the period of the Industrial Revolution—will surely do the trick, as Huntington's own data demonstrate. Europeans or former European colonies, he tells us, controlled 35 percent of the earth's land surface in 1800, 67 percent in 1878, 84 percent in 1914, and even more in 1920, when Britain, France, and Italy divided up the Ottoman Empire. "The West," writes Huntington, "won the world not by the superiority of its ideas or values or religion . . . but rather by its superiority in applying organized violence. Westerners often forget this fact; non-Westerners never do."[29]

In addition, it is hardly the case that members of the same civilization never clash. Islamic nations fought one another bitterly during the twentieth century, and the Western powers did the same (what could be worse, really, than the two world wars?). The historical pattern is clear:

states fight each other over economics, ideology, or territory, and Huntington's argument that this pattern will be different in the twenty-first century, will shift to civilizational fault lines because these fault lines are so old, is unconvincing. They were old fifty or one hundred years ago, and the major conflicts were not civilizational then. Why should they be now? What is the causal factor that will make for a new pattern? Huntington never says.[30]

It is too easy, in short, to dismiss more recent events as superficial and look for inherent, archaic reasons. Consider the following excerpt from a letter I received from an Iranian journalist living in London, in the wake of September 11. "Much of the Moslem world," he writes,

> lives, works with, argues, trades, and generally rubs along pretty well with [the] European powers, some of whom . . . have done terrible things to Moslems in the past, who have been colonial powers who have exploited [them] economically, imposed their military will, or . . . tried to turn Moslem countries into part of Europe. The hostility to the United States of America is due to [the] foreign policy of that government in most of our lifetimes. . . .

My correspondent goes on to say that Islamic fundamentalism has its roots in the 1960s corruption and oppression brought on by Western client states; the failure of the Eastern bloc to offer a viable alternative; the failure of Arab nationalist movements; and the 1953 overthrow, by the CIA, of Iran's democratically elected leader, Mohammad Mossadegh. While there are essentialist or quasi-essentialist differences between Islam and the West, then, I think it fair to say that the recent record (elaborated on later) is rich enough in terms of providing an explanation for the motivations of someone like Osama bin Laden.[31]

This issue of bin Laden's motivations is taken up in some detail in one of the best studies of the "war on terrorism" to have been published in the wake of 9/11, Michael Scheuer's *Imperial Hubris: Why the West Is Losing the War on Terror*. Scheuer, who published the book under the pseudonym "Anonymous," was the CIA's expert on Osama bin Laden and Afghanistan and South Asia for nearly twenty years. Unlike American newspapers, which bury OBL's addresses to the American people in their back pages in heavily excerpted form, and generate a ton of spin around them to the effect that this man is a whack job or a barbarian or an evil monster, etc., and thus not to be taken seriously, Scheuer prefers instead to take the man at his word and to examine what he is saying, *in extenso*. (Just so you know: the Federal Broadcast Information Service provides U.S. leaders with the full text of bin Laden's statements.) And by and large, Scheuer is able to demonstrate that OBL hates us not for who we are (the essentialist argument), but for what we do. He also shows that bin Laden's objections to what we do are quite reasonable, politically speaking, and that unless there are some serious changes in what we do— which Scheuer is not foolish enough to expect—we shall be fighting a bloody, self-destructive war until the cows come home.[32]

Scheuer does, however, point to some essentialist references in OBL's speeches, so it is important to realize that it is not entirely a question of our foreign policy with respect to the Islamic world. In short, who we are is part of the equation as well. One Al Qaeda member, for example, posted something on the *Al-Ansar* Web site in late 2002, that makes the group's contempt clear: "The Disunited States of America," wrote Abu-Ubayd al-Qurashi, "are a mixture of nationalities, ethnic groups, and races united only by the 'American Dream,' or to put it more correctly, worship of the dollar, which they openly call 'the Almighty Dollar.'" Around the same time, bin Laden said in a speech to the American people: "I urge you to seek the joy of life and the after life and to rid yourself of your dry, miserable, and spiritless materialistic existence." Islam, by contrast, he goes on, is "the religion of good manners, sincerity, mercy . . . kindness to others, justice between people, giving rights to the people who deserve them. . . ." (Of course, the Arab despots OBL opposes don't exactly live by codes of kindness and justice, but bin Laden's reasoning—which is not entirely convincing—is that they are apostate regimes, not "really" Islamic.) "This Western Civilization," he stated on 21 October 2001, "which is backed by America, has lost its values and appeal. The immense materialistic towers were destroyed. . . ."[33]

So who we are does make a difference to our enemies; and although the American Dream is more than just a materialistic one, Islamists really do understand how central materialism is to the American way of life. Hence, their avowed declaration to bankrupt the U.S. economy—it's their primary strategy, because they know that this is to hit us where it hurts the most. The problem is that we haven't a clue as to who *they* are.

Americans do not understand that individual freedom is not a universal aspiration, and that other peoples—especially in the Middle East—put other values first, such as honor, order, and tribal loyalty. Scheuer himself admits, "The war is fundamentally religious . . . the enmity is based on creed." Or value system, might be a better way of putting it.[34]

That being said, the bulk of Scheuer's analysis of OBL's statements does support his central point, that it is our behavior that is at issue, not our way of life. Thus Al Qaeda, says Scheuer, is not engaged in Armageddon, a struggle to conquer the globe (this belief on our part is the same mistake we made with respect to the Soviet Union); they are not deranged individuals; and their answer to Bernard Lewis' lopsided question "What went wrong?" is basically "The actions of the United States, as heir to the British Empire in the Muslim world, are what went wrong." In October 2002, for example, OBL declared the war would go on as long as U.S. policies toward the Muslim world remained unchanged. And his indictment, says Scheuer, "is pretty much factual": American support for the Israeli occupation of Palestine, which involves Israeli attacks on the Palestinian people; brutal sanctions against Iraq (and now, its occupation); the 1965 "regime change" and subsequent slaughter of at least a half a million people in Indonesia, whose killers the CIA assisted in coming to power and to whom the U.S. embassy even supplied extensive hit lists; U.S. military presence in the Arabian Peninsula (the shift of troops from Saudi Arabia to Qatar in 2003 fooled nobody); support for (or acquiescence in) oppression of Muslims by the Chinese, Russian, and Indian governments (one wonders, however, why OBL isn't similarly enraged at them); and protection of tyrannical Arab regimes so that we can have access to cheap oil. The reason for their jihad against us, said OBL in a statement to the American people, "is very simple: Because you attacked and continue to attack us. . . . You shall not feel at ease until you take your hands off our nation." In fact, the message of "you fuck with us, we'll fuck with you" has, in so many words, been repeated by OBL over and over (including in interviews with *Time* and CNN), right down to the eve of the 2004 presidential election. Meanwhile, writes Scheuer, we stand by governments trying to exterminate Islamic militants who are fighting against institutionalized barbarism, while our elites go on insisting that violence by Muslims (but never by us) is terrorism, and that none of these people can be regarded as freedom fighters. As a result, he says, we are "in a hell of a fix."[35]

Although there is certainly some truth to the charge that "they hate us for who we are," Scheuer is persuasive in showing that the crux of Islamist (and Islamic) enmity toward us is behavioral and nonessentialist. But Scheuer is no optimist: he does not expect American elites to get it, to wake up, because as he correctly points out, a real public debate on these issues—such as was pathetically missing from the 2004 presidential campaign—would mean drawing attention to issues that are very sensitive, which is something these elites fear. This includes Osama's laundry list of grievances, cited above, and in particular the fact that the United States has inherited the mantle and pattern of nineteenth-century European imperialism: military garrisons, economic control, support for brutal leaders, exploitation of natural resources. After all, we know where all of that wound up.[36]

The West versus the Rest

All that aside, however, we need to get a clearer sense of the general nature and history of American foreign policy, for it turns out that U.S. foreign policy in the Middle East is basically an extension of U.S. foreign policy *tout court*.

One of the most insightful approaches to this topic is that of the eminent historian Charles Beard, whose work was subsequently enlarged upon by William Appleman Williams (*The Tragedy of American Diplomacy*). For Beard, foreign policy was really an afterthought; it grew out of domestic policy, which was essentially about money. The centerpiece of the foreign policy strategy of William McKinley, Theodore Roosevelt, William Howard Taft, Woodrow Wilson, and Warren G. Harding, he argued, was economic expansion—exporting our economic surpluses. This, in turn, meant pushing open the doors of trade and investment everywhere, whether by polite coercion or by military force. It was only via trade and investment, these presidents believed, that the United States could flourish, and the permanence of its domestic order be assured. In that sense, Beard argued, U.S. foreign and domestic policy were two sides of the same coin.[37]

But how far back does this pattern go? According to Williams, Americans thought of themselves as an empire (in terms of the American continent, that is) from Revolutionary days. Alexander Hamilton, for example, referred to the United States as such in *The Federalist*. James Madison wrote Thomas Jefferson in 1786, "Most of our political evils may be traced up to our commercial ones"; and he proposed, as a guide to policy and action, the same kind of argument that historian Frederick Jackson Turner did a century later in his famous "frontier thesis," which explains our prosperity as the result of (westward) expansion. Beginning with the presidency of Andrew Jackson (1829–37) in particular, democracy was seen as intertwined with individualism, private property, and a capitalist market economy, but the process of territorial expansion had already begun under Jefferson with the Louisiana Purchase of 1803. Indeed, during McKinley's war on the Philippines, Senator Albert Beveridge defended the president's actions by saying that McKinley was merely walking the path marked out by Jefferson, whom Beveridge referred to as "the first Imperialist of the Republic." (The Louisiana Purchase—roughly half a billion acres at less than three cents a pop—has rightly been called "the greatest land grab in all human history.") Natural greatness, liberty, and territorial expansion easily morphed into a unified whole, the ideology of which was labeled "Manifest Destiny." Thus Turner wrote that expansion had been the dominant fact of American life for three centuries, and that the frontier was absolutely crucial to American history. What it provided, he said, was a "gate of escape" from existing responsibilities, and it sustained a pattern of relying on external factors for solutions to internal problems. In fact, debates in Congress over Texas, Oregon, and the Mexican War (1846–48) affirmed the idea that Americans could preserve their liberty "by ceaseless constant action."[38]

How this played out during the first half of the nineteenth century is well-known. To take one of the most egregious examples, issues of imperialism were clearly present during the Mexican War under President James Polk, who was trying to subject the predominantly foreign population of California, New Mexico, and possibly all of Mexico to American rule. (The renowned American newspaper editor Horace Greeley, for his part, tried to stem the tide by urging Americans to read "the histories of the ruin of Greek and Roman liberty consequent on such extensions of empire by the sword. . . . Only idiots or demons," he wrote, could seek the glory of conquest that was so harmful to their nation.) The immediate cause of the war was the annexation of Texas in December 1845, along with the American desire to acquire California. When Mexico rebuffed

Polk's attempt to "negotiate" these issues, the United States had no inhibitions about shifting from diplomacy to force: it was going to have these territories with Mexico's approval or without it. The war, which was strongly supported by the expansionist faction in Congress (over the vehement objections of then Congressman John Quincy Adams), began in May 1846 and ended in September 1847, when American troops entered Mexico City. By the Treaty of Guadalupe Hidalgo (2 February 1848), Mexico was forced to cede 40 percent of its territory to the United States.[39] Quite a coup, one might say.

But it didn't stop there. According to Williams, when America ran out of frontier—that is, when Manifest Destiny had run its course and there was no more contiguous land to buy, annex, or conquer—the root impulse got channeled into overseas expansion. It was during the 1890s, when the United States was beset by a severe economic crisis, and it recognized that the continental frontier was gone, that the nation clearly formulated the argument that expansion in the form of a foreign economic (or even territorial) empire was the best way to maintain its own prosperity. The decision for imperial expansion was part of the 1896 platform of the Republican party, which captured the presidency and held it for the next sixteen years. The famous Open Door notes of 1899–1900, written by McKinley's secretary of state, John Hay, advocated not traditional colonialism but rather the policy of "an open door through which America's preponderant economic strength would enter and dominate all underdeveloped areas of the world." Nor did subsequent Democratic presidents (Jimmy Carter excepted) attempt to deviate from this project— one that, says Williams, can accurately be described as a program of *informal* empire. As early as 1902, Princeton University President Woodrow Wilson wrote that overseas expansion was the economic frontier that would replace the American continent as the territorial frontier. In effect, the Open Door notes were merely the doctrine of Manifest Destiny gone global.[40]

The Spanish-American War (1898) is a dramatic case in point (although it finally involved issues of territory more than ones of economics), and a key stepping-stone in the development of America's imperial "career." Between 1870 and 1900, the American share of world manufacturing went from 23.3 percent to 30.1 percent, making the United States the foremost industrial nation. This rapid growth was a big factor in its desire to flex its muscles in the international arena. America worried that the other imperialist powers would cut it off from the world's economic markets; its industrial growth generated the desire for foreign expansion, which created foreign interests that in turn (it believed) required protection; and it also had a yearning for *symbolic* greatness—i.e., the desire to be seen as a major player on the world's stage. Add to this the fact that it was an alliance of Republican businessmen that put McKinley in the White House, an elite clique that advocated an aggressive foreign policy, an active search for markets, and a large navy. These men were empire builders, and under their influence McKinley was emboldened to compel Congress to follow his foreign policy. In that sense, he was perhaps the first modern president.[41]

Congress, however, wanted the war as well. It had a strong expansionist faction; it was concerned about losses of American investment in Cuba, and moved by a growing sense of American influence in the affairs of the Western Hemisphere; and nearly everyone seemed to be inflamed by the "yellow press" (the publications of William Randolph Hearst and Joseph Pulitzer), which distorted the news from Cuba, where local patriots were fighting for independence from Spanish rule. As war loomed, Professor Wilson declared that the United States stood for "the light of day, while theirs was the light of darkness"—betraying a Manichaean consciousness we would revive after World War II and retain right down to Ronald Reagan and George W. Bush. In point of fact, on the eve of the war (April 9–10), Spain agreed to all of our demands, including a cessation of hostilities; but McKinley, eager to go to war, barely mentioned this in his speech to Congress on April 11, when he asked for authority to intervene in Cuba. In May, the U.S. Navy defeated the Spanish at Manila; in July, it destroyed the Spanish fleet in Cuba. In July as well, Teddy Roosevelt and his Rough Riders took Santiago de Cuba; Manila was occupied in August. Under the terms of the Treaty of Paris (10 December 1898), Cuba was granted independence from Spain, under U.S. tutelage; and Puerto Rico and Guam were ceded to the United States, as was the Philippines (the latter for a payment of $20 million). America was now established as an imperial power in Latin America and the Far East.[42]

Noteworthy in this whole series of events is the fact that the United States had no regard for the rights of smaller nations, never consulted with them about their own affairs, and denied Cuba any rights of self-determination under the protectorate. Yale University's William Graham Sumner wrote that such policies of conquest would transform the American republic into "another empire just after the fashion of all the old ones," while Mark Twain, who started out as an expansionist, stated:

> I said to myself, here are a people who have suffered for three centuries. We can make them as free as ourselves, give them a government and country of their own, put a miniature of the American constitution afloat in the Pacific, start a brand new republic to take its place among the free nations of the world. It seemed to me a great task to which we had addressed ourselves. But I have thought some more, since then, and I have read carefully the treaty of Paris, and I have seen that we do not intend to free, but to subjugate the people of the Philippines. We have gone there to conquer, not to redeem. . . . I am opposed to having the eagle put its talons on any other land.

Of course, even putting "a miniature of the American constitution afloat in the Pacific" would have followed the pattern of American imperialism, according to which the world would be remade in our image, but Twain's point about conquest is nevertheless well taken.[43]

This was, then, the context in which the Open Door notes were formulated, and they, and the Spanish-American War, set the pattern for the next hundred-plus years (in particular from 1950 on): what America couldn't get by negotiation or economic pressure it would take by force. The Open Door strategy was adopted by McKinley, Teddy Roosevelt, and their successors, and by 1939—paradoxically, a peak year for American isolationism—U.S. economic expansion encompassed the globe. T.R., in fact, declared that American supremacy would promote the interests of civilization itself, that peace would be the consequence of empire, and that the United States must not shrink from its role as policeman of the world.[44]

What then is the "tragedy of American diplomacy," in William Appleman Williams' memorable phrase? Essentially, it's that we uphold an ideal of self-determination for the peoples of the world, which we then subvert by defining our foreign policy as a process of helping those peoples to become . . . like us! In general, wrote Williams, our foreign policy is guided by three ideas. First, we want to help other people solve their problems. Second, we are committed to the notion of self-determination. Third, we insist that these other people go about solving their problems in the same way we do. The tragedy is not only the inherent contradiction involved in all this, but also the fact that we don't recognize it as such; we don't grasp that it is an oxymoron. In addition, we do not see that in expanding our own economic system—the well-being of which we have, since McKinley, tied to overseas expansion—we make it difficult for others to retain *their* economic independence. As reformer and ex-Wilsonian Raymond Robins wrote of his former hero, "He was willing to do anything for people except get off their backs and let them live their own lives." Wilson's liberalism saw conflicts of interest as mere appearances, and deemed intervention necessary to remove obstacles placed there by "misguided" people. Wilson could literally not conceive that his twin purposes of expanded trade and an Americanized world might ever come into conflict. Every opponent of the United States, says Williams, was thus seen as being confused about the nature of the world—beyond redemption, in a sense. In this way, everybody's business became our business, domestic problems became international ones, and we felt we had the right to remove any restrictions upon our "natural" right to resolve our difficulties at home by means of overseas expansion. There is, says Williams, a complete innocence involved in what is really a total world-view; it seems to Americans like natural law. The upshot was that the liberal state extended the practice of colonialism: local peoples ruled, but within limits defined by their economic ties to the imperial power.[45]

As for the economic motive behind all of this, we should note that prior to 1913, American entrepreneurs were unable to accumulate enough capital on their own to engage in overseas expansion successfully. Between 1913 and 1939, a solution evolved of having the government help the private sector to do this. Beginning with the Wilson administration, taxes collected for individuals were used to provide corporations with loans and subsidies for overseas expansion. In 1915, speaking to the National Council on Foreign Trade, Secretary of State William Jennings Bryan told his corporate audience, "My house is your house. . . . My Department is your department; the ambassadors, the ministers, the consuls are all yours. It is their business to look after your interests and to guard your rights." President Harding continued the program, urging Americans to "go on to the peaceful commercial conquest of the world," in order (he added) to avoid social conflict at home. As for the New Deal, rather than being a revolution, it was a way of preventing one: even in the depths of the Depression, overseas expansion of the American corporate system was regarded as a basic means of economic recovery.[46]

Nobody could have foreseen this, of course, but it was the Open Door policy that set us on the long road to the Age of Terror in which we now find ourselves. The policy undertook to make drastic changes in other societies, societies that were often agrarian and neofeudal. The changes were thus extremely painful, and the efforts we made to enforce them according to our way of thinking served only to intensify the opposition to us. It was not the most fruitful approach one hundred years ago; today, we certainly have no excuse. It is amazing to see contemporary American politicians, apparently ignorant of more than a century of lopsided foreign relations, angry and bewildered at resistance to, or attacks on, the United States when "we are so good," and "obviously" have everybody's best interests at heart. The inability or unwillingness to look at ourselves through foreign eyes, to see those who object to being steamrolled by us as anything but knaves or ingrates, has a very long history. For ours is a total worldview; it has been, and remains, largely impervious to substantive critical feedback.

William Appleman Williams was the first, and perhaps the greatest, of the so-called revisionist historians, and he left behind him a distinguished discipleship (direct and indirect) of scholars and teachers: Lloyd Gardner, Walter LaFeber, Joyce and Gabriel Kolko, Gar Alperovitz, and many others, who expanded his insights in various ways. So much of what he wrote rings true, even more so in the age of the 1991 Gulf war and the 2003 invasion of Iraq (indeed, at times it seems as though he could have predicted, if not actually scripted, these events). But before we continue on with his analysis, it behooves us to ask: Was he right? Is American foreign policy the product of interlocking business and political elites? Is it just an economic Manifest Destiny writ large?

To some extent, yes; it seems to me that much of what Williams argued was correct. We have to remember that Williams was never promoting a conspiracy theory of history or maintaining that the government was the tool of special interests, but rather asserting that there was simply an internalized consensus among the nation's elites as to how economic and foreign policy ought to proceed. Nevertheless, as Michael Hunt says in *Ideology and U.S. Foreign Policy*—and many of Williams' latter-day disciples would agree—the economic emphasis is too narrow. Williams never really demonstrated the concrete link between the economy and the concerns of policy makers, and as early as 1966 conceded that the idea of the Open Door might have drifted away from its economic moorings.

Similarly, historian J. A. Thompson, in a critical review of Williams' work published in 1973, points out that for the most part, American exports have been usually lower than 5 percent of the GDP, and that the bulk of our trade is with other advanced industrial nations, not with the Third World. Williams gets around this, he says, by arguing that political leaders operated on the basis of an unquestioning belief that expansion was necessary for economic survival. But Americans, says Thompson, have often discussed their foreign policy in terms of national security, prestige, racism, and religion as well, and these have sometimes been autonomous from economic issues. The argument would seem to function best when it does not exclude other factors.[47]

What might these be? Ideological factors, it turns out, were also present, and they often overshadowed the economic ones. Thus Michael Hunt defines ideology as a structure of meaning that is part of the culture—so much a part, in our own case, that we take it for granted, are not really aware of it, and regard other ideologies as aberrant. The ideology underlying American foreign policy, he goes on, is coherent, emotionally charged, and comprised of three interlocking ideas, all of which emerged by the early twentieth century, and which together constitute a "civic religion." The first sees the American future in terms of a quest for national greatness, coupled to the promotion of liberty. The second defines attitudes toward others in terms of a racial hierarchy. The third holds that with the exception of the American Revolution, revolution in general is a potentially dangerous thing.[48]

Thus for Hunt, America's territorial expansion, which began with the Louisiana Purchase in 1803, was more an issue of ideology than of economics. Central to the process of Manifest Destiny was a guiding (moral) vision, the United States as the beacon of liberty. The rhetoric of the Jackson era, he notes, was that of Americans as the torchbearers of freedom, always on the move. By 1900, expansionists argued that we would remake others in our own image, to the benefit of both them and us. Indeed, Wilson said as much in 1904, adding that the image involved was specifically an Anglo-Saxon one (not too much of a shock, that). In this way, the notion of national greatness and agent of democracy easily shaded into the second factor, that of racial hierarchy.[49]

Is it purely coincidental, in other words, that most of our imperial ventures or wars of conquest, from Mexico in 1846–48 to Iraq in 2003, involved an "enemy" who was nonwhite? As Hunt says, the United

States, both at home and abroad, always had a system of racial hierarchy in mind, one that put those with the lightest skin at the top and those with the darkest at the bottom. So-called superior peoples, writes Hunt, "spoke English . . . exercised democratic rights, embraced the uplifting influence of Protestant Christianity, and thanks to their industry enjoyed material abundance. Those toward the bottom were woefully deficient. . . ." The idea of racial hierarchy, in short, offered a useful conceptual handle on the world and shaped the way we dealt with other peoples. Our newspaper cartoons depicted blacks as brutes or children, Asians as inscrutable or somnolent. Motion pictures portrayed Latinos as greasers, Latinas as sultry, and Arabs as devious, fanatical, or evil. All of this has a long history. In effect, racial hierarchy permeates our culture and has been used to underwrite our claims to foreign lands and to justify the imposition of Anglo values and institutions. Consciously or unconsciously, race has always played a central role in our foreign policy. Today we have cleaned up our language—we speak in terms of "modernizing" traditional societies—but this, says Hunt, is only a restatement of the old ethnocentric platitudes that were formerly directed at the Philippines, China, and Mexico. Americans still live in a world in which Anglos are on top, Europeans follow, and the Third (read: nonwhite) World sits at the bottom. "Black Africa," writes Hunt, "occupied the lowest rung, just as black ghettos represented the lower reaches of American society." Thus, during the Vietnam war, the enemy were called "gooks" or "slopes," and President Nixon offered a "generous" POW exchange, a ratio of ten Vietnamese to one American G.I.—without even noticing how insulting such an "equation" would be to Asian peoples. Plainly put, Americans don't respect cultural patterns different from their own, and this has facilitated an imperial foreign policy. Nor was any of this necessarily tied to economics (though it often has been).[50]

Hunt's third factor is that political revolution must be orderly—like the American Revolution supposedly was (in fact, we confiscated British property). Revolution has been seen by Americans as a kind of solemn affair, led by respectable middle-class citizens in powdered wigs and harnessed to moderate political goals. The image of revolution potentially out of control is frightening to us; the entire Cold War policy of containment embodied the notion that virtually any social change, nationalistic or otherwise, was a dangerous thing, a threat to freedom everywhere. Thus during the 1960s, as revolution rolled across Latin America, Asia, and Africa, we were unable to see this phenomenon as anything other than a Soviet conspiracy, a challenge to American values, and a violation of what we regarded as "appropriate" political change (which is to say, no change at all). We had no problem backing oppressive dictators who would put a stop to attempts at liberation, what were mostly nationalist movements. Nor did the United States have any problem working with colonial powers. When Belgium, which had run one of the most brutal imperial regimes in the history of the world in the Congo, lost control of that colony, President Dwight Eisenhower labeled it "chaos run wild," and had the CIA mark the popular nationalist leader Patrice Lumumba—"obviously" a Communist dupe—for assassination (one such story out of many, as we shall see). And although economics could and often did play a role in these events, it wasn't necessarily inherent to them. The American Dream involves something more comprehensive than just making money. As Hunt says, it includes Americans' vision of themselves as bringing freedom and the American way of life to the world, being atop a racial hierarchy (although this is no longer expressed overtly), and keeping political revolution at bay. If "American interests" is broadened in this way, the similarity of our situation to that of the late Roman Empire becomes strikingly obvious. As the eminent economist Joseph Schumpeter once put it:

> There was no corner of the known world where some interest was not alleged to be in danger or under actual attack. If the interests were not Roman, they were those of Rome's allies; and if Rome had no allies, then allies would be invented. When it was utterly impossible to contrive such an interest—why, then it was the national honor that had been insulted. . . . Rome was always being attacked by evil-minded neighbors.

Hunt adds: "It is easy to recognize in this portrait more than a faint resemblance of ourselves." It is indeed a difficult habit to break.[51]

Our discussion of foreign policy thus far has largely concentrated on the nineteenth and early twentieth centuries. With this background in mind, what can be said about U.S. foreign policy in the post–World War II era? Did the various themes identified above play out from 1945 to 1989 and beyond in a fairly predictable manner? Given the nature of the enemy, was our policy justified? In what follows, I wish to talk about the period of the Cold War and our role in it, but it will be necessary to omit for now any detailed analysis of our involvement in the Middle East. Given the importance of the latter, that region requires a completely separate discussion. Our relationship with the Middle East is the culmination of a foreign policy that has been building for some time now and will prove to be, I believe, the linchpin of the American downfall. With that in mind, let's look at the imperial project of the postwar era.

~ 4 ~

Pax Americana

Who can doubt that there is an American empire?—an "informal" empire, not colonial in polity, but still richly equipped with imperial paraphernalia: troops, ships, planes, bases, proconsuls, local collaborators, all spread around the luckless planet.

—Arthur M. Schlesinger Jr.,
The Cycles of American History (1984)

THE ONLY THING THAT kept America from establishing a full-fledged empire in the postwar period was the presence of the Soviet Union as a restraining force. As a number of political analysts have observed, no "peace dividend" ever materialized after the fall of the USSR; rather, the collapse of a bipolar world gave the American eagle the opportunity to spread its wings unfettered—which is what it did. In doing so, it revealed the truth: it had been running a *pax americana* all along.

This does not mean, however, that a convincing case can be made for any sort of moral equivalency between the United States and its European allies, on the one hand, and the former Soviet Union or the People's Republic of China on the other. Whatever the United States did during the Cold War—and the record isn't exactly stellar—it did not shove millions of its own citizens into labor camps, or starve them to death, or conduct domestic mass purges and liquidations. With the fall of the Soviet Union and the availability of KGB and other archival material, we now know quite unequivocally that the crimes of communism within that country were especially grim. Thus Stéphane Courtois and his colleagues at the Centre National de la Recherche Scientifique, in *The Black Book of Communism* (first published in France in 1997), show that 25 million people were killed in Russia during the Bolshevik and Stalinist eras, and perhaps as many as 65 million in China under Mao Zedong. In terms of systems of government and how they treat their own citizens, then, let us not be confused about this: democracy wins, hands down.[1]

However, that is not quite the end of the story. As is the case with the "war on terrorism," I believe much of the Cold War was an illusion, a large mythic structure or narrative co-created by the United States and the USSR for their own respective domestic political agendas. On both sides, the presence of a powerful enemy served to generate a huge apparatus of employment and government expenditures, including elaborate structures of espionage, military research and development, scientific research institutes, and the like. The two "threats" thus maintained each other and enabled each system to define itself in opposition to the other. After all, writes Ivan Eland (in *The Empire Has No Clothes*), if the main goal of U.S. foreign policy after 1945 had been to fight communism, the *pax americana* we had established during the Cold War years would have been dismantled after 1991. But our military spending never dropped below Cold War levels after that date. The truth of the matter is that the conspiracy theory of a global red menace threatening to engulf the world was grossly exaggerated by the United States for imperial purposes, to gain public support for military and political intervention in the affairs of other nations and for the huge defense budgets such intervention would require. In this way, the Cold War became the justification for building a global empire. In fact, given the decrepit state of the Soviet economy, some analysts within the U.S. government had contemptuously referred to the USSR as "Upper Volta with missiles." Consider the fact that in the "National Security Strategy" of 2002, the Bush administration admitted that during the Cold War, we faced a "risk-averse adversary"—an admission, says Chalmers Johnson, that would never have been made during the Cold War itself. If KGB archives demonstrate how brutal the Soviet Union was within its own borders (satellite states included, of course), they also reveal that the Kremlin's focus was on internal security, not world domination. The documents show that Russia regarded Germany, rather than America, as its greatest threat; that its modus operandi in the postwar period was basically cautious and reactive; and that Stalin had no master plan to establish a Communist empire. The rhetoric of world Communist revolution was largely hot air, a unifying tool for building a strong USSR. This is why, for example, the Kremlin backed away from supporting the Greek and Italian Communists after the war, and why events in Hungary and Czechoslovakia (awful though they were) can correctly be seen as efforts to bolster a shaky regime, not to extend into fresh territory. Even the invasion of Afghanistan in 1979 was defensive, an attempt to ward off the advance of Islamic fundamentalism toward Russia's Muslim provinces. (At least, this is what Russian archival material thus far examined reveals.) It was Americans who became obsessed and predatory during the postwar period, to a far greater degree than the Soviet Union. It is not that the Berlin airlift and Wall and the Cuban missile crisis were not real, and I am not suggesting there was no threat at all. But that seems to be largely it. Most of the Cold War was smoke and mirrors.[2]

Hot versus Cold Wars

But we didn't start out with an aggressive military posture toward the Soviet Union; that came a bit later. As Ivan Eland observes, from 1945 to 1949 our policy was one of political and economic containment of the USSR; the drift toward military containment began in late 1949 and early 1950. This aggravated Soviet insecurities and expanded our military commitments in peripheral areas, and it was this policy shift that marked the beginning of the American global empire and our own military involvement in many areas of the Third World. Even so, there was a fair amount of purple prose in some of the original rhetoric. The term "containment" was coined by George Kennan in a 1947 essay in *Foreign Affairs* (it was so delicate an issue at the time that he signed the article "X"). Containment was the notion of preventing the Soviet Union from using the power it won as a result of World War II to shape the international order. Kennan had outlined his views earlier in his famous "long telegram" from Moscow on 22 February 1946, in which he argued that the USSR was impervious to external influence, and that the best we could hope for was a spheres-of-influence approach. According to Kennan, the behavior of the Soviets bore little relationship to what the West did or did not do. Rather, they viewed the outside world as hostile, needed to find an enemy, and with Germany out of the picture would fill the resulting void with the United States. "Easily persuaded of their own doctrinaire 'rightness,' " he argued in the "X" article, "they insisted on the submission or destruction of all competing powers"; their ideology taught them "that it was their duty eventually to overthrow the political forces beyond their borders." In their eyes, "no opposition to them can be officially recognized as having any merit or justification whatsoever." They regard their regime as the only true one "in a dark and misguided world." Thus we cannot, continued Kennan, rely on ad hoc reactions; only a long-range policy will do the trick. "In these circumstances," he concluded,

> it is clear that the main element of any United States policy toward the Soviet Union must be that of long-term, patient but firm and vigilant containment of Russian expansive tendencies . . . designed to confront the Russians with unalterable counter-force at every point where they show signs of encroaching upon the interests of a peaceful and stable world.[3]

The "long telegram" and the "X" article met with immediate acceptance in Washington. As Henry Kissinger put it years later, "George Kennan came as close to authoring the diplomatic doctrine of his era as any diplomat in our history." Yet one wonders at the supposedly "revelatory" quality of Kennan's writings. The fact is, the United States had been busy "containing" Russia since Tsar Nicholas II. As Walter LaFeber points out in his classic text *America, Russia, and the Cold War,* the United States tried to stop Russian expansion beginning in the 1890s. In Kennan-like phrases, Teddy Roosevelt wrote of the Russians that they "are utterly insincere and treacherous; they have no conception of truth . . . and no regard for others." Between 1918 and 1920 President Wilson sent more than ten thousand troops to try to overthrow Lenin by force. And between that time and the rise of fascism, America made every effort to "quarantine" the Communist "infection," a campaign that resumed after World War II. Indeed, historian John Lewis Gaddis notes (in *Strategies of Containment*) that containment was on the minds of American officials as early as 1941.[4]

And yet, in the world of diplomacy, turns of phrase—and timing—can be everything. The word "containment" crystallized the attitude, the ideology, and the psychology of an entire era. As Kennan himself later pointed out, official Washington was ready to receive this message on an unconscious level. It was all well and good, he said, to talk about the Soviets needing to fill a void with the defeat of Hitler, but what else were we doing if not the same thing? In his memoirs, Kennan claimed that what he had in mind in the "X" article, with the call for "vigilant application of counter-force," was *political* rather than *military* containment, and that in retrospect he felt as though he had "inadvertently loosed a large boulder from the top of a cliff" and was now witnessing its path of destruction. The truth is that Kennan had conflicting feelings about the Cold War that he seemed to be launching. He was a nuanced and sophisticated thinker, and this came out in a number of ways.[5]

First, Kennan did not believe all people were everywhere the same, and therefore held that our national security could not be contingent upon the diffusion of American institutions. The internal organization of states could not be our concern, he argued; we were certainly capable of coexisting with diverse regimes. The attempt to impose our way of life on others would be so demanding as to alter the character of our *own* way of life, so our diplomatic goal had to be maintaining a balance of power. Second, he went on, not all parts of the world were equally vital to American security; we had to prioritize. We couldn't be opposing communism wherever it appeared, and couldn't intervene in another country's politics where the Communist party come to power there in a democratic election—at least, not without corrupting our own values. Third, the primary challenge from the USSR was psychological rather than military. We couldn't fight the Soviet Union everywhere, and we couldn't intervene to prevent Communist takeovers, which would entangle us in a host of civil wars. "The real purposes of the democratic society," Keenan told his audience at the National War College on 21 December 1949, "cannot be achieved by large-scale violence and destruction." Thus in a subtle way, we had to educate the Kremlin, showing the Soviets that they didn't have to remake the entire world in their image in order to feel safe in it, and we had to resist the same temptation ourselves. Indeed, said Kennan, the process of trying to maintain an empire would generate the resistance sufficient to undermine it.[6] Famous last words, as they say.

As Gaddis correctly observes, Kennan served as both an impetus for and a critic of the Truman administration's activities from 1947 to 1950. He began by believing in a "perimeter" defense, whereby the United

States would confront the USSR at every point, but this quickly evolved into a "strongpoint" concept, meaning we had to concentrate on areas that were vital and let go of the rest. This latter approach included not attempting to impose our way of life on others and striving for a balance of power. As a foreign policy "realist," he regarded the formation of NATO, the creation of an independent West German state, and the decision to build the hydrogen bomb as major mistakes, destined to make the Soviets more paranoid (with good reason). Encircling them with military bases and alliances, he said, narrowed the window of negotiation. Basically, Kennan watched the containment concept go wrong, wherein the process of containment (which now included the notion of becoming stronger than the USSR and of rolling it back) overshadowed the goal that that process was supposed to attain: ending the Cold War. Just the opposite occurred. Process triumphed over policy, and this became the pattern of the future. "It was not 'containment' that failed," Kennan wrote many years later; "it was the intended follow-up that never occurred."[7]

One facet of this was that the follow-up fell into the wrong hands. If Kennan was a man who thought in shades of gray, his successor at the State Department, Paul Nitze, principal author of the top secret National Security Council document known as NSC-68, definitely did not. "Nuts" might be the most appropriate term for this essay; but by the spring of 1950, when Nitze had completed it, he was moving with the ideological fervor of the times—as was his boss, Harry Truman. Indeed, the Red scare and the national security state were well under way. Winston Churchill delivered his strident "Iron Curtain" speech in Missouri in 1946 (characterized by Stalin as an ultimatum to accept Anglo-American rule or prepare for war); the Truman Doctrine, which followed this, conveniently blamed the USSR for all the troubles of the world. (The "axis of evil" of the early 1950s was more like a nail, one might say.) As for NSC-68, the document stated that "a defeat of free institutions anywhere is a defeat everywhere." Kennan's so-called strongpoint strategy was left in the dust, in favor of a "perimeter" defense whereby all the points along the perimeter are regarded as equally significant. In addition, Nitze emphasized the importance of perception, arguing that how we were seen was as crucial as how militarily secure we actually were. This rapidly expanded the number of interests deemed relevant to national security. Finally, in terms of the global defense of our interests (real or perceived), anything goes. "The integrity of our system," wrote Nitze, "will not be jeopardized by any measures, covert or overt, violent or nonviolent, which serve the purposes of frustrating the Kremlin design. . . ." Containment had become a Manichaean vision.[8]

As Gaddis points out, NSC-68 defines American interests in terms of Soviet threats; it never sets out the minimum requirements necessary to secure those interests. There could be no end to it, then: "interests" would expand as threats did, so there was no explicit point at which security could be attained. The self-contradictory and self-defeating nature of our Cold War policy was thus set in motion; frustrating Kremlin design had become an end in itself, no longer a means to a larger end. We became addicted to cat and mouse, spy versus spy. And whereas Kennan's focus was only partly military, NSC-68 concentrates almost completely on this. For all intents and purposes, the document rules out diplomacy as a means of dealing with the Soviets and effectively says that any negotiation the United States undertakes with them should be done as a tactic, nothing more (precisely what we kept accusing the Russians of during most of the Cold War!). In short, it says we should be deliberately devious. And if all our interests were now defined as vital, "negotiation" in our minds effectively meant Soviet capitulation—this, while the document calls for a more moderate Soviet attitude toward the world. Not coincidentally, NSC-68 points out that more money can be made available to the military if the economy can expand, the idea being that the government should manage the economy so that the means of defense could be expanded to protect the new (ever-expanding) security interests. What Eisenhower would refer to, ten years later, as the "military-industrial complex" was well on its way.[9]

The Truman administration felt that selling such a policy to Congress and the public at large would make it necessary, in the telling phrase of Senator Arthur Vandenberg, "to scare the hell out of the American people." Secretary of State Dean Acheson indicated that it would be necessary to use dramatic language, such as "the free versus the enslaved world." As General Douglas MacArthur later put it, the government kept the American people in a perpetual state of fear, and in "a continuous stampede of patriotic fervor." (The same sort of Machiavellian politics, of course, was resurrected when "terrorism" replaced communism after 9/11. Indeed, the similarities between the Truman and Bush Jr. administrations in this regard, and in the tactic of governing through fear, are quite obvious.) Clearly, the stage was set for someone like Joseph

McCarthy, who first came to national attention in February 1950; and shortly after that the Korean war came along, which was a godsend to the State Department. The timing couldn't have been better, in terms of getting Congress to bankroll the NSC-68 agenda. The war seemed to validate Nitze's ideas, in a circular way: since perception was the issue, Korea, which had hitherto been regarded as being of peripheral interest, was now vital—because *all* interests were now considered vital! It was unclear what the Soviet involvement in Korea actually was, and the country had very little actual military or strategic importance to us, but so what? Here was an opportunity to make it symbolic of our "resolve." What should have been a distraction, says Gaddis, was turned into an opportunity, as we foolishly got bogged down in a peripheral war with a secondary adversary. As we know, it wouldn't be the last time.[10]

Circular, self-defeating behavior has, of course, waxed and waned in American foreign policy, but one thing that comes across quite clearly from John Lewis Gaddis' study is that nothing that followed NSC-68 really deviated from it all that much; this is a depressing thought in the light of Gaddis Smith's assertion (in *Morality, Reason, and Power*) that "the philosophy of NSC-68 was fundamentally antidemocratic," and that differences between that document and McCarthyism were ones of tone and style rather than substance. To that we should add the chilling assertion of Joseph McCarthy himself, that "McCarthyism is nothing more than Americanism with its sleeves rolled up"—a sobering thought, indeed.[11]

In any case, the spirit of NSC-68 was fully present in the administration of Truman's successor. In his inaugural address of January 1953, Dwight Eisenhower agreed with the notion that America could not tolerate any victories for communism anywhere. His disagreement with Nitze was with the latter's belief that the nation could *afford* to do whatever it took to achieve security. Ike was a fiscal conservative; he felt that unrestrained defense spending would ultimately damage the economy. He also—much to his credit—argued that the Cold War had to have a goal beyond that of "victory," or the United States would wind up destroying what it was attempting to defend. In his view, you could only have absolute security by creating a garrison state, which, he believed, would wreck the nature of American society.[12]

This was all well and good; the problem was that Eisenhower appointed John Foster Dulles as secretary of state, a man who influenced him greatly. Much like the neoconservatives of a later era, Dulles saw the world, congenitally, in adversarial terms. He believed the United States actually had an interest in being threatened—that it served our purposes—and for him, the adversary was "a vast monolithic system," present everywhere, and bent on "destroying human freedom." The Soviet goal, he said, was to extend state socialism to the entire world—a huge, and politically very useful, misreading of the Kremlin's intentions—and Ike was thereby led to see the hand of the Kremlin at work in nearly everything that happened on his watch. Korea, the Philippines, Vietnam, Laos, Cambodia, Burma, Trieste—it was all evidence of a vast Communist conspiracy bent on conquering the globe. In a famous 1956 interview for *Life* magazine, Dulles said that the United States must not be "scared to go to the brink." As in the case of the Truman administration, what was at work here was a bizarre inversion: whereas neutralization of the Soviet threat had been the original goal of containment, that threat was now the means by which the instruments of containment would be perpetuated as ends in themselves. The door was thus open to nuclear diplomacy, Dulles' foolhardy "brinksmanship." Starting in October 1953, American and NATO strategy was to make the prospect of nuclear war credible— to let it be known that the United States was more than willing to contemplate the use of nuclear weapons. This casual zero-sum game approach was quite crazy, especially once the USSR had the bomb. Ike was only lucky that his bluff was never called, that the Soviet Union was fundamentally "risk-averse."[13]

All in all, concludes John Lewis Gaddis, the Eisenhower administration suffered from a failure of strategic vision. Its anti-Communist zealotry—Dulles' refusal to shake hands with Zhou Enlai in Geneva in 1954, as though recoiling from contagion, was emblematic of this—led it to oppose communism even when the latter took on nationalist forms (or even when the agitation for social change wasn't particularly Communistic). The United States often violated the principles of self-determination it was supposedly trying to preserve. Although I shall deal with the CIA's role during the Cold War in more detail later on, even a hasty glimpse at its record under President Eisenhower is quite stunning: the overthrow of popular governments in Iran (1953) and Guatemala (1954); the attempted overthrow of the Indonesian government in 1958 (finally accomplished in 1965, and resulting in the death of hundreds of thousands of people); guerrilla operations against China and North Vietnam; and the assassination plots that were contemplated against Zhou Enlai,

Fidel Castro, and Rafael Trujillo. Ike gave the CIA a broad mandate, and was willing to lie if necessary to maintain its cover. This is a shabby chapter in the history of American foreign relations, and it only got worse after Eisenhower's time.[14]

As for President Kennedy, progressive rhetoric aside, both he and Lyndon Johnson retained the zero-sum-game worldview bequeathed to them by their Republican predecessor. There was the same knee-jerk reaction to any change in the status quo. The strategy, now labeled "flexible response," was committed to countering any Communist moves, and JFK's inaugural address of January 1961 certainly sounded a lot like NSC-68 ("pay any price, bear any burden . . ."). In a very astute analysis of this address, Louis Menand points out that while we remember the speech as a call to service addressed to the American people, it was actually a message of warning addressed to Nikita Khrushchev. The tone, says Menand, is one of alarm. It is a speech about containment, and "could have been delivered, almost without a word changed, in 1948." So by mid-1964 we had a 150 percent increase in the number of nuclear weapons, a 200 percent increase in deliverable megatonnage, and the construction of ten new Polaris submarines and four hundred new Minuteman missiles. The talk was now of "mutual assured destruction"; Walt Rostow, a key member of the State Department, spoke of "immunizing" Third World countries against the "disease" of communism and argued that it was vital that these countries develop along lines consistent with our own concepts of individual liberty. Programs such as the Alliance for Progress, the Peace Corps, the Food for Peace Program, and the Agency for International Development were all part of this effort, and at the time of Kennedy's death the CIA was planning to sabotage the Cuban economy and, once again, to assassinate Castro.[15]

The point is that even before Vietnam rolled around, we had badly undercut the moral basis of the containment policy. Across much of Asia and Latin America, our allies cared nothing for democracy; their allegiance was to our dollars, not to our values. Nor did *we* care, so long as they let us install military bases and said the "right" things. By allying ourselves with repressive regimes, we aligned ourselves against the populations of those countries. These regimes canceled or rigged elections and jailed or murdered dissenters. We often gave non-Communist dissidents little alternative but to join forces with the Communists, in order to survive; to many countries, we were beginning to look, in the words of the

American historian H. W. Brands, like a "neo-imperialist pariah"—an image that has only gotten worse over time.[16]

The self-destructive character of American foreign policy came to full fruition in what is surely our greatest debacle (to date), Vietnam—"the largest imperial war of the century," according to Brands. The logic of that policy dictated that the defense of Southeast Asia was crucial to world order, that there were no strictly "peripheral" interests. U.S. government claims to the contrary, we were involved in Vietnam from 1950, the year we labeled Ho Chi Minh a "tool of international communism" (he and the Vietminh had in fact been admirers of the United States). In that year as well, we began shipping large amounts of matériel to the French, to the tune of $1 billion annually. By 1954, when Eisenhower espoused the domino theory for Indochina, we were supplying 78 percent of the French budget for the war, and the French air force consisted almost entirely of American planes. We even contemplated the use of atomic weapons. When we did turn it into "our" war in the sixties, the CIA's Phoenix program rounded up, jailed, tortured, and killed more than twenty thousand Vietnamese citizens. Nor is that the worst of it. An exposé published in *The Blade* in Toledo, Ohio, in October 2003 (for which the newspaper was subsequently awarded the Pulitzer Prize) revealed that the famous massacre at My Lai was hardly unique: in 1967, an elite army unit known as Tiger Force went on a seven-month rampage, torturing and butchering hundreds of civilians, mutilating bodies, beating elderly farmers to death with shovels, and cutting off ears to wear on necklaces. The savagery visited by American G.I.s upon an innocent civilian population is breathtaking, and it was conducted with full knowledge of their superiors. In fact, there were hundreds if not thousands of such events; archival research now reveals that My Lai and the Tiger Force atrocities were but the tip of the iceberg of what was basically daily fare. "Vietnam was an atrocity from the get-go," said David Hackworth, the retired colonel who created the Tiger Force unit; "there were hundreds of My Lais." All in all, we wound up killing millions of civilians, laying waste to the land with tens of millions of gallons of carcinogenic herbicides, and generating more than six million refugees. Telford Taylor, who had been the chief U.S. prosecutor at Nuremberg, suggested that General William Westmoreland, Robert McNamara, and Secretary of State Dean Rusk could be found guilty of war crimes under the Nuremberg criteria. And all this because the worldwide order was supposedly at stake.[17]

But the government was never able to say *why* the world balance of power was at stake in this small and distant country. The truth was that Vietnam was symbolic rather than real; intrinsically, it meant nothing at all. Meanwhile, the ante got upped; it would "look bad" to withdraw. The logic was completely circular, as Walt Rostow's brother Eugene (who was undersecretary of state for political affairs from 1966 to 1969) later admitted: we were there, he said, because we were there, defending a "credibility" that was getting destroyed the longer we stayed . . . thus the need to "press on" with the job(!). George Kennan, in fact, suggested cutting our losses in 1965 and was ignored, while Secretary of Defense McNamara acknowledged that five months of bombing hadn't changed anything . . . so he recommended more bombing. The CIA did the same thing in 1966, although its director, Richard Helms, did send President Johnson a secret assessment criticizing the domino theory and saying that the loss of Vietnam would not damage our role as a world power (LBJ ignored the report). By 1968, when we had dropped more tonnage on Vietnam than we had dropped in all of World War II (the total for this war was the equivalent of one Nagasaki A-bomb per week for seven and a half years), the Vietcong continued to funnel men into the south. Across the globe, we began to look like what we in fact were: in Brands' words, "a superpower pounding a peasant country to dust for opposing the American will." And the Americanization of the Vietnamese landscape was an additional pathetic symbol of the war: around American bases all over the country, entire towns grew up advertising Schlitz and Coke, and organized around doing laundry, selling cold drinks, and supplying prostitutes to G.I.s. In the wake of the bombing of a Mekong Delta village in 1968, one air force major candidly stated, "It became necessary to destroy the town, to save it." This remark, says John Lewis Gaddis, "could be applied to the whole American experience in Vietnam." The "flexible response" strategy, he adds, was no strategy at all; it was a vacuum. I suspect the same thing could be said of most of what came out of NSC-68.[18]

The new Nixon-Kissinger strategy of "détente" that followed this arose partly in an attempt to correct it, supposedly returning to the original ideas of George Kennan (the latter remarked that Kissinger understood his views better than anyone in the State Department ever had). The idea was to actually end the Cold War, not perpetuate it for the sake of being at war. No more zero-sum logic, said Kissinger; no more symbolic battles; no more trying to change the nature of other countries. The important thing was the overall calculus of power. Conflict and disharmony, he asserted, were inherent to international life; any quest for superiority would be self-defeating. The goal was stability, not "victory" or reform.[19]

What could be saner? This tolerance for conflict, for difference, was at least theoretically (and paradoxically) the road to peace. Hence the "opening up" of China in 1973—a far cry from Dulles' refusing to even touch Zhou Enlai nineteen years before. And yet . . . the old patterns remained; China proved to be the exception. Nixon secretly bombed North Vietnamese sanctuaries in Cambodia in 1969, and toppled Chile's legitimately elected government in 1973. He and Kissinger never gave up their intolerance of Marxism, even when it took indigenous, popular, and independent forms. In fact, neither of them could accept the possibility that Marxism *could* be indigenous, popular, and independent. Once again, there was a deep concern over "credibility," over how we would look in the eyes of the world. Once again, we claimed to oppose socialism because it denied freedom of choice, but when a nation such as Chile freely chose it, the CIA was called in for dirty tricks operations. Kissinger's comment says it all: "I don't see why we have to let a country go Marxist just because its people are irresponsible." Sure, we are all in favor of diversity, he added, but "we set the limits of diversity." The tragedy of American diplomacy, then: self-determination on our terms; subversion of democracy in order to preserve it. As for human rights, then as now, we didn't make an issue of their suppression in countries that were on the "right" side of the struggle. Jimmy Carter excepted, the NSC-68 ideology was never abandoned.[20]

Case studies of what the U.S. government and the CIA did in the pursuit of our antirevolutionary ideology are quite extreme, as we have just seen concerning Vietnam. A particularly egregious instance of American interference in a legitimate Third World government is provided by the story of Guatemala, which gives a clear picture of what the modus operandi has been. In 1953, Eisenhower, John Foster Dulles, and Dulles' brother Allen, director of the CIA, decided that the democratically elected government of Jacobo Arbenz was "Communist," and had to go. Guatemala's foreign minister objected that the United States was categorizing any manifestation of economic independence, desire for social progress, or even intellectual curiosity, as evidence of communism, but to no avail. The American rhetoric continued: Guatemala was a Soviet

republic, a Communist dictatorship, etc. In fact, the USSR had no interest in Guatemala. It didn't provide the country with any military assistance and didn't even have diplomatic relations with it. Guatemala had
voted closely with the United States at the United Nations on issues of
"Soviet imperialism"; Arbenz had the support of many anti-Communist
groups. What more did the State Department want? But the United
States was angry that Communists were allowed to participate in his government (Arbenz correctly pointed out to the Americans that this was
merely part of democratic procedure, an argument completely lost on
Washington), and that he was interested in land reform. With 2.2 percent
of landowners owning 70 percent of the arable land, and agricultural
workers making an average of eighty-seven dollars a year, Arbenz expropriated large tracts of land and redistributed them to one hundred thousand landless peasants.[21]

Of course—and this is a good example of how the economic factor
gets stirred into the pot—the U.S. government was being pressured by
the United Fruit Company, much of whose (uncultivated) land Arbenz
had expropriated. United Fruit owned much of Guatemala, including
telephone lines, railroads, and banana exports, and it had close personal
ties to Eisenhower, the Dulles family, and the State Department. It had
persistently tried to thwart Arbenz's reform program; when (in March
1953) the CIA approached right-wing officers in the Guatemalan army
and arranged to sell them arms, United Fruit contributed $64,000 to the
effort (the coup was foiled). After that, the Eisenhower administration
went about preparing things more carefully. Soviet weapons were gathered to be planted in Guatemala prior to the invasion. More than two
hundred unattributed articles were planted in foreign and Latin American newspapers, labeling Guatemalan officials "Communists." Thanks to
Francis Cardinal Spellman of New York, a letter was read in Guatemalan
churches on 9 April 1954 urging the people to overthrow the Communist "enemy of God." "Soviet" arms were parachuted into Guatemala;
United Fruit circulated photos of mutilated bodies, claiming these were
of atrocities committed by the Arbenz regime. The CIA and the American ambassador bribed right-wing officers—who then gave Arbenz an
ultimatum to resign—to defect. And so on.[22]

Meanwhile, the man being groomed to head the new government was
a fervid anti-Communist colonel, Castillo Armas. Armas took over as
soon as a CIA plane bombed a military base and government radio sta-

tion. In July 1954, he jailed thousands of "Communists" and tortured and killed many of them. A committee was set up that could arbitrarily declare anyone a Communist, with no right of appeal. Agrarian reform came to a halt; United Fruit got all of its land back; and 75 percent of Guatemalan voters were disenfranchised. All political parties, labor groups, opposition newspapers, and peasant organizations were banned; books (including the works of Victor Hugo and Fyodor Dostoyevsky) were burned. On June 30 John Foster Dulles had declared that the events in Guatemala showed how the Kremlin was trying to destroy the West; the next year, the United States attempted to scuttle the section of the proposed U.N. Covenant of Human Rights that dealt with the right of peoples to sovereignty and self-determination. As for Guatemala, the terror initiated by Colonel Armas continued with hardly a pause for the next forty years. So no: unlike the Soviet Union, we didn't butcher our own citizens; we just helped other countries to butcher *theirs*.[23]

And *mutatis mutandis*, this scenario was repeated in various locations throughout the Third World. To expand on the example of Chile, in 1964 the United States decided that the Chilean election could not be left to democracy, so it underwrote half the presidential campaign costs of Eduardo Frei, the opponent of Socialist candidate Salvador Allende. It also conducted a vigorous propaganda campaign against Allende, allegedly linking him to the Soviet Union (in fact, all of the U.S. intelligence reports of the time showed no such link). Frei was victorious, but in late 1970 Allende finally managed to get elected, despite CIA attempts to get the Chilean military to stage a coup. (A CIA study of 7 September 1970 had concluded that an Allende victory would represent an "advantage for the Marxist idea," which might inspire other countries to consider a socialist solution to their problems.) With the help of International Telephone and Telegraph, the CIA went into high gear, squeezing the Chilean economy and subsidizing strikes. The U.S. campaign against the Allende government was nothing less than terrorism, and included the assassination of René Schneider, the head of Chile's armed forces, which was carried out with funds and submachine guns provided by the CIA. The coup finally took place on 11 September 1973; thousands were killed and tortured, books were burned, and President Gerald Ford went on record hailing the event as being "in the best interests of the people of Chile." This has to be one of the most shameful episodes in the history of American foreign policy.[24]

Once again, we see how the antirevolutionary ideal of the United States led it to interfere violently in the democratic process of another country. As author William Blum remarks in *Killing Hope*, to the United States the real heresy in the Third World is independence. The cost of Vietnam dealt us a crippling economic blow; this, and the repeal of Bretton Woods, mark the real beginning of our decline. But even when the financial cost has not been that great, the moral or spiritual cost has been enormous. How better are we than our enemies? is the disturbing question that hovers over a good deal of American foreign policy. We claim to stand for freedom and self-determination; in reality, we act to destroy these more often than not. Out of a fanatical antirevolutionary ideology, we have delivered millions of so-called Communists—mostly peasants and innocent people—into the hands of dictators and torturers. As the second century of the American republic wore on, our "shadow" was getting increasingly dark.

The issue of the "shadow" brings us to another factor that has propelled U.S. foreign policy—namely, the psychological motivations behind it all. This dimension emerges quite clearly in H. W. Brands' absorbing study of the Cold War, *The Devil We Knew*. Brands allows for strategic, economic, and political factors in the shaping of our foreign policy, and he believes that the United States and the USSR co-created the Cold War and "institutionalized" it, after which it took on a life of its own. But he points out that Kennan's assertion in the "long telegram"—that the Soviet Union was able to function only with an enemy—is a particularly apt characterization of the United States. Recall what Kennan wrote: that the USSR viewed the outside world as hostile, was persuaded of its own doctrinaire rightness, insisted on the elimination of all competing powers and ideologies, believed that no opposition to them could possibly have any merit, and saw their regime as the only true one "in a dark and misguided world." Let's not kid ourselves: it would be hard to find a better description of American postwar foreign policy, right down to today. Whether we are talking about Harry Truman declaring, "The whole world should adopt the American system," which "can survive in America only if it becomes a world system"; or Ronald Reagan with his John Winthrop–ish "city on the hill" versus his Darth Vader–ish "evil empire"; or George W. Bush declaring a "crusade" against "the evildoers" and militarily intending or attempting to make the Arab states over into capitalist democracies—all of this while accusing the *other side* of involvement in a global conspiracy—it has only been by virtue of an enemy that we have had any identity at all. Having a shared enemy has been crucial to the United States because the country lacks a shared ancestry or cultural experience. This was true from the get-go: the Declaration of Independence, after all, derived its bite from opposition to Great Britain. It's always a Manichaean drama, always an enemy "out there" that is the cause of our misfortunes. This psychological divide left no third category for independent nationalist or Communist movements. While it was ridiculous to claim that a victory for China (1949) was a victory for the Kremlin as well, or that our involvement in Korea (beginning in 1950) was really part of a larger cause, we apparently needed to tell ourselves these sorts of things in order to feel okay, or even to feel we had a reason to exist.[25]

Similarly, says Brands, NSC-68 employed lurid language for a top secret document that only a handful of people were going to see, so one has to wonder why the author thought that was necessary. But as Dean Acheson explained it years later, if Truman administration officials were going to be able to "scare the hell out of the American people," they first had to scare the hell out of themselves. NSC-68 was a "psyching up," as it were. Its black-and-white, reductionistic rhetoric made the task brutally simple, and even those who ought to have known better got caught up in it. From that point on, there wasn't much distinction between caution and paranoia; the real appeal of anticommunism was the (phony) psychological security it provided the whole country with, an ontological (or existential, if you will) reassurance to which even finer minds proved to be extremely susceptible—thinking "tribally," one might say. This also enabled us to dismiss the fact that Communists were often, in those early years, freely elected in other countries—a reality we couldn't tolerate because it required the acceptance of ambiguity and complexity. We preferred to fall back on conspiracy theories, which enabled us to cling to an apparently much needed belief in our own righteousness and innocence—something that obviously hasn't changed much in the last fifty-odd years.[26]

And this conspiracy psychology had an obvious additional payoff for certain sectors of government and industry: we armed ourselves to the teeth in the 1950s, setting the national security state in motion as we mobilized on a permanent basis. The outlay for defense was 4.6 percent of the GDP in 1950; by 1953 it had risen to 13.8 percent. In 1940 the federal budget devoted 16 percent to defense; in 1959, more than 50 percent. By 1955, the American alliance system circled the globe, and we were pledged to the defense of practically everybody, including a host of despots and autocrats. The CIA was effectively told it could do whatever was necessary to "get the job done." Blaming communism was really an attempt to "exorcise evil." This phenomenon of "exorcism," it seems to me, can be operating even when the enemy really *is* a nasty regime.[27]

This was a major reason that Jimmy Carter failed so miserably at the polls in 1980, and why his administration is almost universally regarded as a botched presidency: he wanted, at least down to December 1979, to put the containment policy to rest, and this simply would not fly with the American people, who, in Brands' words, "loved the Cold War too much to let it go." They longed for the simple age of right versus wrong, the notion that we were good and our enemy evil and that military strength could give us security. So they were drawn to Ronald Reagan, a man who saw the world in just such simplistic terms, and who pledged to make America great again. His blaming of foreigners for nearly everything wrong with the world gave Americans the (pseudo-)psychological security they badly needed.[28] To this day, tens of millions of Americans—perhaps even the majority—regard Reagan as "wise," a great leader, because he provided a simple Manichaean formula. This says quite a bit about what the United States had become as a nation by 1980.

What the Cold War provided, then, was conceptual simplicity, something Americans found (find) difficult to live without. As with the "war on terrorism," it obviated the need to understand international relations at any depth. All you had to know was "Communist" or "not Communist." This "quick and dirty division of the world into friends and foes," writes Brands, the possession of an "agreed-upon focus of evil against which [Americans] could favorably contrast themselves," perversely led American leaders "to subvert the principles that constituted their country's best argument against communism." The Cold War, adds Walter LaFeber, cost the nation $8 trillion in defense expenditures, took the lives of nearly one hundred thousand Americans, ruined a very large number of lives during the McCarthy era, led the nation into hostile conflicts in Southeast Asia, and, in the 1980s, triggered the worst depression in forty years. A Pyrrhic victory, or so it would seem. Conservatives claim that American pressure was finally responsible for causing the USSR to cave in, but one could more reasonably argue that American antagonism actually prolonged the Cold War. The United States threatened the USSR for forty years with rhetoric, military bases, the arms race and so on, and this meant the Soviets could avoid dealing with their own internal problems—ones inherent to the Communist form of government. Had we not played this game, they—and we—would have been required to confront such problems—exactly what one president, Jimmy Carter, was trying to get us to do.[29]

Failed Presidency versus Failed Nation

The Carter presidency is so anomalous, particularly in terms of the postwar pattern of U.S. foreign policy, that it is initially hard to conceive how it ever happened. Timing accounts for much of it. America had just suffered an ignominious defeat in Vietnam, and the morality of the entire venture looked shabby in the extreme. The Church Committee had conducted a congressional investigation into the dirty tricks of the CIA, focusing especially on the overthrow of Salvador Allende. Gerald Ford had pardoned Richard Nixon immediately after the latter resigned, thus making the squalor of Watergate even more squalid. All in all, U.S. government morality and image were at ebb tide; it was a confused and demoralized time. Enter, in 1976, Jimmy Carter, a "Christian" candidate, low-key and self-effacing, who spoke to the need for some national soul searching. "We're ashamed of what our government is as we deal with other nations around the world," he announced on the campaign trail—astonishing rhetoric, really. "What we seek is . . . a foreign policy that reflects the decency and generosity and common sense of our own people." Over and over, in hundreds of speeches and interviews, Carter reiterated that the United States had gone through a loss of spirit and morality. A foreign policy dominated by rivalry with the USSR, he maintained, was an obsession whose logic led directly to Vietnam (the latter, in short, was no "detour"). The time was over for blaming an enemy for our own problems, he declared; rather, the time had come to look within ourselves, to put our *own* moral house in order. Carter attacked the *realpolitik* of Henry Kissinger and the U.S. role in Chile; the time had come, he maintained (this in 1977), to move beyond "that inordinate fear of communism which once led us to embrace any dictator who joined us in that fear."[30]

For a brief moment in American postwar history, the position of sanity found an echo. The moment, was, however, long enough for the president to suggest a different direction in our international agenda: obsession with communism would not shape every policy; we would work for a more humane world order in our international relations, not seek merely to defeat one adversary; military solutions would not come first; efforts would be made to reduce the sale of arms to developing countries (by 1975 we had become the world's largest arms exporter—$15 billion in sales as compared with $2 billion in 1970); and so on. These were, quite clearly, exceptional times.[31]

But the exception was of short duration; the Carter morality was, within two years, heavily out of step with the return to the usual public demand for a more muscular and military foreign policy. In addition, out-of-office cold warriors closed ranks, forming organizations such as the Committee on the Present Danger, which included Paul Nitze. Their goal—to revive the Cold War—was ultimately successful; Ronald Reagan and CIA-assisted torture in Central America were the inevitable results. And in the course of all this, a picture was formed of Jimmy Carter as weak, bungling, inept, and out of his depth; an ad hoc president who had no coherent conceptual outlook or foreign policy at all. It seems to me that some of this was true, but a genuinely alternative foreign policy simply could not "scan" in the mind-set still with us, that of NSC-68. It was also a case of the inability of nuanced thinking to make any headway with a voting public trained to "think," for so long, in terms of simplistic oppositional slogans. I want to look at these processes a bit more closely, not so much out of an interest in the Carter presidency per se as much as for what they say about the nature of American foreign policy, and why, from Truman (or perhaps even McKinley) to Bush Jr., it has been virtually impossible to alter. That Carter would be perceived as weak, and presidents such as Reagan and Bush Jr. as strong, says a lot about who we are as a people, and how we understand "strength."[32]

As I said, some of the conventional image of the Carter presidency is based on fact. For someone pledging to get beyond the historical knee-jerk reflex of blaming the Soviet Union for all of our problems, Carter made a rather peculiar choice for his national security adviser: Zbigniew Brzezinski, a man clearly in the NSC-68 tradition, and whose visceral antipathy to the USSR was legendary (indeed, Truman was Brzezinski's favorite president). At the same time, he chose Cyrus Vance as his secretary of state, a man who favored conciliation in the exercise of foreign policy and—unlike Brzezinski—thought that human rights ought to be a genuine part of it. Their positions were probably too disparate to be integrated into a single philosophy or administration; indeed, in the end Vance resigned and Brzezinski reigned unopposed.[33]

It is also the case that too many things got overblown or oversold. Loud denunciations of human rights violations did little to sway the violators, for example; the Stragetic Arms Limitations Treaty (SALT) negotiations between the United States and the USSR finally fell apart; and then there was the Iran hostage crisis, and the failed rescue attempt. Most of all, Carter increasingly wavered regarding a "moral" foreign policy and constraints on the military, dramatically so after the Soviet invasion of Afghanistan in December 1979. While this shift could have appealed to the American public, it was a bit too late and appeared inconsistent. More to the point, it was out of character for Jimmy Carter, and the nation recognized this. It was not, however, out of character for Ronald Reagan, who made the case much more convincingly, and thus easily thwarted Carter's bid for reelection.[34]

And yet, as historian Robert Strong points out, this is hardly the whole story; a lot of the negative image had to do with media spin, and—to my mind—the public need for a simplistic "handle" on events. As an example, Strong tells the story of an anecdote about Carter's speech on U.S.-Soviet relations, given in Annapolis in the summer of 1978. The anecdote appeared in a very influential two-part article, "The Passionless Presidency," that was published the following year in the *Atlantic Monthly*. The author, James Fallows, had been Carter's chief speechwriter from 1977 to 1979, and subsequently went on to become the Washington, D.C., editor of the magazine. Fallows reported that the president had thrown the Annapolis speech together by literally stapling one memo from Vance to another from Brzezinski. He suggested that the whole thing had been sloppy, and that the president couldn't reconcile or perhaps even recognize the philosophical differences between his two chief foreign policy advisers. Strong decided to check this story out, went to the Carter Library in Atlanta, dug up the speech, and guess what? No staples or staple holes in it. In addition, he found a number of Carter's drafts, demonstrating very long and careful preparation.[35]

As Strong admits, the staple story may or may not be true, but that is not the crucial point. What *is* important is that the image of the stapled memos, and thus of incoherence and ineptness, stuck; worse, that (as Fallows claimed) Carter was "passionless," an engineer who mechanically moved from problem to problem without seeing the connections among them, a man who had no clear political philosophy and was not able to think in terms of broad concepts—an unimaginative, ineffectual president, in short.[36]

In addition to the absence of staples and the evidence for long and careful preparation on Carter's part, what can be said about Fallows' overall characterization, which, after all, became the heart of the conventional wisdom about the thirty-ninth president? Essentially, that Fallows largely missed the boat. One wonders if he knew very much about Carter's personal history, or about the most formative influence on his career—the civil rights movement in the South. Put this together with Carter's campaign speeches, and his foreign policy position during the first three years in office, and the answer is obvious: Jimmy Carter's overarching political principle was his commitment to human rights. It was this commitment that shaped U.S.-Soviet relations for this president; he believed that in the long run, the USSR would succumb to the global quest for self-determination. In effect, this quest is what Carter believed political life, and perhaps even human life in general, was all about. Certainly, it has been the story of *his* life.[37]

Just consider: Jimmy Carter's mother, Lillian, had long been an opponent of segregation, and the Carter family would not join in the widespread resistance to the U.S. Supreme Court's 1954 *Brown v. Board of Education* decision. As a result, the family business was boycotted. They were also ostracized when they opposed a decision by their church to keep out black worshipers. Jimmy entered state politics on a "one man, one vote" platform, and his thinking was that if the South could end segregation in a few years, why couldn't the world undergo similar changes? Human rights, in general, was central to his worldview.[38]

As president, especially during the first three years, Carter never stopped talking about the subject. He referred to human rights in his inaugural address, and in his first speech to the United Nations in March 1977. At his Notre Dame address that May, he listed five foreign policy objectives; human rights was number one. He staffed the Human Rights Bureau of the State Department with dedicated activists and established mechanisms to ensure that human rights records would be factored into decisions on foreign aid, arms sales, and diplomatic contacts. He also cut military aid to Argentina, Ethiopia, Uruguay, Chile, Nicaragua, Rhodesia, and Uganda because of human rights abuses. The list is quite extensive.[39]

But the staple story stuck, as did the cliché about Carter's being caught between his two advisers. It is true that there were conflicts; it is also true that Carter had an overambitious foreign policy agenda, and that he was forced to modify some of his idealism in the face of right-wing pressure, the changing mood of the nation, and the limits imposed by the real world. But he cannot be fairly characterized as not having a political philosophy or a conceptual approach to foreign policy; the Vance-Brzezinski split, says Robert Strong, got exaggerated because this binary interpretation *was* a sound bite, a simplistic lens through which to view the Carter administration. (In reality, although the two advisers had their differences, they also saw eye to eye on a number of issues.) In addition, two other factors played a part in the view of Carter as being weak and indecisive, factors that may be hallmarks of naïveté but that more likely reflect the man's maturity. Carter had strong convictions, and some have characterized him as stubborn; but he was never doctrinaire or ideological. It is this, to my mind, that makes him so unusual; it sets him off from presidents such as Reagan or Bush Jr.—men who were (are) very doctrinaire and who confuse(d) strength with rigidity (the American public does as well). Carter accepted compromises and contradictions when necessary, and saw the foreign policy arena as one necessarily fraught with conflict and inconsistency. Allied with this, he did not think in oppositional terms, and since that is all the media and public seem to be able to do, his message got lost. It was not his style, like Ronald Reagan's, to deliver repeated rhetorical assaults on communism. Carter was more inclined, writes Strong, to offer up the positive side of the same message; to tell his audience things such as "our philosophy is based on personal freedom." But after a quarter century of NSC-68 and of badly needing binary rhetoric to shore up a sense of disintegrating identity, the nation was far more interested in hearing speeches about the "evil empire" than about anything more complex, or real.[40]

The second factor that created the "inept" view of Carter was his lack of interest in spin and PR. This president made no effort to correct the media portrayal of him as bungling and inconsistent. Of course, not all of the "inconsistency" charge was off base; Carter *did* abandon his pledge to get beyond the containment mentality of the Cold War during his last year in office, and start succumbing to the anti-Soviet feelings of Brzezinski and the rest of the country, even before the Russian invasion of Afghanistan (more on this below). But adapting his human rights idealism to real-world events is not the same thing as weakness, and he was not concerned with correcting (or cultivating) his public image. Carter did not seek out slogans to summarize or advertise his positions, and so the press and the public were stymied in their attempt, Strong says, "to define an administration that would not define itself." To many observers, Jimmy Carter was a kind of mysterious politician who descended from the moon, visited D.C. for four years, and then left—which, given the foreign policy outlook of his predecessors over the previous thirty years, was in a sense correct. He had neither the talent nor the patience for memorable rhetorical appeals; his interest was in the substance of foreign policy issues, not in how they would play in the media. It is no accident that he was defeated by an actor, a not terribly astute, sloganeering individual with an opposite modus operandi. Popularity with the media was at the top of Reagan's list. He was not interested in the substantive details of foreign policy; he probably couldn't even understand them. What interested the fortieth president was rhetoric, public appearances, and ceremonial duties. He had no intellectual curiosity whatsoever; his political philosophy amounted to little more than "us good, them bad," and that was basically what most of the American people wanted to hear. Jimmy Carter (perhaps foolishly) had loftier goals in mind; thus, he was "inept."[41]

If the Fallows article successfully branded Carter as a president with no coherent foreign policy, Jeane Kirkpatrick's widely influential essay in November 1979, "Dictatorships and Double Standards," faulted him for failing to support America's right-wing allies, and for being a "liberal." Kirkpatrick was a member of the Committee on the Present Danger, whose goal it was to resuscitate the Cold War. Her central charge—that Carter's human rights policy "lost" us Iran and Nicaragua—was full of holes, but it carried great weight among the Cold War crowd and beyond (it was squarely in the tradition of the GOP's attacking Truman for "losing" China). The United States, she said, should accept dictators such as Anastasio Somoza and the Shah of Iran as "traditional authoritarians," ones who prevented the triumph of the left. Carter, she went on, was destabilizing our right-wing allies. Our so-called crisis of spirit was simply something being inflicted upon us by liberals. Right-wing regimes were, she asserted, capable of redemption; left-wing ones were beyond it. Furthermore, any nation that describes us as colonialist, expansionist, or racist was an enemy, for we were none of those things (Kirkpatrick apparently hadn't read a whole lot of American history). Not surprisingly, the article attracted the attention of Ronald Reagan, who appointed her ambassador to the United Nations in 1981; and her distinction between "redeemable" right-wing regimes and "irredeemable" left-wing ones provided the basis of much of his foreign policy: the Iran-contra scandal, the repression of the left in Nicaragua and El Salvador, and the CIA torture training that went on in Honduras, to name some of the worst examples. William Casey, Reagan's CIA director, manipulated intelligence reports to exaggerate the Soviet threat in Central America, in order to whip up support for the government's policies. Business as usual, in other words.[42]

Although Kirkpatrick's attack was fundamentally misguided—indeed, Christopher Hitchens remarked that what she really preferred was not authoritarian regimes to totalitarian ones, but authoritarianism to democracy—it must be said that in an American context, it was shooting fish in a barrel. We have seen how continuous the ideology of NSC-68 has been, and how profoundly biased the United States is against revolution or even social change. It's not very difficult to win an election, or stay in power, if you reflect back to the American people the binary way of thinking they are so used to. But anything really different from that—the Ralph Nader green platform of 2000, for example, or the Jimmy Carter human rights platform of 1976—is largely doomed. This is why Carter has to be regarded as something of an accident; his basic orientation flew in the face of our political history, in the face of who we had become as a people. Although (to my knowledge) no actual surveys have been conducted, I suspect that in the case of Vietnam, for example, most Americans, to this day, believe that it was the result of the misapplication of sound premises (we just got temporarily off track); that relatively speaking, few came away from those years thinking that obsessive opposition to communism had logically and inevitably led us down a blind alley, and that the whole basis of our foreign policy needed an overhaul.

Something similar can be said regarding Carter's response to the energy crisis—that we had to reduce our expectations and be prepared to live with a certain level of discomfort, and that unless we moved in a new direction life on earth for most people was going to be much worse in

2000 than it was in 1980. How many Americans want to hear *that?* We love our large, energy-inefficient vehicles, and don't seem to be too preoccupied with the fact that other peoples of the world have to die in large numbers so that we can live an extravagant and wasteful lifestyle. As George Kennan wrote in a top secret report of 1948, "We have about 50 percent of the world's wealth, but only 6.3 percent of its population. . . . Our real task in the coming period is to devise a pattern of relationships which will permit us to maintain this position of disparity. . . ." Clearly, we have succeeded in maintaining a substantial disparity, in ignoring human rights, in deriving our identity from opposition to others, and in projecting our problems—and our military—outward. Jimmy Carter had something more creative, more introspective, in mind. What chance did he possibly have?[43]

This matter of introspection is perhaps what it all comes down to in the end. Americans as a people don't really like to look inward. Our feelings on the subject are much closer to, say, Bush Sr. than to Jimmy Carter. Whenever the elder Bush was asked probing questions, his immediate response was "Don't stretch me out on the couch."[44] When Carter asked us to look at our wasteful energy policy, our self-contradictory foreign policy, and our questionable political morality, he was asking us to reflect on ourselves, on who we were and what we really wanted. And this would have inevitably led to looking at ourselves from the outside, seeing ourselves as others saw us. Given our track record, few people outside the North Atlantic region, as Carter understood, saw communism as a greater enemy than colonialism and institutionalized inequality. We had aligned ourselves with colonial and reactionary regimes that flouted the principles we supposedly fought to vindicate. The Third World regarded us as imperialistic, self-serving, and hypocritical, endlessly employing a double standard. We backed right-wing regimes across the globe; Vietnam looked like neocolonial repression of indigenous nationalism. It wasn't exactly a glowing record, and it had been generated by largely faulty premises.

In his "crisis of spirit" speech in the summer of 1979, Carter spoke of a "national malaise," and said that America had two possible paths it could take. One, he said, led to fragmentation and self-interest—"a certain route to failure"—whereas the other led to "common purpose and the restoration of American values." The latter path, he added, "leads to true freedom." Now I am not sure how much choice we really had in 1979; given the powerful economic and technological factors discussed in chapter 2, it seems to me that fragmentation and self-interest—the life we lead today, in these end-of-empire times—were pretty much inevitable. But the Carter years (one thinks, by comparison, of Pope John XXIII and the Vatican) were perhaps the only time the window was open on a different possibility, a nonoppositional world in which the problem lies not in domestic liberals or foreign Communists, but in ourselves. As Gaddis Smith says, during the Carter administration an effort was made to think in terms of a lasting world order beneficial to all, rather than to make every decision based on gaining a short-term advantage over an enemy. Carter failed, he concludes, "because he asked the American people to think as citizens of the world with an obligation toward future generations." But who, then, really failed: Jimmy Carter, or the American people?[45]

History is of course nothing if not ironic, and sometimes tragically so. Carter certainly wanted to get the country off the path of NSC-68 and the knee-jerk reaction to the Soviet Union, but even for him, it was easier said than done. He made two very serious mistakes toward the end of his administration, ones that would eventually play out as Bush Jr.–Cheney agendas. As noted earlier, the Soviet invasion of Afghanistan in December 1979 was very likely a defensive move vis-à-vis Islamic fundamentalism, an attempt to head off "Khomeini fever" (as Cyrus Vance put it)—that is, the emergence of hostile Islamic states on Russia's southern border in the wake of the Iranian revolution. There was no master plan to drive the United States out of the Persian Gulf. As with Vietnam and so many other places, Afghanistan was a nonstrategic country; we could have let it go. But spurred on by Brzezinski, Carter's reaction was to see the invasion through the time-worn distorting lens of containment; and so, in his State of the Union address one month after the invasion, the president enunciated the Carter Doctrine: "An attempt by any outside force to gain control of the Persian Gulf region will be regarded as an assault on the vital interests of the United States of America, and such an assault will be repelled by any means necessary, including military force." Thus began the long military buildup in the Gulf, which (according to Michael Klare in *Blood and Oil*) led to a whole series of military engagements in that region, culminating in the 2003 invasion of Iraq.[46] (Carter, as an elder statesman made wise through time, was deeply opposed to that latter venture; the tragedy is that it was the stepchild of his own abrupt and misguided shift in foreign policy.)

The second major error that followed from the containment ideology is quite well-known: Carter was persuaded by Brzezinski—even before the Russian invasion—that this was an opportunity to entrap the USSR in a Vietnam-style quagmire. Thus his administration (and that of Reagan's as well) trained the Islamic militants, the mujahideen, to fight the Soviets; and after the Russians withdrew, the radical Islamists won control of Afghanistan and used it as a base from which to launch terrorist attacks against us. This was a remedy that was much worse than the disease, one that led to 9/11 and—no fault of Jimmy Carter's—the use of that event by the Bush-Cheney administration to cement an openly imperialist policy. As in the case of the "hands off" policy in the Persian Gulf, one can only wonder whether the former president now spends much time pondering the strange twists of fate.[47]

"To transcend tragedy," wrote William Appleman Williams in *The Tragedy of American Diplomacy*, "requires the nerve to fail. . . . [This] has nothing at all to do with blustering and self-righteous crusades up to or past the edge of violence." Rather, he goes on, it is the quiet acceptance of limits, and the understanding that this does not mean the end of existence itself. It means abandoning what Frederick Jackson Turner called "the gate of escape" provided by the frontier, and it means radically changing our foreign policy. Without that, Williams concluded, we shall have gone from childhood to old age without ever having matured (and of course that is exactly what has happened to us). One can point to Jimmy Carter's mistakes in office—they were real, and the two just cited above, which were based on falling back into containment logic, were the worst of the lot. But the overall impulse, it seems to me, of trying to get us off the path of lurching blindly ahead with the logic that took us into Vietnam, and of trying to get us to see ourselves as others see us, was fundamentally sound. We did not, as it turns out, have the "nerve to fail"; the window shut, and we chose "self-righteous crusades up to or past the edge of violence." The blowback from this is going to be the theme of the twenty-first century, as we continue to weaken ourselves through endless war and oppositional logic, and the attempt to project our military into every corner of the globe. "The traditional effort to sustain democracy by expansion," wrote Williams at the conclusion of his book, "will lead to the destruction of democracy." This is, by now, our imperial destiny, and there does not seem to be any way to alter it.[48]

Republic versus Empire

Let me, then, revisit an earlier thesis, namely that U.S. foreign policy is about the economy—"dollar diplomacy," as it is sometimes called. It would indeed seem that the economic factor is always present. Sometimes it is dominant; sometimes it is overshadowed by the other factors we have discussed. But even in a case such as Vietnam, where economics does not seem to have played much of a role, one can argue that it was never very far from the minds of the policy elite. George Kennan's 1948 secret memo about our goal being one of preserving the economic disparity between the United States and everyone else remains a persistent theme. It was echoed recently in the 1998 "Long Range Plan" of the U.S. Space Command (written with the help of seventy-five corporations that do business with the military), which states that the gap between the rich and poor will widen, and that the U.S. needs military space development in order to contain the regional unrest that will inevitably ensue as a result. The Long Range Plan also declares that the way a nation makes wealth is the way it makes war—a thesis that leaps right out of the pages of Beard and Williams.[49]

There is simply no getting around these basic facts:

✦ There *is*, as Dwight Eisenhower said in his farewell address, a military-industrial complex.

✦ During the Truman administration the military-industrial complex insisted on, and got, a permanent war economy (one that generates vast wealth for American defense contractors).

✦ After World War II the American republic was essentially replaced by a national security state, largely exempt from congressional oversight and answerable to practically no one.

And while often masked by other factors, the economic motif runs consistently through the history of the United States during the twentieth century. It was all well and good for Ike to have warned the nation about the dangers of the military-industrial complex, but in fact from 1952 on (i.e., commencing during his campaign) he himself emphasized the importance of being able to trade freely with those countries from whom we obtain or could obtain vital raw materials. He repeatedly talked about manganese, cobalt, tungsten, and tin; and both he and John Foster Dulles agreed that "the chief American interest in the world was access to the world." In that sense too it is a bit creepy—if not that much of a shock—that the president's "National Security Strategy" of September 2002 speaks of the right to be able to buy and sell things, and comments, "This is real freedom. . . ." *Cherchez l'argent* remains a faithful guide to much of American foreign policy.[50]

It is the economic factor, combined with the militarization of American foreign policy, according to Andrew Bacevich, director of the Center for International Relations at Boston University, that has been key to the transformation of the republic into an empire. Bacevich claims that we had a "globalization" strategy in the 1890s and that it was still operative one hundred years later. Then as now, the goal was to create an integrated international order that offered no barriers to the flow of goods, capital, and ideas, and that is administered by the United States. The whole world is to become a free-market economy, and the U.S. military is there to remove any opposition to this process. And since there will be those who will not be happy with this project and will resist it, our foreign policy necessarily has to become, in essence, a military one. Thus, says Bacevich, "the politicoeconomic concept to which the United States adheres today has not changed in a century": an "open" order based on commercial integration and technological innovation, with the rapid deployment of the armed forces to maintain that order, if necessary. This vision has been the strategic consensus of the foreign policy elite of both major political parties, long before George Kennan, and long after him as well.[51]

All of this was quite in evidence during the Clinton administration. One month after he took office, Clinton gave a speech at American University saying that our challenge now was to master the emerging global economy, and that American enterprise needed to operate on a global scale if it was to avoid failure. The passage of NAFTA in November 1993, which relied heavily on GOP votes, demonstrated the Democratic commitment to corporate interests, and was hailed by Henry Kissinger as crucial to our foreign policy. Clinton's message to China's Jiang Zemin, when the president visited that country in 1998, was that there finally was no real alternative to the American system. Indeed, by the end of his second term, the *Boston Globe* was referring to the outgoing president as the "pied piper of capitalism."[52]

As must be extremely obvious, the success of the expansionist agenda depends on having the U.S. military as the enforcer of all of this. The economic payoff that results from involving the Defense Department (DoD) is twofold:

1. We are enforcing a worldwide economic order in which the deck is loaded in our favor (globalization = Americanization).
2. An expanded military budget means lots of business for American defense industries and weapons manufacturers.

We can see how this works if we take a closer look at the dramatically expanding role that militarization has come to play in American political and economic life.

It is sobering to realize that in the 1920s and 1930s, the United States deployed an army that was roughly the size of Portugal's. Today, America has a quarter of a million troops and civilians stationed in 130 countries. It is, by far, possessor of the largest military establishment in the world and is the world's largest arms exporter. (The U.S. share of the global arms trade doubled after the Cold War ended, so that America now sells roughly half of all the weapons sold worldwide.) By 1990, Pentagon property was valued at nearly $1 trillion, the equivalent of 83 percent of all of the assets of all U.S. manufacturing industries. With an annual budget (during that time) of $310 billion, the Pentagon was (and presumably remains) America's largest company: 5.1 million employees, 600 fixed facilities nationwide, more than 40,000 properties, and 18 million acres of land. Indeed, the Pentagon's economy is twice as large as all of Japan's. In 1997, the government spent $37 billion on military research and development, nearly two-thirds of what the entire world spent on the same. In 1998, while the entire world spent $864 billion on military forces, the American fraction of this was nearly one-third. Although it is true that during the 1990s military expenditures amounted to only 3 or 4 percent of the GDP, the figure is misleading, because when we look at the discretionary budget, the fraction is huge: nearly 50 percent during Fiscal Year 2001 (the last Clinton budget). Indeed, Gore Vidal claims that during the Reagan years the military fraction of the discretionary budget was nearly 90 percent, and we are, as of this writing, set to go through the roof once again: in the wake of September 11, Bush's $2.13 trillion dollar budget (which would put the country $80 billion in the red) would increase the Pentagon's annual account to $451 billion by 2007—more than the budgets of the next fifteen largest militaries combined. As of 2003, the U.S. was spending more than $400 billion per year on defense and another $100 billion a year for fighting in Iraq and Afghanistan.[53]

The scholar who has done most to trace the history of these developments is the late Seymour Melman, in books such as *Pentagon Capitalism* and *After Capitalism*. After World War II, he writes, the DoD dominated the affairs of more than thirty thousand industrial laboratories, and the government became the largest financier of research and development in science and technology. From 1952 to 1994, the annual increases made available to the Pentagon exceeded the combined net profit of all American corporations. After 1991, the war economy was maintained at over $250 billion per year in military budgets, and from 1940 to 1996, leaving $5.8 trillion spent on nuclear weapons programs aside, military outlays totaled $17 trillion (measured in 1996 dollars). The sum of all new weapons plans announced by the Pentagon during 1996–97 amounted to more than $1.5 trillion, and some DoD officials estimated that the actual cost could be twice as great. The truth, says Melman, is that the DoD is the largest industrial entity in the United States, and the president is its CEO.[54]

As for the militarization of foreign policy, the *Washington Post*'s Dana Priest has documented the increasing tendency of American leaders to turn to the military to solve political and economic problems. "This," she writes, "has become the American military's mission and it has been going on for more than a decade without much public discussion or debate." The latest version of this, of course, is the plan to vanquish terrorism, about which General Anthony Zinni told Priest, "there is no military solution to terrorism." But certainly the Republican leadership doesn't want to hear this. As for the Democrats, it is ironic, says Priest, that Clinton had such an "antimilitary" reputation, given the fact that he relied so heavily on the military to do his foreign policy for him. He sent Zinni to India and Pakistan, for example, to defuse tensions between the two countries, and then to Jordan to negotiate the handover of terrorists. A gulf, says Priest, had developed between America's new leadership role in the world and what the country's civilian leaders were willing to do to fill it. Quietly, and behind the scenes, the military stepped into that gap, and on Clinton's watch "the military slowly, without public scrutiny or debate, came to surpass its civilian leaders in resources and influence around the world." Clinton even began to assign the military tasks such as humanitarian disaster relief and disarmament programs. As we know, Clinton's successor basically discarded diplomacy in favor of military "solutions," but as Priest points out, the pattern had already begun as far back as the 1970s and 1980s. Thus politicians "asked infantry and artillery officers and soldiers to help build pluralistic civil societies in countries that had never had them. They required secretive Special Forces to make friends with the nastiest elements in foreign militaries and turn them into professionals respectful of civilian authority." The invasion of Iraq in 2003—when no weapons of mass destruction were in fact present—and the assignment of the rebuilding of the country to the U.S. armed forces indicate just how far this process has gone.[55]

It was, in particular, after the Gulf war that the U.S. military evolved into a global constabulary, a kind of imperial police force. Between 1989 and 1999, the country engaged in forty-eight open military interventions, as opposed to sixteen during the entire period of the Cold War. Thus Andrew Bacevich notes that after the Cold War, there was a greater reliance on coercion as an instrument of foreign policy, with "the emergence of a new class of uniformed proconsuls presiding over vast quasi-imperial domains." What we saw under Clinton, he goes on, was

the appearance of American troops in all sorts of out-of-the-way locales, many of them hitherto remote from even the loosest definition of U.S. interests: periodic demonstrations of U.S. capability in places like Kuwait and Kazakhstan; emergency interventions to set things right in Somalia and Haiti; the establishment of quasi-permanent garrisons in Bosnia, Macedonia and the Persian Gulf; and the continuous dispatch of training missions and liaison teams throughout Latin America and the former Soviet bloc.

With this too came a growing tendency to use the military to initiate foreign policy in areas where we didn't have easy access, such as Algeria and Yemen, and to rely on it periodically to punish those we didn't like: the Serbs, the Sudanese, the Afghanis, and of course, Saddam Hussein. By the end of the nineties, "a militarized foreign policy was something most Americans took for granted."[56]

So Clinton paved the way, but the final conversion of America from republic to empire was planned in the closing years of the Bush Sr.

administration, and then officially unveiled when it was really safe to do so: after 9/11. There are enormous costs to all of this—not just financial, but also moral, political, and social. Gore Vidal writes:

> Our Congress has been hijacked by corporate America and its enforcer, the imperial military machine. . . . We have allowed our institutions to be taken over in the name of a globalized American empire that is totally alien in concept to anything our founders had in mind. I suspect it is far too late in the day for us to restore the republic that we lost a half-century ago.[57]

It is a sad state of affairs, the more so because it is likely that 99 percent of the country has never heard of the Project for the New American Century (which I'll discuss below), or knows what the 2003 invasion of Iraq was really about, or understands that a very small group of individuals managed to administer the final coup de grâce and push the nation over the edge into an overtly imperialistic agenda. But I am making it sound too precipitous. The truth is, it hardly happened overnight, and it had great psychological continuity with the whole Cold War mentality—the enormous reassurance that comes from having an enemy. The German philosopher Hegel referred to this as "negative identity," the process of creating an identity for yourself by defining yourself *against* something. Ultimately, he said, it never works, for to say "I am not *that*" is at root empty; it doesn't tell you who you actually are, and in essence enables you to hide from that question. And the United States has been hiding from that question at least since the Truman Doctrine; even Manifest Destiny, as Frederick Jackson Turner wrote, provided a "gate of escape" from the problem of true (internal) identity. Only Jimmy Carter, as we saw, out of a genuine Christian inspiration, wanted the nation to turn the searchlight inward—and we just weren't having that. Given this virtually congenital unwillingness to seek (some would say recapture) a positive identity, it was inevitable that when Mikhail Gorbachev pulled the rug out from under us by declaring that the Cold War was over, we had no place to stand. We were suddenly disoriented, cast adrift. We had been "anti-Communists" for so long that besides being consumers, we *had* no other identity. (We did have a "civil religion" of America itself, which I shall discuss later; but even that had gotten processed through the anti-Communist filter.) To make things worse, the president who inherited the post–Cold

War scenario was one of the emptiest, identity-less individuals to ever occupy the White House: George H. W. Bush, whom Garry Trudeau (*Doonesbury*) rightly caricatured as a feather, someone with no substance. As has so often been stated, the man had no vision. He had no convictions about anything and no historical imagination whatsoever. What he needed was another war, and he found it first in a phony "war on drugs" (which cost $20 billion and led to nothing), and then by having Saddam Hussein rescue him, conveniently fall into his lap. But at that time, the Gulf war—which was also a phony war—had no real staying power; it didn't fit into any clear post–Cold War pattern. We were, for example, not dependent on Kuwaiti oil and didn't give a damn about the country until Iraq invaded it. Thus Bush Sr. often spoke of the Gulf war as part of a "new world order," but it was merely a platitude; he had no idea of what this emerging order might be. The American people may conceivably have seen how empty the man was (although I suspect their real concern was with the economy); but because they were pretty empty themselves, they didn't want to be reminded of it. Rather, they wanted someone to *fill* the void—like Reagan, say—even if the filling were little more than cotton candy (but it had to *look* real). After Bush Sr. was voted out of office, he declared that the international scene was nothing more than a blank slate; which it was—to *him*. Thus he was unable to fathom the meaning of German unification, the collapse of the Soviet Union, or the Gulf war. George H. W. Bush was sleepwalking, unable "to articulate a rationale for the exercise of U.S. power in a post–Cold War world."[58]

Bill Clinton's solution, of course, really didn't work either. All he could offer the American people was an expanding consumer economy. This worked for a time, but ultimately it lacked the grand mythological appeal of combating an "evil empire." When you get down to it, globalization, besides being an updated euphemism for imperialism, is not much more than the elite version of shopping. If the 1890s have been labeled "gay" by past historians (in the sense, of course, of being exuberant and upbeat), I suspect that future historians will call the 1990s "frivolous," given the sheer triviality of that decade: the overblown "information highway," yuppies on the make (followed by the bursting of the dot.com bubble), O. J. Simpson and Monica Lewinsky and impeachment. It was a lost decade, with America flailing around, trying to fill the void that shopping, or heroic tales of investment and globalization, ultimately could not fill. Meanwhile, the right-wing "junta" that was temporarily out of office bided its time, networked, and waited for the opportunity to mount a neo-Reaganite comeback. When Supreme Court partisanship and corruption put Bush Jr. in the White House, and when Dick Cheney became, as vice president, the de facto president (it being generally understood that Bush Jr. lacked the ground-level gray matter necessary for the job), the neocons saw their chance. The Big Idea they had in mind to fill the national void was world hegemony, "a level of military mastery without historical precedence": "Full Spectrum Dominance." How, exactly, did this come about?[59]

There was, in fact, a coherent foreign policy forming in the aftermath of the fall of the Berlin Wall, but in the wings, as it were. Dick Cheney, then secretary of defense, drew around him Paul Wolfowitz (undersecretary of defense for policy), Lewis Libby (his chief of staff), and Donald Rumsfeld. He asked them to think about foreign policy at the grand strategic level, and Wolfowitz presented his vision on 21 May 1990. This eventually evolved into the Defense Planning Guidance (DPG) of 1992, which was essentially a blueprint for American global hegemony in perpetuity. In nearly final draft form, the classified forty-six-page memo was distributed to the top brass in the military on 18 February 1992. This then got accidentally leaked to the *New York Times* the following month, which published a front-page story saying that the Pentagon was planning to see to it that we would have no other rivals in the next century, that no other nation would ever become a great power. It also advanced a policy of the use of preemptive military force against states suspected of developing weapons of mass destruction; foretold a world in which our military intervention would become "a constant feature"; and stated that we had the right to ensure our access to the oil of the Gulf region and could act independently in lieu of collective action if we chose to do so. It made no mention whatever of the United Nations.[60]

The *Times* article provoked furious criticism from both the left and the right. The DPG draft was labeled "arrogant" and "un-American"; Senator Joseph Biden called it a prescription for "literally a *pax americana*." Cheney tried (very unconvincingly) to distance himself from the document; a Pentagon spokesman even claimed that Cheney never saw it, although the DPG explicitly states that it had received "definitive guidance from the Secretary of Defense." The Pentagon also denied that the document said what it said, claiming that they had no ambitions for world domination and that the goal of the DPG strategy was to sustain the democratic alliances and collective internationalism that had been shaped over the last forty years(!). The Bush Sr. administration quickly disowned the document, "depicting it as the musings of an insignificant lower-tier appointee acting without official sanction." There was, interestingly enough, one discordant (read: honest) voice in all this, that of the chairman of the Joint Chiefs of Staff, Colin Powell. Shortly before the document got leaked, the general told members of the House Armed Services Committee that the United States required military power sufficient enough to deter any other nation from even dreaming of challenging us. "I want to be the bully on the block," he declared; and in the wake of the press leak, he flatly stated that he saw nothing wrong with America running the world. After all, he added, our European allies were not afraid of our military power because they knew that it "will not be misused."[61]

Powell excepted, however, the DPG of 1992 was rejected by the Bush Sr. administration, and more or less branded as a species of lunacy—something important to keep in mind when evaluating the foreign policy ideas of the government a mere ten years later. According to Andrew Bacevich, the document implied a radical departure from the conception of international politics from Wilson to JFK, which embraced a framework of liberty and universal ideals. The DPG of 1992, on the other hand, "had a decidedly alien ring" to it. Alien or not, the whole thing refused to die. Out of office in 1996, Wolfowitz wrote an article arguing for a preemptive attack on Iraq and for ditching the policy of containment. In 1997, William Kristol and Robert Kagan of the right-wing *Weekly Standard* drew on a number of neoconservative think tanks, such as the American Enterprise Institute and the Center for Security Policy, as well as on members of the military-industrial complex, to form the Project for the New American Century (PNAC), a group dedicated to the Reaganite policy of military strength and "moral clarity." In September 2000, as a blueprint for a new Republican administration, they issued *Rebuilding America's Defenses*, which advanced the ideas of U.S. global hegemony and preemptive war, including recommendations for "regime change" in China, Iraq, North Korea, and Iran. Unsurprisingly, the plan would have immediate rewards for U.S. weapons manufacturers; its principal author, Thomas Donnelly, was PNAC's deputy director until he was recruited by the world's largest such manufacturer, Lockheed Martin.[62]

Of course, the idea of America as an empire was very much in the air by this time. Condoleezza Rice already stated in 1999 that the world had room for only one hegemon; General Henry Shelton, in an unguarded moment in October 2000, referred to the post–Cold War armed forces as "the new centurions." Richard Haass, who would become director of policy planning in the Bush Jr. State Department, said shortly after the 2000 election that Americans would need to "reconceive their global role from one of the traditional nation-state to an imperial power." And the heavy militarization that would make this possible was in the works as early as 1989, when John Collins published *Military Space Forces: The Next Fifty Years*, which had been commissioned by Congress. This book, which forms the basis for much U.S. policy regarding the militarization of space, provides what can only be called the final version of the frontier thesis—Manifest Destiny now gone cosmic. It discusses mining the moon for natural resources and the need to be able to protect those investments by being able to fight from and in space. This would include biological and chemical warfare, as well as space satellites. In 1998, as we have noted, the U.S. Space Command drew up its "Long Range Plan," which calls for "a seamlessly integrated force of theater land, sea, air, and space capabilities through a worldwide global defense information network." A major tool in that project is the global positioning system, which can monitor events on earth very closely, and has been used to guide precision bombs to their targets in bad weather.[63]

Ideas and sentiments such as these unsurprisingly found their way into *Rebuilding America's Defenses*. Noting that "space has become a new 'international commons' where commercial and security interests are intertwined," the report calls for "a galaxy of surveillance satellites" and says that we must be able to deny others the use of space. But the report is about much more than space weaponry, and it is interesting that it uses the phrase *pax americana* a number of times, and in a positive sense. It assumes that American military control of the world and the shaping of the international security order in line with America's interests are in the interests of virtually everybody. However, on the remote chance that some opposition to this might arise, it suggests that we need a "worldwide archipelago of U.S. military installations," whose soldiers will act as "the cavalry on the new American frontier." As for the Persian Gulf, the report states that "while the unresolved conflict with Iraq provides the immediate justification, the need for a substantial American force presence in the Gulf transcends the issue of Saddam Hussein"—he's just a pretext, in other words, for our getting control of Middle Eastern geopolitics. In addition to installing a permanent army unit in the Gulf region (troops in Saudi Arabia being seen as not qualifying for this role), America will have to raise its military strength in East Asia in order to cope with "the rise of China to great power status." The report singles out Iraq, Iran, and North Korea as potential enemies and calls for a dramatic increase in defense spending. (It also heavily denigrates the Clinton-era army as inadequate . . . which nevertheless managed to overrun Iraq in twenty-six days less than three years later.)[64]

I confess that if I were a psychiatrist, and somebody walked into my office with the sort of worldview in his or her head as is represented in the pages of the PNAC report, raving about the need for a "world-wide command-and-control system," I would rapidly conclude that he or she was a paranoid schizophrenic and suggest (prolonged) hospitalization along with (heavy) antipsychotic medication. This notion of having to be in constant control of everything, of needing to watch and monitor the activity of the planet in minute detail—what else to call it but insane? Let us remake the entire planet in our image; and if a country should, for some unimaginable reason, disagree . . . well, what else is the U.S. military for? As Arnold Toynbee's granddaughter Polly wrote in the wake of the 2000 presidential election: "God's chosen people, uniquely blessed, nurture a self-image almost as deranged in its profound self-delusion as the old Soviet Union. The most advanced . . . nation on earth knows nothing of itself, irony-free and blind to the world around it."[65]

When the final outcome of that election was still in doubt, Dick Cheney was put in charge of the presidential transition team and, writes Michael Lind, used the opportunity "to turn the foreign policy executive into a PNAC reunion." He stacked the new administration with his allies, men who took advantage of Bush Jr.'s ignorance and inexperience. Raised in Texas, Bush Jr. had absorbed the surrounding culture of machismo, anti-intellectualism, and religiosity, and turned to Christian fundamentalism during a midlife crisis. It is not clear that he ever understood the grand strategy that was unfolding around him; rather, he was picked to play the role of a not too bright front man, and he did it very well (in general, it would be hard to find someone more unconscious). Thus a July 2002 *New York Times*/CBS News poll revealed that 45 percent of Americans thought that "other people are really running the government"—a remarkably intuitive insight for a remarkably uninformed population.[66]

Nevertheless, the PNAC crowd did not harbor any high hopes of immediate implementation of its hegemonic scenario because of the traditional aversion of the American people to "foreign entanglements." Hence *Rebuilding America's Defenses* observed that "the process of transformation . . . is likely to be a long one, absent some catastrophic and catalyzing event—like a new Pearl Harbor." Now that is what might be called a rather prescient remark. In May 2002 I was invited to do a lecture tour in Germany, and I noticed that occasionally, someone in the audience would raise the question as to whether 9/11 had been engineered by the U.S. government. This line of inquiry was even more pronounced the following October, when I was doing something similar in Mexico. It was clear to me that a significant percentage of my Mexican audiences believed in a conspiracy theory about September 11. I told them I personally believed in no such thing, but the tragic events of 9/11, while certainly not wished for by the Bush administration, clearly proved to be a great gift to it. Bush, who up to that time had no idea what he was doing in office save following in his father's footsteps and giving handouts to the rich, suddenly found his mission in life. Within days, he began making speeches that were coherent, free of the usual gaffes and grammatical errors. Meanwhile, behind closed doors, Wolfowitz, Libby, and Rumsfeld began calling for an invasion of Iraq, on the shaky premise that Saddam Hussein must have helped bin Laden (at the time, Bush rejected this). The bottom line is that September 11 enabled the PNAC crowd to realize their dreams of a new American empire, for the horrendous events of that day reduced the public's usual resistance to American military involvement overseas.[67]

And so, after the ensuing war on Afghanistan, the president found himself introducing the PNAC doctrine to the public in a speech at West Point on 1 June 2002. He had already, in his State of the Union address, labeled Iraq, Iran, and North Korea as an "axis of evil," and said we "would not wait on events." Now, he added that we must uncover terror cells in one-third of the world, and "must take the battle to the enemy." The administration would work to impose a universal moral clarity between good and evil, a moral clarity that would be part of the U.S. arsenal. We will strike preemptively when there is a threat, he declared, and *we* will define what constitutes a threat. We shall also, his speechwriter managed to slip in, act to prevent the emergence of a rival power. The audience applauded wildly.[68]

That September, the White House released the "National Security Strategy" (NSS), to which we have already referred. It is a slightly milder version of the PNAC report, but the message is the same. We shall "rid the world of evil," it fatuously declares; we shall act preemptively; we shall act alone if necessary; and *we* shall decide who is or is not an enemy, and deserving of "regime change." In a word, we are going to militarily rearrange the world to suit ourselves. The war on Iraq began almost exactly six months later.[69]

Critiques of the document, and there were many, turned on the notion of how discontinuous all this was with traditional American foreign policy. William Pfaff, writing in the *International Herald Tribune*, even claimed that the NSS was a break with the modern state order that had existed since 1648, when, at the end of the Thirty Years' War, the Peace of Westphalia recognized the sovereignty of states as the basis of international order. Now, he pointed out, the United States won't respect this, but instead bases its right on a national security that subordinates the security of every other nation. In fact, Pfaff continued, the United Nations Charter (largely drafted by the United States) states that the use of force against any independent sovereign state is outlawed, and he noted that preemptive war was treated as a war crime at the Nuremberg trials.[70]

Similarly, Hendrik Hertzberg of *The New Yorker* argued that the NSS was "a vision of what used to be called, when we believed it to be the Soviet ambition, world domination." The document, he claimed, was a prescription for a benevolent American dictatorship, as well as for perpetual war. A regime in which the cops have to answer only to themselves, he pointed out, had a name: police state.[71]

Finally (to take just one more example), David Armstrong, writing in *Harper's*, pointed out that when the DPG of 1992 got leaked to the *New York Times*, it provoked a furor precisely because it smacked of the lunatic fringe, constituting as it did a right-wing break with long-standing notions of cooperation and multilateralism in favor of domination and preemption. The United States, he wrote, once rejected such attacks— such as Pearl Harbor—as barbarous, unworthy of a civilized nation. We also criticized the Soviet Union for (supposedly) trying to rule the world and now seemed to be hell-bent on doing it ourselves. Having gotten rid of the evil empire, said Armstrong, "we now pursue the very thing for which we opposed it."[72]

What are we to make of this? Leaving the 2003 invasion of Iraq aside for the moment, we need to get a bird's-eye view of the overall foreign policy picture that emerged over the years 1992–2002, a development that highlights the precise nature of America's late-empire phase and gradual turn toward a Dark Age. To wit: Is the Bush Doctrine a major rupture in a century-long—and especially, post–Cold War—American foreign policy? Certainly, the PNAC crowd believes this, because it sees its strategy as a rejection of containment or, more exactly, a going-beyond the ideas of NSC-68. And yet I am led to wonder. . . . Wasn't the Mexican War preemptive? Wasn't the Spanish-American War a bid for global hegemony? Wasn't all the CIA activity described in this chapter a bit of both? Let's face it: the only reason we weren't directly preemptive in a "bipolar" world is that it was far too dangerous to attack our adversary directly. For that reason, we had to be content with sharing the power on the world stage, and attacking peripheral, nonstrategic "enemies." Once the USSR collapsed, the gloves could come off; our real (imperial) strategy could be revealed once and for all. Andrew Bacevich is right in labeling the DPG of 1992 as having a "decidedly alien" character, but as he says, the real indiscretion here was semantic. Paul Wolfowitz had merely been candid about what the United States was really up to; his mistake lay in failing to couch it in appropriate-sounding euphemisms. Similarly, even as he castigated the Bush administration's foreign policy, William Pfaff pointed out that its plan for American hegemony was just another version of Manifest Destiny, and that the goals of the PNAC crowd represented an attempt "to turn what has been a loose and consensual American world leadership into actual hegemony." Absent the USSR, in short, we *did* run the show. Again, Wolfowitz's error was merely to say so, in explicit and unadorned form.[73]

Still, language is not unimportant, and differences of degree—for this is what I have been arguing—often do turn into differences of kind. (Pluck a man's hair out, one strand at a time, and eventually he's bald.) In the case of the Bush Doctrine, coupled with the Bush administration's assault on civil liberties, I think it can be argued that we have been in the midst of a slow-motion coup d'état, one that has, in fact, been building since the late seventies, and that can now, in the wake of the 2004 presidential election, finalize its program for a one-party system and a theocratic plutocracy. It was in the 1970s, you may remember, that out-of-office cold warriors began to mobilize, forming organizations such as the Committee on the Present Danger. Their goal was to discredit the introspective Carter and install the militaristic Reagan, and of course they succeeded. But—would that the left (what's left of it) had such stay-ing power!—they didn't rest on their laurels. To realize their dream of a *pax americana*, Wolfowitz, Rumsfeld, Cheney, et al. relied in the 1990s on a number of think tanks and front groups that have interlocking direc-torates and shared origins in those earlier organizations: the American Enterprise Institute, the Center for Security Policy, and the Center for Strategic and International Studies, among others. They provided the Bush Jr. administration with policy advice and personnel. They also relied on right-wing media empires to blanket the public space with their mes-sage, in much the same way—if more powerfully—that the yellow press of Hearst and Pulitzer did during the Spanish-American War. Thus Rupert Murdoch disseminates propaganda via Fox News, and the *Weekly Standard* is a mouthpiece for defense establishment intellectuals (for instance, Richard Perle, who is also a fellow of the American Enterprise Institute). There is also the *National Interest* and the *Washington Times* (the latter owned by the Reverend Sun Myung Moon), which also owns the UPI newswire. The result is a "seamless propaganda machine" that has effectively destroyed public discourse in the United States, to the point that we now dwell in a kind of right-wing propagandistic fog. Research into the tax records of right-wing groups has revealed that since the 1970s, conservative backers—basically, nine immensely wealthy families (Olin, Coors, Mellon Scaife, etc.)—have poured upward of $3 billion into financing a war of ideas that has managed to move mainstream thinking in America toward the right. The money has gone into a whole host of institutions that market the conservative message to American citizens, and the investment has clearly paid off. Add to this the link to the military-industrial complex, exemplified by Lockheed Martin, whose employees sit on the boards of right-wing think tanks such as the Heritage Founda-tion and the Center for Policy Studies. Meanwhile, Cheney was formerly the CEO of Halliburton Oil; Andrew Card (White House chief of staff) a vice president of General Motors; Donald Rumsfeld the CEO of G.W. Searle and later of General Instrument; Condoleezza Rice on the board of directors of Chevron—the list goes on and on. If you doubt for a moment that there is a "vast, right-wing conspiracy" in this country, you must be living on another planet.[74]

All this is to say that if America has finally wound up in a very strange and brutal place, it has not been without long and careful preparation on the part of people wishing to take the vision of NSC-68 to the next level, until the United States morphed into the New Roman Empire. It was not for nothing that in 2001 the new secretary of defense commissioned a private study of the great empires, with a view to finding out how they maintained their hegemonic positions. Yet as crazy (or heroic, if one chooses to see them that way) as one might find the PNAC crowd, as robotic (or wise) as one might find their presidential mouthpiece (leader), the individuals in question are really beside the point. Neocon cabal or not, the *pax americana* is not an accidental empire; indeed, I doubt if there *is* such a thing, historically speaking. We have arrived at this point in our history as a result of an inexorable momentum, shaped by a whole host of factors. If we are finally at the end-of-empire phase of this process, then we should not see these men and women as "evildoers," despite the enormous destruction they are causing the world and especially the United States. They are, truth be told, history's agents, in the same way that George W. Bush is theirs. Remember that Barry Goldwater (who ironically became a GOP outcast and something of a liberal toward the end of his life) garnered 27 million votes in 1964—an impressive number—but failed to get elected president because despite his great popular conservative appeal, his time had not yet arrived. But as the years passed, and we tore ourselves apart with Vietnam, the Bretton Woods repeal, expanding technological meaninglessness, and a Manichaean foreign policy, it was inevitable that the conservative minority—the Limbaughs and the American-style Likudniks and the Lockheed Martin folks and the Mellon Scaife crowd—would eventually triumph, ushering in the death of the American republic in the name of saving that republic, with the majority of Americans now too ignorant or out of it to realize this, or to even care. It is for this reason that when I read, for example, Hendrik Hertzberg insisting that the animating vision of our foreign policy should not be *pax americana* but a world of law and consent, that I wonder whom he thinks he is talking to. It's a little like Robert Putnam declaring, at the end of *Bowling Alone,* that "we must revive community." Gosh, let's get right on that; and while we're at it, let's reverse the earth's gravitational field as well. There is no question that we are on a downward path now; as Henry Kissinger recently put it, "hegemonic empires almost automatically elicit universal resistance, which is why all such claimants have sooner or later exhausted themselves."[75] What it would take now to pull back from the edge, let alone reverse course, requires a grace, a flexibility, and an imagination that I suspect we simply don't possess.

We have, as Georges Clemenceau said of the United States long ago, gone from barbarism to decadence without the intervening stage of civilization—or, at least, without much of one. The blowback Kissinger refers to will come to us now increasingly in the twenty-first century in the form of terrorism—an enemy we cannot defeat because it is, strictly speaking, not an enemy, but rather a technique, the only weapon available to those who object to the violence of the American empire and how it impacts them, and who have not been able to get their objections heard. Nor is it an accident that this terrorism will be coming at us almost exclusively from the Arab world. In order, then, to grasp the meaning of 9/11, we have to retrace our steps and fill in the missing link, up to now largely omitted: our relations with the Middle East.

~ 5 ~

Axis of Resentment: Iran, Iraq, and Israel

Power always thinks it has a great soul.

—John Adams

They create a wasteland and they call it peace.

—Tacitus

WHAT THE UNITED STATES did in the rest of the world, it did with a vengeance in the Middle East. The same overzealous policy of military containment, which created so much havoc at home and abroad, proved to be especially destructive in its application to countries such as Iran and Iraq. Once one knows the history of all this, it is no great stretch of the imagination to conclude that the events of September 11 were the tragic but inevitable outcome of our foreign policy in that part of the world.

One could argue that the larger drama behind all this, in addition to that of containment, was the de facto replacement of one empire by another—that is to say, the need America felt, after World War II, to pick up where Great Britain left off. As one colonial power waned, another one waxed, so that the United States substituted for the United Kingdom in its colonial role, by proxy arrangements if necessary (for instance, Israel acts as our "surrogate" in the Middle East). In that sense, we are really talking about one two-hundred-year-long Anglo-American empire. As she ruled the waves less and less, Britannia passed the torch on to the

United States. Fortunately or unfortunately, America has no one to pass the torch on to; rather, the imperial project will be her undoing. We have come to the end of this way of life.

A major factor in the unraveling process is that of economic and military "overstretch," in which our strategic adventures will become too costly to bear. Indeed, they are already. Another is that of blowback, terrorist strikes against us that will generate more overstretch and thus more blowback in a negatively reinforcing spiral that we are apparently unwilling or unable to arrest. Forcing other people to be like us, in the name of "democratization" or modernization, or remaking the world for our own economic or geopolitical purposes, is a big part of this self-destructive cycle. Once again, the tragedy of American diplomacy: "self-determination, American style," is a contradiction in terms. Despite the obviousness of this, it is something the U.S. government, and perhaps the majority of the American people, cannot seem to grasp, and there is no indication that it or they are going to do so any time soon. Yet the reality of overstretch and blowback is quite literally staring us in the face.

And on an unconscious level (at the very least), the ideology of our foreign policy is as fully operative today as it was fifty or even one hundred years ago. It includes the belief that we have a mission and are the torchbearers of freedom; the commitment to a hierarchy of race (aka white knows best); and the profound aversion to any but the most modest of social or political changes in the Third World—unless we are the author of those changes.

Three case studies illustrate all of the above themes quite clearly. Our imperial interference in the Islamic world, at least in the postwar period, begins with Iran, specifically with the CIA coup (known as Operation Ajax) that toppled Mohammad Mossadegh, the immensely popular Iranian prime minister, in 1953, and restored the brutal Shah of Iran (Mohammad Reza Pahlavi) to power. This triggered a whole chain of events, set a pattern for years to come, and shaped the way millions of Muslims came to view the United States.

The second case study is that of Iraq, which certainly antedates the Gulf war of 1991 and the American invasion of 2003. Indeed, American interference in that country goes back to the early 1960s, but our really active involvement came in the wake of the Islamic revolution of 1979 in Iran—which was in turn blowback from the coup of 1953. Given the hostage crisis of 1979–80, Iran's hatred of the United States, and the need for someone—Saddam Hussein, as it turned out—to replace the shah as our "point man" in the Middle East, we were only too happy to back Iraq in its 1980–88 war with Iran and to secretly stock its arsenal. Our *volte-face* of 1990, the sudden decision to turn on Hussein, had very little to do with the latter's invasion of Kuwait; and the twelve years of sanctions that ruined Iraq and led to the death of half a million Iraqi children hardly went unnoticed in the Islamic world.

Finally, there is Israel/Palestine, the central running sore in the list of Muslim grievances against the United States. This is a long and complicated story, but America's support of Israel—in economic terms, $3 billion a year—and its general lack of interest in the plight of the Palestinians, has generated enormous rage among Muslims. When they sit in front of TV sets around the world, watching satellite networks broadcasting pictures of Palestinian children dying from Israeli gunfire, they are hardly unaware of the part that American financial, political, and military support for Israel plays in these events.

This, then, is the "axis of resentment" that led to 9/11. It doesn't make the killing of three thousand American civilians justified, and I hope the reader will understand that I am not asserting any such thing. But it certainly makes it explicable; and if we cannot grasp that the events of September 11 were retaliatiory rather than "insane" or "evil," we shall have little hope of putting an end to terrorist attacks upon us. It behooves us, then, to take a closer look at our postwar involvement in the Middle East, and see if we can connect the dots.

Iran

Our story begins in 1908, when a British petroleum company hit a gusher in what was then known as Persia. Recognizing the strategic importance of this, the British government arranged for investors to organize the Anglo-Persian Oil Company, and five years after that Winston Churchill, as First Lord of the Admiralty, persuaded the government to buy 51 percent of the firm. From that point on, the interests of Great Britain and the oil company were inseparable. The desert island of Abadan, in the Persian Gulf, became the center of oil refining and was organized as a "classical colonial enclave"—an idyllic existence for the rulers, sheer misery for the ruled. The Anglo-Persian Agreement of 1919 gave England control of Persia's army, treasury, transport system, and communications network. Ruled by martial law, it was, in effect, reduced to the status of a British protectorate. As the company began extracting huge amounts of Persian oil, the resulting wealth enabled Britain to stay at the pinnacle of power while most Iranians lived in poverty.[1]

The harshness of this arrangement was modified slightly in 1933 under the nominal ruler of Iran, Reza Shah Pahlavi, and the firm was renamed the Anglo-Iranian Oil Company, or AIOC (the country itself was renamed Iran two years later). But the structure of colonial exploitation remained firmly in place. The AIOC paid no taxes to Iran, gave more than half its profits to the British government, additionally paid millions annually in taxes to Great Britain, sold oil to the Royal Navy at a fraction of the market price, and had no Iranian directors on its staff. In 1941 the company extracted 6.5 million tons of oil; by 1945 the figure had risen to 16.5 million. In 1947 the AIOC reported an after-tax profit of £40 million, of which it gave Iran £7 million. Discontent, naturally enough, began to grow over the AIOC's privileged position, and the Iranian parliament, or Majlis, finally asserted itself, passing a law directing the government to renegotiate the arrangement—an event that marked the beginning of a long, drawn-out battle with Great Britain. The deputy who wrote the law was Mohammad Mossadegh, an upper-class Iranian who spoke for the common man. His reputation for decency and integrity was legendary, and his commitment to democracy and self-determination absolute—which made him the obvious foe of the AIOC. He was, in fact, the country's first genuinely popular leader, and is revered in Iran to this day.[2]

Under Mossadegh the opposition gained momentum. When an independent audit of the AIOC in 1949 revealed that the company was using accounting tricks to cheat the country out of huge sums of money, the Majlis began talking of splitting profits with the company on a fifty-fifty basis, or else nationalizing the industry outright. Later that year, the Arabian-American Oil Company (Aramco) reached a new agreement with Saudi Arabia, under which it would share profits equally, and this strengthened the opposition's case even further. President Truman suggested to the British government that it would do well to follow Aramco's example, but Great Britain would have none of it. Herbert Morrison, who became foreign secretary in 1951, said that he regarded the conflict as "a simple matter of ignorant natives rebelling against the forces of civilization." As for the shah—Mohammad Reza Pahlavi, who had succeeded his father when Reza Shah Pahlavi had been forced to abdicate in 1941—his only interests appeared to be in building a bigger army, buying weapons from the United States, and attempting to rig parliamentary elections. Demonstrations ensued, leading to the formation of the National Front, with Mossadegh as its leader, to coordinate opposition to the shah and the British. In March 1951 Mossadegh submitted a bill calling for the nationalization of the oil industry, which became law on May 1, establishing the National Iranian Oil Company to take the place of the AIOC. Given the huge popular support for nationalization, the shah had little choice but to sign this into law, and on May 6 Mossadegh took office as prime minister.[3]

The British were of course furious about these developments, and responded by trying to foment a coup against Mossadegh, which backfired when the latter got wind of it and broke off diplomatic relations with Great Britain, ordering all British personnel—intelligence agents included—out of the country. This left Britain with no alternatives: if there was to be a coup in Iran, the Americans would have to stage it. Truman, however, was not sympathetic; he felt the British should cut a fair deal with Iran, as Aramco had done with Saudi Arabia, and be done with it (privately he referred to the British as blockheaded). He and Secretary of State Dean Acheson also believed that Mossadegh was part of a nationalist revolution sweeping the Middle East and that the eloquent and colorful prime minister was in fact a bulwark against communism. Finally, Truman was worried that the use of force against Iran might trigger Soviet intervention. There would, he said, be no U.S. support for a coup, adding that a mishandling of the Iran crisis would produce "a disaster to the free world."[4] (Little did he know how prescient this remark was.)

Great Britain's second line of attack—taking its nonexistent case to the U.N. Security Council—was even more foolish. (Mossadegh at one point called the British argument an attempt to persuade the world that the lamb had devoured the wolf.) Mossadegh himself came to the United Nations to defend the Iranian cause in person. Arriving in New York on 8 October 1951, he couched the struggle in terms of the wretched of the earth versus the rich and powerful—the more convincing because it was true. He related the tale of how a "cruel and imperialistic company" had stolen the resources of a "needy and naked people," and found a sympathetic audience. American officials at the United Nations gave him a warm welcome;

the prime minister had himself photographed in Philadelphia pointing to the Liberty Bell; and he subsequently wound up on the cover of *Time* as Man of the Year, being characterized by the magazine as "the Iranian George Washington." As for the British, they lost their case and sat in their chairs at the United Nations with egg on their faces.[5]

It was not that the Truman administration was "soft on communism," as its Republican critics were constantly charging (shortly after taking office as vice president, Richard Nixon referred to "Dean Acheson's college of cowardly Communist containment")—this much should be obvious from the previous chapter. Paul Nitze's NSC-68, which was a declaration of containment, had its own momentum, and the events of the Cold War, the coup in Iran included, followed from its inexorable logic and the political climate it created. But things were perhaps not quite as rabid in 1951–52 as they would soon become, and some degree of clarity and nuance was occasionally still possible during the pre-Eisenhower years. In the case of Truman, Acheson, and their circle, they simply recognized the obvious: Mossadegh was no Communist. Yes, there was a Communist party in Iran, called the Tudeh, but Mossadegh refused to accept their cooperation. And for the most part, the Communists opposed him, accusing him of being an American puppet. Middle-level analysts at the CIA regarded him as an Iranian nationalist and also believed (correctly) that the Tudeh was too weak to do much of anything, politically speaking. As for the USSR, it never made a move during the entire Iranian drama, nor did Mossadegh ever ask Moscow for help. In a word, Mossadegh didn't fit the Communist profile.[6]

But the British simply couldn't let it go, and in the fullness of time, they got their chance. First, while Mossadegh was speaking in New York, Winston Churchill and the Conservatives were elected to office. Churchill's goal was to perpetuate England's role as an imperial power, and in particular to hold the line against Third World nationalism. But even more important was the American presidential election of 1952, which brought Dwight Eisenhower into office, along with the appointments of John Foster Dulles as secretary of state and his brother Allen as director of the CIA. With this changing of the guard, the administration in Washington made the transition from ideology to what, in retrospect, seems like a species of insanity.[7]

Not that Eisenhower fell into the latter category. At first he was, like Truman, averse to the idea of overthrowing a democratically elected government. He also felt that Mossadegh was Iran's best hope. While the Dulles brothers kept harping on the supposed possibility of a Communist takeover in Iran, Ike raised a more interesting possibility at the 4 March 1953 meeting of the National Security Council, wondering aloud why it wasn't possible "to get some of the people in these down-trodden countries to like us instead of hating us." (Imagine that!) Unfortunately, he failed to answer his own question, and proved to be weak-willed on the subject, letting Dulles and his cohorts run the show. Regardless of the president's own views, he was surrounded by a clique who had definite plans for American foreign policy even before he was sworn into office (obviously, not the last time this would happen in American history).[8]

And things were also in motion on the other side of the Atlantic, prior to the American election, when the Tory government invited CIA operative Kermit Roosevelt (grandson of T.R.) to London to discuss overthrowing Mossadegh under the rubric of what they labeled Operation Ajax. Roosevelt, who would become the principal architect of the coup, flew to Tehran the day of the election, and Christopher Woodhouse, a senior agent of MI6 (Britain's secret intelligence service), met with the CIA and the State Department in Washington less than two weeks later. Britain's goal, of course, was to recover control of the oil industry, but Woodhouse was shrewd enough to pluck the Dulleses' Manichaean strings instead, pitching the project as crucial for countering a Communist threat. Shortly after Eisenhower's inauguration, a British delegation came to Washington to meet with the Dulles brothers and recommend that Roosevelt head up the operation, while Loy Henderson, the U.S. ambassador in Tehran, began contacting certain Iranians about the possibility of overthrowing Mossadegh. In February the British organized a phony rebellion against the Iranian leader, which event the Dulles brothers used in their discussions with the president as evidence of the instability of Mossadegh's regime (Eisenhower had no idea that the protest had been a put-up job). Allen Dulles also told him that if the Communists got control of Iran, 60 percent of the world's oil reserves would fall into their hands. Meanwhile, the U.S. embassy in Tehran was very active in overstating the strength of the Tudeh and Mossadegh's relationship with it.[9]

In the end, then, obsession proved to be far more seductive than reason, and the new administration found it much easier to see nationalist movements as Communist ones, rather than analyze situations on a case-by-case basis. It gave no real consideration to the alternative to a coup: providing support for Mossadegh and his non-Communist allies. As for Eisenhower, he made it clear that he didn't want to know the details of what was happening, and in fact stayed away from the crucial meeting of 25 June 1953, at which John Foster Dulles picked up the final planning report and declared, "So this is how we get rid of that madman Mossadegh!"[10]

Eisenhower's role was intriguing here and, in many ways, irresponsible. One has the sense that he knew what Dulles was doing was immoral, but he let it happen anyway. He could have shut Ajax down at any time; he could have bailed Mossadegh out. But he chose to choose by not choosing. The truth is that Eisenhower often knew better with regard to foreign policy decisions, but tended to defer to Dulles rather than rein him in. His actions and his words often didn't match. As for Dulles, he can be said to have been riding a historical wave. It's an old question, of course: Does the man make the age, or vice versa? A bit of both, most historians would say. The "age" was that of America's rising imperial role: opposing the Soviet empire, replacing the British one. Like Paul Nitze a couple of years before him, and Henry Kissinger a couple of decades after him, Dulles was an agent of that wave. He was moving with the tide, but he also did much to accelerate it. Those opposed to it—such as Roger Goiran, the CIA chief of station in Tehran, who warned Allen Dulles that the coup would result in Iranians forever viewing the United States as a supporter of colonialism—were quickly pushed aside (Dulles fired him). Ike's role was to allow it to happen, and then not want to know about it. He too was an agent of America's imperial destiny.

In any case, what then unfolded—the CIA's scenario of dirty tricks— is another dark stain on the record of U.S. foreign relations. Ajax agents manipulated public opinion against Mossadegh, portraying him as a Communist; roughly 80 percent of Iranian newspapers were under CIA influence, and articles in them were written by the agency in Washington. Thugs were hired to attack religious leaders, throw rocks at mosques, and then make it appear as though this had been on Mossadegh's orders; army officers and members of the Majlis were bribed; and the heavily funded Kermit Roosevelt hired a mob to stage a pro-shah march through the streets of Tehran, as well as attack the offices of pro-Mossadegh newspapers and political parties. Knowing the prime minister's reputation for Old World courtliness and hospitality, Roosevelt also put Loy Henderson up to going to Mossadegh and inventing a story that

Americans in Iran, children included, were being viciously harassed. The trick worked: angered by the notion that guests in his country were being mistreated, the prime minister called his police chief and ordered him to attack the demonstrators—some of whom were his own supporters—and to ban all further public demonstrations. He thus cut himself off at the knees, which proved to be a fatal mistake. After a pitched battle on August 19 that left three hundred dead, Fazlollah Zahedi, a man who had had close connections with Nazi agents during World War II, was installed as the new prime minister, and he promptly named two of Roosevelt's Iranian agents to his cabinet. As for the shah, who had fled the country prior to the coup, he now resumed his throne, declaring that Mossadegh was "an evil man," willing to sacrifice the Iranian people for his own personal power. The CIA immediately gave $5 million to the new government, and put an additional $1 million in Zahedi's pocket.[11]

The aftermath of all this bordered on the surreal. A little more than two years after being fêted in New York and Philadelphia as "the Iranian George Washington," Mohammad Mossadegh was put on trial in Tehran, a trial that was a complete sham. He told the court that his only "crime" had been to free Iran from colonial rule, after which the court sentenced him to three years in prison, followed by house arrest for the rest of his life (he died in 1967). A new oil consortium was organized, giving the AIOC (which later became British Petroleum, appropriately enough) 40 percent of the shares and five American oil companies another 40 percent (the remaining shares were divided between a Dutch company and a French one). Eisenhower proclaimed that he had saved Iran from communism and awarded Kermit Roosevelt the National Security Medal. (Roosevelt quit the CIA a few years later to take a job with Gulf Oil, one of the U.S. firms in the consortium, eventually becoming a vice president.) As for the shah, during the next decade he received more than $1 billion in American aid. Representative government was finished in Iran; the Majlis elections of 1954 were blatantly rigged, and the parliament became a rubber stamp. In Tehran, police patrols rode through the streets in jeeps marked with the U.S. aid insignia.[12]

It is interesting that almost nobody at the upper levels of the U.S. government saw anything wrong with this picture. At our instigation, democracy in Iran was completely destroyed, and in the aftermath we declared the abysmal results a victory for democracy. We have been fond of calling our enemies "fanatics," but what exactly were (are) we? Officials such as the Dulles brothers and Kermit Roosevelt, says *New York Times* reporter Stephen Kinzer, were driven men, turning Iran into a battleground for a misguided crusade. They were driven by a near rabid ideology; preemptive coups and actions against threats that had not even materialized seemed perfectly reasonable to them. Roosevelt later wrote of the debriefing session of 4 September 1953 that John Foster Dulles was "alarmingly enthusiastic. . . . His eyes were gleaming; he seemed to be purring like a giant cat" as he planned similar ventures. The next year, as we saw in the last chapter, brought with it the coup against Jacobo Arbenz in Guatemala, which led to hundreds of thousands of violent deaths. When individuals "get religion"—and there is really no other name for the Manichaean anticommunism that gripped America during the Cold War—reason and even common decency typically fly out the window, and the results are frequently horrific.[13]

"It is difficult to imagine," writes Kinzer, "an outcome that would have produced as much pain and horror over the next half-century as that produced by Operation Ajax." For his political survival, the shah relied on Savak, his secret police, who were trained by the Israeli Mossad and the CIA (which set up seminars in Tehran, as well as at the International Police Academy in Washington). Savak's record of torture, says historian Barry Rubin, was "equal to the worst ever devised." Between 1953 and 1979 ten to fifteen thousand people lost their lives at Savak's hands. Survivors told of six-year-old children being tortured, of women being given electric shocks in their vaginas, of bodies being scorched. By 1978, prisons were so crowded that torture chambers had to be converted into holding cells, and the torture carried out in hallways. Estimates are that more than half a million people were beaten, whipped, or tortured during the shah's regime, and the entire population was subjected to an all-pervasive terror. The police were everywhere, and had carte blanche to arrest almost everyone. In 1976 Amnesty International wrote that Iran had the highest rate of death penalties in the world, no valid court system, and "a history of torture which is beyond belief." Not without reason, the Iranian people (along with much of the Muslim world) came to identify what was happening to them with the United States. "It is not far-fetched," writes Kinzer, "to draw a line from Operation Ajax through the Shah's repressive regime and the Islamic Revolution [of 1978–79] to the fireballs that engulfed the World Trade Center in New York." But this is only one part of the fallout from Operation Ajax. The coup in Iran taught tyrants and aspiring tyrants [in the Middle East] that the world's most powerful governments were willing to tolerate limitless oppression as long as oppressive regimes were friendly to the West and to Western oil companies. That helped tilt the political balance in a vast region away from freedom and toward dictatorship.[14]

This lesson was certainly not lost on the shah. Huge amounts of money and arms flowed in his direction, as the Iranian people watched oil revenues that could have been used to improve their lot being spent on vast quantities of American weaponry. The shah became a big favorite of the Nixon administration in particular, which believed he would act as the American surrogate in the Middle East—a "pillar of stability," as Henry Kissinger put it (along with Israel and Saudi Arabia). They saw him as a bulwark against Soviet influence and as our "proxy" in the region as the United Kingdom began withdrawing its forces from the Gulf (which was already in progress during the Johnson administration). This was central to the Nixon Doctrine of 1969, according to which we would "anoint" certain Third World allies to act on behalf of American economic and geopolitical interests. Thus Kissinger declared that the shah would "fill the vacuum left by British withdrawal, now menaced by Soviet intrusion and radical momentum." He would, in short, police the Gulf on our behalf, and to that end Iran became a weapon salesman's dream. Nixon promised the shah he could buy anything from the United States short of nuclear weapons, and the resulting shopping list was off the charts. During the 1970s, one-third of all purchases of U.S. military equipment were made by Iran.[15]

If the shah could not overcome the taint of the coup, whereby he was seen as an American puppet ruling an illegitimate throne, he was not doing much to correct that impression. A 1963 poll of Iranian youth revealed that 85 percent believed U.S. aid to Iran made the rich in their country richer; in 1964, the spiritual leader (mullah) Ayatollah Khomeini declared that the shah's policies had "reduced the Iranian people to a level lower than that of an American dog." Inflation was rampant; the shah's lifestyle was extravagant in a country where the annual per capita income was $350. Americanized neighborhoods of Tehran were islands of wealth in a sea of poverty. Symbolically enough, former CIA director Richard Helms was appointed ambassador to Iran in the seventies; Nixon and Ford praised the shah's record on human rights as the torture and repression increased. Meanwhile, the shah's so-called White Revolution, his campaign for modernization, left rural areas impoverished, and those who moved to the city were unable to find work. Eventually, these people turned to religious leaders for guidance, to find meaning in their lives, and anti-shah demonstrations began in earnest in 1978. The dissatisfaction boiling beneath the surface was thus as much spiritual as it was material, but Jimmy Carter, who had inherited this mess, was not able to see this. As Khomeini gained support, Carter sent riot-control equipment to the Iranian army; when troops fired on demonstrators on December 27, the crowd chanted: "Carter gives the guns, the shah kills the people." The shah was finally forced to flee the country on 16 January 1979, whereupon Khomeini returned from exile and denounced America as "the Great Satan." Given the experience of the Iranian people at the hands of the U.S. government, the fact that America had callously turned Iran into a living hell, the epithet struck a deep chord. By early November fifty-three American diplomats were taken hostage, and the new government began channeling money to anti-American terrorists.[16]

Why wasn't it possible for the United States to get people in these "down-trodden countries" to like us instead of hate us, as Eisenhower had asked? The answer is obvious—or ought to be. By the time of the 1979 revolution most Iranians understood that the shah had sacrificed the nation's economy, social welfare, and cultural integrity so that he could rule within the framework of America's strategic objectives. They saw how billions of rials went into the pockets of U.S. military advisers, and how a small elite had become wealthy because of its connections to the shah. They also saw Americans housed in opulent villas, having access to subsidized food, giving lavish parties—all at the expense of the Iranian people. As for the modernization campaign, they watched how imported plastic goods—often made from Iranian oil—destroyed the livelihood of the village potter, herder, tanner, shoemaker, retailer. They watched American TV progams, and rightly found the material trashy and offensive. "Why should we want a civilization which is worse than savagery?" Khomeini thundered to his receptive audience in June 1980. For their own purposes, he said, the Americans "have turned us into the area's policeman." "The world-devouring United States," he called us contemptuously. As the saying goes, the man may have been crazy, but he certainly wasn't stupid.[17]

The hostage crisis had a number of dimensions to it. First, it served to restore Iranian national pride, having a great psychological impact on the country. We have been pawns in your international chess game long enough, was the message; now, you'll dance to *our* tune. Second, it was about justice (or, perhaps more precisely, retribution). As one member of the Majlis put it, "Our purpose . . . is to put America on trial, so that we can prove to the world the oppression and tyranny suffered by this deprived nation at the hands of the American government and the CIA organizations [*sic*], and to expose their crimes." But above all, the taking of the hostages was an insurance policy against the possibility of a repeat performance of 1953. In late 1979 the shah was in the United States (for medical treatment); the Iranian assumption was that America would try to foment another coup and put him back on the throne. Paranoid, maybe, but in the light of history, hardly delusional. Possession of American hostages gave the new government leverage against this possibility.[18] Meanwhile, the American public sat at home, watching these developments unfold on television, with a sense of personal hurt and outrage, the names of John Foster Dulles and possibly even Dwight Eisenhower (the American school system being what it is) unknown to most of them. ("How can they do this when we're so good?" wondered George W. Bush after the events of 9/11. How indeed.)

The events of 1979, rooted as they were in the coup of 1953, led to three further developments that then moved inexorably toward September 11: the Iranian funding of terrorism; the Soviet invasion of Afghanistan and the consequent CIA backing of Islamic militants; and the American choice of Saddam Hussein as our "golden boy" during Iraq's war with Iran. The ironies involved in all of this are breathtaking but, as in the case of the hostage crisis, largely lost on the American public.

The funding of terrorism can be dispensed with fairly briefly. In a word, the new Iranian government, in its rage against the United States and Israel, spent much of the 1980s financing and arming Hamas and Hezbollah. In addition, its revolutionary leaders became heroes to fanatics in many countries. The Afghanis who founded the Taliban were inspired by the Iranian example, and gave Osama bin Laden the base (*al-Qaeda*, in Arabic) from which he would later launch his attacks on the United States. Indeed, in his 1998 *fatwa* calling for a jihad against the United States, bin Laden cited the presence of American troops in Saudi Arabia, the sanctions against Iraq, and the general Western humiliation of the Arab peoples as the key elements of "the continuation of the calamitous Crusader occupation." And sympathy for bin Laden is hardly restricted to hard-core Islamic militants. Rather, it is quite widespread, as millions see him as the "conscience of Islam." There is a sense throughout the Muslim world that they are "in this together" against a West that regards them as inferior peoples to be exploited for economic or geopolitical advantage or as dangerous fanatics who have to be militarily contained. How surprising is it, really, that Iran harbored and protected the Al Qaeda leadership, including a son of bin Laden's, after the fall of the Taliban in 2001? There is of course a lot of demonization of the West involved in this worldview, but it was hardly conjured up out of thin air. And when you don't have the military resources of your opponents, impotence turns into violence, and terrorism becomes the "logical" alternative. It's an old cliché: our terrorists, their freedom fighters. It depends on who writes the history.[19]

As for the Soviet invasion of Afghanistan of December 1979 and the American support of Islamic mujahideen, the usual story is that in response to the Soviet invasion the United States aided the mujahideen so that they could eject the Russians from their land. In fact, as Zbigniew Brzezinski revealed in an interview with *Le Nouvel Observateur* in 1998, the United States had begun arming the mujahideen six months prior to the Soviet invasion(!). He and Carter (he said) went ahead with this decision not *despite* the likelihood that this would increase the probability of such an invasion, but *because* of it. "It had the effect," he said, "of drawing the Russians into the Afghan trap." Thus on 6 April 1979 a committee chaired by Brzezinski instructed the CIA to develop a comprehensive plan for a secret war in Afghanistan backed by the United States. Three months later, Carter signed the document authorizing the agency to begin helping the mujahideen, and the Pakistani intelligence services quickly got on board, running guns to the rebels. As William Blum puts it, "Afghanistan was a cold-warrior's dream."[20]

Having thus succeeded in doing this, the U.S. government poured nearly $3 billion into Afghanistan over the next decade, a sum that was matched nearly dollar for dollar by Saudi Arabia. In addition, Green Berets were deployed to infiltrate the country and teach the rebels how to use high-tech weapons, since arms were provided to the mujahideen in large quantities. The plan eventually worked; the USSR began its withdrawal in 1988, with Mikhail Gorbachev declaring that Afghanistan had been "a bleeding wound." A year later, the Soviet Union began to unravel, and it is clear that the Afghan adventure was a factor in this development. Yet the logic of "the enemy of my enemy is my friend" was a dubious one, and it had a powerful chain reaction. Afghan casualties included one million dead, three million wounded, and five million who were rendered refugees—in all, about one-half of its population. (Since the United States no longer had use for the country by 1992, it just walked away from the entire mess. This too did not go unnoticed by the Arab world.) For all intents and purposes, Afghan society was destroyed, and the Taliban subsequently rose on its ruins. In the wake of September 11, the causal links are pretty obvious. Part of our funding for the operation found its way into the hands of Osama bin Laden, who was then a Saudi engineer in his late twenties. By the late 1980s, Saudi intelligence was, with America's approval, using bin Laden to channel millions of dollars to the rebel forces. Through Pakistani intelligence, he was indirectly trained by the CIA (we trained his trainers, in effect). According to a 2001 BBC report, in 1987 the CIA began illicitly issuing visas to unqualified applicants from the Middle East and bringing them to the United States for training in terrorism for the Afghani war in collaboration with bin Laden—an operation that apparently continued into the 1990s. Indeed, in the wake of 9/11, *Newsweek* reported that five of the hijackers had received training at secure U.S. military installations during the previous decade.[21]

A "fixation with combating the Soviet threat," writes historian Douglas Little, "had led a generation of U.S. policymakers to neglect the appeal of revolutionary nationalism and radical Islam among the peoples of the Muslim world"—an appeal that our actions served to deepen. "That the Pakistani and U.S. intelligence services helped stoke the fires of radical Islam among bin Laden and the Afghan mujahideen during the 1980s is one of the cruelest ironies of the Cold War," says Little; both bin Laden and the Taliban, he points out, "were to some degree Frankenstein's monsters created by U.S. and Pakistani political experiments that were too clever by half." (In the 1980s, Reagan compared the mujahideen to America's Founding Fathers!) While it is true that a good part of the resistance to the Soviets was indigenous, the fact is that we instigated an anti-Communist "proxy" war that resulted in worldwide terrorist blowback. If, concludes Little, we had had some sympathy for revolutionary nationalism in the 1950s, for figures such as Mossadegh and Egypt's Gamal Abdel Nasser—whose aspirations were hardly those of a clash of civilizations—we might have avoided Khomeini and bin Laden. The problem, of course, as already indicated, is that such sympathy could not get a hearing in the context of the imperial role that the United States was hell-bent on assuming. After September 11 it should have become clear that America was doing itself in. Unfortunately, this observation couldn't get a hearing either, thus foreclosing the possibility of any real solution.[22]

Iraq

And Iran led to Iraq. As with Iran, the Iraqi story has its origins in the British Empire. In the aftermath of World War I and the breakup of the Ottoman Empire, the League of Nations made Mesopotamia a British mandate. A treaty signed with King Faisal I (whom the British themselves had installed as king) placed military and economic control of the country in British hands, and Britain more or less retained that control for the next few decades. In 1931, the Iraq Petroleum Company (IPC) was set up, with shares being held by British, French, Dutch, American, and Portuguese companies. The British intervened to overthrow a nationalist regime ten years later, and after the close of World War II the government passed a law requiring the IPC to pay half of its profits in taxes. Given this familiar Middle Eastern scenario, nationalist sentiment continued to fester, and on 14 July 1958 a career officer by the name of Abdul Karim Qasim led a successful military coup against the pro-British government. This event, which included the execution of King Faisal II and his family, is seen in Iraq to this day as the moment of liberation from British domination.[23]

Qasim, in any case, demanded that the IPC grant Iraq 20 percent ownership and 55 percent of the profits. They refused, so in 1961 he issued a decree stripping the company of 99.5 percent of its concession as of 1963 and establishing a state-owned Iraq National Oil Company. Although Qasim was a nonaligned nationalist, willing to work with the USSR on an economic basis but capable (in 1959) of putting down a Communist uprising if he had to, Washington inevitably saw the nationalization move as pro-Soviet. The Kennedy administration thus began encouraging dissident army officers to overthrow Qasim, and the CIA got involved in numerous attempts to rub him out, including an assassination plot using a poisoned handkerchief (which failed) and a coup (which succeeded) in February 1963, shortly before the new law was to go into effect. This brought the Ba'ath party into power, and in 1965 the new regime reaffirmed IPC's control over Iraq's richest oil fields. Yet Iraq remained in turmoil until 1968, when stability was achieved with the help of an anti-Western Ba'ath zealot named Saddam Hussein.

Feelings of nationalism continued to ride high in the Arab world, however, and struggles with the IPC continued, until the Iraqi government finally nationalized the company in 1972—making it the first Arab nation to take over a Western-owned oil corporation. By 1979, oil output and exports provided Iraq with more than $47 billion in income. And unlike the situation of Iran under the shah, petroleum revenues filtered down to ordinary citizens: the country had a strong public sector, extensive free public services, and a large body of small landowners. This continued even after Hussein became president of Iraq in 1979; petrodollars began to dry up only after Iraq got embroiled in a war with Iran the following year. That aside, Hussein ruled ruthlessly from the start. His presidency, in fact, began with a purge.[24]

Just about everything you've heard about Saddam Hussein, as it turns out, is true. As Middle Eastern tyrants go, he was among the nastiest and had been violating human rights ever since he became vice president of Iraq in 1975. The problem is that with the exception of Truman's compassion for the Iranian people, and the first three years of the Carter presidency, the United States was simply not concerned about human rights in the Middle East, one way or the other. As one Clinton administration diplomat told Mideast scholar Fawaz Gerges in 1995, America's Middle Eastern foreign policy is about its own interests, nothing more. The American strategy is to put on a show of indignation when doing so might further those interests, and to look the other way when it does not (Iran, Saudi Arabia, Kuwait, Bahrain, Qatar, Egypt, Jordan . . .). The 1990–91 or 2002–3 "discovery" of Hussein as the latest incarnation of Hitler played well with an American public ignorant of history (and completely indifferent to it, in any event), but it was both hype and hypocrisy. When Hussein, for his own political purposes, invaded Iran in September 1980, there was no hue and cry from the U.S. government about it; indeed, we secretly supported him. Invasion per se has never bothered the United States. When Vietnam invaded Cambodia in 1979, America said nothing at all; the Israeli occupation of parts of Syria and Lebanon (let alone Palestine) did not generate any outrage on its part; and in general, the United States doesn't really care about the illegitimacy of border disputes unless it believes its interests are at stake. As far as Hussein's invasion of Khomeini's Iran goes, we were only too happy to have him attack it, and we also saw him as a bulwark against Soviet influence in the Gulf region. Some scholars believe that in the context of the hostage crisis, President Carter actually encouraged the invasion through diplomatic back channels, although it is more likely we gave Hussein a green light by flashing him no explicit red one—a pattern that would be repeated on the eve of the Gulf war.[25] Our basic Middle Eastern policy is by now fully transparent to the Islamic world: the United States supports whoever serves and extends its power, and that can change at a moment's notice.

Hussein's decision to go to war with Iran, which lasted from 1980 to 1988, was largely a result of his own opportunism, part of his plan to emerge as the "new Nasser" of the Arab world. Oil also played an obvious role: even a partial victory in Iran could have given him control of 20 percent of the world's oil consumption. With Iran tied up in its own revolutionary chaos, Hussein envisioned a quick victory, and a heroic triumph. As it turned out, Iran proved to be less of a pushover than he expected; and it was at this point that the United States, which definitely wanted Iran to be defeated and for Hussein to replace the shah as one of our proxies in the Middle East, stepped in. In his meticulous and scholarly study (*With Friends Like These*) of America's support for Saddam Hussein from 1980 to just before the Iraqi invasion of Kuwait, Bruce Jentleson reveals how the Gulf war had nothing to do with the stated reasons for the American campaign, which were confused and contradictory in any case. That the United States "suddenly" found Hussein in violation of international agreements and human rights, and that he "suddenly" was found to be amassing WMD and was supposedly comparable to Hitler, were ludicrous justifications in light of our apparent eagerness to stock his arsenal for nearly a decade. The U.S. government contributed heavily to his chemical and biological warfare program, selling him materials that made his WMD possible. It also sold him helicopters, provided him with sensitive intelligence information, and then squelched all congressional queries about this activity. It deliberately turned a blind eye to his terrorist activities and increasing hostility to the United States. All of this has been massively documented, not only by Jentleson but also by scholars such as Mark Phythian (*Arming Iraq: How the U.S. and Britain*

Built Saddam's War Machine) and Kenneth Timmerman (*The Death Lobby: How the West Armed Iraq*). At one point Jentleson provides a six-page chart of Hussein's pursuit of WMD from the 1970s through April 1990, all of which the U.S. government knew about. I don't wish to bore the reader unduly with all of these data, but an overview of the highlights might not be totally out of place.[26]

✦ To keep Iran from winning the war, the Reagan administration secretly provided Hussein with satellite photos of Iranian troop movements in 1982 and later funneled black market arms to Iraq.

✦ Even though intelligence reports made it clear that Hussein was supporting terrorism, the Reagan administration took Iraq off the state terrorist list as of 26 February 1982, and the Bush Sr. administration kept it off. This meant that the country was eligible for U.S.-financed export credits, and that controls on arms and technology sales would be relaxed.

✦ On 1 November 1983 Secretary of State George Shultz received intelligence reports showing that Iraq was using chemical weapons almost daily. The following February, Iraq used large amounts of mustard gas and also the lethal nerve agent tabun (this was later documented by the United Nations); Reagan responded (in November) by restoring diplomatic relations with Iraq. He and Bush Sr. also authorized the sale of poisonous chemicals, anthrax, and bubonic plague. Along with French supply houses, American Type Culture Collection of Manassas, Virginia, shipped seventeen types of biological agents to Iraq that were then used in weapons programs. In 1989, ABC-TV news correspondent Charles Glass discovered what the U.S. government had been denying, that Iraq had biological warfare facilities. This was corroborated by evidence from a defecting Iraqi general. The Pentagon immediately denied the facts.

✦ American air force officers were sent to work with the Iraqis in July 1986; in October, the U.S. Navy sank three Iranian patrol boats and two offshore oil platforms. In 1988 U.S. forces blew up two oil rigs and put half of the Iranian navy out of action.

✦ In the 1970s, America knew that Iraq was trying to develop a nuclear weapons program; in the 1980s, military exports were knowingly sent to Iraqi nuclear installations. By 1989 it became clear that Iraq was trying to develop an atomic bomb, yet Iraqi personnel were allowed to visit Los Alamos and to attend the ninth annual Symposium on Detonation, which discussed nuclear weapons applications. In terms of obtaining nuclear-related technologies, all the Bush Sr. administration required was Iraq's word for it that these items were for civilian use.

✦ On 16 March 1988 Iraqi forces attacked Halabjah, a Kurdish town northeast of Baghdad, with mustard gas and nerve toxins, killing three to five thousand civilians. Five days after the Iran-Iraq war ended (20 August 1988), Hussein's forces dropped chemical bombs on thirty Kurdish villages. Several American-made helicopters, which had been sold to Iraq for "crop dusting," were used in these attacks. To deflect any possible condemnation of Iraq for the Halabjah massacre, the Pentagon concocted a story that Iran was partly responsible for it, and the State Department directed its diplomats to do the same. Yet Halabjah, and the gassing of the Kurds, was cited by Bush Sr. in the buildup to the Gulf war, and by Bush Jr. in the buildup to the war of 2003, as one of the reasons for going to war.

✦ Hussein's backing of Palestinian terrorists led to the death of 241 Marines in Lebanon in 1983; an Iraqi missile was fired at the USS *Stark* in 1987, killing 37 sailors. In response to the latter, the Reagan administration accepted Iraq's explanation for the *Stark* incident— that it was an accident—without batting an eyelid, and then successfully pressured Congress to drop a bill that would have put Iraq back on the terrorist list.

✦ In late 1989 the United States granted Iraq $1 billion in credits, asking the country to put pressure on the Palestinians to be flexible regarding the Arab-Israeli peace process. Iraq then created a "Popular Arab Front" to support the intifada, and Hussein made a speech hostile to the United States.

✦ On 15 February 1990 the Voice of America ran an editorial discussing Iraq's abysmal human rights record; April Glaspie, the American ambassador to Iraq, was subsequently ordered to send the Iraqi foreign minister, Tariq Aziz, a note of apology for this, and all future VOA editorials were to be cleared by the State Department. Senator Alan Simpson personally told Saddam Hussein that the members of the American press were "bastards."

✦ The Iraqi president made some vitriolic speeches against the United States and Israel in February and April 1990; all the while the Bush Sr. administration continued to oppose any sanctions against Iraq, and in late July worked to block congressional legislation canceling $400 million in agricultural credits to Iraq because of its human rights violations. Four days before Iraq invaded Kuwait (August 1, Washington time), Bush Sr. actually sent a conciliatory cable to Hussein—by now, over Pentagon objections—saying "we desire better relations with Iraq."

Quite a record: a litany of shame that we were only too happy to condone or participate in. Yet all of this, which had been perfectly acceptable to Reagan and Bush Sr. down to the invasion of Kuwait, and which had been ignored or denied by those administrations through the end of July 1990, was suddenly "discovered" and elevated to the level of criminal status. The exact information that the Pentagon and the State Department had worked so hard to cover up or keep out of the public eye, so that our (perverse) support of the Hussein regime could continue undisturbed, was now thrust *into* the public eye as justification for going to war with that regime! At the very least, this suggests that the causes of the Gulf war lay elsewhere. What, then, *was* the war about?

Oddly enough, not even the Bush Sr. administration seemed to know. Before and after the war, it seemed to be flailing around for reasons, which it trotted out and then subsequently contradicted or abandoned. These included: Hussein was evil; he was threatening us with WMD, including nuclear weapons; he had an appalling record of human rights violations and had even gassed his own people; and we needed to ensure that we had access to the oil reserves of the Gulf region (explicitly stated by General Norman Schwarzkopf and by CIA Director William Webster). The low point was reached when Secretary of State James Baker finally announced that the war had been fought for the sake of "jobs." Not true, but about as tawdry a justification as one could imagine. Some analysts have argued that the whole thing was a conspiracy; that we wanted the war and lured Hussein into a trap. Perhaps, but that still doesn't answer the question of why we wanted the war in the first place. There was, no doubt, a hidden agenda, because none of the stated reasons (with the exception of access to oil) make a whole lot of sense (they were all easily discredited). A deeper answer is the geopolitical one (which includes the oil issue but is larger than it): as Reagan and Bush Sr. saw it, Hussein would pick up where the shah had left off—our proxy in the Middle East. The problem is that the two presidents were not terribly clued in as to how Hussein was responding; they somehow were not able to grasp the fact that this imagined scenario was not what was happening in the real world.[27] This is certainly true, it seems to me; but as indicated in chapter 4, it also suggests that Bush Sr. was clueless in a deeper sense: he didn't really understand what was happening historically. Thus he kept going on about the "new world order," but the phrase was nothing more than buzzwords to him. Hence the stumbling around, the transparent lying to the American people, and so on. An intellectual lightweight who didn't really know what he was doing, Bush Sr. was quickly pushed aside by history after he had fulfilled his role as a catalyst for certain events. By the time his son came to power, the new world order—that is, global American hegemony and the final phase of empire—was pretty much in place. Being a lightweight—or a vacuous marionette, in George Jr.'s case—was not a liability but actually an asset; that Bush Jr. was (is) a hollow mouthpiece for a self-destructive imperial project is an arrangement that makes that project all that much easier to fulfill. That "he's a real nowhere man" is not an obstacle for a nation sliding into chaos while it is trying to convince itself that it is in charge of the world. Indeed, it's a perfect fit.

All this confusion notwithstanding, the Gulf war did not materialize out of thin air. The American version of the events—which is partly true—goes something like this: in 1988 Iraq emerged the victor from its war with Iran, but was deeply in debt as a result. One of its biggest debts was to Kuwait, from which it had borrowed something on the order of $12–14 billion. Relations between Kuwait and Iraq had always been strained, owing to a border dispute that went back to the breakup of the Ottoman Empire; and in an attempt to settle that dispute, Kuwait took the opportunity to put financial pressure on Iraq by exceeding its OPEC quota for oil production. This flooded the oil market and drove prices down. By 1990 Kuwait and the United Arab Emirates had depressed the price of oil from eighteen to eleven dollars a barrel, and Iraq was losing $20 million a day as a result. As Saddam Hussein pointed out, war can be economic as well as military, and he asserted that this amounted to war against Iraq. According to the official version of events, Iraq began massing troops along the Kuwaiti border toward the end of July, and invaded its neighbor on August 2 (local time), catching the United States off guard. Saudi Arabia was fearful that it would be invaded as well, and asked the United States to post troops on its soil, which it subsequently did. Meanwhile, America demanded that Iraq withdraw from Kuwait, sought a diplomatic solution to the crisis, but found that Iraq was intransigent. Therefore, after amassing a large force in the Gulf region ("Desert Shield"), it attacked Iraq on 16 January 1991 ("Desert Storm"), "liberating" Kuwait in short order. *Sic semper tyrannis!*[28]

It's a great, heroic story, one of Good triumphing over Evil—which is how Bush Sr. presented it to the American public—but the reality is a bit different. Here are some of the holes in the fabric.

First, was there a legitimate threat to Saudi Arabia? Did Iraq actually mass troops in Kuwait or on the Saudi border? On 30 July 1990, the Defense Intelligence Agency reported the presence of more than 100,000 troops on the border with Kuwait, and on August 6 Secretary of Defense Dick Cheney flew to Saudi Arabia to show King Fahd satellite photos of Iraqi troops. By mid-September, citing top secret satellite images, the Pentagon announced that something like 250,000 Iraqi troops stood on the border with Saudi Arabia. The problem is that there is reason to believe that both of these estimates were greatly overblown. Jean Heller, a reporter with the *St. Petersburg Times*, published stories on 30 November 1990 and 6 January 1991 that revealed the existence of satellite photos of Kuwait from August 8 and September 13, and of Saudi Arabia from September 11. Satellite experts said these photos didn't show an Iraqi force in Kuwait of even 20 percent the size claimed by Bush, and in the case of the Saudi border there were no troops at all—just empty desert. Heller attempted to contact Dick Cheney three times about this, and got a bureaucratic brush-off. To this day, the Pentagon's photos of Iraqi troop buildup remain classified.[29]

All of this suggests that Saudi Arabia never really had anything to fear from Iraq, and in fact, the story that the desert kingdom invited us in is a lie. The purpose of the Cheney visit of August 6, and the (phony?) satellite photos, was to persuade Saudi Arabia that it was in danger and that it should *let us* put troops on its soil. (The G.I.'s came for six months and stayed for twelve years—a major source of Al Qaeda's rage against the Saudi government and the United States, given the proximity to holy places of Islam.) Nevertheless, fear of a possible invasion of Saudi Arabia was certainly on the American government's mind in the early days, and was part of the reason that Bush Sr. didn't quite know how to respond during the first few days following the invasion of Kuwait. There was no sense of "outrage" at Saddam Hussein; Bush's August 2 statement to the press was rambling and confused. At a meeting at the White House the next day, Colin Powell, chairman of the Joint Chiefs of Staff, asked the president if we would be willing to fight for Kuwait, and the president did not reply. On August 6, however, Bush declared his intention to eject Iraq from Kuwait, a sudden decision that caught the military by surprise.[30]

The second hole in the fabric is that, for whatever reason, America gave Saddam Hussein a green light to invade Kuwait. I say "for whatever reason" because the facts here—in particular, that the United States could have easily warned Iraq explicitly not to invade Kuwait and didn't—can be used to support the theory that the whole thing was a conspiracy designed to lure Iraq into war, *or* the theory that Bush Sr. was an incompetent bungler. Economist and media analyst Edward Herman has argued that both are true: the Bush administration blundered into inviting Hussein to invade Kuwait, and once that was done, began to see that the situation could be useful. As a former oilman, Bush had to have understood the economic threat Kuwait was posing to Iraq, and certainly could have urged Kuwait to negotiate with its neighbor. Instead, within a few days of the invasion he set a course of racheting the whole thing up to war.[31]

In any case, the blundering—or the conspiracy, or the blundering conspiracy, depending on your point of view—definitely involved giving Hussein a green light, in both immediate and long-term ways. On the immediate level, Hussein had many reasons to conclude that the United States would not react strongly to an invasion. On July 24 Margaret Tutwiler, State Department spokesperson, told the press "there are no special defense or security commitments to Kuwait," and there were similar messages that got floated out around this time. And then on July 28, Bush sent the Iraqi president that conciliatory cable. But the crucial statement—although it was an affirmation of existing U.S. policy and not a departure from it—came from Ambassador Glaspie in a meeting with Saddam Hussein on July 25. Glaspie, who was fluent in Arabic, told the Iraqi president that "we have no opinion on the Arab-Arab conflicts, like your border disagreement with Kuwait." Her tone was very reassuring; and months later, in House testimony, she admitted that she never told Hussein that the United States would fight him if he invaded Kuwait—adding that to do so would have amounted to "a change in our policy." Glaspie was made the fall guy for this, but she was in fact toeing the party line. Not once during the crisis period did any administration official state that America would defend Kuwait if it was attacked. In addition, the government was granting dual-use export licenses even in the last, pre-invasion days and opposing an economic sanctions bill against Iraq that Congress was trying to pass. Hussein could draw his own conclusions.[32]

Yet, as we saw above, the entire history of U.S. foreign policy toward Iraq during the 1980s and early 1990s was one big green light. Hussein was "our man"; we had—as in the case of the shah, and as a substitute for him—armed the Iraqi president pretty heavily. In the aftermath of the Gulf war, Bush Sr. claimed that we had not enhanced Hussein's WMD capabilities, but the United Nations Special Commission and other inspection teams were finding evidence for it daily. Equally important was our attitude toward his use of such weapons. After Hussein had killed large numbers of Kurds in August 1988 with poison gas, the Reagan administration refused to impose economic sanctions. If *this* fell within the bounds of tolerable behavior, what *didn't*? The point is, we had no deterrent credibility; there was no reason for Hussein to assume a negative response to an invasion of Kuwait, especially when one factors in the "make nice" gestures of the U.S. administration in the final days. Bush Sr. denouncing him as "Hitler" was complete hypocrisy; if he could so be labeled, then one would have to say that he was "our" Hitler.[33]

Hole number three was the claim that the United States was seeking a diplomatic solution to the crisis while Iraq refused to budge. Just the opposite is true: Saddam Hussein attempted to negotiate with us a number of times and was rebuffed in each case. In fact, olive branches were extended to the United States no fewer than five times in August 1990; all of them were ignored or rejected. On 9 January 1991 James Baker met with Tariq Aziz in Geneva, handing the Iraqi foreign minister a letter from President Bush that informed Saddam Hussein he had to capitulate to U.S. demands or be crushed by force (the letter even mentioned the possible use of nuclear weapons). All of this has been documented by serious journalists and scholars, and some of the offers were reported on at the time by newspapers such as the *Financial Times* of London. There is, in short, no doubt as to who wanted a diplomatic resolution of the crisis and who wanted war.[34]

To ensure that the war would take place, as well as to create the veneer of its being an international effort, nations were bought off or threatened with loss of foreign aid (a pattern that would be repeated in 2003). Egypt was forgiven $7 billion in debt; Syria, China, Turkey, and the USSR, inter alia, received military or economic aid and World Bank or IMF loans, or had sanctions lifted. As a PBS special on the war pointed out, Syria was forgiven many of the very same sins of which Iraq was accused. On the other hand, when Yemen opposed the war, it suffered a steep reduction in U.S. aid. Meanwhile, Kuwait spent $10 million on a propaganda campaign in the United States; in the fall of 1990 "Nayirah," a fifteen-year-old girl who claimed she had been a volunteer in a Kuwaiti maternity ward, wept as she testified before a congressional caucus that Iraqi soldiers took 312 babies out of incubators and left them on the cold hospital floors to die. (She later turned out to be the daughter of the Kuwaiti ambassador to the United States, with no connection whatsoever to the hospital in Kuwait. Instead, she had been coached by the world's biggest PR firm, Hill and Knowlton in Washington, which held a $10 million contract with Kuwait.) Subsequent to her testimony, Bush Sr. appeared on TV, speaking indignantly about this "outrage," and in the weeks following publicly invoked the incubator story four more times. The final propaganda ploy came after a *New York Times*/CBS poll in November 1990 suggested that the one reason that resonated with the American public for fighting Iraq was the possibility of the latter's having nuclear weapons. Within days, Bush Sr. was claiming that Iraq was only a few months from detonating a crude nuclear device (the reality was five to ten years).[35]

And so, to war. The "coalition" bombardment of Iraq began on 17 January 1991 (Baghdad time) and went on for forty-three days. The operation can be described as the use of a sledgehammer to kill a fly. Overall, 99,000 to 140,000 tons of explosives were dropped on the country, the equivalent of five to seven Hiroshima blasts. The level of American firepower was unprecedented; as political scientist David Hendrickson notes, the United States "used force on a scale that was off the charts in comparison with its past record in the Arab world." As many as 200,000 people died. Targets chosen included water and sewage treatment plants, electrical generating plants, oil refineries, transportation networks, factories, bridges, roads, and irrigation systems, much of which bombing constituted violations of international law. According to a June 1991 article in the *Washington Post*, a lot of the damage that was described during the war as collateral and unintended was neither. Rather, the goal was that of "disabling Iraqi society at large." (The Pentagon later admitted that the objective was a total demoralization of the citizenry.) Hundreds of thousands of Iraqi children would die of treatable diseases during the next decade, as a result of what were basically war crimes. There was also a kind of demonic violence exercised against retreating Iraqi forces, who were massacred in flight on February 26–27, after a cease-fire was already in place (also a war crime, in violation of the Fourth Geneva Convention). American pilots exuberantly referred to the slaughter as a "turkey shoot" and pounded the retreating army with glee. Iraqi troops were desperate to surrender; the majority were never given the chance. Upward of 30,000 people were killed in the event; *Newsweek* reporter Tony Clifton said it "looked like a medieval hell." Civilians who tried to escape by fleeing to Jordan were bombed on the highway—this in broad daylight, with luggage piled atop buses, taxis, and cars. It was not exactly America's finest hour, and it made an enormous impression on the Arab world. As the University of San Francisco's Stephen Zunes notes, most of that world cared little for Saddam Hussein, but our manufacture of a war to advance our hegemonic goals in the region, and the delight and brutality with which that was executed, created new hatred toward the United States. Many began to view Hussein as a hero. Tens of millions of Arabs were now bitterly hostile to the United States, and the suffering America caused became the soil in which Al Qaeda flourished, and from which Osama bin Laden would find his recruits. Indeed, the ongoing U.S. military presence in the Gulf has been cited as the primary motivation for bin Laden's becoming our main adversary, for it was a reminder to all there of the neocolonial ties that the Gulf monarchies have with the United States. The "Gulf War and its aftermath," writes David Hendrickson, "played an important role in the inculcation of that implacable hatred that led to 9/11."[36]

What *about* the aftermath, then? The toll exacted by the severity of the U.S.-led U.N. economic sanctions against Iraq was even heavier that the

Gulf war itself; they certainly caused a whole lot more deaths. The supposed rationale was to put pressure on Saddam Hussein—apparently, pressure to get him to resign from office, which we must surely have known was not going to work. It was not Hussein who suffered from the sanctions but the Iraqi people; the sanctions served only to consolidate his grip on power. In 1999 UNICEF published a survey revealing that half a million Iraqi children had died in the eight years since the Gulf war, and that one-third of children under age five were chronically malnourished. Diarrhea had reappeared as a major killer, and cholera had spread rapidly. During this decade and after, the United States, by means of its fiat in the U.N. Security Council, fought aggressively to keep humanitarian goods from entering Iraq. In the face of enormous suffering, it blocked purchases necessary to generate electricity, as well as dialysis, dental, and firefighting equipment; water tankers; and milk- and yogurt-production equipment. Despite the ghastly data on malnutrition, in 2000 it blocked a contract for flour milling. It blocked a billion dollars' worth of medical equipment, and even child vaccines (until the *Washington Post* and Reuters embarrassed the administration by making the vaccine story public in March 2001). Heart and lung machines, water pumps, agricultural supplies, wheelbarrows(!), detergent(!), toilet paper(!), hospital blood bags, morphine, drugs for dysentery—all kept out. What else to call this, asks Dennis Halliday, former director of the U.N. Iraq Program, but genocide? "U.S. policymakers," adds Joy Gordon in a 2002 *Harper's* article, "have effectively turned a program of international governance into a legitimized act of mass slaughter." As was the case in Vietnam, there was almost a kind of joy, or at least grim satisfaction, on the part of the U.S. government in destroying the innocent people of a Third World country. The documentary film *The Hidden Wars of Desert Storm*, released in 2000, shows gruesome scenes of sick and starving children, and babies dying from lack of oxygen supplies. The United States also kept moving the goalposts: as soon as Iraq would comply with some bureaucratic regulation, America would have the United Nations throw up another obstacle. The truth is that we never had any intention of eliminating the sanctions, short of Hussein leaving office. On 12 May 1996 CBS did a *60 Minutes* segment called "Punishing Saddam," during which Madeleine Albright, the American ambassador to the United Nations, was confronted by the data of half a million dead Iraqi children. "We think the price is worth it," she replied.[37]

The "massive destruction of innocents," writes Joy Gordon, "is something that is unlikely to be either forgiven or forgotten."[38] It would be hard to believe that events of this sort had nothing to do with September 11. Pictures of starving and malnourished Iraqi children are burned into the minds of Arabs and Muslims everywhere (the more so with the emergence of popular Arab cable television), and these people attribute what they see to America, not to Saddam Hussein. They understand quite clearly that Muslim lives mean absolutely nothing to us. Indeed, it takes a particular level of cruelty and violence to see to it that a dying civilian population cannot obtain morphine or toilet paper or children's vaccines, let alone to add that the resulting deaths were "worth it." If the United States is not intentionally the enemy of Islamic civilization, it is doing a pretty good job of imitating a nation that is.

But the question of our own motives still remains. Why this national obsession with Iraq, which was never a threat to us? This is where the larger picture is important, because it seems likely that one reason for the Gulf war is that we are a dying empire. In a 2003 interview with the *Neue Zürcher Zeitung*, the French demographer Emmanuel Todd remarked that "theatrical military activism against inconsequential rogue states . . . is a sign of weakness, not of strength. . . . This is classic for a crumbling system." He went on, "The final glory is militarism." The fact that we are dying, and perhaps know it on an unconscious level, may account for the virulence of our attack on an infinitely weaker nation. A major motivation for the Gulf war was "kicking the Vietnam syndrome," as Bush Sr. described it—thereby demonstrating that the United States was still able to throw its weight around and could get what it wanted by armed intervention. ("What we say goes," he declared arrogantly after the war was over.) Indeed, at the conclusion of the war, Colin Powell said it was a "feel good" not seen since the end of World War II. On a personal level, this translated into a kind of redemption for career officers such as Norman Schwarzkopf, who was haunted by the defeat in Vietnam, or for Air Force Brigadier General William Looney, who was head of U.S. Central Command's Airborne Expeditionary Force, and who declared, "We dictate the way they live and talk. And that's what's great about America right now."[39] As for Bush Sr., what was he really trying to prove, what was he saying to Saddam Hussein, if not "See? My dick is bigger than yours after all!"

Along with this was the desire of the Pentagon and State Department not to dismantle the national security state that had been in place since Paul Nitze and NSC-68. The end of the Cold War raised exactly that specter. Not only was this threatening to the military establishment, but it could also wreak havoc with an economy heavily dependent on weapons sales and manufacture. But having to put out (or create) "brush fires" around the world meant there would be no need to scale down, as a number of newspapers and high-ranking officials observed at the time. The Gulf war enabled the defense establishment to claim that there was still a need for continued funding.[40]

Then, of course, there was the matter of having access to the oil reserves of the Middle East, along with the desire to have geopolitical supremacy in one of the most politically sensitive regions of the world. America wanted unrivaled hegemony in the region and an environment conducive to our economic and strategic interests. Since Europe and Japan get most of their oil from the Middle East, control of it is also a way of controlling them. But as philosopher Douglas Kellner points out, there was really no single reason that the United States went to war; rather, it was "overdetermined," a confluence of political, economic, and military considerations all coming together. Yet the most suspicious aspect of the whole affair, according to foreign policy expert Christopher Layne, was the Bush administration's inability to articulate a coherent rationale for it, which suggests that the core reason lay in the values and premises of the foreign policy elite—principles that they themselves couldn't clearly articulate—regarding the concept of a new world order. This was the reason for the bungling or "sleepwalking" quality of the whole event, especially at the beginning. As noted earlier, with the collapse of the Soviet Union, history was undergoing a large techtonic shift. As the "plates" separated, a huge existential chasm opened up. Containment had been everything to us. Absent that, we had no idea of who we were. We were thus poised to step into the huge abyss that resulted, but . . . with what? It was as though the whole culture began unconsciously scanning for a target, an enemy, and Bush temporarily found one when he declared a (spurious) "war on drugs." Then Saddam Hussein, who was understandably reading the signals we had sent him all along as positive—which they were—but who, like Bush, didn't realize the significance of the Soviet collapse nor grasp how rapidly things were changing, did absolutely the wrong thing at the wrong time and thus walked into the trap that history, not George H. W. Bush, had laid for him. So I believe Edward Herman is right: this *was* a conspiracy, but a kind of accidental or bungled one. By shifting our focus from Communists to odious dictators to (ten years later) terrorists, we never had to confront the void or the negative identity game, never had to see the handwriting on the wall: these were, and are, our declining years. What seemed like a new world order with us in charge was in reality the beginning of the end: we don't have the wherewithal to survive this century, except in severely attenuated form. As sociologist and historian Immanuel Wallerstein has written, we can learn to fade quietly or—much more likely—insist that what we say goes, and "thereby transform a gradual decline into a rapid and danger-ous fall." More on these choices later. For now, we need to look at what is probably the flashpoint of the whole East-West conflict, the question of Israel and Palestine.[41]

Israel/Palestine

In many ways, the story of modern-day Israel really begins with the destruction of the Second Temple by the Romans in A.D. 70, after which the Diaspora began in earnest. Since they no longer had a homeland, the Jews migrated from country to country, typically making a huge cultural or economic contribution, until the nation they happened to be resident in decided it had a "Jewish question," one that could best be resolved by expelling them. Exactly what this "question" was, beyond "How do the Jews manage to outshine everybody else?," has never been clear to me; but the historical record indicates that with the exception of a very few tolerant host nations, nothing—complete assimilation included—ever worked, in the sense of altering this pattern of forced migration. The most extreme and horrific response, of course, was the one formulated by Nazi Germany: the *Endlösung*, or Final Solution, in which the Jews were to be wiped off the face of the earth. About one-third of the world Jew-ish population was eradicated as a result. In the aftermath of the Holo-caust, nineteen hundred years of guilt finally worked their way upward into the consciousness of Christian Europe: the Jews, it was decided, had a right to a state of their own. In May 1948, then, the United Nations attempted to solve the Jewish question by creating an Arab question, and neither Jews nor Arabs have had a moment's peace since.

It is the details of these events that constitute the bone of contention between Israelis and Palestinians, and rivers of blood (as well as ink) have been spilled in the course of this debate. Nearly sixty years later, however, things seem to be almost as murky as they were in 1948. As Palestinian scholar Ibrahim Abu-Lughod once observed, it is unclear whether an authoritative interpretation of those events can ever emerge. "The more you look into the history of this conflict," writes one *New York Times* editor, "the more difficult it is to assign blame clearly."[42] The Israeli version has been one of beleaguered heroes in a new land, forging a new identity, far from the experience of Auschwitz, and thrust into a war of independence to regain their ancient homeland. The Palestinian version is that they, not the Jews, were the residents of that particular patch of Middle Eastern property, and they got evicted from their land at gunpoint. In this version, the events of 1948 are *al-Nakba* ("the Catastrophe"). Both of these stories, as it turns out, are true; the question is *how* true, and exactly where the "line" of truth should be drawn.

One of the advantages of living in a democracy (or disadvantages, depending on your point of view) is having the right to publish extremely unpopular views; and this began to happen in Israel in the late 1970s as a number of "revisionist" historians started calling the state mythology into question. Their main point was similar to that of American revisionist historians who argue that the settling of the United States was predicated on wiping out the Native American population and herding the remainder onto reservations (refugee camps, in effect): there's a skeleton in the closet, an "original sin" that was present at the very birth of the nation. In the case of Israel, that skeleton (according to the revisionists) is the dispossession of the Palestinians, which made the creation of the state of Israel possible. And skeletons, as we know, eventually start rattling; they have a way of coming back to haunt us.[43]

So Israeli scholars such as Benny Morris (*The Birth of the Palestinian Refugee Problem, 1947–49*) and Tom Segev (*1949: The First Israelis*) have taken it upon themselves to exorcise these ghosts. As their documentation reveals, it's not a pretty picture. At Deir Yassin, a village near Jerusalem, the Irgun, under Menachem Begin, slaughtered about 250 civilians on April 9–10. There were also a number of small-scale massacres, and about a dozen rapes. All in all, the lesson was not lost on the local population: 50,000 people fled Ramla, Lydda, and the neighboring towns, for example (a fact that Israeli censors forced Yitzhak Rabin to excise from his memoirs). Asked by General Yigal Allon on 12 July 1948 what to do with the Arabs, Prime Minister David Ben-Gurion replied, "Expel them" (*garesh otam*). Most chose exile to avoid Jewish rule or what they feared would be death at the hands of Israeli commando groups, and expulsions went on into 1949 and beyond, when it became official policy to shoot Palestinians trying to return to their homes. All in all, the number of refugees amounted to something like 700,000 people.[44]

The whole thing, however, is a little more complicated than one of a deliberate assault on a civilian population. A lot of this was anxiety ridden and reactive, motivated by the trauma of the Holocaust itself, which the Ashkenazi Jews could never overcome, and which became a sad subtext in Israeli-Palestinian relations. But some of this antedates the Holocaust: Arab riots and pogroms against the Jews in 1920–21 and 1929 (including a massacre of sixty-six ultra-Orthodox Jews in Hebron), for example, or the victimization of Jews during an Arab revolt in Palestine in 1936–39. The U.N. vote of 29 November 1947 on partition was met by a wave of anti-Jewish terrorism, and the new year saw three more massacres of Jews. When the state of Israel was declared on 14 May 1948, Jordan, Syria, Egypt, and Iraq all invaded within the next forty-eight hours, determined to strangle the new state at birth. And when all is said and done, the Palestinian Arab exodus was the product of a war that the Palestinian Arabs had started. The Jews certainly had reason to believe that if they lost the war of independence, they would be slaughtered.[45]

It is also the case that the expulsion of the Palestinians was not a deliberate policy, but an incidental—if favorably regarded—part of military operations. Thus even in late 1948, the Israel Defense Forces tended to leave Arab communities in place; events depended on local circumstances and individual company commanders. Many Arabs left because of the general chaos and anarchy that followed in the wake of the withdrawal of British rule, and also because of orders or advice from Arab officials, who (rightly or wrongly) feared for the safety of those who might choose to stay, and thus wound up encouraging a Palestinian exodus. Ben-Gurion's unfortunate remark aside, the "policy" was a tacit one, that of taking advantage of the limited flight of the Palestinians so as to transform it into a permanent mass depopulation. While there can be no doubt that the Zionist vision was to turn an Arab-populated land into a Jewish state, Ben-Gurion never enunciated an explicit expulsion policy because he was aware that it was morally questionable. He thus preferred to hint at it instead. In essence, once the exodus began, the opportunity to reduce

Arab numbers was too tempting for the Israeli government to forgo; so the unofficial policy became, The more Palestinians that leave, the better. Hence, there was an expulsion, but it was situational rather than programmatic. As Benny Morris says, the events of 1947–49 were so complex and varied that "a single-cause explanation of the exodus from most sites is untenable." Nevertheless, it cannot be said to be Israel's finest hour. Complex or not, there is no way the expulsion can be regarded as voluntary. And so the end of one community, so to speak, became the beginning of another.

As for the American role in all this, in 1949 the United States demanded that Israel take back 250,000 refugees, but it never really pressured the Israelis about it. That July, Israel finally offered to take back 65,000 to 70,000, but the Arabs rejected the proposal. U.N. Resolution 194 of 11 December 1948 had affirmed that refugees wishing to return should be permitted to do so as early as possible, but as time passed the United States was less committed to this. The Truman administration felt that economic development would be the best solution for the Palestinians, but the latter saw this approach as dismissive of their political aspirations. By 1951 the U.S. government position was that the Palestinians would do best to resettle outside of Israel. As for the Palestinians, they felt they had been sold out; the whole series of events left them with a great bitterness toward the United Nations and the United States.[46]

It's not that the United States had any particular love for the Jews, post-Holocaust sympathy notwithstanding. In fact, the story of the government's attitude toward the Jews is a multilayered one. During the period between the wars, the State Department, which was notoriously anti-Semitic, was pro-Sunni Arab. The State Department scenario of future Mideast relations was heavily based on the Open Door policy, especially as it might affect American oil interests, and State also envisioned American hegemony increasing as British colonial influence receded. Basically, the general idea was to outmaneuver the British, ward off the Soviets, and encourage the Arab states to be sovereign, pro-American, and—of course—receptive to American business and investment. Zionism was thus viewed as a potential threat to this scenario, because if the Arabs were to believe that the United States was partial to the Jewish cause, American influence among them would suffer.[47]

The result was that the State Department bet on the wrong horse, historically speaking. It dismissed Zionism as "chimerical," favoring instead the rise of Arab nationalist movements that, it somehow believed, would operate under the guidance of benevolent American leadership. In doing so, it encountered opposition from higher echelons in the government, as well as from its own Europeanists. It even favored, during the war, seeking help from the Soviet Union in curbing Zionist efforts in Palestine. As far as the subsequent establishment of the state of Israel, however, none of this made any difference. As the war ended and Franklin Roosevelt—who was in fact indifferent to the plight of the European Jews, and who vetoed every effort to save them—died, world opinion began to favor a Jewish homeland, leaving the State Department out in the cold. It was at odds with the Truman White House, which was sympathetic to Zionist aspirations. So even though the attitudes of the State Department (along with the War Department) had translated into policies that had murderous results for European Jewry, Foggy Bottom ultimately failed in its pro-Arab, anti-Zionist campaign. It was essentially out of touch with postwar realities.[48]

And the new realities meant that private sentiments had no bearing on public policy. Thus, although a diary discovered in 2003 revealed that President Truman was actually quite anti-Semitic, his personal feelings made no difference for his strong support of the establishment of a Jewish state. Or to skip ahead for a moment, Richard Nixon, who was crudely anti-Semitic (as we learned from the tapes he made of his discussions in the Oval Office), was guided by what he perceived as the national interest, not by his antipathy toward Jews, and was easily persuaded by Henry Kissinger that Israel had a "strategic role" to play in the Middle East. All in all, Washington's support for Israel has been fundamental; very few presidents have questioned it.

This is, however, a drama with many acts (and actors). If some branches of government were anti-Zionist and committed to Arab nationalism, there was nevertheless an important cultural current at work that was sluggishly moving in the opposite direction, and that eventually triumphed. This predated the Holocaust, and was a lot more subtle and amorphous than postwar sympathy for the Jews; but ultimately, the fact that America was more easily able to identify with the Jews than with the Arabs from a racial point of view may have been just as important in influencing U.S. policy in the Middle East. The reason for this, according to Douglas Little in *American Orientalism*, is the issue of modernization, which seems to have played a major role in perceptions of Semitic peoples in the decades leading up to 1948 and after. Since Arab societies tend toward the traditional and religious, and Western ones toward the scientific and technological, the filter of modern-versus-traditional has a lot to do with how the Middle East got perceived by the United States. "Modernization" was often a cover for racial bias, in other words, a way of saying that a sensible world is a world that is more like ours.

An early example of this is a feature article that ran in 1934 in the widely popular magazine *National Geographic* on how the new European immigrants were transforming Palestine, "modernizing" it, and thereby raising the pastoral Arab peoples to a "higher plane of life." (There were 85,000 Jews living in Palestine in 1914, 350,000 by 1939.) This view of Arabs as backward and exotic (and occasionally dangerous) as contrasted with "can-do" Westernized Jews and Israelis became the staple of *National Geographic* coverage and made its way into books and movies after World War II, shaping American Middle East foreign policy in subtle ways. More and more, Arab aspirations for self-determination were seen as politically primitive, whereas Zionism, being Western and European, was perceived as having greater legitimacy. Thus a State Department report of 1948 describes Muslims as "fanatical and overwrought"; Eisenhower believed Arab thinking was rooted in "violence, emotion, and ignorance." The film *Exodus*, released in 1960, portrayed the heroism of Jews during the struggle for independence, and in general Hollywood projected images of noble Israelis surrounded by unruly Arabs. Lyndon Johnson frankly equated the PLO, Nasser, and Arab nationalists with the Vietcong and welcomed the Israeli victory of 1967. The Six Day War, in fact, completed the transformation, in American eyes, of Jews from victims to victors. The Arabs, in contrast, were seen as losers, weak and inferior.[49]

Literature also had a role to play in this process. T. E. Lawrence's *Revolt in the Desert* (1927), for example, depicted Arabs as noble (if brutal) savages, in need of Western guidance. Fast-forward a few decades and we find no Arab equivalent to Leon Uris' runaway best-seller, *Exodus*, nor any Arab studies that attempted to combat the negative stereotyping that can be found in the work of Raphael Patai (*The Arab Mind*, 1973; it is favorite reading among the neocon crowd, as it turns out), which talks of the "fossilization" of Arab culture, or John Laffin (an early version of Bernard Lewis), who wrote (in *Arab Mind Considered*, 1975) about how history had "turned wrong" for the Arabs. Then there was Uris' *The Haj* (1984), which had a print run of about two million copies in its first year, and which portrayed Palestinians in a very pejorative way. All of these sources—books, films, and magazines—evoked an image of Arabs as primitive and malevolent. Indeed, the only thing I've seen that could be (partially) interpreted as a popular response (it's more like a swipe) is the stunningly prescient movie by Edward Zwick, *The Siege* (1998), in which an Arab terrorist says to an FBI agent, "You have to learn the consequences of telling the world how to live."

It was this view of Arabs as backward versus Israelis as Western, European, white, secular (mostly), and modern—like us, in short—that paved the way for Israel's emergence as a strategic asset in American relations in the Middle East. There is no way to prove this, of course, but it seemed to have conditioned the whole atmosphere of the "proxy" relationship, i.e., of its possibility. There was an internal shift after 1967; many in Israel became more interested in land than peace. The West Bank, the Golan Heights, and East Jerusalem were important to conservative prime ministers such as Begin and his successors Yitzhak Shamir, Benjamin Netanyahu, and, of course, Ariel Sharon. As Israel's ambitions became increasingly territorial, hatred festered in the squalid Palestinian refugee camps. Dean Rusk warned LBJ that "Israel's keeping territory would create a revanchism for the rest of the twentieth century," and in 1972 a retired State Department expert on the Middle East wrote that the repeated humiliation inflicted by Israel would unleash a "collective need for vengeance" on the part of the Arabs. But these were minority voices. As for the Arabs, if they were intransigent before 1967, says Douglas Little—and their basic, unrelenting desire was nothing less than the annihilation of the state of Israel—the Israelis were intransigent after; and for the most part, the United States did not oppose Israel's expansionist policy. Israel did not want to talk about repatriating refugees or allowing for a Palestinian state, and it was at this point that it began to pursue the building of settlements in order to consolidate its control over the occupied territories. After the Six Day War, writes Michael Ben-Yair, Israel's Attorney General from 1993 to 1996, Israel "chose to become a colonial society." In effect, he goes on, "we established an apartheid regime."[50]

The issue of the settlements has probably been the major immediate cause of Palestinian violence. As Henry Siegman, a former director of the American Jewish Congress, has written, the settlement enterprise is "nothing less than the theft of Palestinian land in broad daylight, a theft made possible only by Israel's vastly superior military force"—whose tanks and helicopters bear the legend MADE IN USA. In 1977, when Prime Minister Begin refused President Carter's request to freeze settlement activity (Carter called the settlements illegal), there were 7000 settlers living on the West Bank. By 1990 there were 76,000 settlers there and in Gaza, and as of 2002 (if one includes East Jerusalem and the Golan Heights), 400,000 in the occupied territories. President Reagan reversed Carter; he declared that the settlements were not illegal. In addition, his administration did little to discourage Israeli Defense Minister Ariel Sharon from invading Lebanon in June 1982, which led to the infamous massacres at Sabra and Shatila. The Bush Sr. administration, in a rare move for the American presidency, called on Israel to abandon its expansionist policy, whereas Clinton was and Bush Jr. has been much less outspoken. (Clinton never insisted that Israel cease building new settlements, even though he knew the building of them would make peace more unlikely.) But whatever U.S. policy has been on the settlement question, the one thing the United States has decidedly not done is force the issue by threatening to pull the plug on the huge amount of foreign aid it gives Israel each year. The reason for this lies in the latter's role as our proxy in the Middle East.[51]

The cultivation of Israel as a geopolitical asset fits the general pattern of U.S. foreign policy: we wanted to prevent the USSR from filling the vacuum created by Great Britain's gradual withdrawal from its empire, mistakenly believing the Soviet goal to be world domination. After 1945, notes Douglas Little, America effectively made the Monroe Doctrine the template for the Middle East. But as time went on, it became clear that we couldn't police the whole region by ourselves, and our special relationship with Israel grew out of the fact that we were determined to contain the Soviet Union without having another Vietnam on our hands. Again, the Six Day War can be taken as the key moment: with that victory, Israel staked out a position at precisely the time that the United States, thanks to Vietnam, was getting interested in limiting its involvement in the Third World. But even prior to that, Israel anticipated a proxy role for itself. For example, a spokesman for the Israeli foreign office was quoted in the *New York Times* of 12 June 1966 as saying: "The United States has come to the conclusion that it can no longer respond to every incident around the world, that it must rely on local power . . . as a first line to stave off America's direct involvement. Israel feels that it fits this definition." LBJ, for his part, approved the sale of large numbers of tanks and planes to Israel before the Six Day War; the year after the war, Prime Minister Levi Eshkol declared that "the value of Israel to the West in this part of the world will . . . be out of all proportion to its size." The Nixon Doctrine—that certain countries in key regions of the world would play the role of "local police" under the direction of the U.S.—followed in 1969, with the *New York Times* reporting that December that, in the view of the Nixon administration, only Israel's strength could "prevent a call for direct American intervention." Thus in 1970, when Syrian troops entered Jordan in support of militant Palestinians who were struggling with King Hussein, Kissinger invited Israel to act on America's behalf when the king asked for U.S. protection. Israel deployed its forces, and the king engaged the Syrians, who then withdrew. Israel, said Kissinger, proved it could "keep the peace" in the Middle East. By 1973 the CIA and Mossad were comparing notes on Arab radicals, and during that year's Yom Kippur War Kissinger called for a $3 billion aid package to Israel (it had been $30 million in 1970), a level sustained annually ever since. The geopolitical pattern of Israel as America's proxy was by now firmly in place.[52] (Whether Israel actually does serve U.S. interests in the Middle East is, of course, a whole other question.)

And so where are we now, at the beginning of the twenty-first century? We have seen decades of violence, with not much end in sight. (Whether the death of PLO chairman Yasser Arafat in 2004, or the Israeli withdrawal from Gaza in 2005, will really change anything remains to be seen.) We have a colonized population economically dependent on people they view as their oppressors, sometimes employed picking crops on lands once owned by their families. We have terrorist attacks on innocent civilians on one side, and the daily brutality of an occupying power, using maximum force indiscriminately in heavily populated areas, on the other—state terrorism, in short. We have the Bush Jr. administration confusing cause and effect, insisting that Palestinian terrorism is preventing the Palestinians from achieving their freedom, when it is the denial of freedom—a harsh and humiliating occupation—that has led to terrorism as a desperate response. (Israeli Defense Minister Binyamin Ben-Eliezer conceded in April 2002 that the military operations themselves "become the hothouse that produces more and more new suicide bombers.") And finally, we have General Moshe Ya'alon, the Israeli army chief of staff, stating, "The Palestinians must be made to understand in the deepest recesses of their consciousness that they are a defeated people"; and the late General Rafael Eitan, a former army chief of staff, at one point calling the Palestinians "drugged cockroaches in a bottle."[53] And because Israel serves as America's proxy, supposedly protecting U.S. economic and strategic interests; because Muslims the world over know about the $3 billion subsidy and where Israeli weaponry comes from; because they see the United States consistently voting against the Palestinians, and for the Israelis, in the United Nations, even on human rights issues—for all these reasons, they despise the United States, and cite the Israeli-Palestinian conflict as the key sticking point in their relations with the West. (Ironically enough, a survey conducted by the Pew Research Center in May 2003 revealed that 47 percent of Israelis see the United States as unfairly favoring Israel over the Palestinians!) True, the conflict is often a political football used by Arab governments, a way of distracting their own populations from problems at home. Nevertheless, it is a real football: the issues are not invented. Consider the following events, all of which took place in 2004:

+ An Israeli officer pumped the body of a thirteen-year-old girl full of bullets, then announced that he would have done the same thing if she had been three years old;
+ Ultra-Orthodox soldiers mocked Palestinian corpses by impaling a man's head on a pole and sticking a cigarette in his mouth;
+ An Israeli officer stopped a Palestinian violinist at a roadblock near Nablus and made him "play something sad," while soldiers stood around and ridiculed him (this provoked an outrage among Israelis because it was reminiscent of Jewish musicians in concentration camps being forced to provide background music to mass murder).

This, I thought when I read these reports, is where the Jews have wound up, after five thousand years of persecution? All I can feel is a sense of sadness and shame.[54]

Just so there is no confusion, let me be clear: I am not suggesting that Gaza is Auschwitz—of course not. The Israelis are not herding the Palestinians into gas chambers, and I am not asserting any type of moral equivalency here. But that is cold comfort, as far as I am concerned. Quite obviously, not being Auschwitz cannot become the standard of what is politically and morally tolerable.

I am also, once again, not arguing that murdering civilians, whether at the World Trade Center or a Jerusalem pizza joint, is justified by any kind of moral calculus. It isn't. What I *am* saying is that these things cannot and do not arise in a political vacuum. Avraham Burg, who was speaker of the Knesset from 1999 to 2003, is no longer shocked at the Palestinian response to the occupation, and he urges his fellow citizens to understand why:

> Israel, having ceased to care about the children of the Palestinians, should not be surprised when they come washed in hatred and blow themselves up in the centers of Israeli escapism. They consign themselves to Allah in our places of recreation, because their own lives are torture. They spill their own blood in our restaurants in order to ruin our appetites, because they have children and parents at home who are hungry and humiliated.[55]

As for reactions to America, many Palestinians danced in the streets upon hearing the news of 9/11, which pretty much says it all. Ever oblivious of history and context, the American people reacted to this with hurt and anger; but as in the case of Iran and Iraq, if you don't have a historical memory, or—which goes along with this—you have a government that is easily able to mystify your experience, then behavior such as this is incomprehensible. But Arab and Muslim peoples have a very *good* historical memory, and neither America nor Israel will be able to rest easy until their grievances are addressed.

It seems to come down to something like this: the U.S. government, and apparently most of the American people, have not yet figured out the laws of cause and effect. Nor do they show any noticeable signs of being on the edge of discovery. This brings to mind a talk Bill Clinton gave on 28 May 2003 at the Kennedy Library in Boston, in which he made a comparison between what he called the practical mind and the theological one. If the practical mind digs itself into a hole, he said, its reaction is to stop and think about what it is doing and what the alternatives might be. If the theological mind does the same thing, its response is to call for a bigger shovel. Now the former president was talking about domestic rather than foreign policy, but one would have to say that when it comes to the latter subject (as with so many others), the approach of the Bush Jr.

administration is, as is well-known, "faith based." Given our record in the Middle East over the last fifty-odd years, there are—as should be self-evident by now—a number of lessons to be learned. The most important of these is surely that unless you want to provoke a terrorist backlash, you scrupulously avoid militarily imposing your will on the countries of that region. Yet instead of reflecting on the obvious and deciding to work toward reversing a self-destructive foreign policy, Bush Jr. and his inner circle called (and are calling) for a bigger shovel. In effect, they adopted the Israeli model of exacerbating terrorism by raising the military ante. They have thus guaranteed that the cycle of attack and retaliation (which is in essence what they take foreign relations to be) will be with us for many years to come—and, I predict, seriously debilitate us. That is because, historically, insurgent resistance to foreign domination is the Islamic world's métier; as a result, our victories in this arena are likely to be short lived, and Pyrrhic ones even if not. Much of what America has been doing in the Middle East resembles a man with a headache convinced he can make it go away by repeatedly hitting himself over the head with a hammer. Gulf war—the Sequel is a case in point.

The Meaning of 9/11

I too love jeans and jazz and *Treasure Island*
and John Silver's parrot and the balconies of New Orleans.
I love Mark Twain and the Mississippi steamboats and
Abraham Lincoln's dogs.
I love the fields of wheat and corn and the smell of Virginia
tobacco.
But I am not American.
Is that enough for the Phantom pilot to turn me back to the
Stone Age?
I need neither oil nor America herself, neither the elephant
nor the donkey.
Leave me, pilot, leave my house roofed with palm fronds and
this wooden bridge.
I need neither your Golden Gate nor your skyscrapers.
I need the village, not New York.
Why did you come to me from your Nevada desert, soldier
armed to the teeth?
Why did you come all the way to distant Basra, where fish
used to swim by our doorsteps?
Pigs do not forage here.
I only have these water buffaloes lazily chewing on water
lilies.
Leave me alone, soldier.

Leave me my floating cane hut and my fishing spear.

Leave me my migrating birds and the green plumes.

Take your roaring iron birds and your Tomahawk missiles. I
  am not your foe.

I am the one who wades up to the knees in rice paddies.

Leave me to my curse.

I do not need your day of doom.

—From Saadi Youssef, "America, America"
(translated by Khaled Mattawa)

THE AMERICAN INVASION OF IRAQ in the spring of 2003 was about
a lot of things, but it certainly wasn't about Iraq. Nor was it intended to
be, although the Bush Jr. administration obviously could not say so publicly. As *Rebuilding America's Defenses*, the PNAC report, clearly states, Saddam Hussein was nothing more than an "immediate justification" for a
larger goal, that of having "a substantial American presence in the Gulf."
Indeed, on the eve of the 2003 attack, George Bush and Tony Blair, from
their odd, symbolic isolation on the Azores, declared that Britain and the
United States would invade Iraq even if Hussein left the country(!). But
as the report makes clear, American hegemony is hardly to be limited to
the Middle East; the neoconservative agenda is about control of the
entire world (as well as outer space), and about imposing the American
political and economic model on that world. Bush Sr. may not have been
particularly astute, but at least he was living in a finite universe. With Bush
Jr. we enter a kind of surreal terrain; the Void is now so vast as to be
incomprehensible. The framework has become eschatological, building
on a post-9/11 vocabulary: "crusade," "infinite justice," and so on. The
enemy—"evil"—can never be defeated by definition; there are no possible criteria for what a victory would consist of. As the renowned Sloven-
ian philosopher Slavoj Žižek put it, "What if the true purpose of the war
is to pass to a global emergency state?" In effect, the goal becomes war
itself, war without end, Hegel's "negative identity" now made into a permanent planetary condition. But none of this is about Iraq per se; Iraq
was merely the target of a convenient, if paranoid, psychological projection. As the British journalist George Monbiot predicted even before the
"National Security Strategy" was issued by the White House in September 2002, "If the U.S. were not preparing to attack Iraq, it would be

preparing to attack another nation. The U.S. will go to war because it needs a country with which to go to war."[1]

Earlier I raised the question of whether all of this constituted a rupture in American foreign policy or a continuation of it, and suggested that it was both. Gore Vidal was right: with NSC-68 the republic got hijacked into becoming an empire; but the 2002 "National Security Strategy," with its doctrines of global hegemony and the "right" of preemptive strike, is "hijacking squared," so to speak. The neoconservative "cabal"— Paul Wolfowitz, Richard Perle, Douglas Feith, Elliot Abrams, Dick Cheney, Donald Rumsfeld, et al.—did not create the agenda of "full spectrum dominance" out of thin air, quite obviously; but an Orwellian vision of world domination and permanent war can hardly be called business as usual.

The Lies

The sordid tale of how the neocons and the Bush administration tricked the country into war has been told, *mutatis mutandis*, many times by a variety of journalists and scholars across the political spectrum, from Hans Blix to Patrick Buchanan, as well as by government insiders whose versions of events echo and corroborate each other's. Particularly comprehensive is the study by Stefan Halper and Jonathan Clarke, *America Alone*, and a lengthy article in the May 2004 issue of *Vanity Fair*, "The Path to War." Briefly, the story goes something like this: given the fact that Iraq had been in the neocon crosshairs since 1992, and that the PNAC report blatantly stated that invading the country would require another Pearl Harbor, the inner circle around Bush wasted no time making their move in the wake of 9/11. While the rest of us were in shock and mourning, they began a deliberate, cynical manipulation of the political situation. To implement their plans, they would conflate Iraq with 9/11 and terrorism. Thus by 2:40 P.M. on September 11, Donald Rumsfeld raised the possibility of going after Iraq, and less than a day later told the inner circle that this was preferable to going after Afghanistan inasmuch as the former had "better targets" (and this guy is still employed?). Also on 9/11, Rumsfeld said to his aides: "Go massive. Sweep it all up. Things related and not." Conflation was definitely the name of the game. Richard Clarke, then head of counterterrorism, and other officials were soon being pressured

(Clarke describes it as attempted intimidation) to find Iraq–Al Qaeda links. As *New York Times* columnist Paul Krugman writes, "The Iraq hawks set out to corrupt the process of intelligence assessment." The fix was in; this was a war they were simply going to have, come hell or high water. "Truth" was not part of the equation.[2]

So on 17 September 2001, the president signed a top secret document for going to war against Afghanistan that also directed the Pentagon to begin planning military operations for a war on Iraq. This plan was known only to the inner circle, and not told to the opponents of military action—such as the State Department, which didn't know about it until it was a fait accompli. No paper trail was kept, no record of meetings. Condoleezza Rice told Bush that he needed to go after all rogue nations' weapons of mass destruction. One official later said the entire program was theological: "It's almost a religion—that it will be the end of society if we don't take action now." Bush subsequently signed a secret intelligence order directing the CIA to undertake a covert program to topple Hussein, which included assassination. In short, the decision to invade Iraq was made almost immediately after 9/11, but kept under wraps for several months.[3]

The next step, then, was to make up a story and sell it to the American people; the State of the Union address of January 2002 would be the opening wedge of this campaign. Bush's speechwriter, David Frum, recounts in his memoir that in December 2001 he was told to come up with a justification for war against Iraq that would go into that address. Thus was born the "axis of evil," a phrase chosen for its theological resonance, according to the neocons, with Bush darkly hinting at the new direction: "I will not wait on events, while dangers gather." In April, Bush told a British reporter, "I made up my mind that Saddam needs to go." After that, administration discussion was all about tactics, and General Tommy Franks, head of the U.S. Central Command, began visiting the White House to brief the president on plans for the war. Next came the West Point speech of 1 June 2002, announcing the new policy of pre-emptive war; the next month, when Richard Haass, the director of policy planning for the State Department, intended to go to the White House to raise some objections, Rice told him that the decision had been made and he shouldn't waste his breath arguing about it.[4]

The problem, however, was that not enough people wanted war. A Gallup poll of mid-August 2002 showed support for the war at 53 percent, down 8 percentage points from two months before. To make things worse, elite opinion—including that of figures from earlier administrations, such as Brent Scowcroft (Bush Sr.'s national security adviser, who argued that an invasion of Iraq would dilute the war on terrorism and lessen the cooperation of nations needed to fight it), Henry Kissinger, former secretary of state Lawrence Eagleburger, and conservative Republicans in Congress—was heavily against it. All of these men felt that the Bush Jr. administration hadn't made the case for Iraq being an imminent threat. "There is scant evidence," wrote Scowcroft in an op-ed piece in the *Wall Street Journal*, "to tie Saddam to terrorist organizations, and even less to the September 11 attacks."[5]

What to do? One tactic was to keep repeating a lie—namely, that Iraq and Al Qaeda were linked. Thus on 25 September 2002 both Rice and the president publicly insisted on the Iraq–Al Qaeda link; the day after that Rumsfeld declared he had "bulletproof" evidence of ties between Hussein and Al Qaeda; and in a speech given in Cincinnati on October 7, Bush claimed that Iraq was an immediate threat and might strike U.S. territory with the help of terrorist groups using WMD on any given day. Unfortunately, also on October 7, CIA director George Tenet wrote a letter to Congress that did not support these assertions. CIA analysis in general concluded that Iraq had little reason to provoke the United States; it was simply not its modus operandi. This was also the consensus of the U.S. intelligence community as given in the National Intelligence Estimate on Iraq, which circulated within the administration in October. But the Bush administration had an important lever: after September 11, Tenet was under attack because of the CIA's failure to prevent the events of that day. Indeed, a number of congressional leaders wanted the director to resign. Hence, tactic number two: Bush kept Tenet on, but the president and the inner circle pressured him to endorse key elements of the case for war even when this required ignoring CIA findings. And so Tenet caved; he began to make concessions, ambiguous statements about the possibility of Iraq–Al Qaeda contacts, along with his later infamous "slam dunk" remark about Iraq's possessing WMD. When Richard Clarke, along with CIA and FBI experts, wrote a report showing that no such contacts existed, Condoleezza Rice's office sent it back, saying: "Wrong answer. . . . Do it again."[6]

Which brings us to the third tactic, for which the Bush Jr. administration borrowed a leaf from the Bush Sr. administration's book: manufacture a nuclear threat. That was the trump card for war in 1991 (along with phony or distorted atrocity stories), and it worked just as well the second time around. The major "campaign" for this was scheduled for September 2002 as well, to coincide with tactic number one, but Cheney made two speeches in August to prepare the terrain. In a question-and-answer session at the Commonwealth Club in San Francisco on August 7, he told his audience that it was "the judgment of many of us that in the not-too-distant future, [Saddam Hussein] will acquire nuclear weapons"; in a talk to the national convention of the Veterans of Foreign Wars in Nashville on August 26, he declared, "We know that Saddam has resumed his efforts to acquire nuclear weapons." Cheney cited Lieutenant General Hussein Kamel, a son-in-law of Hussein who defected in 1995, as one of his sources for this "knowledge," which illustrates an interesting pattern in the type of disinformation the administration was putting out. Kamel had been head of the Iraqi weapons program—nuclear as well as chemical and biological —for ten years, and he became famous for exposing Iraq's deceptions regarding WMD. But what he also told the U.N. inspectors, and the International Atomic Energy Agency (IAEA), and which was additionally told to the CIA, was that he personally ordered the destruction of Iraq's WMD, nuclear weapons included, after the Gulf war. Cheney was referring to Kamel's testimony about the earlier deceptions, and conveniently neglected to mention that Kamel had destroyed Iraq's nuclear capability in 1991. It was also the case that Kamel had returned to Iraq and was killed in February 1996, so he could hardly have been a source for what U.S. officials knew in 2002. In any event, *Newsweek* broke the story regarding Kamel's destruction of Iraqi nukes on 24 February 2003; during the four months prior to that, the Kamel story was cited four times by writers on the *New York Times* op-ed page as evidence for Iraq *having* nuclear weapons, and therefore as a reason to go to war. Bush also referred to it in his Cincinnati speech of 7 October 2002; and Colin Powell selectively used the Kamel information in his presentation to the U.N. Security Council on 5 February 2003, again as an argument for Iraqi nuclear capability. Prior to the attack on Iraq, however, and for the most part after it as well, no major newspapers or TV shows picked up on the *Newsweek* story, and the whole thing fell off the proverbial radar screen.[7]

Another instance of the administration's disinformation pattern occurred in September, when Bush cited an IAEA report that, he said, showed Saddam Hussein was only months away from obtaining nuclear weapons. In fact the report said no such thing, and for just a few hours MSNBC reported, on its Web site, that this was a misstatement. After that, the notice vanished from the site.[8]

One particularly egregious case of disinformation was a story that Iraq was trying to procure a certain kind of high-strength aluminum tube in order to be able to enrich uranium for a nuclear weapon. In reality, evidence was accumulating that these tubes—which Iraq was indeed attempting to purchase—were for conventional artillery, as Iraq had claimed. Classified CIA reports made available to Senators Bob Graham and Richard Durbin indicated clearly the problems involved in the "nuclear" interpretation, whereas declassified versions of these omitted the strong countervailing evidence (or at best, shoved them into the footnotes) and played up the nuclear version that the government wanted to promote—which it did, with a vengeance. In September 2002, it leaked the aluminum tubes story to the *New York Times*, and Cheney, Rice, and Rumsfeld went on the talk shows to trumpet the discovery. Rice even insisted, in a CNN interview of September 8, that the only application such tubes could have was in uranium centrifuges, which was a lie. Many intelligence analysts were appalled by these interviews, but government scientists who disagreed were expected to keep their mouths shut. (Linda Rothstein, editor of the *Bulletin of the Atomic Scientists*, wrote in July 2003 that many of the charges against Iraq that had been trotted out to the media "failed the laugh test.") Bush stated the tubes story as a fact in his address to the United Nations on September 12, and on September 24 George Tenet declared that the tubes were intended for producing enriched uranium. That same day the British government made public a dossier—later revealed as largely bogus—saying the same thing. The effect of all this showed up in the polls: by the last two months of 2002, 59 percent of Americans were in favor of war, 90 percent believed Hussein was developing WMD, and 81 percent thought Iraq was a threat to the United States (polls by Gallup, the *Los Angeles Times*, and ABC/*Washington Post*, respectively). The campaign was working so well that Bush cited the aluminum tubes in his State of the Union address of 28 January 2003, and Colin Powell referred to it in his presentations of February 5 and March 7 at the United Nations (his staff had actually been briefed about the falseness of the claim prior to the latter date). On March 7 Mohammed ElBaradei, the IAEA director, presented the final results of expert analysis of the tubes, which the United States conceded behind closed doors as being accurate. Yet nine days later, Cheney assaulted the credibility of ElBaradei and the IAEA on *Meet the Press*.[9]

A second bit of "nuclear persuasion" was the claim that between 1999 and 2001 Iraq had tried to buy five hundred tons of uranium oxide ("yellow cake") from Niger. As with the tube story, this was published in the spurious British dossier, and it too made its way into Bush's 2003 State of the Union address. But significantly, the claim had been excised from a draft of Bush's 7 October 2002 Cincinnati speech on the direct intervention of George Tenet. Tenet got it struck on the very day of the speech on the grounds that intelligence didn't support it. And what was that intelligence? In point of fact, Cheney's office had received the documents on this matter a year earlier and handed them over to the CIA, which then asked Joseph Wilson, a former ambassador and prominent diplomat, to go to Niger and check the story out. Wilson discovered that the documents were obvious, amateurish forgeries. (One IAEA official said that some of the errors could be spotted by using Google.) He subsequently told the State Department and the CIA that the charge was bogus, and his report went directly to Cheney. Yet administration officials kept citing the Niger story, and someone put it into the State of the Union address, knowing, said Wilson some time later, that it "was a flat-out lie." In the days before and after that address, the claim was repeated by Rice, Powell, Rumsfeld, and Wolfowitz, and got inserted into two documents sent out by the White House. All of these high-ranking government personnel knew the claim was false, but it was just too hot a trump card for them not to play. In the wake of subsequent revelations, Tenet dutifully performed the role of fall guy, at least for a while; but on 22 July 2003 the CIA revealed that top White House officials knew that the CIA had seriously disputed the Niger story long before the president's address, and had fought to keep it out of the text. The administration's cover was blown.[10]

What was pretty clear in the aftermath of all this was that the decision to go to war drove the intelligence, not the reverse. The Bush administration, writes one columnist, disseminated information "that ranged from selective to preposterous"; but the crucial internal message was, If you value your job, you'd better get with the program (members of the Defense Intelligence Agency, or DIA, report being told this explicitly). Quite a few intelligence experts at the CIA and other agencies (most speaking on condition of anonymity) later told reporters that they had been pressed to distort evidence or tailor it to conform to the administration's views—in particular, to state that Iraq had WMD and terrorist links. As Richard Clarke discovered, if they wrote reports skeptical of these views, they were encouraged to "rethink" it and to "go back and find the right answer." Professionals in the Pentagon and elsewhere who had dissenting views—including a number of senior officers assigned to the Joint Chiefs of Staff—were excluded or marginalized. One former official with the National Security Council told reporters at *The New Republic* that the government's approach "was a classic case of . . . rumor-intelligence plugged into various speeches and accepted as gospel." Most administration officials, according to these reporters, "probably knew they were constructing castles out of sand."[11]

And yet serious dissent did exist. As Scott Ritter, a former chief U.N. weapons inspector, pointed out in February 2004, when so many pundits were wringing their hands about "How could we have gotten it wrong?," not *everyone* got it wrong. Rather, those who broke with the party line, so to speak, couldn't get a hearing. "On virtually every single important claim made by the Bush administration in its case for war," writes former senior White House adviser Sidney Blumenthal, "there was serious dissension." When Bruce Hardcastle, a senior officer at the DIA, told the Bush administration that Iraq was *not* engaged in a nuclear weapons program or the renewed production of chemical weapons, they not only fired him, they abolished his job altogether. Analyses submitted by the State Department's Bureau of Intelligence and Research (INR), which contradicted the claims about WMD or the Iraq–Al Qaeda link, were simply shunted aside. Greg Thielmann, who retired as INR chief in late 2002, later remarked, "Everyone in the intelligence community knew that the White House couldn't care less" about contradictory information. "I'm not sure," said Thielmann, "I can think of a worse act against the people in a democracy than a president distorting critical classified information."[12]

A good example of the latter activity was Colin Powell's presentation to the U.N. Security Council on 5 February 2003, in which he made the case for WMD and links to terrorists. It was a smooth performance, and certainly garnered enormous praise from the press, which, along with Powell, apparently forgot the remarks he made at a February 2001 press conference in Cairo, where he stated that containing Saddam had worked. "He has not developed any significant capability with respect to weapons of mass destruction," declared Powell. "He is unable to project conventional power against his neighbors." As for the U.N. speech, while the evidence appeared to be overwhelming, listeners had to take Powell's word for it that the Iraqi activities depicted on the tapes he was showing were indeed illicit. One saw trucks moving around, for example, but that hardly meant that warheads were being transported. Powell praised the British dossier of September 2002, which had large sections lifted from magazines and academic journals (a lot of it was obsolete data). Hans Blix, the chief U.N. weapons inspector, easily cast doubt on much of Powell's evidence. The talk proved to be based on hyped and incomplete intelligence; it was full of holes, rehashing the aluminum tubes story and presenting very tenuous evidence for Iraq–Al Qaeda ties. As confident as Powell appeared, in other words, the reality was something else. According to *U.S. News & World Report,* Powell junked much of what Cheney's office and the CIA had given him, tossing pages into the air and exclaiming, "This is bullshit." He met with his British counterpart, Jack Straw, at the Waldorf-Astoria Hotel just before his speech, expressing serious doubts about the WMD data; Straw, for his part, felt that much of the intelligence was just assumptions, nothing more. (Straw later denied that such a meeting took place, but that was a hard sell after diplomats leaked transcripts of it.) So the secretary of state, the good soldier who could always be counted on to do what was asked of him, publicly trumpeted arguments he suspected or knew were fictitious, gave the White House the talk that it had essentially wanted, and then in June, once the war was over, said that questions regarding the justification of the war were "outrageous." A stellar performance, all in all.[13]

What is outrageous, of course, is how the war came to pass, and the hoodwinking of the American people. One thing Powell complained about to Straw was the influence wielded by the Pentagon's Office of Special Plans (OSP), which Powell candidly dubbed a "Gestapo office," and which had been set up under the directorship of Undersecretary of Defense (for Policy) Douglas Feith, who was referred to by General Tommy Franks as "the fucking stupidest guy on the face of the earth." In October 2001, Wolfowitz, Rumsfeld, and Feith organized this special intelligence operation within the Pentagon to offer an alternative analysis to the CIA, which they didn't trust to come up with the "right" answers. The job of the OSP was thus to "reassess" CIA information—or as journalist James Bamford says, to tout trumped-up evidence against Saddam

Hussein, which the CIA was then pressured into endorsing. Basically, the neocons had developed their own intelligence-gathering methods, relying on sources outside of the State Department and the CIA, and principally on stories supplied to them by an exile group known as the Iraqi National Congress (INC)—information dismissed by the other agencies as unreliable. Thus a report issued in October 2004 by Senator Carl Levin of the Senate's Armed Services Committee shows that the administration's argument for an Iraq–Al Qaeda link was essentially fabricated by the OSP, and that Feith's claims had already been refuted by the CIA and DIA—as Cheney, Rumsfeld, and Wolfowitz knew all along. As for the INC, its track record, given its extremely biased agenda, was not very good. Defectors have a strong motive to tell interviewers what they want to hear, and the INC frequently manipulated information. Led by Ahmad Chalabi, who was being groomed to be the postwar Iraqi leader, the INC pushed a tainted case for war, exaggerating the threat posed by Iraq and painting rosy pictures of American G.I.'s being welcomed in the streets. They spun stories of Iraq–Al Qaeda links, provided the erroneous information on biological weapons factories that Powell used in his U.N. speech, and fed journalist Judith Miller a bogus tale of twenty "known" WMD sites in Iraq, which then appeared on the front page of the *New York Times* (20 December 2001). As it turns out, it looks as though, by feeding this sort of information through the INC, Iran may have manipulated the American government into war (in order to pave the way for a Shia-ruled Iraq). Apparently, Chalabi and his intelligence chief were double agents. But the neocons can hardly cry victim here: as a former CIA officer put it, Chalabi "was scamming the U.S. because the U.S. wanted to be scammed." Chalabi, said General Anthony Zinni, was the neocon crutch. These were no unwilling dupes.[14]

So the neocons got their war, after which—given the absence of any WMD—they began to play down the importance of these. In a May 2003 interview with *Vanity Fair*, Wolfowitz matter-of-factly stated: "The truth is that for reasons that have a lot to do with the U.S. government bureaucracy, we settled on the one issue that everyone could agree on, which was weapons of mass destruction as the core reason"—a convenient excuse, in short. On June 3, in a lecture Wolfowitz gave in Singapore, he said that the real goal of the war all along was oil. The next day, Cheney lunched with GOP senators and told them to block any investigation into the evidentiary basis for the war. None of this bothered the

American people, the great majority of whom were supportive of the war. A poll taken by the *Washington Post* just before the second anniversary of 9/11 revealed that 70 percent of them thought that Saddam Hussein had been directly involved in the attacks, that the 9/11 hijackers were Iraqis, and that Hussein had used chemical weapons against our troops. Another poll, taken in June 2003, indicated that 41 percent believed that WMD had been found (or they weren't sure), and 75 percent thought Bush showed strong leadership on Iraq. On 18 July 2003 Bush said the reason America went to war was that "Saddam refused to let the inspectors in," when in fact he did—they left for their own safety once Bush decided to attack the country. The statement created no stir whatsoever; it was barely noticed. Nor did Bush allow himself to be engaged at press conferences on the subject of whether he tricked the nation into war; instead, he just repeated several simplistic assertions over and over, in the tradition of Ronald Reagan, and most of the American public was perfectly fine with this.[15]

The role of the former Soviet Union in all this, as a kind of ghost at the banquet, is quite remarkable. I am talking not only of the Carter Doctrine and our policy vis-à-vis the Persian Gulf, or the CIA training of the mujahideen, which ultimately resulted in 9/11, but also about the mistaken framework in which the "war on terrorism" was conceived and executed. As James Mann shows in *Rise of the Vulcans*, Bush's war cabinet grew up steeped in Cold War ideology and never managed to get off that track. They never stopped fighting the Cold War, and this is why they could only see *state* enemies—"dictators" rather than terrorists. Both before and after 9/11, the neocons paid little attention to actual terrorism. So the USSR was long gone, but, writes Stephen Holmes in his review of Mann's book, "the psychological need to confront 'evil' states remained." And of course, the whole country got drawn into their *mishegas*.[16]

The other "contribution" of the USSR is perhaps more ominous. The campaign leading up to the war, write Stefan Halper and Jonathan Clarke, was a "great conjuring trick," a process known as the "discursive representation of reality." Columbia University's Kathleen Hall Jamieson describes this phenomenon as the creation of "frames," which is the development and dissemination of interpretations that are accepted by the press and public, and so "become the lenses of which they are unaware but nonetheless shape how we think about political affairs." Neocon "discourse" was very effective; Iraq was practically pulled out of a hat (in retrospect) as an immediate danger. The neocons linked their preexisting agenda to a separate event, 9/11, and thus created an entirely new reality. This co-opted government agencies in a pattern of deceit. "They manipulated the institutional power of their own positions," write Halper and Clarke, "to draw the American public into what can best be described as a synthetic neurosis that supported their template for regime change in the Middle East. . . . The case for war against Iraq was an argument of disconnected claims and images . . . many of which turned out to be false or uncorroborated." So the war was not only an extension of the image of the external world held in the minds of the neocons, but also an extension of the same as it had been created in the minds of the American people. These techniques of mass persuasion, conclude the authors, are the same as those practiced by the former Soviet Union.[17]

As for the war itself, from the viewpoint of the attackers it was a cakewalk (at least until it was officially over). The battle plan was called "shock and awe," the idea being that America would strike with such speed and overwhelming force (aerial and cruise missile bombardment) that the Iraqi citizenry would be psychologically demoralized, thereby willing to give up without a fight. Indeed, on the eve of battle, American newspapers were reporting that "the United States has assembled a force with more firepower than ever seen before in a single battle." There was something surreal, or "mental," about all of this: why would we need to assemble such a force, to go at it in this way, especially since the American government really didn't believe the war was about WMD or the evil nature of Saddam Hussein or any genuine threat to the United States? I recall, around this time, listening to an interview on the Diane Rehm show on National Public Radio with one of the military strategists close to the battle plan. The violence involved, as he described it, reminded me of Picasso's *Guernica*, or the firebombing of Dresden. As the man told Diane and the listening audience how the plan worked, his voice became increasingly excited. Innocent human beings, apparently, were not part of the equation . . . or maybe that *was* the point. This kind of sadism always has an odd sexual feel to it; I couldn't help thinking how the politics of empire had finally rotted the American soul. When a civilization finally hollows itself out, there is nothing much left for it to do except turn into a case study from a textbook by Wilhelm Reich, in which you get off on the cruelty you can visit on the powerless. Disturbingly, this is a lot of the psychology that hovered over the torture or slaughter in Vietnam, during the Gulf war, or at Abu Ghraib. And when a powerful nation can pick fights only with the small and the weak, it is because appearances to the contrary, it is weak itself.[18]

The war began on 19 March 2003 (Washington time) and "ended" about April 8. According to initial Iraqi estimates, civilian deaths numbered between 6100 and 7800. In fact, the damage we wreaked on that miserable country proved to be much worse. A study released by a research team at Johns Hopkins a year and a half later put the civilian death toll at 100,000, adding that more than half of the deaths caused by the occupation forces were women and children. Subsequent surveys by the United Nations indicated that 400,000 young children in Iraq were "wasting"—that is, suffering from acute malnutrition. As Dr. Richard Horton, the editor of the British medical journal *The Lancet* (which published the Johns Hopkins study), acerbically put it, "Democratic imperialism has led to more deaths, not fewer."[19]

The U.S. government, of course, repeatedly emphasized the "liberatory" aspect of the invasion: after all, Saddam Hussein was widely feared and hated, and there were a great many Iraqis who were quite happy to see him go. Thus much was made of the toppling of the statue of the Iraqi leader in Baghdad on April 9, in front of huge, cheering crowds, an event that seemed to say "It was worth it, after all." Like a great deal associated with this war, this was far more image than substance: it was an American soldier, not an Iraqi citizen, who pulled the statue down, and there *was* no crowd in the town square. U.S. newspapers did not reproduce the full image, but the picture available on the Internet showed three American tanks and a few dozen Iraqis gathered nearby, in a small section of the square. Close-up photos suggest that the active participants were members of the INC, who rode in on the back of the tanks. As in the case of Bush's postwar arrival on the aircraft carrier USS *Abraham Lincoln*, this was largely PR, a misleading form of symbolism—although it played extremely well back home.[20]

Talk about bringing "democracy" to Iraq was also PR; it also played well to a gullible American public, but the U.S. government's actions render the claims dubious. Thus when the Baghdad Shiite weekly *Al Hawza* began running anti-American articles, Paul Bremer, the temporary military governor of Iraq ("proconsul"), had American soldiers chain and padlock the doors of the newspaper's offices. Bremer also empowered an appointed electoral commission to "eliminate political parties or candidates" it disapproved of. Ayad Allawi, the interim prime minister chosen to act as our puppet after Ahmad Chalabi suddenly fell from grace, moved (in August 2004) to shut down the Baghdad offices of Al Jazeera when it refused to adjust its editorial policies to his liking. In addition, he armed himself with the power to declare martial law and reinstated the death penalty. Worst of all, this was a leader who had no popular mandate. Labeling the whole thing a charade, Scott Ritter makes the obvious point: "Allawi's government," he writes, "hand-picked by the United States from the ranks of anti-Saddam expatriates, lacks not only a constituency inside Iraq but also legitimacy in the eyes of many ordinary Iraqi citizens."[21] This is, at best, a Potemkin democracy.

One very significant event that took place during the invasion, but which failed to capture much attention in the United States, was the looting of the archaeological museums in Baghdad. This struck me as being highly symbolic, but having a powerful level of reality to it as well. Indeed, the Nigerian novelist Ben Okri, writing in *The Guardian* on 19 April 2003, felt that those of us in the West were now "at the epicenter of a shift in the history of the world." American forces moved in to protect the oil fields; the matter of ancient Mesopotamia, of Iraq's museums and libraries, was of no consequence to them. In fact, Marines defaced some of the ancient walls at the site of the Sumerian city of Ur (near modern-day An Nasiriyah), the famous Ur of the Chaldees excavated by Leonard Woolley in the 1920s and 1930s, and the legendary birthplace of Abraham. For the most part, in the days after the fall of the Iraqi government, the U.S. military just stood by while looters picked these institutions clean. In fact, the Pentagon was repeatedly warned of this possibility in advance of the war, writes *New York Times* columnist Frank Rich, but at the highest levels of the White House, the Pentagon, and Central Command, no one cared. From presidential press secretary Ari Fleischer to Donald Rumsfeld, they simply trivialized the whole thing. ("Stuff happens!" cried Rumsfeld, and made a joke out of it.) "By protecting Iraq's oil but not its cultural mother lode," writes Rich, "America echoes the values of no one more than Saddam. . . ." Thus U.S. armed forces allowed tablets containing bits of the Gilgamesh epic to be stolen, but somehow managed to secure the lavish homes of Hussein's elite, "where the cultural gems ranged from videos of old James Bond movies to the collected novels of Danielle Steele." All of this, writes Okri, represents "a signal absence of the true values of civilization."[22]

And this is really the point. After all, if your "values" are those of corporate consumerism, you don't really *have* a civilization. So why worry if manuscripts, books, and cuneiform tablets from Sumer and Babylon are stolen or burned? How many Americans, do you think, can define "cuneiform" or identify Mesopotamia? Someone like George W. Bush would probably be only too happy to bulldoze these museums and libraries and replace them with shopping malls—the "real freedom" referred to in the 2002 "National Security Strategy." Thus Okri writes, "The end of the world begins not with the barbarians at the gate, but with the barbarians at the highest levels of state."[23] True, but it takes barbarians in the streets cheering the barbarians at the highest levels of state to make a new Dark Age a reality. The American government didn't care about the destruction of our Western heritage because, like the American people, it no longer identifies with it, and couldn't care less about it. Future historians may record this shift as the real, symbolic significance of the 2003 Iraqi war, although obviously it has been building for decades.

The Costs

At some point after my last book, *The Twilight of American Culture*, was published, it was reviewed by a newspaper in San Francisco. The reviewer was led to reminisce about the Fourth of July celebrations of his childhood, as compared with the most recent one he attended in 2001. "In my childhood," he wrote, there was

> something stirring about the whole business, a sense that the country wasn't a giant corporation or a land of dunce-filled strip malls but a true and enduring revolution in self-government, an ongoing experiment in human freedom that . . . was worthy of respect and defense and even a kind of love. I was that little boy and am no longer, and the United States was that country and is no longer. And I wonder what country it has become.[24]

Alas, that America is long gone; we are never going to get it back.

When a civilization has reached a kind of critical mass and goes into its final phase, the only people who can rise to the top are typically those who will, in the name of "national greatness," actually promote that process of disintegration. We began this phase in earnest between 1971 and 1975, as George Modelski's "long cycles" theory states. Jimmy Carter was a temporary reaction against the causes of decline, but other than that we have been on a downhill course ever since. This decline can clearly be seen in a president who is little more than a fundamentalist marionette, mechanically uttering slogans and inanities, and dishonestly taking us into a foolish war while he gives huge tax breaks to the rich. Meanwhile, until recently, the majority of Americans approved of this war, and the majority still approve of this president and his administration. A great many journalists applaud him, often hailing his empty platitudes as "wisdom." What are we to make of a legislative body (the House of Representatives) whose members get so petulant over the fact that France will not endorse America's illegal neocolonial venture, that it orders its food services to change its menu listing from "French fries" to "freedom fries"? Could anything be more childish? When I first glanced at a newspaper article on this, I thought it was referring to something that was going on in a high school cafeteria in the Midwest, until I looked more closely and discovered it was happening on Capitol Hill. A headline in the *Washington Post* subsequently got it right: "Liberté, Egalité . . . Stupidité." But the incident goes much deeper than mere stupidity, for it is symbolic of an emptiness at the core, an America that has effectively stopped being a republic and whose official representatives cannot tolerate any other opinions than their own.[25]

There even seems to be an inability to grasp that there *can* be more than one opinion on a subject, when it comes to American foreign policy. Thus on 17 May 2003 Chris Hedges, a Pulitzer Prize–winning *New York Times* reporter, was booed off the stage by students at Rockford College in Illinois when he tried to criticize the war in his commencement address. The college president, Paul Pribbenow, much to his credit, tried to explain to the students that this was freedom of speech, and that the job of a college education was to expose them to different points of view. Apparently, Rockford had failed these graduating seniors, since they literally couldn't understand what Pribbenow was talking about, and resorted to screaming "God Bless America." Remarkable, how much things have changed since Vietnam.[26]

The United States has yet to figure out the damage it has done to itself as a result of the damage it has done to the Middle East over the last fifty-plus years. Only a very small minority in this country understand, or want to understand, the reciprocal relationship between inner and outer, core and periphery. "The dirt done at home," mused Graylan Hagler, the pastor of Plymouth Congregational Church in Washington, D.C., a few weeks after September 11, "is reflective of the dirt done abroad."[27] This brings to mind Arnold Toynbee's comment that a civilization doesn't die from being invaded from the outside, but rather commits suicide. On the opening day of the invasion of Iraq, an advertisement placed in the *New York Times* by an online public interest journal, TomPaine.com, captured these sentiments quite exactly. It shows a sketch of Osama bin Laden in the style of the old Uncle Sam army recruitment poster, saying: "I Want YOU . . . to Invade Iraq." It continues, "Go ahead. . . . Your bombs will send me a new generation of recruits and fuel their hatred and desire for revenge. So go ahead. Squander your wealth on war and occupation— America will be weaker for it. Divide your people, divide the world, isolate yourselves! Perfect!" The truth is that we gave bin Laden exactly what he wanted: America's getting stuck in a quagmire in Iraq was his wildest dream, the best jihadist recruitment tool he could ever hope for, and we delivered it in spades. The damage of September 11 is nothing compared to the damage we did and are currently doing to ourselves as a result of our reaction to that event. In a bizarre kind of way, Rumsfeld, Perle, Abrams, Bush, Cheney, Wolfowitz, Rice, Feith, and their ilk are bin Laden's comrades in arms.

It is important, then, to get a clear understanding of the costs we engendered as a result of intensifying our imperial agenda rather than pulling back from it. There are three categories here: moral or spiritual corruption, including the erosion of civil liberties; domestic costs, which are social, economic, and cultural; and military costs, the weaknesses we have now created in terms of our ability to protect ourselves.

As far as our moral or spiritual life goes, the key factor is the return to a system of military protectorates and de facto colonialism. It rots the presidency, the government, and the body politic. John Quincy Adams effectively predicted such ventures would backfire as far back as 1821. Let it be said, he declared, that "America goes not abroad, in search of monsters to destroy." For if she were to do so, he went on, "the fundamental maxims of her policy would insensibly change from liberty to force. . . . She would be no longer the ruler of her own spirit." Well, we are very clearly no longer the ruler of our own spirit; Jimmy Carter's 1979 assertion of the existence of a general "malaise" pervading the nation is by now an enormous understatement.

There are other factors contributing to this malaise. American companies were lining up for government contracts in Iraq even before the war ended. Almost all Arab companies were excluded, of course, and—amazingly enough—so were most British ones. Bids were invited for billions of dollars in work, including reconstruction of roads, water systems, seaports and airports, government buildings, schools, irrigation systems, and public health facilities—everything we destroyed during the two wars we visited upon the country and the decade of sanctions in between. These bids, furthermore, were invited only from companies that had strong political links to the Republican party, such as Halliburton and its subsidiary, Kellogg Brown & Root (Cheney was Halliburton's CEO from 1995 to 2000); the Bechtel Group (a number of its senior executives were Reagan appointees); and the Fluor Corporation (which has ties to the Pentagon and the intelligence community). By the end of 2003 the main beneficiaries of an $8 billion bonanza in government contracts for rebuilding Iraq went to major Republican campaign donors; and of the $18.4 billion voted by Congress for this purpose, only 2 percent got spent on it. By late 2004, nothing had been spent on construction, health care, sanitation, and water projects; the bulk of what was spent went for administration. A special development fund was set up, but it turned out that occupation authorities used Iraq's own money (nearly $20 billion in oil revenues) for this purpose. By all appearances, we invaded Iraq for the sake of American business. As one critic put it, the story of the war is "kick their ass and take their gas." Indeed, it would be hard to find a clearer (or more cynical) example of Dwight Eisenhower's military-industrial complex.[28]

These contracts, in fact, look like what they are: payoffs to politically favored businessmen, and they reinforce the impression that the war was waged for venal purposes. Bechtel, for example, is now in line for the long-term reconstruction of Iraq, which could cost $100 billion or more. While U.S. taxpayers foot the bill for the war, Bechtel and the other administration favorites reap huge profits. So American soldiers fight and die in Iraq, many thousands of Iraqis are killed, and the classic "merchants of death" clean up. Like the rest of the Bush administration, Paul Bremer regarded the war as a good business opportunity, and wasted no time rolling out the red carpet for U.S. multinationals. Meanwhile, Iraq's first Burger King set up shop at the Baghdad airport; Bremer allowed duty-free goods and packaged food to flood across the border, leading to large numbers of local bankruptcies; and the occupation authorities went ahead with the privatization of dozens of state-owned companies, pre-empting the decision of any elected Iraqi government.

ANOTHER AREA of corruption is the role of the media during this war, which, as in the case of the Gulf war, was largely that of a cheering section. As veteran journalist and former CNN and ABC producer Danny Schechter notes, U.S. news coverage "sold the war even as it claimed to be just reporting it." Indeed, he says, the war spectacle that was released was the result of a virtual merger between the Pentagon and the media. Thus two detailed 2004 studies, which examine news articles and editorials that were published in America's elite press in the months leading up to the invasion of Iraq, "paint a disconcerting portrait of a timid, credulous press corps that, when confronted by an administration intent on war, sank to new depths of obsequiousness and docility." True, the *New York Times* op-ed page ran a number of essays critical of the war, but the front page was largely war propaganda—as the newspaper grudgingly and belatedly admitted (26 May 2004) in a lukewarm apology to its readers (on page 10). As the *Washington Post* noted on the same day, few news organizations reported on WMD claims as aggressively as did the *New York Times*. It used Iraqi defectors and exiles as its sources, without bothering to get their agenda-driven (mis)information independently verified, and it gave "prominent display" to "dire claims about Iraq," while it buried follow-up articles that threw these claims into question. Judith Miller was particularly responsible for this brand of journalism, with stories such as the one of 8 September 2002 ("U.S. Says Hussein Intensified Quest for A-Bomb Parts," co-authored with Michael Gordon), which reported that Iraq had tried to import aluminum tubes in order to produce enriched uranium and, eventually, an atomic weapon. The tubes, as we saw, were a key prop in the administration's case for war, and the *Times* played a crucial role in legitimizing this bogus claim. When Miller was subsequently asked why her stories didn't include the views of skeptical WMD experts, she replied: "My job isn't to assess the government's information. . . . My job is to tell readers of the *New York Times* what the government thought of Iraq's arsenal." But as playwright Wallace Shawn put it, the *Times* editors are not dummies; they had to know that the discussion of WMD was effectively "the public relations branch of preparing for war." The editors and reporters, he goes on, seem to have a need to believe that their government, while sometimes wrong, of course, is not utterly insane, and must at least be trusted to raise the right questions. These writers just can't bear the thought of being completely alienated from the center of their society, their own government. Thus, although they themselves would have considered a "pre-emptive" invasion of Iraq two years ago to be absurd and crazy, they now take the idea seriously and weigh its merits respectfully and worry gravely about the danger posed by Iraq, even though Iraq is in no way more dangerous than it was two years ago, and in every possible way it is less dangerous.

The dispassionate tone of the "debate" about Iraq, said Shawn, in the newspapers as well as on every television screen, "seems psychotically remote from the reality of what will happen if war actually occurs." As for the *Washington Post*, which was rabidly pro-war, between August 2002 and 19 March 2003 it ran more than 140 front-page stories that focused heavily on administration rhetoric against Iraq. According to Karen DeYoung, a former assistant managing editor, "We are inevitably the mouthpiece for whatever administration is in power."[29] *Inevitably?* What's wrong with this picture?

You get a public voice by telling power what it wants to hear. By putting out an anti-Arab position—for instance, "these people only respect force"—people such as Middle East scholar Fouad Ajami, Bernard Lewis, and Thomas Friedman rise to positions of significant public influence and visibility. It is not easy to locate alternative voices in this country; the notion of "the liberal media," as Eric Alterman has written, is pretty much a joke. What to think of NBC, which fired Phil Donahue (in addition to veteran war reporter Peter Arnett), the only TV network host opposed to the war? Or CNN, which attacked Scott Ritter, who had headed the U.N. weapons inspections from 1991 to 1998, as "an apologist for and defender of Saddam Hussein," because he claimed that the case for Hussein being "a threat to the U.S. worthy of war" had yet to be made? (Kyra Phillips practically called him a traitor during their interview, and Paula Zahn told CNN viewers that he had "drunk Saddam Hussein's Kool-Aid.") And then, much of the news coverage of the war came via media owned by Rupert Murdoch, who owns not only the Fox News Channel, but Twentieth Century–Fox film studios, the *Times* of London, the *Weekly Standard*, the *New York Post*, and a number of other newspapers. The airwaves were saturated with slogans, to the point, write Stefan Halper and Jonathan Clarke, that the media created a kind of "echo chamber," in which the government's rationale for war was repeated over and over again, until they "disabled a fundamental aspect of American governance." As for the American press corps, reporters themselves admit that if they write anything too negative, they'll be kicked out of the White House press pool, lose access to the centers of power, and thus potentially damage their careers. Thus they felt obliged or pressured to cooperate with Bush Jr.'s "scripted" press conference of 6 March 2003, in which they politely submitted to pre-approved questions and even pretended to be spontaneous. These questions were frequently on the order of asking Bush how his faith was guiding him (the president nearly cried, and replied that he "prayed daily that war can be averted"). At one point the president slipped, actually indicated that the questioning was scripted. Yet newspaper accounts the following day didn't even mention it (except for one mild reference in the *Washington Post*). The obsequiousness of all this is terrifying, because what, exactly, *is* the role of the press in a democracy? Surely not ass kissing as we go off to an unjustified war. Surely not kowtowing to transparent government propaganda. If reporters can't ask difficult or embarrassing questions, if they cannot write anything too negative, then they no longer perform anything akin to a real function anymore—right?[30]

There is something really shameful about all this, because as journalist Nicholas von Hoffman notes, these folks are little more than "war whores." During both the Gulf war and the Sequel, he says, the "performing seals" of TV news brought to the coverage of these events "a certain lubricious quality . . . as they strained to infect viewers . . . with the upside of death and disfigurement." What we saw in their glistening eyes and happy agitated voices, he says, was an erotic energy invested in "their talk of freedom, courage and victory" over a two-bit opponent; and in the aftermath, they outdid themselves in their praise of the Pentagon, while never bothering to give their viewers any real news, the story of what was actually going on.[31]

A THIRD instance of corruption—the American practice of torture—shows, perhaps more than anything, how different a place the United States has become. Abu Ghraib, of course, is the most notorious torture story to come out of the invasion of Iraq, but our abuse of human rights is hardly limited to one Iraqi prison. The irony of Abu Ghraib, however, was that the place had been used for the similar purposes by Saddam Hussein. The photographs that were turned up by Seymour Hersh's investigation form a vivid portrait of part of the American imperial psyche: sadism, depravity, and utter contempt for Third World peoples. In this regard, it is perhaps illuminating that it was Hersh who in 1969 broke the story of the massacre at My Lai, and that some of the techniques used in Iraq can be found in a 1963 CIA torture manual drawn up for Vietnam. For example, the famous picture of a hooded man standing on a box, with electrical wires attached to various parts of his body ("the Statue of Liberty," as the Iraqis sardonically called it; the man, Satar Jabar, was nothing more than an accused car thief), is a technique known to interrogation veterans as "the Vietnam." And the same sadistic joy that prevailed in Southeast Asia now obtains among U.S. forces in the Middle East. We see (or now know about) men with wires attached to their genitals; being threatened by attack dogs (which were subsequently unleashed); piled together in a "pyramid" while naked and hooded; being forced to masturbate in front of female soldiers, or be sexually fondled by them; sodomized by a chemical light; and so on—and all the while, American soldiers posing for the camera, grinning, laughing, giving a thumbs-up sign (for example, over a battered corpse), and in general, expressing unabashed glee. Some of the soldiers subsequently admitted that their purpose in much of this had been "entertainment"; they found it hysterically funny. All of this, it turns out, was but the tip of the iceberg; indeed, not just Seymour Hersh, but even Donald Rumsfeld, indicated that the full range of pictures and videos was much worse, and much more extensive, than the American public got to see. (I myself spoke with the wife of a man stationed in Iraq and working for military intelligence, who had told her that the practice of sexual humiliation was extremely widespread and involved a fair amount of bestiality.)[32]

In terms of impact on the Arab world, it is hard to imagine what could be worse. Even the Israelis don't treat the Palestinians this way. For Muslims, there isn't anything more degrading and shameful than public nudity and sexual humiliation. Yet here we are, gleefully brutalizing prisoners in precisely the way Muslims find most repulsive. The photos, writes one *Washington Post* reporter, "capture exactly the quality and feel of the casual sexual decadence that so much of the world deplores in us." Indeed, sexual torture as "entertainment" confirms the worst beliefs that Muslims have about the United States: depravity, a total lack of moral values. Thus the editor of the London-based *Al Quds al-Arabi* wrote, in the wake of the Abu Ghraib revelations, that Arabs see this behavior as representative of the United States, and do not accept our government's line that this is the work of "a few bad apples." Rather, he writes, "it is the result of an official American culture that deliberately insults and humiliates Muslims."[33]

It is hard to refute the charge that the whole thing was systemic, and designed in particular for a Muslim population. After all, how are a bunch of kids from rural West Virginia or wherever going to know what is particularly humiliating to Arabs, about whom they know literally nothing? Is it really likely they would do all this on their own initiative? As commentator Mark Shields argued on *The NewsHour with Jim Lehrer* (7 May 2004), this was no accident. It was, he asserted, choreographed at the highest levels; privates and corporals don't think in these terms. The dominant force inside Abu Ghraib, Seymour Hersh found out, consisted of military intelligence teams, including CIA officers and interrogation specialists from private defense contractors; and it was this group that—at least at the immediate level—set the agenda. The report on the abuses drawn up by Major General Antonio M. Taguba, writes Hersh, "amounts to an unsparing study of collective wrongdoing and the failure of Army leadership at the highest levels." The Red Cross similarly weighed in on the issue, reporting a wide, systemic pattern of abuse and torture in U.S.-run Iraqi prisons, and rejecting completely the government's claim that Abu Ghraib was an aberration.

Hersh subsequently found out that the "roots of the Abu Ghraib prison scandal lie not in the criminal inclinations of a few reservists but in a decision, approved last year by Secretary of Defense Donald Rumsfeld, to expand a highly secret operation, which had been focussed on the hunt for Al Qaeda, to the interrogation of prisoners in Iraq." This Pentagon operation, which was known as "Copper Green" (among several other code words), encouraged physical coercion and sexual humiliation of Iraqi prisoners. It was a transfer of techniques that were already being used at the interrogation center at Guantánamo Bay in Cuba, to Baghdad, with a much expanded scope. The idea of employing sexual humiliation came in part from Raphael Patai's rather dubious analysis of Arab culture and psyche, *The Arab Mind*, described as "the bible of the neocons on Arab behavior," which contains a full chapter on Arabs and sex. So while the abuses of Abu Ghraib were being explained as a contradiction or exception to the American occupation, the truth was that they were a logical extension of it. A Red Cross investigation also revealed that doctors working for the U.S. military there, as well as at Guantánamo, collaborated in the interrogation and abuse of detainees.[34]

As it turns out, the process by which Abu Ghraib became possible involved a fundamental subversion not only of values but also of law. The matter of legal expediency is no small matter: if you have a government of men, and not laws, you are going to get into serious trouble. As Karen Greenberg and Joshua Dratel document in *The Torture Papers*, a series of dubious legal memos were used to pave the way for interrogation practices forbidden by international law, in order to evade legal punishment for employing them. These memos from the Defense and Justice Departments and the White House, says Anthony Lewis, "read like the advice of a mob lawyer to a mafia don on how to . . . stay out of prison." For example, White House Counsel Alberto Gonzales (since promoted to Attorney General for his efforts in this direction) wrote that the war on terror "renders obsolete Geneva's strict limitations on questioning of prisoners and renders quaint some of its provisions." Similarly, a report on interrogation methods prepared for Rumsfeld says that the president has unlimited authority in this regard and provides legal justifications for disregarding the laws governing the use of torture. To implement this, the Justice Department conveniently narrowed the definition of torture in an infamous memo of 1 August 2002, signed by Assistant Attorney General Jay Bybee (who has since been made a federal appeals court judge for *his* valuable contribution to American justice). Written for the CIA and addressed to Gonzales, the memo states that for interrogation to qualify as torture, it "must be equivalent in intensity to the pain accompanying serious physical injury, such as organ failure, impairment of bodily function, or even death." It adds that the president can authorize such techniques without violating international or federal law. In short, it's acceptable to torture prisoners to death, if you claim it was done in the interests of national security.[35]

It doesn't take long for the disregard of the law and of basic human rights to migrate from the foreign arena to the domestic one. In the case of post-9/11 developments, the two went hand in hand. In his book on Abu Ghraib, Hersh asks how it was possible for eight or nine individuals to get such extensive control over the government, to the point that what distinguishes us as a democracy is severely attenuated. A good question.

One answer is that democracy is a lot more fragile than we think. For example, on 19 July 2004 *Newsweek* broke the story that the White House and the Justice Department had, for several months, been discussing the possibility of postponing the November 2 presidential election, which would have been a first in American history, if it had come to pass. If power at all costs is the game, then democratic elections, protection against torture, civil liberties—all of the things we used to take for granted—become expendable, and practically overnight. As America morphed from a republic into an empire, these sorts of changes began to occur quite naturally; the unthinkable became perfectly thinkable, after all. Nor have most Americans, it must be said, been overly concerned about this new direction in which we are moving. Indeed, a large percentage of them are probably not even aware of it.[36]

Once again, we see that the membrane between foreign and domestic policy is quite osmotic. The use of torture, write the editors of the *Washington Post*, carries enormous dangers for us, because our willingness to engage in it corrodes democratic values. The administration can talk "democracy" all it wants, but if you are practicing torture, it becomes unclear in what sense you are still a democracy. The whole thing is a slippery slope. If you entertain the moral argument that if you have a captive who knows of an imminent attack that will cost thousands of lives, torture is justified, the question then arises as to where the cutoff point is. Why stop with the captive, after all? Why not his family, or his friends? It was in precisely this way that the practice of torture rapidly spread through the French security apparatus in Algeria. In Israel, it went from rare exception to nearly standard practice, in a misguided effort to prevent civilian acts of terrorism. And once it becomes common, it undermines a society's democratic norms, whereby a nation is defending what it stands for by subverting its own values in order to defend them.[37]

Furthermore, if torture is justified in the defense of our way of life, then why get exercised over the curbing of civil liberties, which is obviously a much milder issue in comparison . . . at least for the time being. And that development can't be laid at the door of John Ashcroft and the Bush administration alone. The curbing of civil liberties associated with the prevention of terrorism actually got under way with Janet Reno in 1996, when the government passed the Effective Death Penalty and Anti-terrorism Act, authorizing the Justice Department to prosecute individuals based on their political beliefs and associations, loosen the carefully crafted rules governing federal wiretaps, criminalize fund-raising for lawful activities associated with unpopular causes, jail permanent residents merely for their affiliations or political activity, even when lawful, with no judicial review, and use secret evidence (that only the judge can see) in trials and detention hearings (the burden of proof being placed on the accused).[38]

Five and a half years later, we have the USA Patriot Act, which takes all of this to the next level. It allows the government to conduct secret searches and the FBI to obtain access to personal and financial records of individuals without a court order or without even establishing probable cause of crime. The government can also jail American citizens indefinitely, without a trial, without being charged, or without being able to confront witnesses against them. Representing, says one reporter for the *Seattle Times*, "the largest expansion of police powers in decades," the Patriot Act enables the FBI, with very few judicial obstacles, to monitor phones and computers and investigate library borrowing records. The FBI can force anyone to turn over records on customers or clients and it can gag the recipient of a search order from disclosing the search. It can also conduct "sneak and peek" searches on individuals (enter your home and copy the contents of your hard drive, for example, or plant a "bug" in your living room) without notifying the subjects until long after the search has been executed. It can wiretap without showing probable cause or reasonable suspicion of criminal activity, and the definition of "terrorism" is so broad that it can be used to target environmentalists or any other domestic political protesters whom the government happens not to like. Indeed, by September 2003 it was revealed that the powers of the Patriot Act were being used quite widely, to include nonterrorist cases and garden-variety crimes.[39]

All of this was an unfortunate consequence of September 11, but the constant waging of a "war on terrorism" makes it easier for legislation like this to get enacted. Thus in 2002 John Ashcroft issued new guidelines that increased the freedom of government agents to spy on individuals and organizations, and for a while the Bush administration was trying to put through a system called TIPS (Terrorism Information and Prevention System), whereby people would be encouraged to spy on one another—the staple of totalitarian regimes. Another program being entertained in one form or another is TIA (Terrorist Information Awareness, originally called Total Information Awareness), which provides for massive surveillance of citizens, merging large numbers of data banks and setting up extremely sophisticated technological recognition systems, including eye (the iris) and gait (style of walking), which can be measured by a radar-based device (the Pentagon has enlisted the Georgia Institute of Technology and Carnegie Mellon University in this effort). The new technologies are quite creepy, going "beyond even the wildest dreams of Orwell's Big Brother," as one expert in the field has remarked. Their use will take on a life of its own, setting the stage for an information security apparatus that will alter our democracy forever. It also involves video surveying with the global positioning system, now extended from foreign spying to the domestic arena. It is not for nothing that a survey found that 31 percent of corporate chief security officers believe that the United States was in jeopardy of becoming a police state, and that former House majority leader Dick Armey called the Justice Department "out of control" and "the most dangerous agency of [the] government."[40]

What has happened to our democracy in the name of defending it—the waging of war partly for venal, corporate purposes; the self-emasculation of the press; the approval of torture at the highest levels of government, and subsequent practice of it; and the dramatic erosion of our civil liberties—reminds me of a remarkably prescient episode of the popular comic strip *Blondie*, published on 28 October 2001. The cartoon shows Dagwood Bumstead and his neighbor, Herb Woodley, struggling to put up a large American flag and flagpole in front of Dagwood's house. It's so unwieldy that the pole keeps smashing into the house. They finally manage to get the pole and flag up, and everybody in the neighborhood is standing around, hands on hearts in Pledge of Allegiance posture, saying what a beautiful sight it is. Behind them is the house—windows broken, door smashed in, roof and gutters damaged. The caption reads "United we stand."

The second major category of costs, after that of the moral and spiritual, involves the domestic ones—social, economic, and cultural. Given the nature of the Bush Jr. administration, some of this was underway before September 11, of course; the war on terror provided an excuse to accelerate the process. To summarize just a part of the damage: during the first three years of Bush's tenure, nearly 3 million jobs were lost in the private sector; 1.3 million more Americans fell below the poverty line; 2.3 million more were without health insurance; long-term unemployment just about doubled; overall economic growth amounted to 1 percent, the lowest for any administration in fifty years; the stock market lost $6.65 trillion in value; a projected budget surplus of $5.6 trillion became a deficit of $400 billion; $2 trillion got transferred from Social Security taxes to the non–Social Security budget; and forty-five states were left struggling with severe budget problems. A good part of this was due to the sharp increase in military spending, the lion's share of which is for advanced weaponry that has nothing to do with fighting terrorism. In addition, monthly operations in Iraq are costing taxpayers $3.9 billion, and the total tab is estimated to reach a possible $600 billion. (Adjusted for inflation, the monthly bill for U.S. military missions in Iraq and Afghanistan, as of September 2003, was almost that of the monthly expenditure for the war in Vietnam—$5.15 billion.) We are now spending almost as much on "defense" as the rest of the world combined, which has resulted in a freeze on money for domestic programs, eliminating or severely reducing vocational and after-school services, rural development, family literacy and poverty programs (including school lunch subsidies), public housing, and community service grants to dispossessed neighborhoods. Across the nation fire stations, zoos, and hospitals have been shut down, teachers, police, and social workers fired. Since federal tax cuts under Bush led to a $10 billion drop in state revenues, the cumulative shortfall (as of May 2003) for forty-one states was in excess of $78 billion, and we can only expect the trend to get worse. Funding for the arts was hit particularly hard, with heavy reduction in arts spending or outright elimination of state arts budgets in at least twelve states. Symphony orchestras across the nation were unable to pay their musicians; some simply ceased operations altogether. Meanwhile, a Treasury Department study of 2002 revealed that the U.S. faces a future of chronic budget deficits totaling at least $44 trillion (this report got shelved and Treasury Secretary Paul O'Neill got fired). The echo of the Roman pattern is obvious. As Cicero famously put it, "The sinews of war are infinite money." Who has infinite money?[41]

As for the third category of costs, the military weaknesses that have resulted from the mishandling of the war on terror, these include a willful neglect of the actual terrorist threat and the pursuit of self-destructive policies that will guarantee Islamic backlash and the strengthening of Al Qaeda worldwide. As of this writing, half the army's combat strength is tied down in Iraq, a key factor in our imperial overstretch. Administration policy also involved a maddening lack of interest in homeland security. The spending that does exist focuses on parts of the country that need it the least—the "red states" of the interior, which voted for Bush. Thus while the most natural targets lie in or near large metropolitan areas, the government spends seven times as much protecting each resident of Wyoming as it does each resident of New York. As for Washington itself, much of the $324 million allocated to the capital was, two years after the 9/11 attack, left unspent, or spent on things such as leather jackets for the D.C. police force or a custom-made boat for a small volunteer fire department in Virginia. In addition, the Bush administration has repeatedly blocked proposals to enhance security at obvious potential domestic targets, such as ports and nuclear power plants. Rand Beers, a top White House counterterrorism adviser who finally resigned in March 2003, asserted that the homeland security policy was only rhetorical, and that the administration was making things less, not more, secure. A study undertaken in 2002 by former senators Warren Rudman and Gary Hart concluded that the government was not taking the necessary steps to protect the country from another attack, which they (along with many individuals in the intelligence community) believe is certain to occur. Rudman and Hart also produced a 2003 report for the Council on Foreign Relations, in which they note that homeland security remains "drastically underfunded" and that the country is "dangerously unprepared" to cope with another catastrophic attack. Meanwhile, although defense spending is going through the roof, most of it, as noted above, is for advanced weaponry that has no relevance to protection against terrorism. Looked at practically, writes Stephen Shalom of William Paterson University, the government's war on terror "is a fraud. It has only increased the dangers of terrorism abroad without protecting us from terrorism at home." In a word: when sarin gas gets released in the D.C. metro, or the Sears Tower in Chicago is blown away, or botulism toxin gets poured on the floor of the American Museum of Natural History in New York, whose fault will it be, do you think?[42]

Another reason for the neglect of the terrorist threat may well be our long-standing and perverse relationship with Saudi Arabia, a repressive, fundamentalist regime whose population is virulently anti-American. (If we are opposed to radical Islam, we should be going after the House of Saud, not just Osama bin Laden.) Fifteen out of the nineteen September 11 hijackers were Saudi nationals, yet the Bush administration chose to go after Iraq. The spread of Wahhabism (a purist and reactionary form of Islam) since the 1970s is in part a by-product of a U.S.-Saudi alliance that was historically based on anticommunism and oil, and we have propped up that regime so it would serve our ideological and economic interests. This apparently incestuous relationship between the United States and Saudi Arabia is the subject of former CIA officer Robert Baer's *Sleeping with the Devil* and Craig Unger's *House of Bush, House of Saud* (which formed the basis of much of Michael Moore's film *Fahrenheit 9/11*). A good deal of the evidence for links between the two governments, and between the Saudi royal family and the Bush dynasty, is circumstantial, and it isn't necessary to repeat it here. But the reader should be aware that the amount of this evidence is so large, and the economic relationship between the two countries (based on arms and oil) so dense, that it would be perhaps a bit naïve to conclude that that relationship did not play some role in our lack of interest in Saudi Arabia as a possible source of the terrorist threat. There was, in short, a strong motivation for the Bush administration to leave Saudi Arabia alone, and to go after Iraq instead.[43]

As for an inevitable backlash, we have already seen this in worldwide Islamic revulsion toward the United States and a resultant jihadist recruitment for Iraq, which fuels the continuing insurgency there. In effect, we took a country that was not a terrorist threat and turned it into one. Even without the travesty of Abu Ghraib, severe blowback against the United States over the next few decades is virtually assured. With the outbreak of the war, the killing of civilians, and pictures of crushed babies and armless children being broadcast by Al Jazeera around the world, Arab newspapers everywhere expressed their outrage at America. The feeling was that the United States might actually be trying to exterminate Arabs, that America was the enemy, and that terrorist attacks on it would therefore be justified. American troops, the newspapers reported, were callous killers. The general belief was that the United States was evil and that it wanted to "devour the Muslim world." One senior U.N. official, in the wake of the 19 August 2003 bombing of U.N. headquarters in Baghdad, told *New York Times* columnist Bob Herbert: "This is a dream for the jihad. . . . The American occupation is now the focal point, drawing people from all over Islam into an eye-to-eye confrontation with the hated Americans." In short, if we didn't have a "clash of civilizations" before the Iraqi war, we certainly do now.[44]

The Choices

What would it take for us to start doing something different? Two days after 9/11, Chalmers Johnson remarked in an interview, "I know it sounds cruel to say, but the people of New York were collateral damage of American foreign policy." Iraq was part of our Middle Eastern "shadow," left over from 1991; September 11 was the delayed collateral damage that ensued—the shadow made manifest. Instead of figuring this out, the U.S. government chose to repeat the cycle (after a short, and apparently botched pursuit of Osama bin Laden) with even greater intensity, completing the process whereby the Cold War was replaced by the Terror War. And terror, as Patrick Buchanan rightly remarks, is the price of empire; the two go hand in hand.[45]

On 6 December 2004 *The New Yorker* ran a magazine cover that I found extremely haunting. The artwork, "In the Shadows," is by Carter Goodrich. The picture is of a street scene, perhaps in midtown Manhattan, with Americans, festively dressed, doing their Christmas shopping. And there, in the background—in the shadows—dressed like Santa and ringing a Salvation Army bell, is Osama bin Laden, a watchful and sober expression on his face. The message is very clear: here, in the midst of luxury—luxury enjoyed at the expense of Third World poverty and misery—is America's guilty conscience. For whom does the bell toll, then? For us; but we don't seem to be able to hear it.

How long before Al Qaeda detonates a nuclear device in a major American city? Something like that is coming, for Osama bin Laden is no fool: he doesn't expect the American people to pay any attention to anything he says. Rather, the purpose of his public statements is to win sympathy from the Arab world for such an attack, having said, in effect: "I warned them again and again, but they just wouldn't listen." Graham Allison of Harvard University's Belfer Center for Science and International Affairs, the author of *Nuclear Terrorism*, points out that it is not all that difficult for a terrorist group to manufacture a nuclear bomb if it can acquire the requisite amount of weapons-grade uranium-235. Reflecting on the possibility of this happening, a friend of mine wrote: "We can change our policies now toward a legitimized form of the global rule of law, or after one or more cities are destroyed and/or our economy goes totally bankrupt." I responded, "I have no doubt as to what our choice is going to be."[46]

Oddly enough, I believe the culture already understands this on an intuitive level; these sorts of predictions or insights frequently surface in a creative context (as on *The New Yorker* cover). In an episode of the TV series *Jack and Bobby*, which aired in December 2004 (this is a narrative that partly projects a future scenario of America in the 2040s, when we are no longer the world's leading power), a politician looks back on the events of 12 September 2041 and relates how an Islamic fundamentalist group drove a truck into midtown Chicago and detonated a nuclear warhead. The only thing dubious about this scenario, I'm guessing, is that it probably won't take thirty-plus years for such an event to occur. By failing to grasp the meaning of 9/11—one dials 911 in America, of course, in cases of emergency—we managed to convince ourselves that what was in fact profound structural weakness was instead the apex of American power. This is a tragic confusion ("denial" would be more accurate), and it will cost us dearly. "Rome," writes Harvard University's Joseph Nye, "succumbed not to the rise of a new empire, but to internal decay and the death of a thousand cuts from various barbarian groups." If the meaning of 9/11 was a wake-up call, the lesson of 9/11 is that we learned nothing at all.[47]

And beneath this willful ignorance is the deeper layer I mentioned earlier: the Void. It is this that we fear, above all else. Just a century ago the Greek poet Constantine Cavafy wrote a poem called "Waiting for the Barbarians," in which he describes the Romans, assembled in the Forum, waiting for the barbarians to show up at the gates. They wait and wait, but the barbarians fail to come. Cavafy concludes:

Why this sudden bewilderment, this confusion?
(How serious people's faces have become.)
Why are the streets and squares emptying so rapidly,
everyone going home lost in thought?

Because night has fallen and the barbarians haven't come.
And some of our men just in from the border say
there are no barbarians any longer.

Now what's going to happen to us without barbarians?
They were, those people, a kind of solution.[48]

Putting the enemy "out there" is indeed "a kind of solution," a way of keeping the Void at bay. It solves the problem of having no inherent purpose—or, perhaps, no purpose at all (and as the Buddhists say: Would that be so bad?). As long as we can't live with empty space, so to speak, our choices are not really choices; they are merely compulsions. Reviewing Robert Lowell's *Collected Poems*, Tom Paulin comments that Lowell "knows the heart of darkness in the American imperial sublime." Here is the end of his poem "Waking Early Sunday Morning":

> Pity the planet, all joy gone
> from this sweet volcanic cone;
> peace to our children when they fall
> in small war on the heels of small
> war—until the end of time
> to police the earth, a ghost
> orbiting forever lost
> in our monotonous sublime.[49]

So we missed the boat on 9/11; we decided to continue "policing the earth" more dramatically than we ever had, "until the end of time." This decision is turning us into ghosts, as we enter the Dark Ages in earnest. Choosing "the road not taken" (to quote a different Robert) would have required something really remarkable, and I don't think history provides us with a single example of a nation that managed to take that path.

Yet the problem of choosing the wrong road is not limited to our foreign policy. William Appleman Williams was right, after all, when he claimed that foreign and domestic issues were inextricably linked. If we have taken a series of wrong turns in one arena, the chances are good we did something similar—something related—in the other as well. Before we evaluate America's fate as an empire, it will be instructive to retrace our steps domestically, and examine some crucial forks in the (historical) road. What could we have done differently at home, and what might have been the corresponding result?

- 7 -

The Roads
Not Taken

There is no more potent tool for rupture than the reconstruction of genesis: by bringing back into view the conflicts and confrontations of the early beginnings and therefore all the discarded possibles, it retrieves the possibility that things could have been (and still could be) otherwise. And, through such a practical utopia, it questions the "possible" which, among all others, was actualized.

> —Pierre Bourdieu,
> "Rethinking the State"

. . . that dominant individualism, working for good and evil . . .

> —Frederick Jackson Turner,
> "The Significance of the Frontier in American History"

Every force evolves a form.

> —Shaker proverb

IN HER MASSEY LECTURES for the Canadian Broadcasting Corporation in 1985, which she entitled "Prisons We Choose to Live Inside," the British novelist Doris Lessing stated that future historians might be puzzled by the fact that Western civilization had the knowledge it needed to avoid its collapse, but apparently chose not to use it. This is—or will be, I believe—true of America in particular, but how much flexibility we have in terms of deliberate choice remains an open question. Every civilization is a "package deal," as it were, and that configuration means that it necessarily follows a particular trajectory determined by the constraints of that deal, which are both positive and negative, and which typically crystallize in a specific pattern or direction very early on. It also means that every civilization is dialectically structured—that is to say, the particular factors that made its rise to power possible prove to be, in the fullness of time, the very factors that do it in. This is because in its rise to power, the civilization in question had to repress those factors that pointed in a different (and often opposite) direction; it had to be, in a word, lopsided, and this lopsidedness provided it with an enormous amount of energy. But the phenomenon of lopsidedness also leads any such system to become increasingly out of kilter, and at some point the rejected pathways or lifeways come back to haunt it, because they represent tendencies that are necessary for balance, for the overall health of the organism. But by then, it is usually too late to shift gears (if I may be permitted to mix metaphors); collapse or decline can be avoided only if the repressed alternatives, the "roads not taken," are substantively incorporated into the dominant paradigm. Since this constitutes what might be called "shadow" material, the resistance to it is fierce, and so decay is, historically speaking, the rule.

The analogy might be that of an organization that has become dysfunctional, or perhaps that of an individual skirting the edge of a nervous breakdown. A friend of mine, a therapist who works with organizations as a consultant and who is called in when things have gotten rocky, tells me that these organizations typically pay no attention to his recommendations unless they are on the verge of bankruptcy. Once they reach that point, their ability to listen increases exponentially. They suddenly find his suggestions extremely compelling, but by that time it is usually too late. The situation is always paradoxical, he says: the thing they most need is usually the very thing they refuse to consider—until circumstances leave them no choice. At that point change may indeed be undertaken, but it tends to be cosmetic, fiddling with certain aspects of design but leaving the basic structure more or less intact. Individuals, it would seem, are like this as well. As W. H. Auden put it many years ago in his poem "The Age of Anxiety," "We would rather be ruined than changed."

In terms of civilizations, we might ponder the current unfortunate conflict (or clash) between the United States and the Islamic nations. As we saw in chapter 3, if every civilization is a package deal, then they are all some combination of tribal and secular. There are no purely secular societies, and there are probably no longer any purely tribal ones either. Going too far in the secular direction creates the anomie of a society expanding economically and technologically for no other purpose than expansion itself. It becomes a society without intrinsic meaning, devoid of any real human connections. Going too far in the tribal direction, however, creates a situation in which things are so totally interconnected that you feel you can never breathe. (As *Newsweek International* editor Fareed Zakaria, who grew up in India, once put it: "Whenever someone says the word *community*, I want to reach for my oxygen mask.") Intellectual stagnation and cultural repression are quite common in such societies. But Bernard Lewis' loaded question "What went wrong?" would not be so loaded if he had been willing to ask it of the West, not just of Islam. In many ways, contemporary Islamic civilization is a failure, for reasons already discussed. But it could also be argued (and many millions of Muslims do) that our so-called success is a failure as well—a human failure. Our purported material wealth is, quite clearly, heavily skewed toward the wealthy; but even beyond that, as Mother Teresa said when she visited America, we are a poor nation overall in the spiritual sense. America's poverty, she said, is worse than that of India's, for it is that of a terrible loneliness that come from wanting the wrong things.[1]

I recall, several decades ago, my high school history teacher telling the class that the United States was different from, say, India, because we were not "primitive." As an example of this "primitiveness," she cited a newspaper article that described people in India getting crushed to death by a stampede of the devoted during some Hindu ritual. Well, I would agree, that's pretty bad—barbaric, in fact. But before we start shaking our fingers, let's consider an event that took place on 28 November 2003 in Orange City, Florida. A woman in line at a Wal-Mart store to buy a DVD player (on sale) was literally trampled underfoot by frenzied shoppers, who wouldn't even get out of the way when the ambulance crew came to take her to the hospital. The paramedics found her slumped unconscious over a DVD player, while (the *Chicago Tribune* reported) "seemingly oblivious shoppers all around her continued to snap up items." Newspapers labeled the shoppers "a frothing mob," and indeed there is nothing less barbaric or demented about this than there is about the Hindu mob deplored by my history teacher.[2] In fact, it's worse: at least the Hindus were frothing about Shiva or Vishnu; the Americans, about Sony or Panasonic. "What went wrong?"

The American story is one of a nation that moved along a certain trajectory, "choosing," at a number of crucial junctures, options that seemed glorious and exciting at the time—technology over craft, individual achievement over the common weal, innovation over tradition, automobiles over mass transit, suburbs over cities, power over compromise, economic expansion over social welfare, competition and autonomy over community (to name but a few)—but that finally landed us at the nadir of our civilization, namely in a Florida Wal-Mart trampling some unfortunate woman into unconsciousness for the sake of a $29 DVD player. (Don't kid yourself: these people are your neighbors.) It is not that technology, individualism, economic expansion, and all the rest are necessarily "bad"; that would be a rather foolish conclusion. It's that any of these pushed to the limit—which entails rejecting the opposite pole—becomes pathological; in addition, historically, all of these factors interacted synergistically to produce an even more extreme result. The lopsidedness that originally energized us is now threatening to take the whole system down. The fragmented character of American society, writes Alex Marshall in *How Cities Work*, is due to the fact that "at every fork in the road, we have chosen the individual over the collective."[3] Just the reverse can probably be said of the Islamic nations. They seem to have taken things such as community, group solidarity, and tradition to *their* extremes and created their own type of pathology and civilizational failure (especially in modern times). Each civilization swung too far in a particular direction, which is why they are now mirror images of each other—fundamentalist in their own ways. Both have arrived at a moment of crisis.

In very rough terms, the central drama of American history is that of an expanding capitalist economy that gained momentum, moving faster and faster, feeding greedily on technological innovation (especially after World War II), eventually steamrolling all other values except those of a market economy, and heavily influencing U.S. foreign policy in its wake. This is, I grant you, a bit simplistic; the reality is a lot more nuanced than this, as I hope we have seen above. But as a broad historical overview, it's not completely off the mark. And it does raise two interesting questions. What would it mean, at this point, to recover (or even *discover*) our "shadow"? What would it mean to take a serious look at the "parallel universe" that got so decisively rejected? Shadows, having (usually) been denied for a long time, contain a lot of repressed energy. We are desperate today for community because we have been lonely and alienated for so long. We ache for silence (well, some of us do) because our environment is saturated with fatuous commercial noise. We resonate to beauty—when we do encounter it—because we swim in an ocean of gadgets and garbage. Our typical idea of the perfect vacation is to go somewhere that has escaped the ravages of "progress," or that can create the illusion of having done so, because we are disgusted by urban decay and suburban sprawl and meaningless jobs to which we commute an hour or more every day. And we want to be taken care of; we yearn for an economic safety net, because we are exhausted by the sheer pace of things, the relentless and demoralizing struggle for survival, and of having to live in a society whose real motto is not "In God We Trust" but rather "There Is No Free Lunch" or, perhaps more precisely, "What's in It for Me?" If we seek to know how we got to this point, it will be necessary to understand where we came from.

The American Character

The concept of national character is very much out of fashion these days, violating as it does the much more popular notion of multiculturalism. Surely in a land as diverse as ours, containing large percentages of blacks, Hispanics, and Asians, for example, it makes no sense to speak of a central set of traits that characterize "the American people." There are, so the argument goes, many Americas, not just a single (let alone unified) one. And yet, once we get past the tedious rhetoric of political correctness and identity politics, what do we see? Blacks and Hispanics, for all their community and family and (often) religious orientations, essentially want a larger share of the economic pie. That is their "vision" for America, and for themselves in America. A few disaffected white liberals aside, the only people in the United States who view the American Dream as a nightmare are Native Americans, and then only some of them.[4] In fact, any group or individual that rejects the dominant ethos in this country and sees it as a species of illness is going to pay a very high price. Regardless of race, religion, historical background, or country of origin, everybody in the United States is effectively a Protestant capitalist individualist whose life is grounded in the ideology of an expanding market economy. When it comes down to the basics, America is about as diverse as a one-string guitar.

The scholar who (to my knowledge) first argued this from a behavioralist and social science perspective was the historian David Potter, in his *People of Plenty* (1954). Despite certain problems with it half a century later, it is impressive to see how well his argument has held up. Wittingly or not, writes Potter, all historians employ the concept of national character because history shapes culture and culture molds the national character. Americans are not an arbitrary conglomerate united by nothing more than geography or location; rather, they possess "distinctive traits and social adaptations which characterize them as a group." One can certainly appeal to things such as the influence of corporations or the presence of a frontier or any other causal factors, in order to argue that this national character is not genetic—some sort of "racial" property, as it were—but what's the difference? Regardless of the forces that have shaped the American character, the bottom line is that there *is* one: the forces involved generated a modal personality, a dominant psychology, and a mainstream way of behaving. This configuration, asserts Potter, is based on the expectation of material abundance, of inexhaustible plenty— of living in a nation whose streets will (and should) be paved with gold, if they aren't already. The error of the eminent American historian, Frederick Jackson Turner, according to Potter, was to see the frontier strictly in terms of geographical territory, which is far too narrow a framework. Turner ignored the *psychological* frontier, which in America is based on the interaction of technology with the environment. The promised expansion, as a result, is endless. Historically, the promise of abundance and the social mobility attendant on that created a social flux that deprived Americans of the psychic comfort of having a place in an organic social order. This means that the individual has very weak ties to the community (such as it is), and that the American idea of social justice is not to redistribute wealth but just to make more of it (the specious trickle-down theory). Ultimately, as some scholars have argued, this vision of plenty led to the relentless commodification of life, to consumption as literally a mode of perception. And if a few Native Americans and white middle-class "greens" or "reds" view this as a collective pathology, well, the collective definitely does not.[5]

Fifty years after the publication of Potter's book, Walter McDougall, who is a Pulitzer Prize–winning historian at the University of Pennsylvania, came to much the same conclusion, expressed in somewhat starker terms. There certainly is an American character, says McDougall in *Freedom Just Around the Corner*; it's called "hustling." We are a nation of people on the make, he argues, and this certainly antedated Enron and Halliburton. To be sure, he says, this hustling has a sunny, upbeat face to it, the Yankee "can do" mentality. But the dark side is no minor aspect, and it was present from Day One: nearly everyone in early America, he suggests, had little interest in what was good for the colony or the nation, and a very great interest in "what's in it for me?" The overall picture is that of a scramble for profit, and the result has been a nation that is not only endlessly competitive, but remarkably violent.[6]

The "infancy" of a nation may have some similarities with human infancy, in an individual sense, because in both cases we can recognize the formative power of the early years. The Jesuits were fond of saying, "Give us the child for the first seven years; after that, nothing much matters." Or, as Heraclitus put it nearly 2600 years ago, character is destiny; once the tramlines of personality are laid down, modifications will occur in the course of a person's growth, but there is no avoiding the fact that "the child is father to the man." After a certain point, changes are at most variations on a theme; nothing is going to be terribly different. The same may be true of civilizations. Thus in his discussion of the history of the "counterculture" in American history—which he defines as the attempt to subordinate the material to the ideal, or the spiritual—historian David Shi, in *The Simple Life*, does a good job of tracing the dominant culture back to the early seventeenth century. In 1616, he notes, Captain John Smith observed that most of the Virginia colonists, religious sentiments notwithstanding, were in the New World for material gain. "I am not so simple to think," wrote Smith, "that ever any other motive than wealth will erect there a Commonweal." Of course, this was not quite correct; religion was a very strong current in colonial America, with Quakers, Puritans, and other groups playing a significant role. Yet none of this managed to derail the individualistic and commercial ethic of American society, and the two aspects probably went hand in hand. The early Puritan merchants, for example, often wrote "in the name of God and profit" at the top of their ledgers. John Winthrop, the first governor of Massachusetts Bay Colony, kept warning his followers that they would have to be vigilant to ensure that the "good of the public oversway all private interests." But by the time he died, in 1649, it was reported that "men were generally failing in their duty to the community, seeking their own aggrandizement" instead. A communitarian outlook never seemed to really take root in the culture at large. "The pristine vision of the [Massachusetts Bay] colony's founders," writes Shi, "continued to be dashed upon the rock of selfish individualism." This was the pattern set in America's formative years, and it has been repeated again and again down to the present time. Deviations from it—whether we are talking about the Shakers, the Amish, the arts and crafts movement of the late nineteenth century, the progressives, Lewis Mumford, Jimmy Carter, Marxism, Buddhism, whatever—were easily suppressed, co-opted, or brushed aside. Even the Depression did little to alter the basic commercial outlook and individualistic way of life, and ultimately wound up strengthening them. Sokei-an, America's first Zen master (who died in 1945), once wrote that introducing Buddhism to the United States was "like holding a lotus to a rock and hoping it will take root." Like all of the alternatives discussed in Shi's book, Buddhism took root to some tiny extent, but ultimately the rock remained the rock, and has so to this day. The "Coca-donald Society" is ultimately where all of us live.[7]

Of course, the materialist and individualist tendencies of seventeenth-century America were light fare compared with what came later. One could conceivably make the argument that things were still fluid, at that point, still up for grabs; that, as Pierre Bourdieu says, things could have turned out otherwise. Looking back, the crucial period for things starting to congeal was that of the American Revolution and a bit after, when the ideals of the Founding Fathers got subverted into something very different (to their deep disillusionment). Even in the eighteenth century, life in the colonies was still tied to a European mind-set, which included allegiance to tradition, notions of the greater good, and a system of reciprocal obligations. All of this was to change quite dramatically, particularly in the 1790s. In order to really understand the phenomenon of the "untaken roads," then, we need to look at these formative years in American history, and their role in determining the national character.

Perhaps the clearest and most concise summary of these developments is Joyce Appleby's brilliant *Capitalism and a New Social Order*. According to Appleby, the colonial understanding of social organization turned on the concept of virtue. The classical republican (small r) definition of "virtue" was "the capacity of some men to rise above private interests and devote themselves to the public good." It was this capacity that made republics possible, in the classical view: free men realized their human potential in service to the commonwealth. This definition was the dominant one in the colonies for most of the eighteenth century, but by the 1780s it had already become blurry, often being modified by the word "disinterested." By 1800, the definition had undergone a complete inversion; "virtue" now meant the capacity to look out for oneself and one's family.[8]

The crucial factors here were the Industrial Revolution in England, the Enlightenment in France and Scotland, and the influence both of these had on the future United States. The Enlightenment, after all, was an assault on the feudal order of medieval Europe. Its (liberal) concept of freedom was individualistic and instrumental, the opposite of the classical notion. It was also abstract and universalist, asserting that all human beings were everywhere the same. In the view of Adam Smith—who modeled his economics on Newtonian physics—self-interest in motion, like restless atoms, was the philosophical basis of the free enterprise system and the market economy. Ceaseless striving characterized human nature, in this view; for Smith, a proper society was a commercial one, with every man basically a merchant. Smith's ideal of human conduct was anathema to a traditionalist such as the Reverend Thomas Hooker, the seventeenth-century colonial clergyman. "For if each man may do what is good in his owne eyes," wrote Hooker, "proceed according to his own pleasure, so that none may crosse him or controll him by any power; there must of necessity follow the distraction and desolation of the whole." In Smith's world, by contrast, it was the collective result of individual selfish actions that somehow (through the "invisible hand" of the market) added up to the greater good. The profit motive underlay everything, he argued, and market relations amounted to a natural, and benevolent, system.[9]

All of this fell on increasingly receptive ears on the other side of the Atlantic. In general terms, the Federalists held on to the classical republican definition of virtue, whereas the Jeffersonian Republicans were drawn to the world of Adam Smith and the concept of laissez-faire. It was during the 1790s, says Appleby, that the new nation began to shed its European ethos, and the aristocratic model of an organic society, consisting of reciprocal rights and obligations, was attenuated. We go forth, proclaimed one Republican writer, "in pursuit of new commodities." In

Political Arithmetic, Thomas Cooper wrote, "The consumers form the nation." (Thomas Jefferson distributed Cooper's work as election campaign material in the 1800 presidential campaign.) A few of us might laugh at Condoleezza Rice's identification of freedom with shopping in the "National Security Strategy" of 2002—what could be more superficial?—but it is as American as apple pie.[10]

In any case, Jefferson's victory of 1800 was an enduring one; Republicans controlled the federal government for the next twenty-four years. The Federalists were attacked as being counterrevolutionary; their classical, aristocratic, and communitarian vision, in which the public interest preceded the private one, was eclipsed. This turn of events proved to be decisive for the future of the American republic, resulting, says Appleby (quoting the historian Richard Hofstadter), in "a democracy of cupidity."[11]

A much lengthier and more nuanced version of these events is provided by Gordon Wood in *The Radicalism of the American Revolution*. What emerges from his account is that the Founding Fathers found themselves defeated by their own success. In pushing the anti-organic, anti-aristocratic line, they unleashed a politics that they couldn't control and that wound up in a place they could not have anticipated—much to their chagrin. In a nutshell, says Wood, during the Revolution the colonists abandoned their monarchical allegiance, leaving them without a glue to hold their society together. They thus turned to Enlightenment values to replace the traditional ones; but these values, with their emphasis on "natural virtue," proved to be too idealistic in actual practice, and so the glue of the new society eventually became nothing loftier than the freedom to make money.[12]

In order to understand how radical these changes were, says Wood, we have to grasp how unprecedented the American Revolution was. We tend to focus on the political dimensions of the event—the war of independence and the break from England. But this was much less of a rupture than we think. The real revolution, according to Wood, was social, a complete transformation of the relations that bound people to one another. In fact, the Revolution rejected aristocracy as it had been understood in the West for more than two thousand years; the country went from monarchy and hierarchy to egalitarianism and commerce practically overnight (although the institution of the Senate was there to guard against complete democracy). After all, the gross inequalities of the classical and medieval world were balanced by a huge emotional payoff: everyone counted for something, everyone had a place. No one was ever alone or unattached. Republicanism (capital R) dissolved these ties in the twinkling of an eye.[13]

"Republicanism," during those years, was a catch-all phrase for everything opposed to the monarchical world. (John Adams once remarked that the word meant anything, everything, and nothing.) Yet the Revolutionary leaders were hardly opposed to the classical definition of virtue, the sacrifice of private interests for public ones; they just didn't believe it required a hereditary aristocracy to carry that out. Jefferson, for example, held to the notion of a "natural aristocracy," one of talent, to be peopled by a landed, gentlemanly elite. The problem was that unlike the situation in Europe, things were rather murky in the colonies. Many of the American gentry were involved in commercial enterprises, for example, which raised what we now call conflict-of-interest issues for the Founding Fathers. For various reasons, colonial society was torn between monarchical and republican tendencies, and the Revolution brought this tension to the surface. The revolutionaries wanted not just independence from England, but the independence of individuals from all personal networks. Property was now seen as the key to social independence, which assumed the status of an ideological imperative. The dream of the Revolutionary generation was a utopian one derived from the Enlightenment, that the new rulers would be men of merit who governed only in the public interest—"natural virtue." Love, in effect, would be the social equivalent of gravity, the principle of attraction that would hold everything together.[14]

Alas, it was too great a stretch. In the absence of an aristocratic, hierarchical framework, it required a level of virtue to which few people in the colonies could aspire. As Wood puts it, "the ink on the Declaration of Independence was scarcely dry before many of the revolutionary leaders began expressing doubts about the possibility of realizing these high hopes." The citizenry was involved in trade and moneymaking and not particularly interested in the nation at large. The new popular leaders exploited the Revolutionary rhetoric of liberty and equality for their own narrow political advantage, and for the local interests of their constituents. The goal was the buying of new consumer goods. "Instead of creating a new order of benevolence and selflessness," writes Wood, "enlightened republicanism was breeding social competitiveness and individualism." The Revolution, he says, was "the source of its own contradictions." After all, the leaders wanted to draw a line between republicanism and democracy, but since the latter was a logical extension of the former, they couldn't maintain this distinction without repudiating the Revolution itself. The result was "a scrambling business society dominated by the pecuniary interests of ordinary working people," which the Founding Fathers saw as a failure of their grand experiment. Jefferson perhaps excepted, the Founders were, after all, not levelers; they believed in rank and social distinctions and had never imagined that the upshot of their efforts would be a society that equated personal quality with money, and virtue with pure self-interest. They regarded direct democracies, such as those of ancient Greece, as unstable; the fate of Socrates was an object lesson for them. George Washington was deeply disillusioned; John Adams and James Madison, as early as 1787, began to speak privately of the benefits of monarchy, and many Federalists wanted to bring back some of its "adhesive" qualities. As one Scottish visitor put it, America was a society of "discordant atoms," badly in need of a principle of cohesion (like gravitational attraction, one might say). Yet the citizenry was undaunted: commerce, the national obsession, seemed to be glue enough for them. Benjamin Rush's fear that a society such as this "would eventually fall apart in an orgy of selfishness" was not one that was widely shared. The Philadelphia physician was right, as it turns out; it just took a bit longer than he had imagined.[15]

In a very real sense, then, the American nation was *born* bourgeois. Unlike Europe, it never went through a feudal phase. For sociologist Seymour Martin Lipset, this absence is the key to "American exceptionalism," one aspect of which is that social and political alternatives to the American mainstream—communitarian ones in particular—have never been able to get off the ground. Individualism, laissez-faire economics, and the pursuit of private interests were locked in from the beginning; deviations from that norm never really had a chance. Whereas Europe had a feudal tradition of *noblesse oblige*, which in the modern period took the form of welfare, public housing and employment, and other ways to help the less fortunate, the United States offers its underclass only the ideology of individual mobility and personal achievement. The ethos of the Revolutionary period, says Lipset, loaded the dice, making America the most antistatist nation in the world. It is the only major industrial nation without a general allowance program for families with children and without national health insurance. It also has the highest percentage of people living in poverty among the developed nations. Yet surveys taken from the 1930s through the 1980s reveal very little sympathy for the idea of wealth distribution—even during the Depression. Given the successful Revolutionary attack on hierarchy, aristocracy, and organic community values, this should come as no surprise. As political scientist Walter Dean Burnham once put it, "no feudalism, no socialism"—that is, feudalism was the historical template on which a communitarian ethos was built. Being "taken care of" is regarded as un-American; instead, the emphasis is almost wholly on individual success. Individualism has become the moral standard by which everything is judged, and of which Americans are aggressively proud. Yet by 1994, reports Lipset, two-thirds of the American public said the country was seriously off track.[16] Shadow material knocking at the door, perhaps.

Of course, this is not to suggest that traditional aristocratic society is something that needs to be revived, or that it represents a happy ideal on which we should look back with nostalgic longing. To most of us raised in the modern democratic world, the notion of having a daily reminder of one's subservience to others, one's supposedly inherent inferiority, is repugnant in the extreme. My point is that because civilizations are a package deal, there is a price to be paid either way. Recall the classical criteria of excellence, for example, as listed by Albert Borgmann. Do you admire these? Do you think they give life real meaning, as opposed to the shallow criterion of commercial success? So do I. But let us be clear about this: they derive from sharply vertical societies, in particular from a gentlemanly or noble tradition according to which one is expected to be well versed in science, literature, and history, play music, do a sport, speak several languages, and be charitable (assist the poor and the unfortunate). All well and good, but only a tiny upper crust of these societies could afford to have this sort of life. Similarly, do you believe that a society of "discordant atoms," which is what we really have in the United States, is empty and pathetic? So do I . . . but societies with a commons, with real communities of place, with a commitment to providing a safety net, are (again) historically derivative from profoundly inegalitarian arrangements. Do you find American culture vulgar, materialistic, violent, disturbingly anti-intellectual, and basically vapid? Me too . . . except that without America's tradition of political democracy and civil liberties, including its willingness to provide asylum to millions of immigrants and refugees seeking the "good life," my parents and perhaps yours would have been murdered in eastern Europe (or somewhere), and I wouldn't be sitting here writing a critique of their adopted country, nor would you be reading it. The downside of American democracy, says Woods at the end of his book, is very large; but "there is no denying the wonder of it, and the real earthly benefits it brought to the hitherto neglected and despised masses of common laboring people. The American Revolution created this democracy, and we are living with its consequences still."[17]

Two of these consequences, however, are the collapse of quality and the absence of any astute or enlightened guidance, themes elaborated upon in a book I wish everybody would read, *The Future of Freedom*, by Fareed Zakaria. He too is not advocating a return to a closed order and government by elites; rather, he argues that with the major post-1960 assault on authority, it is not that the elite disappeared, but that it shifted to another locus. Radical democratization may have been touted under Thomas Jefferson, but we still remained tied to the European model to some degree. For much of the twentieth century, says Zakaria, professionals in the United States formed a kind of modern aristocracy that was concerned with the nation's welfare. In terms of museums, symphonies, public parks, and libraries, "American democracy was well served by public-spirited elites," who set the cultural standards and whose guiding principle was quality. If they acted on behalf of equality and of the democratization of culture, they "did so by elevating people rather than bring the standards down." The 1790s notwithstanding, there remained enough of a public service ethic to act as a brake on unbridled power and pure commercialism. That remnant finally ran out, over the past few decades, and the new elites are lobbyists, special-interest groups, and even fanatics, who have moved in to fill the void left by the collapse of hierarchy. This phenomenon might be called "misplaced egalitarianism," and its result is that the only thing that matters anymore—in the arts, education, urban design and so on—is mass appeal. What we get, says Zakaria, is a loss of definition, of cutting edge. Popular opinion is thus the lodestar of today's elites, which means that American life and culture are almost completely consumerist in nature. So if today's elites are concerned about the public, it is only to take its commercial pulse, because the market lurks behind everything in this country. Their horizon, in short, is not the larger public good. "The greatest danger of unfettered and dysfunctional democracy," concludes Zakaria, "is that it will discredit democracy itself."[18]

As for the American tradition of political liberty, as great as it is, it still boils down to Isaiah Berlin's "negative freedom," the freedom to be left alone so as to be able to pursue one's private interests. When it comes to meaning—which is to say, *positive* freedom—commercialism, materialism, and individualism make for pretty thin gruel. It was for this reason that quite early in the game, the democratic revolution broke through the rational crust of the Enlightenment, as powerful religious currents flowed underneath the secular surface of public life. Protestant sects multiplied and rapidly came to dominate American culture. And yet, as is the case today, it didn't quite work, because this was a very fragmented form of religion, and actually separate from society as a whole. If something were to hold the nation together, it had to be a common belief; and the source of that belief proved to be the Revolution itself. "It has been our fate as a nation," wrote Richard Hofstadter, "not to have ideologies, but to be one." Americanism, in short: that is our religion.[19]

The presence of a "civil religion" in America was first pointed out by sociologist Robert Bellah nearly forty years ago and, as already indicated, it is the flip side of the "atomized" society. The separation of church and state, wrote Bellah, has not denied the political realm a religious dimension, for the transcendent goal that America feels charged with is the obligation to carry out God's will on earth. Thus the Declaration of Independence contains four references to God, and religious expression permeates Washington's first inaugural address. The Founding Fathers talked a lot in these terms, but they were not referring to any particular religion, Christianity included. Rather, writes Sidney Mead in *The Nation with the Soul of a Church*, the American religion is that of fulfilling a mission, of bringing a New World into being. It is an activist and moralistic religion, not an inward or contemplative one—a fact that is just now coming home to roost. For many Americans, the nation "came to occupy a place in their lives that traditionally had been occupied by the church." More than that, the nation was seen by its inhabitants as the primary agent of God's activity in history. Only America, wrote Lyman Beecher in *A Plea for the West* (1835), could provide the "moral power to evangelize the world." So our "moral" foreign policy was slated to work in tandem with our commercial domestic one, and both of these reflect and reinforce our specific individual behavior and our value system on a daily basis.[20]

This evangelizing kind of zeal has also been a major factor in closing off any alternatives to the mainstream. As Lipset correctly states, Americanism is an ism in the same way that communism was. They functioned as mirror images (which is why we now need terrorism—badly—to replace our lost *doppelgänger*; in general, religion cannot function without a satanic figure). While other nations have a sense of themselves derived from a common history—one cannot become un-English or un-Swedish, for example—being an American is regarded as an ideological or religious commitment and is not a matter of birth. Hence, those who reject American values are "un-American" by definition. "Americans," writes Lipset,

> are utopian moralists who press hard to institutionalize virtue, to destroy evil people, and eliminate wicked institutions and practices. A majority even tell pollsters that God is the moral guiding force of American democracy. They tend to view social and political dramas as morality plays, as battles between God and the Devil, so that compromise is virtually unthinkable.

As noted, individualism is the center of that religion, the moral standard by which everything is judged.[21]

The Car Culture

If American history shaped the American character, the reverse is also true. The value system of at least 90 percent of the American population (at a conservative estimate), down through the decades, has acted to exclude a number of options that are essential for a healthy society. On one level, one might say that America takes away love and gives its citizens gadgets in return, which most of them regard as a terrific bargain. But it is much larger than this, extending out to all of the "discarded possibles" hinted at by Pierre Bourdieu. I am thinking, in particular, of the things that are part and parcel of the feudal-organic society that the American Revolution attenuated: community, meaning, the craft tradition, silence, "nonrestlessness," a deep appreciation of art and music, inwardness, spirituality, and the criteria of excellence cited above—the sort of things that don't hold much interest for a mass, business-oriented society but that nevertheless make life worthwhile. (One can, by now, throw a rigorous liberal arts education onto the scrap heap as well.) Spurned as "elitism," these things fall into the category of an "inner frontier" (as opposed to Turner's outer one) and got repressed from the very beginning. Thus Sidney Mead comments that there was a loneliness and remorse in the frontier adventure, expressed in sad folk songs and gospel hymns of the pioneers, but that this was always "a minor refrain, drowned in the great crashing music of the outward events that mark in history the conquering of a continent and the building of a great nation"—the building of our "domestic empire," as it were, also known as Manifest Destiny. This conquest, he says, has been "told and retold until it has overshadowed and suppressed the equally vital, but more somber, story of the inner experience."[22] The story of the lost inner frontier is unfortunately beyond the scope of this book, although it inevitably seeps out between the lines from time to time. My deliberate focus in this chapter, in terms of "roads not taken," will be on the *literal* roads, the design of the urban landscape. How this has fallen out will be, as Alex Marshall said, a direct result of the relentless American habit of choosing the individual solution over the collective one. Nor is it some minor aspect of American history. The design of our cities, including the rise of a car culture, the growth of the suburbs, and the nature of our architecture, has had an overwhelming impact on the life of the nation as a whole, reflecting back on all of the issues discussed so far: work, children, media, community, economy, technology, globalization, and, especially, U.S. foreign policy. The physical arrangements of our lives mirror the spiritual ones, in other words, and in that sense the inner and outer frontiers cannot truly be separated.

As far as the outer frontier goes, Frederick Jackson Turner wrote that movement literally defined the American character. Sidney Mead emphasizes that in America movement has always been spatial in nature. Whereas we had a relatively low population density, Europe and Asia had just the reverse. For Europeans and Asians, he says, space has always been at a premium, and so these peoples expanded into time—they found freedom for the human spirit in duration, in the endless flow of events. Thus, he concludes, in America "space has played the part that time has played in the older cultures of the world." The pioneer felt free as long as he or she could move on, and the postwar rush to the suburbs was part of the same mental landscape. The equation of freedom with movement through space has been a dominant motif in American culture, and it is surely no coincidence that a scant fifteen years after Turner announced the closing of the frontier, Henry Ford opened the stationary assembly line for the manufacture of cars (the moving version followed five years later, in 1913). What we have, then, is yet another version of Manifest Destiny: having mapped and settled the continent, Americans would now retraverse it in a Model T. Although this is still a geographical frontier in many ways, it is nevertheless a psychological one as well—a truth that was not lost on the president of the Studebaker Company: "In highways," he declared,

> lies a new national frontier for the pessimist who thinks frontiers have disappeared. It challenges the imagination and spirit of enterprise which have always been the distinctive marks of American life. And even the gloomiest of men admit that America never ignores challenges of a new frontier, geographical or otherwise.

The real importance of the psychological frontier is the illusion that there is something "out there" that can fill up the emptiness inside—hence, the endless restlessness that is so characteristic of America.[23]

Finally, the closing of the frontier (which was actually made official by the Census Bureau in 1890), combined with the commercial ethos of the United States, worked to redefine American urban culture in the 1890s. As many scholars have argued, technology by itself makes no difference; what really matters, in the words of the anthropologist Alfred Kroeber, "are the patterns it encounters in the culture at whose door it is knocking." Thus there were early experiments with steam vehicles in the 1870s and 1880s, but no one took any notice. What happened in the 1890s, however, was that urban residents began to think of their streets as trafficways rather than as open public spaces. Like much else in the United States during this era (described in detail by William Leach in *Land of Desire*), space was rapidly turning into a commodity; it was part of a new "market." The first use of the word "artery" to mean "street," for example, occurs in an engineering journal during this decade. Streets were increasingly seen in purely functional terms, as opposed to being regarded as part of the neighborhood. Both psychologically and materially, then, the way was open for the car to move in and fill the vacuum left by the closing of the geographic frontier.[24]

In *The Car Culture*, James Flink picks up on the notion of the way for the car being "paved" as much by attitudinal and institutional contexts as it was by asphalt. For example, the diffusion of the automobile occurred much more rapidly in the United States than in Europe. Why should that be? Greater availability of space was an obvious factor; another was the industrial background: in the United States, the mass production of standardized commodities (including the mechanization of processes) had become well established by the late nineteenth century. In Europe, on the other hand, things were still influenced by the feudal craft tradition, and so there was small-scale, individualized production of cars. As Flink points out, "soft" factors may actually be more significant here. What the private passenger car plugged into, in the United States, was the core value of individualism. The car promised to put the cost of an urban transportation system on the individual, not on the state. In fact, the combination of car and highway promised to preserve and enhance American individualism. Finally, the car offered something dear to the American way of life: a technical as opposed to political solution to the problems of the nation—a panacea, as it were, for some of the country's major ills.[25]

This last factor is no small point. As Michael Hunt argued for the foreign arena, the United States has an almost morbid aversion to actually working through social and political problems, because it is extremely nervous about real change. This is no less true of the nation on the domestic level. A logical consequence of this is that it prefers to find an anodyne, and technology is one of the best ones around. Consider Henry Ford's recipe for urban reform: "We shall solve the city problem," he declared, "by leaving the city." During the progressive era of the early twentieth century, one popular answer to the presence of slums was the notion that everyone should buy a car and commute from the suburbs— which would also (just coincidentally) be good for business, since it would lead to a boom in suburban real estate. Similarly, the New York highway commissioner asserted in 1902 that commuting would not only put an end to the slums, but also solve the conflict between labor and capital. An approach like this was dear to the American heart, says Flink, "because it did not involve collective political action," and because it offered to preserve traditional cultural values. One thus looked at structural problems—for instance, urban poverty and congestion, or class conflict, which could be solved only by collective political decisions—and found a nonsolution for them that *looked* like a solution: viz. a private, individualized technological device. One reason technology has had so great an appeal in the United States is that it typically offers to change things without really changing them. Indeed, it buries the problem (whatever it may be) under a façade of "progress." In that sense, it is quite congruent with our civic religion, which is always projecting outward.[26]

From its introduction, the car was greeted with huge enthusiasm. As early as 1907 it was referred to as a necessity, and by 1910 America had become the world's foremost automobile culture, with nearly a half million cars registered. By 1926 a Model T could be purchased for $260, and U.S. motor vehicle sales during that year had a wholesale value of more than $3 billion. That year alone, Americans spent more than $10 billion on automobile operating expenses, and traveled 141 billion miles. In 1929 the total production of American cars was in excess of 5.3 million units. By 1933, the President's Research Committee on Social Trends reported the existence of an "automobile psychology" in the United States, stating that the American citizen had become dependent on the car. The New Deal wound up spending vast sums on streets and highways—$4 billion over the period 1933–42. The fantasy of "automobility," writes Jane Holtz Kay (in *Asphalt Nation*), endured alongside the grim realities of the times. Gas lines paralleled soup lines; eight years after the crash of 1929, there were 3 million more cars on the road. Americans literally drove to government offices to collect the food dole. When one local transit company offered people free rides to a Works Progress Administration site, they refused, preferring to drive. As for the WPA itself, the road-to-rail funding ratio during its history was twenty to one. All in all, the combined highway expenditures of local, state, and federal governments between 1947 and 1970 was $249 billion; during the same period, only 1 percent of what the federal government spent on transportation went for urban mass transit.[27]

American society was essentially reshaped to fit the car. Streetcars declined dramatically between 1929 and 1940, since Americans wanted private and individual control of the road. As Clay McShane points out in *Down the Asphalt Path*, trolleys contradicted basic American values. They were dirty and overcrowded and made it impossible for the middle class to isolate itself from the lower classes—blacks and immigrants in particular. Meanwhile, by 1932 General Motors formed a consortium of tire, oil, and highway companies to buy and then shut down streetcar systems, bribing local officials when necessary. In the next quarter century, as 1974 Senate antitrust hearings revealed, GM, by means of monopolies

and interlocking directorates, killed off more than a hundred electric surface rail systems in forty-five cities.[28]

It was in 1956 that the Interstate Highway Act (National System of
Interstate and Defense Highways) was passed, which committed the federal government to paying 90 percent of the construction costs of 41,000
miles of toll-free expressways. While American cities fell over themselves
to get on the bandwagon, European cities revived passenger trains, built
subway systems, and rebuilt old transit systems. As the latter became
vibrant as a result, our own cities participated, quite eagerly, in their own
demise. Between 1945 and 1965, the United States spent $1.5 billion on
local public transportation, as opposed to $51 billion on cars. After some
agitation during the 1960s for mass transit, the federal government pro-
ceeded to spend $400 million on these utilities and $24 billion on the
car. Between 1968 and 1976, the citizens of Los Angeles voted mass transit down no less than three times. The government continued to subsi-
dize road building, as city after city looked more desolate and forlorn. By
1975 Lewis Mumford's comment on the American city was "Make the
patient as comfortable as possible. It's too late to operate." As for the
1980s, Ronald Reagan predictably hailed the automobile as "the last
great freedom," and actively discouraged the use of passenger trains. In
1992, consumers spent more than $600 billion on cars (including repairs,
gas, and insurance), as compared with $5.7 billion to ride public transit.[29]

The romance of the motor vehicle, which accompanied the above
developments, is a story in itself. The car, says Clay McShane, was a
metaphor as well as a machine, a symbol of psychic liberation. Starting in
the 1890s, publicity surrounding it was intense: banquets of the elite
Automobile Club of America, the annual auto show in Madison Square
Garden, races and parades. Photos showed royalty riding around in cars;
cars were given animal or mythological names (Green Dragon, Wolver-
ine) to suggest wildness and adventure. Between 1905 and 1908 more
than 120 songs were written on auto themes, joined over the course of
the century by a thousand more. Many were sexual: "When He Wanted
to Love Her (He Would Put Up the Cover)," and so forth. Early films
exploited the theme of the use of cars by young people to escape the
"tyranny" of their parents; car chase scenes were also very popular. On a
symbolic level, America had a love affair with the car, and reports to the
contrary, it's hardly over (check out the latest ads on TV).[30]

The impact of all this was quite baleful. The spread of the automobile gutted our cities, destroyed (through highway construction) cohesive urban neighborhoods and city parks, contributed to the declining tax base of central cities, generated endless suburban sprawl, and alienated racial minorities. The assembly line and mass production provided the employee with little opportunity for individual creativity or camaraderie with fellow workers, thus accelerating the denigration of craft and community already in progress. The car culture opened larger trading areas, diminishing the viability of the village general store and threatening small banks. In the form of the tractor, the motor vehicle displaced the horse and made the small family farm obsolete. The car privatized the life of American citizens more than ever before, and the damage it has done to the environment, via pollution, is incalculable. Yet for the vast majority of Americans, all of this is a small price to pay for the maintenance of their individualized lifestyle and ideology. The truth is, mass transit never really had a chance in this country.[31]

As the reader is well aware, the nation has moved on to even larger and more fuel-inefficient vehicles. The first modern sport-utility vehicle was the Jeep Cherokee in 1984; then came the suburban utility vehicle (SUV), introduced by Ford in 1996, which generated something of a feeding frenzy. Later also called the sport utility vehicle and manufactured by a host of car makers, the SUV gives the driver the illusion of safety (he or she sits up high and "dominates" the road), while the reality is that the too-high center of gravity causes these vehicles to flip over much too easily. It is clearly tied to the militarization of American society and to our imperial foreign policy, for which it is the perfect metaphor. Because it uses huge amounts of gas, it hooks us into ever greater oil dependency and a pathological need to dominate the Middle East. Some of our new "cars," such as the Hummer, which came out of the Gulf war, are really military vehicles, and represent the subsumption of our domestic life under our imperial program (as of 2004 it cost at least sixty dollars to fill the Hummer's gas tank, and the figure increased dramatically by late 2005). One can only wonder how long it will be before General Motors comes out with some version of the Abrams tank as a "new family recreation vehicle." And all of this because business and extreme individualism reign supreme in the United States.[32]

Assessing the car culture a few years ago, Anne Mackin claimed that the American love of the automobile was an essential element of our national character. We don't really want to live close to one another, she said, and in addition, we are committed to progress for the individual, not for the community. The "landscape we have created with the car," she wrote, "is as close to a national portrait as we are likely to get." It may be worth our while, then, to take a closer look at that landscape.[33]

The Sub/Urban Landscape

First, let's look at the broader picture of urban history, out of which our landscape developed. Because (again) if the car shaped that landscape, it was also the case that the type of landscape we wanted created a use for a device such as the automobile. But it is about much more than the car, of course. We didn't wind up with gated "communities" and no real ones, as well as wasted cities, de facto segregation, and an environment devoid of all sense of place, filled with alienated "atoms" fighting with one another for survival, by accident. What I am trying to demonstrate here is that the details of our individual lives (as, for example, they are embodied in the physical design of where we live) ground our foreign and domestic policies. These things are all the product of the same historical pressures and are derived from the same system of values. Inasmuch as these things co-created one another, and excluded other values that are basic to the health of *any* civilization, we can see in both the workings of an "imperial vector," one might call it, allowing us first to expand and now moving us inexorably toward our decline. To grasp all of this in some detail, we need, once again, to look at America in the colonial period.

One of the most imaginative discussions of American cities is that of the historian Eric Monkkonen, who points out that since the American city developed in a postfeudal context, it was always conceived of as an economic project rather than a social one. The crucial issue, he says, is the wall. The medieval cities of Europe were surrounded by walls, and this meant that they had clear boundaries, ones that imposed restraints on physical growth. As Lewis Mumford remarked, this gave the towns a tight urban form, encouraged community and street life, and yet also provided sanctuary and solitude. The shift away from this, according to Monkkonen, began in the sixteenth century with the rise of the nation-state, during which time the state began to escape from its strictly urban base (for example, the French court moved from Paris to Versailles in the seventeenth century). This meant that the city no longer had to be defended by a wall, a pattern that was picked up (Wall Street in New Amsterdam—later New York—notwithstanding) by the cities of the American colonies. As a result, the American city has more in common with a business corporation than with its European counterpart; in fact, it differs from virtually all of the cities that had preceded it. Once again, we have American exceptionalism, completely predictable along the lines sketched by Lipset, Appleby, and Wood. This lack of an edge, combined with the emerging spirit of capitalist individualism, meant that the individual was far less responsible for the fabric of urban life, and American cities epitomized this tendency. Their very formlessness heralded a new era, and thus Monkkonen argues that the seeds of suburban sprawl were planted very early on. Without clearly defined edges, obvious demarcations between what was city and what was not, American cities did not have a sense of critical constraints on their planning. They were part of the frontier, really—anarchic and individualistic. We should not then be surprised that the automobile swept America in the early twentieth century, because its individualistic and mobile appeal would, in such a context, be irresistible.[34]

All this, in turn, contributed to (and was also stoked by) the bourgeoning laissez-faire environment. Colonial cities decreased demands on the individual as a citizen; they tended to be seen in utilitarian terms— i.e., as "stages" on which individuals were expected to pursue their private goals. And whereas the renovation of cities such as Paris under Baron Georges-Eugène Haussmann was state sponsored, the American pattern has been random and unplanned, largely determined by banks, real estate developers, and other private interests (Washington, D.C., is the notable exception). This, says Monkkonen, was planning disadvantage masquerading as "natural freedom." Places such as Paris or Barcelona emerged from an aesthetic vision, whereas Dallas and Houston are the product of free-market commercialism. The result was a radically new type of urban environment, one that lacked a real center, or heart. This is why, according to urban historian Witold Rybczynski, America never had the notion of cities as repositories of civilization— quite remarkable, when you think about it.[35]

The matter of "planned nonplanning," of laissez-faire urbanization in

America versus government subsidy in Europe, is a crucial factor in what happened historically. American cities, says Rybczynski, are socially fragmented and "recklessly entrepreneurial." Whereas European values had it that land was the "physical container for community values," according to James Howard Kunstler (in *The Geography of Nowhere*), American law has it that land is merely a commodity, something for capital gain. So while European cities were or are centers of political, ecclesiastical, military, and commercial power, in America it was only the commercial aspect that mattered. On the Continent, government intervention made the reshaping of the urban core for agreed-upon bourgeois uses possible; in Britain and the United States, laissez-faire economics turned the core into a bunch of competing uses. Thus in 1853, Napoleon III made Haussmann prefect of the Seine, and subsequently enabled developers to obtain large loans from government-sponsored banks under Haussmann's direction. Money was pooled, so that the government could direct the building process. This is not to say that the state is always going to get it right and have the best urban design; one look at the Soviet realism of the 1930s should be enough to disabuse anyone of that notion. But it is also clear that the suburban configuration that dominates the United States is the achievement of the laissez-faire approach, whereas the boulevards of Paris are the result of centralized planning. So while Haussmann's urban renewal destroyed much of medieval Paris and replaced it with vibrant business and residential districts, American urban renewal, engineered on an ad hoc free-market basis, destroys the fabric of the older city only to replace it with things that are worse than what was removed. Most American cities lack a sense of place; they have become alien worlds for most people, who withdraw from any community involvement. In the main, single-family houses and an elaborate highway system constitute the American landscape.[36]

There was, however, an "American Haussman," as it were, and the struggles of his life are indicative of the great differences between the American and European systems. I am referring, of course, to Frederick Law Olmsted, the father of modern landscape architecture and the single most important figure in American planning. Olmsted cofounded (with Calvert Vaux) the urban parks movement—Central Park in New York City is his most famous achievement in this regard—which was based on European traditions of incorporating nature into the city. "Much of the intercourse between men when engaged in the pursuits of commerce," he wrote in 1870, "has . . . a tendency to regard others in a hard if not always hardening way." To Olmsted, the American priority of making the city a place for moneymaking was a terrible mistake, and he wanted to "break the city up," provide it with "lungs," so to speak, which would transform it into a place for leisure and contemplation. This was hardly a popular view in the United States; as late as 1909, at the First National Conference on Planning, attempts to beautify cities were derided as a species of vanity. As historian Geoffrey Blodgett points out, Olmsted's inspiration was European in more than just the sense of urban design. It had much in common with aristocratic notions of hierarchy and deference, and the classical notion of virtue. Superior talent, wrote Olmsted, should be exercised for the benefit of the community.

Olmsted was part of a circle of post–Civil War reformers who believed that democracy could work only if it was responsive to the cues of a cultivated leadership, without which it would be a purely materialistic venture. This cosmopolitan elite, which included Charles Eliot Norton and Henry Adams, struggled to translate the private ethics of the gentleman amateur into efficient public conduct and placed great emphasis on the inner frontier—tranquility and self-containment. In Olmsted's eyes, the urban park was an antidote to the mass consumer society, the restless materialism of the majority. He saw the park as a work of art and a place for the sacred and the contemplative, and believed it would inspire communal feelings in people. But as Blodgett notes, the public reaction to this elite circle was one of unrelieved scorn; they had no use for these ideas (or thought they didn't, at any rate). True, Central Park, as well as Prospect Park in Brooklyn, did get built; but Olmsted's association with the city of New York was one of constant struggle, because what was involved was a conflict of worldviews. He was ousted from the New York City Parks Department in 1878 and remained embittered by the public's failure to grasp, let alone share, his vision. Lewis Mumford's later (1931) praise for Olmsted for what he had accomplished was a view not widely held, and in fact by then Olmsted had become a rather obscure figure.[37]

The American failure to understand cities in terms of civilization shows up, unsurprisingly, in the way our cities look. In "The Highway and the City" (1957), Mumford comments on the irony of the American who trashes his cities and has no aesthetic environment to walk around in, so goes on holiday to Europe in order to enjoy historic urban centers. As James Kunstler points out, Berlin is now in better shape than the cities of its chief destroyer, while Detroit (to take the most egregious example) looks like it was bombed. Whereas European cities are beautiful, urbane, and healthy, Atlanta and Las Vegas are gigantic wastes. While in Paris even the handwriting on the grocer's chalkboard displays gracefulness, St. Louis is a "virtual mummy's tomb," Baltimore a "flyblown carcass," and Buffalo, Memphis, Nashville, and Little Rock near total disasters. Even a casual look at Allan Jacobs' lovely book, *Great Streets*, reveals how magical places such as Rome and Barcelona are, with their buildings of similar height, their interesting façades, their windows that invite viewing, their trees and intersections, and the spaces they provide for leisurely walking. As for American cities, it is questionable whether they even *have* a future. It took a major uproar, in 1958, to stop Robert Moses from building a four-lane highway through Greenwich Village; most places were not so lucky. There are, of course, some important exceptions, even beyond that of New York: San Francisco, Boston, parts of Washington, D.C., and the very successful urban redevelopment of downtown Philadelphia come easily to mind. Cleveland has made something of a comeback, and Pittsburgh has been ranked as one of the fifteen most livable cities in the United States. Yet overall, the current fashionable talk about a purported nationwide urban revival is not borne out by the data. Both recovering (Pittsburgh, Cleveland, Philadelphia) and struggling (Detroit) cities have experienced population declines over the last decade, and the fast-growth areas are, and have been for some time, the suburbs and the exurbs. A Fannie Mae housing survey of 1997 found that only one in ten Americans wants to live in a major city.[38]

A crucial factor contributing to this unhappy state of affairs is the architectural movement known as modernism, which was officially "founded" in 1933 (it had been around since the 1920s), and which was based on the vision of the Swiss architect Le Corbusier (Charles-Edouard Jeanneret). His real goal, some have said, was to do away with historical time, with the organic feel of the traditional city; indeed, "kill the street!" was one of his favorite sayings. The organic city is a thing of the past, said Le Corbusier; it belongs to the age of handicrafts. The new city, on the other hand, is a city in motion; it is about speed and rational order. This had great appeal in the United States; thousands of buildings were erected on these principles. The constellation of skyscrapers and expressways became the model for postwar American urban renewal because it fit the needs of real estate speculators and corporate clients. Streets were regarded as nothing more than conduits for transportation; sidewalks were replaced with malls; and buildings, now isolated from the rest of the city, were made to stand free in plazas instead of lining the streets. The box style favored by the Bauhaus crowd was copied by nearly every architectural firm in America, and soon everything—high schools, hospitals, hotels, and apartment buildings—began to look like boxes. "An architecture of aloof anonymity," as it has been called, became the symbol of corporate America.[39]

Modernism caught on in the United States because the crux of its style is mechanical isolation, as opposed to the organic relatedness of the traditional European city. As Kunstler says, America doesn't have great public spaces because in order to have them, a culture must first esteem the idea of the public realm itself, and we don't. "What once were the experiences of place," writes Richard Sennett, "appear now to be floating mental operations." This lends itself to a purely instrumental view of life, the isolated atom (ego) acting upon the environment for its own benefit, with no regard for those around it. The physical space we move in is seen by Americans as lacking any inherent value; it's just a large, empty "box." The net effect of this is cold, even hostile; social life in America often feels as though it's a form of war. Again, this is a major reason that the automobile was able to make such rapid headway here, because space that is geometrically conceived is something you pass through, nothing more.[40]

As bad as all this is in the city, it is in the suburbs that the isolated, atomized life attained its apotheosis. Mies van der Rohe's famous statement, that architecture was the "will of the epoch translated into space," attains a special poignancy in the suburban landscape. For the will of the epoch here is "Leave me alone," and suburbia is the logical extension of that mentality. The paradox of this arrangement was not lost on Lewis Mumford, who described suburbia as "a collective effort to live a private life." In many ways, this goes to the heart of the matter, for it is a project based on self-contradiction—the tragedy of American domestic policy, one might call it.[41]

It is also, according to urban historian Robert Fishman, a powerful cultural ideal, specifically, a bourgeois version of utopia. The world, in this view, is characterized by exclusion: work is separated from residence, middle class from working class, white from color, "pristine" periphery from "polluted" core. Fishman defines the word "suburb" as a low-density environment characterized by the primacy of the single-family house located in a parklike setting. (The difference in population density between the United States and Europe is a partial explanation of why suburbs took off in the former and not the latter; although they were popular in Great Britain as well.) Once again, the notion of the frontier had a major role to play here, for in this case the frontier was the urban periphery, with its cheap, undeveloped land.[42]

Still, it took more than psychological ideals to turn the suburban vision into a reality. The Federal Housing Administration was established in 1934, and it reduced down payments on houses and extended the length of mortgages, so that the self-amortizing twenty-five to thirty-year mortgage became the norm throughout the United States. In the thirties, in fact, an FHA mortgage meant fifty dollars down and thirty to fifty dollars a month. The FHA also insured up to 90 percent of the houses' values—houses largely being the single-family detached ones in the suburbs—giving developers an assured supply of capital. Conditions for explosive suburban growth were thus firmly in place. Further legislation was passed at the end of World War II, enabling easy mortgages under the Veterans Administration. These immense market subsidies had the desired effect, for they spawned a huge housing industry that made suburban homes available with virtually no down payment. Thus William Levitt built 150 houses per day on Long Island, until 17,000 of them formed Levittown. The monthly mortgage for a suburban home was less than the rent on a city apartment, so for increasing numbers of Americans, the temptation was hard to resist (not that they wanted to resist it). True, they had to give up mass transit, cultural institutions, and the traditional continuities of community life, but as these were all replaced by cars and TV, most thought it a worthwhile exchange. Between 1950 and 1970, central cities grew by 10 million people, while the suburbs gained 85 million.[43]

It is, of course, Los Angeles rather than Long Island that is the paradigm case. It was *born* decentralized, and is our first suburban metropolis. The city has no central core, and no truly effective mass transit system. It was shaped by the promise of a suburban home for all, a promise that had its origin in the streetcar era. By the time the automobile came along, it was merely a more efficient tool for achieving a vision already agreed upon. In fact, when, in the 1920s, L.A.'s mass transit system threatened the viability of the single-family home, it was quickly tossed aside. By this time L.A. had the highest ratio of cars to people of any city in the world. A streetcar system would have raised land values along the rail lines, making the single-family house there very expensive; whereas a car system would open up the whole region to economic development. Since the economy of L.A. was closely tied to real estate development and speculation, the result was a foregone conclusion. Citizens overwhelmingly voted against a new rail and trolley station and in favor of a completely decentralized, car-based city. So the commercial areas became shabby, the whole pattern was centrifugal (requiring huge amounts of gasoline to enable the constant driving that was necessary to live there), and each family was its own "core." By the 1930s, all of the roads were congested, so what followed was the high-speed expressway, imposed over the city as a grid. Eventually, more than nine hundred square miles of agricultural land were transformed into suburban tract developments, and five hundred miles of expressways were constructed. When the city finally ran out of land, Los Angeles was forced, in the 1980s, to start building skyscrapers and a subway system—reinventing the wheel, in effect. But although the suburban metropolis—aka sprawl—proved to be a contradiction in terms, it remains oddly alive (if not well) in the United States, a testament to our unique combination of corporate dominance and radical privatization.[44]

The "end product of all this furious commerce-for-its-own-sake," writes James Kunstler, "was a trashy and preposterous human habitat with no future." Indeed, as a model of "urban" design, says British architect Lord Richard Rogers, the suburban one is the least sustainable in the world. Pollution and ecological devastation aside, there are human, communitarian, and spiritual dimensions that we cannot now recover because too many Americans are completely unaware that these ever existed. A sustainable design, according to Lord Rogers, is "compact, polycentric, ecologically aware and based on walking," and it promotes social inclusion. Truth to tell, we have lived car-centered lives for so long that we have forgotten what a great landscape or city is about. The culture of good place-making is a set of skills, and this body of knowledge has not been passed on. So Americans sit in Starbucks drinking homogenized, commercial coffee, talking on cell phones, staring into their laptops, and having no notion of what real café (or even social) life is all about. They spend huge amounts of time sitting alone in steel boxes on highways, driving to work and to huge shopping malls, their new "communities." They have no understanding of sacred spaces, places of quiet, or ones of

relaxed public assembly. From a European point of view, says sociologist
Ray Oldenburg, American suburbs are like prisons. There is no contact
between households, and one rarely knows one's neighbors. There are no
places to walk to, or cafés to sit where people drop in and socialize or
read the newspaper. And the "war," the endless me-first competition that
we conduct with one another (any appearance to the contrary), in lieu of
having any real community, is echoed in our foreign policy. Although our
interest in geopolitical control of the Middle East is a complicated issue,
certainly one aspect of that ill-fated project can be limned in the following equation:

$$car\ culture\ +\ suburbia\ =\ oil\ dependency\ =\ war\ culture$$

This war culture can be seen not only in our foreign policy, but also in
the details of how we live, both physically and emotionally. As Kunstler
points out, "Indulging in a fetish of commercialized privatism, we did
away with the public realm, and with nothing left but private life in our
private homes and private cars, we wonder what happened to the spirit of
community. We created a landscape of scary places and became a nation
of scary people." We live, says Richard Sennett, as though attack-and-
defense were the correct model of our subjective lives. As Mother Teresa
suggested, what could be more tragic?[45]

But if huge numbers of Americans are scary, they are also scared, and
the foreign policy of "Fortress America," coupled with an imperial policy, finds its domestic expression not only in the suburb but even more in
the gated "community." This quasi-military arrangement has had phe-
nomenal success in the United States; the number of people living in
such places went from four million in 1995 to sixteen million in 1998,
which ought to tell us something. Most residents surveyed say that security is a key issue for them; and indeed, with gated communities, neighborhoods are redefined by walls and guards. Social order is maintained by
policing and segregation, so as to generate a controlled and homogeneous environment. All of this, writes Setha Low in *Behind the Gates*, is
part of the militarization of America—in effect, an extension of the
national security state. The irony, she reports, is that the vigilance necessary to maintain this arrangement actually heightens the residents' anxiety and sense of isolation. This way of living mirrors the psychology of
the SUV, as well as a foreign policy that seeks to control the world but
which increases terror and instability instead. "A commanding residence

for the privileged few," reads one real estate ad for such a place. It could well become our national epitaph.[46]

IS THERE no way out? Both yesterday and today, a number of solutions to the whole sub/urban dilemma have been proposed, and it will be instructive to look at them, because their fate (or likely fate) reveals much about the possibilities for America in general in the twenty-first century. These alternatives—if that is what they really are—include the so-called garden cities of the early twentieth century (in England), and (in America) the Depression-era greenbelt cities and the 1960s suburban experiments (such as Columbia, Maryland, and Reston, Virginia) that took the garden city model as their inspiration; the emerging "edge cities" or "technocities" of the high-tech age; and the creative designs of the New Urbanism movement of the 1990s and beyond. What are these alternatives, and did they implement, or do they represent, a new vision for America? Are there, in other words, "roads not taken" that we can now revisit and recover, to our everlasting benefit?

The Restored Environment?

To start, then, with the garden city concept: this was the brainchild of the English planner Ebenezer Howard, whose book *Garden Cities of To-morrow* (1902) is one of the most influential works to be written on the subject of sub/urban design. Howard was really a social reformer; planning was part of his search for a cooperative commonwealth. He had been influenced by the English utopian tradition, and also by the Russian anarchist Pyotr Kropotkin, who had drawn attention to the importance of scale, and who promoted the notion of small communities in a decentralized society. For Howard, the garden city was a way of going beyond capitalism to a just society, an era of brotherhood. In order to do this, he said, we must decongest the city; and the key to this was the construction of small cities in the countryside. These towns, at most thirty thousand in population, would be cooperatively owned and economically independent; they would not be bedroom communities for a large metropolis. Howard saw the countryside dotted with hundreds of these towns, each surrounded by a green area (what planners would later call an "urban growth barrier"), with various clusters linked by rapid transit. The towns themselves would be models of small-scale cooperation and direct democracy. Rents on properties would be low, and wages high. There would be a mixture of quiet neighborhoods, commercial-industrial areas, and places for cultural activities. Howard called his central idea the "town-country magnet"; it would be a marriage whose "joyous union" would bring forth "a new hope, a new life, a new civilization."[47]

These ideas were revolutionary at the time: urban decentralization, zoning for different uses, the integration of cities with nature, use of green buffer zones, and the development of self-contained communities outside of central cities. They laid the groundwork for an important tradition in the evolution of American city planning, one that continues to this day. Indeed, Howard's book influenced every proposal for urban reform subsequently made by Lewis Mumford, who viewed the garden city concept as a utopia brought down to earth: socialism without the pain, as it were. Embedded in this work was an idea that would inevitably become very popular in an American context, and one that is really a variation on the theme of the technological fix: that design by itself was an alternative to revolution and that it could (apolitically) solve socioeconomic problems.[48]

The success and failure of the garden city concept were thus woven into the same fabric. Again, we come back to the point that technology is not really a value, and that if you try to make it one, the vacuum it represents politically is going to be filled by the dominant values of the culture. And just what would these be? Basically, money and profit, which is why the convergence of city and nature never materialized. "Instead," writes Robert Fishman, "both communitarian regionalism and metropolitanism proved vulnerable to a program of rapid economic development on the standardized corporate model."[49] This was the fate of Ebenezer Howard's project, as well as most of its American spinoffs. What else would one expect? All planning alternatives in the United States got swamped by the corporate model of life (or "life," I suppose I should say), business values, the Republican (1790s and after) definition of virtue, and the American penchant for extreme individualism. Plainly put, to have different cities you would have to have a different country. You aren't going to find Annecy or Portofino in Nebraska or Illinois.

Ebenezer Howard saw the world of the garden city as one in which "the little man has finally won out." But when the conference to make the dream a reality met in Bournville, England, in 1901, the "little man" was conspicuously absent. To raise the money for his project, Howard effectively had to compromise the project away. At his side in Bournville were millionaires and government officials, big men who could—and did—bankroll the project, but only once the social change elements were jettisoned. For them the garden city was merely a planning concept designed to relieve urban overcrowding; it was something that would preserve capitalism, not reform it. If the resulting company was going to sell shares, for example, it would have to present itself as a good business investment, nothing more. Thus the first two garden cities in Great Britain, Letchworth and Welwyn (both in Hertfordshire, north of London), had no true green buffer zones around them, but merely parks; and they were not independent economic entities. Certainly, they were not socialist experiments, or communally owned. The garden city concept, in short, lost its commitment to social change and became a city planning movement in the narrowest sense of the term.[50]

This pattern of co-optation got repeated in the United States, although there were a (very) small number of victories. One of these was Sunnyside Gardens, which was the first garden city built in the United States. In 1923, Lewis Mumford helped found the Regional Planning Association of America in New York City and drew its attention to the garden city concept. The plan for such a community in the borough of Queens was prepared by the City Housing Corporation, working together with the architectural firm of Stein & Wright. Sunnyside Gardens, completed in 1928, was designed for workers and the lower middle class. Houses were small, many of them fronting inward toward common greens. There are public courtyards, and service roads behind the houses. The area, which is bounded by Skillman Avenue (aka Lewis Mumford Way) and Thirty-ninth Avenue, and by Forty-third and Forty-ninth Streets, still retains a villagelike atmosphere, although this lovely garden community is now a fairly upscale neighborhood (as a local real estate agent informed me) and privately owned. Mumford and his wife, Sophia, lived there for a number of years, as did Frank Lloyd Wright, and Mumford later described the time as the happiest years of his life. Its success lay in the fact that it broke with the corporate model. Commenting on Sunnyside in the *New York Times* in 1972, Ada Louise Huxtable wrote:

Public ownership of land, one of the basic premises, made possible a planned community, rather than speculative piece-meal exploitation. . . . It was simple physical planning—the kind of humane, paternalistic, thoughtful layout that dealt clearly and primarily with a better way to live.

As originally conceived, then, Sunnyside was "un-American," and walking around the place, one can still feel the ambience and hear the echo of a very different social orientation and value system.[51]

Most of the other experiments in this genre did not fare as well. The garden city movement was one of the first challenges to the corporate ideology of the modern Anglo-Saxon world; but as Mumford pointed out in 1927, without a complete reorientation of values, these types of communities would not be able to survive in a culture dominated by the drive for profit and expansion. This reorientation, of course, never came to pass, which is why the garden cities that followed tended to be long on shadow and short on substance. Greenbelt, Maryland, for example, built in 1937, does have a library, a museum, and a community center. Although some of the residents work close by, at Goddard Space Flight Center or Lockheed Martin, 80 percent drive to Washington (thirteen miles) or Baltimore (thirty miles) for work. Like most of the garden city experiments in the United States, it is largely a "dormitory" for commuters. Greenbelt does have a Metro station and bus service, but the town practically sits on the Beltway (I-495) and is largely car dependent. It has no bookstore or traditional coffee shop for hanging out, and while the community center offers numerous classes in art, tai chi, and similar activities, the locals don't seem to congregate there. On the Saturday I visited, the people manning the desk at the center were not from Greenbelt and were not able to answer elementary questions about the town or its history. Greenbelt is racially mixed, but the statistics are deceptive, because the black population is "walled away" from the central town area by a major highway. All in all, the flavor of the place is that there is no there there.[52]

The level of community once present in Sunnyside, or halfheartedly attempted in Greenbelt, is the sort of exception that proves the rule. Moving against the corporate grain is almost impossible in the United States, which is why the few garden city towns remain curiosities, while the suburban home-and-highway formula spread dramatically. One would think that the Depression would have forced the nation into moving toward a different sort of landscape, but just the opposite proved to be true. The Roosevelt administration created favorable conditions for large corporations to invest in new areas, and dam and highway electrification projects sought to make rural regions profitable for corporate expansion. In addition, notes Robert Fishman, it was through regional economic development that corporate America got a huge boost after the Depression, which included building an industrial and defense complex in the metropolitan periphery or the Sun Belt—a process that accelerated during the Cold War. The "decentralized terrain where the regionalists [Mumford, for example] had expected to build their participatory society," he writes, " . . . has become the area in our society most dominated by centralized power and standardized culture."[53] Wal-Mart, not Sunnyside Gardens, would carry the day.

Moving ahead to the 1960s, we see some version of the garden city concept in a town such as Columbia, Maryland, which opened in 1967. It is not clear what sort of cutting-edge concept the architect, James Rouse, thought he was generating, but the place is utterly suburban, as Alex Marshall points out, and one of a string of "incoherent places that hide their disorder under a veneer of privatized central planning." Signs directing one to the purported "town center" lead, in fact, to a huge shopping mall. Indeed, the place has no center at all; it's just a series of look-alike, well-to-do residential areas. Ninety percent of the residents are commuters; the average household income is about $90,000. It comes off like a prettified Los Angeles without the cultural amenities, and one wouldn't walk the streets of Columbia any more than one would those of L.A. It's basically a giant bedroom community for Washington and Baltimore, a kind of trendy parody of the traditional suburb.[54]

Equally instructive for our purposes is the town of Reston, Virginia, designed by Robert E. Simon (an admirer of Mumford). Simon somehow managed to operate outside of heavy corporate control when he built the first of the five Reston villages, Lake Anne Village, which opened in 1964. True, there is no mass transit in the vicinity, the place is car dependent, and the town seems fairly posh. Nevertheless, Lake Anne Village catches one by surprise: it looks like a small Italian town and is situated on a lake, to boot. Cars are set apart from the village center, or plaza, which boasts a coffee shop, a few cafés, and a friendly, fair-sized used bookstore that hosts book clubs and readings. The arrangement is conducive to a high degree of human interaction.[55]

This atmosphere, however, was largely lost in the four remaining villages. The key differences from Lake Anne Village are that they have no distinct center and cars are an integral part of village life. Enter Hollywood Video, Burger King, Dairy Queen, and the usual suspects. These four Restons come off like typical suburbs, and have a corporate feel to them. Unlike Lake Anne Village, they seem to have no places to sit. Lake Anne Village, apparently, was an accident, Simon's one lucky shot at the brass ring.

In the 1970s, we find one experiment that, like Sunnyside Gardens, one might label "un-American": Portland, Oregon. As James Kunstler puts it, one wonders if the city is actually in this country: it has a vibrant downtown area, sidewalks full of people, electric trolleys, and inviting storefronts. The place is alive day and night, full of bars and cafés, with people from different class backgrounds living in proximity to one another (Portland deliberately rezoned to create diversity-of-income neighborhoods). In the 1970s, when other cities were building expressways along their rivers and harbors, Portland tore down an old four-lane highway and reconnected the city with its waterfront. In 1975, it canceled a planned freeway that would have devastated part of the city and invested the resulting available federal funds in light rail. It also established an Urban Growth Boundary (UGB) that forbade the building of commercial projects beyond a certain point, along with an agency with the power to enforce it (and it's not an easy sell to tell people in the United States how their land is going to be used). Portland treats land-use planning as a legitimate expression of community interest and puts restrictions on private actions. Thus it passed zoning laws requiring buildings to have their display windows at street level, and built out to the sidewalk. It put a cap on the height of high-rises and on the number of downtown parking spaces. Portland also set up a pedestrian-oriented downtown that is a true regional hub. In general, the city is one of those rare places in the United States where one can live without a car. The business district has parks full of fountains and greenery. In 1994–95, the voters agreed to tax themselves for the acquisition of more parks, open spaces, and light-rail construction. All in all, says Kunstler, "it was Lewis Mumford's dream come true: authentic [i.e., centralized, government-directed, popularly voted] regional planning."[56]

How did this happen? And most important for America's urban future, are the conditions that made the revitalization of Portland possible unique, a one-shot deal, or are they capable of being reproduced elsewhere? This is no minor issue, for there is no getting around the sad truth that there are very few cities in the U.S. that possess this sort of urban brilliance and that are, in a word, "European." Portland developed in ways that ran counter to the powerful trends shaping American cities and suburbs in the postwar era.[57] So we have to wonder what factors created a trajectory of urban renewal so different from that of the rest of the country. And when we look closely, we see a combination of factors, including that of sheer luck, that would lead one to believe that the Portland experiment is ultimately not for export. These factors, which break with the corporate model, include (1) cautious economic expansion; (2) an environmental ethic that has attracted people who are disaffected from the American mainstream and who in turn promote that environmental ethic (which in turn attracts more such people, and so on); and (3) a political culture that harks back to the classical notion of virtue. Let me discuss these briefly.

Regarding economic expansion, Portland failed to catch the postwar economic boom. While sprawl engulfed the rest of the nation, Portland grew slowly in the period from 1945 to 1970, which made for a rather dingy downtown area by the latter date. At the same time, this translated into slow suburbanization and the slow development of expressways, which meant that the prospects for constructing a lively urban center, when this was finally undertaken after 1970, had something of a chance. Second, the state is, in general, a bit of an odd duck: physician-assisted suicide and the legalization of marijuana for medical purposes are two examples of a political outlook that breaks with the dominant culture. Since the 1960s Oregon has attracted a disproportionate share of individuals with a strong urban and environmental ethic, people who don't want their landscape destroyed by suburban sprawl. When Governor Tom McCall, a maverick Republican, denounced "coastal condomania" (associated with California, in particular) in the early 1970s and the Oregon Senate responded by passing a bill that led to the establishment of statewide goals (including a farmland protection program and the UGB), he and it were speaking for a large percentage of Oregonians. During the early 1970s as well, Portland had a visionary mayor, Neil Goldschmidt, who later became secretary of transportation under Jimmy Carter. Third, the political environment that was created by such a proactive and progressive citizenry and leadership was one in which it was possible, even desirable, for that leadership to talk in terms of "moral obligation"—that is, to behave according to the classical definition of virtue, whereby the community counts for more than one's own personal ambitions (allowing here for some degree of overlap). As Portland State University's Carl Abbott points out, the political style in Portland is one of coalition building. The community views politics as service to the public good, and so over time, he says, moralistic politics squeezed out the individualistic variety.[58] A miracle, in short.

One problem with miracles, of course, is that they tend not to be replicable. Indeed, there are already signs that the Portland model won't endure. In November 2004 Oregon voters passed a ballot referendum known as Measure 37, which rolled back many of the state's unique land-use regulations. To supporters of the law, Measure 37 was a defense of individual property rights—which in the United States, of course, count for far more than environmental values or concerns. To its great loss, Oregon may be on its way to "rejoining" the rest of the country.[59]

But even if Portland does manage to hold the line, it is possible that its idiosyncratic history is rooted in something that may be the most significant factor of all: race. Portland politics does not revolve around race because the place is one of the whitest cities around, and Oregon one of the whitest states. Given the absence of the "white flight" factor endemic to much of the United States, there hasn't been that great a motivation for suburban housing in the greater Portland area. The town never experienced an influx of blacks or had any racial polarization. There isn't much of an "other" in Portland to "protect" oneself from, in other words; the place is largely homogeneous. And this makes for a depressing conclusion. For while all the other factors mentioned above are real, and probably nonexportable even without the issue of race, this last factor may be the nail in the coffin, so to speak. If I had to venture a guess, I would say that the success of Portland was due to a combination of unlikely factors, not just any single one of them. But one has to wonder what the American landscape as a whole would have looked like if race had not played such an enormous role in American history. It just may take racial homogeneity for an American city to work—not a happy conclusion for us, as Americans, to have to come to (if it's true).[60]

What I *do* find inspiring in all of this, however, is that even though it is extremely marginalized in the United States, thinking about the environment in the tradition of the garden city movement, Lewis Mumford, and

Frederick Law Olmsted has refused to lie down and die. It has a long countercultural history (Jane Jacobs' *The Death and Life of Great American Cities* is a major milestone), and even if it serves as little more than a mirror to our follies, and to the self-destructive path we are on, it remains a tradition one can point to that is truly healthy—what civic life needs to have in order to serve truly human purposes.

This brings us to the New Urbanism, an attempt to recapture this alternative tradition, to literally take the roads not taken, which emerged in the late 1980s and early 1990s. Popular in urban design circles, the New Urbanism has had an interesting career; one that, in my view, is iconic of the possibilities for real social change in the United States. It can be regarded in part as an attempt to return to the classical notion of virtue. Thus the *Charter of the New Urbanism* declares that its proponents "stand for the restoration of existing urban centers and towns within coherent metropolitan regions, the reconfiguration of sprawling suburbs into communities of real neighborhoods and diverse districts, the conservation of natural environments, and the preservation of our built legacy." "Community planning and design," say its advocates, "must assert the importance of public over private values." The key to this would be the creation of streets, squares, and parks as settings for the conduct of daily life; neighborhoods with diverse types of people and activities; and a relatively car-free environment. All of these design principles were ignored for more than sixty years.[61]

So far so good, and the formula was employed in the design of Seaside and Celebration in Florida, and of Kentlands in Maryland (among other places), which have been referred to as "neotraditional towns." These are not urban centers, but rather contemporary versions of the garden city concept; they constitute attractive alternatives—so their proponents claim—to postwar suburban sprawl. In fact, they evoke the feel of an America long gone: quiet, neighborly, cohesive, and (at least in theory) community oriented. Yet what seems to be a success on the surface starts, upon closer scrutiny, to dissolve. Seaside, for example, is elegant, very beautifully designed; it definitely breaks with the ubiquitous Florida condo-and-motel-strip atmosphere. However, it mostly consists of second homes, and as such is basically a resort town for the wealthy. In the first decade of its existence, residential lot prices increased tenfold. Writing in the *Wall Street Journal*, Christina Binkley observes that "there's no school, no church, no supermarket here—just gourmet food boutiques and upscale shops. Community life is nil. And nearly everyone around town is a tourist, architecture buff, or second-home shopper." In brief, the place is upper class, completely homogeneous, and something of a fishbowl. As for Celebration, this is a New Urbanist subdivision built by the Walt Disney Company that has the quality of a stage set and where in October and December, machines attached to street lamps blow fake leaves and snow, respectively, onto the streets. All in all, the most perceptive comment I have read on the New Urbanism is that of Andrew Ross, who lived in Celebration for a year, to the effect that New Urbanist towns are *commentaries* on urban problems, not solutions to them.[62]

The New Urbanism did not really accomplish what it set out to do, and this, I believe, can teach us quite a bit about what has gone wrong with the United States. To begin with, its conceptual basis contains two major fallacies that were also part of the garden city movement: that social, economic, and political problems can be solved by planning and design (the technological fix argument), and that a vision for design can actually break with the dominant ethos and escape being co-opted by mainstream corporate forces. For the most part, neither the garden cities nor the New Urbanist towns developed an independent economic base, sustained any real income diversity, or avoided basic car dependency. In the end, New Urbanism replaced ugly suburban sprawl with prettified, upper-income suburban sprawl; the basic idea remains the same. In fact, some argue that New Urbanism may be turning into a justification for *more* sprawl. These places have no real community, because community cannot be "manufactured"; and in any case, Americans want privacy and isolation, not community. Even beyond this, writes architect Michael Sorkin, New Urbanism represents "the enclaving of communities against the threat of genuine plurality, a new style of apartheid," and it "asks us to believe that a shell of a city really is a city, that appearances are enough." What you see in the New Urbanist suburban towns is uniformity of appearance, scale, and demographics, and an absence of true public space and commercial activities. Mainstream co-optation is clearly the norm: if you flip through the real estate section of almost any American newspaper, for example, you'll see that many new developments are superficially adopting New Urbanist design principles as motifs or buzzwords to enhance their marketing strategies. Indeed, claims Alex Marshall, New Urbanism was from the first a developer-driven organization; their conferences tend to be like trade shows.[63]

A different approach to suburbia, however, was first proposed by Robert Fishman with the concept of the "technocity," and subsequently elaborated upon by Joel Garreau in *Edge City*. The crux of Fishman's argument is that appearances to the contrary, suburbia as we have traditionally understood it is coming to an end, giving way to the emergence of a new form of decentralized city. Suburbs will no longer define themselves with respect to a central urban core, inasmuch as the periphery has become the favored locale for the new global economy. The basis of this cluster of "technoburbs," as it were, is the new growth engine of high-tech industries and telecommunications. It is these that string out, in Silicon Valley and elsewhere, into extended regions or technocities (fondly known to their admirers as "nerdistans"). Once managerial office employment, advanced technology labs, and production facilities shifted from the core to the periphery, says Fishman, everything changed, for the technoburb "has become the true center of American society." These suburbs are nontraditional in that they constitute viable socioeconomic units in and of themselves, and so the commute to work is no longer to an urban center but laterally, along the edge, to another technoburb. In fact, by the early 1990s twice as many people were commuting to work along the edge than into the old downtowns. Hence the phrase "edge city."[64]

Fishman and Garreau are optimists; they believe that since things don't get planned in the laissez-faire market economy anyway, we should be tracking on how things are *actually* unfolding, and perhaps even embrace it all—put a positive spin on it, as it were. The problem with this approach, however, is whether a positive spin makes for a positive reality. For one thing, since the technoburb phenomenon is tied to globalization, it has generated an even more severe dichotomy between rich and poor than before, excluding huge numbers of people from the edge city economy (nearly 40 percent of the nation's poor now live in the suburbs, as compared with about 20 percent in 1970). Not surprisingly, this burb lacks any communitarian ethic whatsoever—it basically represents an affectless, throwaway consumer society with no civic spirit (think Tyson's Corner, Virginia, or Atlanta, or Silicon Valley). Finally, the phenomenon binds us even more tightly to the oil-based economy, which has no future except one of imperial (military) overstretch in the Middle East (a venture that also has no future). No matter how you slice it, suburban design, which is the physical manifestation of the American psyche, finally ties back into our other domestic arrangements and our foreign policy, adding up to an increasingly dysfunctional state of affairs.[65]

The truth is that cities and civilization are nearly synonymous, and if the former die out, so does the latter. Nor does renaming a phenomenon change it. Techno-oriented or not, the new suburbs continue the trend of racial and class segregation; have not become independent economic entities; are destructive of the environment; epitomize the culture of consumption; and lack the diversity, cosmopolitanism, political culture, and public life that real cities have. The ethos of the technocity remains what the suburban ethos has always been: resistance to heterogeneity, and the desire to live apart. It also represents the enduring triumph of the private over the communitarian and the Jeffersonian Republican definition of virtue over the classical republican one.[66]

So our problems simply cannot be solved by new design techniques. Joel Garreau has been criticized for saying that if edge cities are becoming dominant, it's because that's what the American people want. True, this ignores the fact that Americans are largely oblivious to other alternatives, and it ignores the historical forces that promoted suburbs over cities; but the man clearly has a point: for whatever reasons, Americans do want this. We cannot squirm away from the fact that we got the landscape that reflects our values, the one that says who we are and how we choose to live. A changed landscape would require different values, along with different relations of power; all of which are closely sewn together with our use of technology, the nature of our economy, and our imperial foreign policy. Pierre Bourdieu's argument, that we actualized one possibility and discarded the others, suggests that things could have been otherwise; and I'm guessing this is probably true (if debatable). But Bourdieu is also arguing that they could *still* be otherwise, and this I simply do not see. Not even the Depression, which shook us to our very foundations, was able to make any substantive difference; if anything, American-style capitalism emerged all the stronger for it. Hence, we cannot realistically expect very much. What are we to make of the fact that even after 9/11, in March 2002, sixty-two senators (including nineteen Democrats), according to the *Washington Post*, "rejected higher fuel-efficiency standards for automobiles, which would have reduced dependence upon Persian Gulf oil"? Republican Senator Christopher Bond of Missouri declared, "I don't want to tell a mom in my home state that she should not get an SUV because Congress decided that would be a bad choice."[67]

So who *should* tell her, then? Who should tell some typically oblivious American citizen, living a fantasy life of total individual autonomy, that buying a huge, unsafe van that gets twelve miles to the gallon is not a very good idea and has ramifications that go way beyond her own private concerns? As *The New Yorker's* John Cassidy writes, Americans think they "are entitled to cheap fuel, regardless of how much they consume." So let's just stay tied to an oil-economy, an unending "war on terrorism," a national security state, a ruined physical landscape, an illusion of security, and a near total absence of community, and (above all) remain totally ignorant of how these factors knit together. Clearly, "dysurbanism," and the social, economic, and political configuration that goes with it, are going to be with us for a very long time. The likely scenario is one of cosmetic changes in the context of a disintegrating civilization, nothing else. (For example, developing a "hybrid" SUV—sort of like diet cheese-cake. Once again, political reality is avoided with a technological fix.) Optimism is no doubt an admirable position, but only, in my opinion, when it has some basis in fact.[68]

The optimism I retain, personally, is the one already mentioned above: the alternative tradition remains a testament to the human spirit, and that spirit will endure beyond the eclipse of American civilization, and (shades of Hegel) probably on a different part of the planet. In the context of our civilization, however, men such as Mumford and Olmsted, or the planners of Portland, may be freaks, but let's face it: they are *American* freaks, and a civilization that produced them, even as an antidote to its own self-destruction, can't be all bad. In terms of saving that civilization, however, their extreme marginalization remains the central problem, as Robinson Jeffers tells us in his unbelievably prescient 1925 poem "Shine, Perishing Republic":

> While this America settles in the mould of its vulgarity,
> heavily thickening to empire,
> And protest, only a bubble in the molten mass, pops
> and sighs out, and the mass hardens,
>
> I sadly smiling remember that the flower fades to make
> fruit, and the fruit rots to make earth.[69]

Decay, then, is inevitable; and if renewal does eventually happen, I suspect it will not occur on the American empire's home turf. This—

resurrection elsewhere—is how things played out in the case of Rome, and I think it likely that we are going to follow a similar pattern. The reason is that our imperial destiny emerges not only from our foreign policy and our domestic arrangements, but also from the nitty-gritty details of American life, in which these things are rooted: values and daily behavior. Such things go very deep; they make real change almost impossible. In the chapter that follows, then, we shall need to examine them a bit more closely.

8

The State of the Union

Every day I ask myself the same question: How can this be happening in America? How can people like these be in charge of our country? If I didn't see it with my own eyes, I'd think I was having a hallucination.

—Philip Roth,
The Plot Against America

As democracy is perfected, the office of president represents, more and more closely, the inner soul of the people. On some great and glorious day the plain folks of the land will reach their heart's desire at last and the White House will be adorned by a downright moron.

—H. L. Mencken, "Bayard vs. Lionheart,"
Baltimore Evening Sun, 26 July 1920

We have this ability in Lake Wobegon to look reality right in the eye and deny it.

—Garrison Keillor

THE GREATEST OBSTACLE TO progressive change in the United States is probably the American people themselves. It would be nice to think that we could somehow "go in," "fix" things, and set the United States on an upward trajectory once again. But beyond the deep structural patterns we have analyzed thus far, which are now working against us, the sad fact is that daily American life contains a great amount of violence and ignorance and is pervaded by a lot of (repressed) alienation and spiritual emptiness. How, then, could we go in and fix things? Who is the "we" who would do this, exactly where would they go, and what would they do?

It is, of course, heresy to talk in these terms, especially if one is a politician. As Fareed Zakaria notes, the sacred cow in the United States is the American people, to which politicians have to pay ritual homage if they value their careers. No matter how manifestly stupid the people's behavior is, American politicians praise their sagacity. Uttering the phrase, "the American people," says Zakaria, is tantamount to announcing a divine visitation; anything has the force of biblical revelation if it is ascribed to this mystical, all-knowing entity. Yet what if "the American people" are, in the words of Nicholas von Hoffman, a collection of "asses, dolts, and blockheads"? Americans, says Hoffman, are living in a glass dome, a kind of terrarium, cut off from both reality and the outside world—"bobbleheads in Bubbleland. . . . They shop in bubbled malls, they live in gated communities, and they move from place to place breathing their own, private air in the bubble-mobiles known as SUVs." They unquestioningly take their "truth" from the government, whereas in other countries grown-ups know there is no truth teat to suck on, and if you want it you have to go dig up the information for yourself. If, for example, Americans had wanted to know the truth about our record in the Middle East, there was enough reliable literature on the subject for them to do so. But they have no interest in these sorts of things; instead, von Hoffman continues, they are "taken up with more important things than war and peace, like pro football and self improvement." The only way out of this destructive American insularity is for "the masses of moron manipulatees to demoronize themselves."[1] What are the chances, really?

It is, in any case, not easy to find an analysis of our national decline in terms of individual behavior, but one sociologist who was not willing to let "the people" off the hook was Philip Slater. Slater was determined to talk about the American crisis in terms of our values, our psyches, our ideologies, and our day-to-day way of living. Thus, comments Todd Gitlin, Slater saw the excess of individualism as it was encapsulated in the suburb and the isolated family as "the root of the military and economic and cultural mobilization which has been institutionalized since 1947 in the national security state." For Slater, for example, Vietnam could not be dismissed as a "regrettable mistake," as though such a costly debacle and irrevocable turning point in our history "could be attributed to nothing more than faulty calculation." No, this war arose from a particular culture, was the expression of a major part of the psychology of that culture, and afforded us a certain psychic payoff—as did all of the Cold War, of course, and as the "war on terrorism" does now. "The people," he maintained, are not "innocent of their rulers' military expeditions."[2]

This is strong stuff; certainly, the American left (such as it is) has never been willing to utter it. Michael Moore, for example, styles himself a populist, and argues that the Bush foreign policy program was conducted against the popular will (which is, for the most part, not true); Noam Chomsky has stated or implied that people do not get the government they deserve, that their consent is manufactured, and that they might eventually (he hopes) throw off the yoke of their oppressors and create a more socialist form of government. Well, there may be a grain of truth to some of this, but I am skeptical that legitimacy can be attained without a wide degree of popular sanction. It seems to me that the people *do* get the government they deserve, and even beyond that, the government who they are, so to speak. In that regard, we might consider, as an extreme version of this, *Hitler's Willing Executioners*, the very controversial attack on the German people by Daniel Jonah Goldhagen, which has been sharply criticized as being racist and "essentialist," but which retains a ring of truth nonetheless, to the effect that Hitler was as much an expression of the German people at that point in time as he was a departure from them.[3] While the analyses of Goldhagen, Slater, and von Hoffman will not win any of them a popularity contest, I don't feel that an honest appraisal of why positive social change is extremely unlikely in the United States can realistically skirt such issues. I am not saying that these behaviors or tendencies are uniquely American, but the constellation of the particular factors I am going to discuss may be. We do display them, and quite dramatically; taken together, they do seem to render any kind of new healthy direction for the United States a rather dim prospect. While we have many admirable qualities and can be generous to a fault, we also possess a number of dark aspects that operate at a bedrock level, and that have led directly to the civilizational morass in which we now find ourselves. Chomsky and Moore would, metaphorically speaking, say that we have been raped by the corporate-consumerist-military establishment, but I suspect it was more like a seduction: if this was sex, it was definitely consensual. Let's see if we can't shine some light on the shadows, in any case.

Emptiness

In the previous chapter, I noted that in the nations of the developed world, one can have fundamental disagreements with the government or even the dominant value system and it is perfectly all right: one won't be attacked as "un-Italian" or "un-Danish," let's say. But America is quite different in this respect: one is immediately branded as being "un-American" if one breaks with the pack, which includes voicing any fundamental criticism at all. This relates to our discussion of America's civil religion, wherein the United States and its history are effectively elevated to divine status. The American Dream—basically, shopping (captured in David Potter's discussion of abundance), radical individualism, and the "religion" of America (including its God-given mission to democratize the rest of the world)—is so fiercely held that it can rightly be characterized as an addiction. Hence, the rage that emerges when it is challenged, even slightly. But as with all addictions, it masks an emptiness at the core. Our violence as a people, for example, emerges in part from the subliminal and haunting awareness that as a belief system, this dream has become something of an illusion. This is why Osama bin Laden can say to us, in his statement of 29 October 2004, "you have no Guardian or Helper," and why Patrick Buchanan writes that our "faith" is by now nothing more than MTV culture: individualism, consumerism, and hedonism.[4]

Shopping, of course, is a pretty pathetic religion, but if "God" can be said to be where someone puts most of their attention, then the data are in. Americans spend far more time in shopping malls than in church, for example, and by 1987 the country had more malls than high schools. And yet none of this compulsive consumerism is really about objects per se. As sociologist Sharon Zukin notes, "The seduction of shopping is not about buying goods. It's about dreaming of a perfect society and a perfect self." We are looking, she says, "for truth with a capital T.... In a society where we no longer have contact with nature or beauty in our daily lives, shopping is one of the few ways we have left to create a sense of ultimate value." We are, she concludes, "searching for our dreams," and seek to fulfill them in stores.⁵

Anxiety about the dream also accounts, in part, for the powerful emergence of Christian fundamentalism in this country, which is a way to hang on to *something* transcendent, at least. Ultimately, it's not really much of an answer to the American spiritual crisis, and is in fact only another manifestation of it. It certainly won't stave off the disintegration of our civilization and is more likely to hurry the process along. Like George W. Bush, it has no real spiritual depth, but merely represents one more addiction, one more unconscious reaction. Real spirituality—what I have called "the inner frontier"—could conceivably save us, but we are too far gone to know what that is anymore. Hence, we thrash around, searching for substitutes (New Age-ism included). The Jesuit scholar John Courtney Murray once observed that if American democracy is ever overthrown by the yearning for monism, for a single faith or an all-encompassing worldview, it will have happened because the United States

> will have undertaken to establish a technological order of most marvelous intricacy, which will have been constructed and will operate without relations to true political ends: and this technological order will hang, as it were, suspended over a moral confusion; and this moral confusion will itself be suspended over a spiritual vacuum.

This is by now a pretty close description of our situation, it seems to me, and the final result was captured by the Egyptian novelist Sonallah Ibrahim, who taught Arabic literature at Berkeley in 1998: "I despised the total individualism . . . the values of life, just living to eat, drink, fuck, have a car, and that's all." This is not everybody, of course; but it does describe a great many.⁶

Alienation

All of this segues into extreme individualism and the alienation that goes with it. We couldn't now, at this point in our history, be further from the republican (small r) notion of virtue, which sees cultures as composed of communities, not just individuals, and sees those communities as the bearer of values. The results of our obsessive individualism show up in numerous international surveys of happiness that have been conducted in recent years, where Americans score so badly. But personally, I find the anecdotal evidence even more compelling, because debacles such as the Enron scandal are really the logical end point of this aspect of the American Dream. Thus the epitome of this value system is captured by the story of a staff assistant on Capitol Hill, Jessica Cutler, who slept with a number of men concurrently (a senator's staff member, a married Bush administration official, and so on) and then posted a chronicle of her bedroom activities on the Web. The portrait of her—and this extended to everything, not just sex—is one of someone who, as she put it, created and inhabited her own moral universe. Her very first blog entry stated that she had no interest in politics whatsoever; it was just that the Senate job looked good on her résumé, and Capitol Hill was a great place for meeting men and showing off her clothes. There was no question here of public service's being socially important, or of sexual activity's being loving or meaningful. Without any ethical grounding to provide direction for her life, the private "moral universe" Jessica created just coincidentally happened to be the dominant secular ethos of the contemporary United States, in which it's all about pleasure, PR, and (self-)promotion. The upshot of it all was pretty predictable: posing for a pictorial with *Playboy* and netting a six-figure book deal. The cover story in the *Washington Post Magazine* commented that the whole affair "raised a ton of questions about where America is headed"—but quite honestly, I don't think there is any question as to where America is headed.[7]

Note that from the standpoint of Republican virtue (capital R), Jessica Cutler was an outstanding student. She "made something of herself," controlled her own destiny, put herself first, manipulated others for her own benefit, maximized her opportunities in a competitive market, etc.—a fast learner in the school of market capitalism and obsessive individualism, one would have to say. Should we be surprised that her efforts were crowned with "success"?

It is really fascinating how, under the regime of American-style individualism, everybody loses, and yet it continues to be celebrated as the greatest gift to the human race. Surely, Jessica Cutler is but one story among millions. Here is another: a few years ago, the novelist Stephen King announced that he would publish his next book online, in installments. To do so, he made a deal with his readers: they would send him a dollar each time they downloaded a chapter, and he would promise to keep writing until the book was finished. However, said King, if he did not receive payments for at least 75 percent of the downloads, he would pack it in, and the book wouldn't get finished. And so the first chapter of the electronic novel, *The Plant*, appeared and generated more than 120,000 downloads. Chapter 2, however, generated only 40,000 downloads, and of these only 46 percent were paid for. So King pulled the plug, the novel never got written, and everybody lost out.[8]

If the philosophy of "me first" is not working out very well in the United States, the sadness involved in this modus vivendi goes back a long way. I received a stark reminder of this a couple of years ago when I happened to be in London and caught an Edward Hopper exhibition at the Tate Modern. There are few American artists, or even artists period, whose work is as psychologically haunting as Hopper's. In paintings such as *Automat* (1927) or *Nighthawks* (1942) one sees quite clearly the results of American individualism: an isolation and pervasive melancholy that lurks underneath the surface bombast. Americans, I remember thinking, must be the loneliest people on earth; they just don't know it. Certainly, no one managed to capture the soullessness of a life devoted to power and "success" as well as Hopper did; and if, on an unconscious level, life in the United States was this bleak in the 1920s, 1930s, and 1940s, what would his paintings look like, I wondered, if he were alive today? An article on the exhibition in Barcelona's *La Vanguardia Magazine* of 11 July 2004 makes just this point: "The pertinent question is how he would have painted the crueler, more fundamentalistic, and more divided United States of George W. Bush." Hopper, the article concludes, was a dissident mirror of a society "happy in appearance, but full of moral doubts (as it is now), and above all infinitely lonely."[9]

Part of the process of Americanization, of course, is giving people the means to hide from the alienation that Americanization leaves in its wake. I suspect that if Hopper were to paint *Nighthawks* today, the people in the painting would be on cell phones or Prozac (more likely, both), staring into TV or computer screens, and perhaps stuffing themselves with Big Macs. Can the process of Americanization be arrested? Left to its own devices, this nation could well turn every face on earth into an empty one, every European café into a scene out of a Hopper painting. Study after study of the effects of Americanization show that if a country buys the neoliberal package, the American way of life comes with it; this means wealth for a small upper class and a culture of competition, extreme individualism, and loneliness forced onto everybody else. This is the "freedom" we seek to export to the rest of the world.[10]

Violence

There are many problems with this type of radical individualism, and one of the most pernicious, as Will Hutton observes, is that it "eats away at the capacity to empathize." In a Hobbesian world of all against all, "the very stuff of human association is undermined." Indeed, one of the points made by Stephen Carter in *Civility* is that Americans treat one another quite badly on a daily basis almost as a matter of course. True, this may not be the violence of, say, Bosnia, and it tends to be invisible in our culture; but it is definitely present, and it takes a heavy psychological toll.[11]

An interesting, if somewhat confused, take on the causes of violence in the United States occurs in *Bowling for Columbine*, the film by Michael Moore. Ostensibly designed to show how a lack of gun control is responsible for the huge numbers of shootings and homicides in America, the documentary—despite its clever exposé of National Rifle Association president Charlton Heston—unexpectedly winds up confirming the old NRA saw that people, not guns, are the real cause of these events. Or at least, *American* people: when Moore and his crew venture north to Canada to explore why the per capita homicide rate there is so much lower than in the United States, they discover that per capita gun ownership up there is much higher. The logical conclusion is that the United States is a violent nation, and the data bear this out. To a question on a 2000 U.S.-Canada survey as to whether "a little violence" is okay if you are frustrated, 31 percent of Americans said yes, as compared with 14 percent of Canadians. In response to the question "Is it acceptable to use violence to get what you want?," 24 percent of Americans said yes, as compared with 12 percent of Canadians.[12]

These data are mirrored by the data on homicide. The average rate of homicides per one hundred thousand people in the European Union was 1.7 during 1997–99, while the U.S. rate during the same period was 6.26, nearly four times that number. Rates of childhood homicides, suicides, and firearm-related deaths in the United States exceeded those of the other twenty-five wealthiest nations in the world. In fact, the homicide rate for American children was five times higher than for the children of those twenty-five nations combined.[13]

American attitudes toward the death penalty are also an indication of the climate of harshness and vindictiveness that pervades the nation. Whereas European opposition to the death penalty runs very deep, two-thirds of Americans are in favor of it. Americans are big on retribution, it would seem; they believe that people sentenced to death are merely getting what they deserve (this despite the growing number of cases in which DNA evidence has exonerated death row inmates). As of 2003, thirty-eight states had capital punishment.[14]

"The astonishing openness of American society," writes Johns Hopkins anthropologist Sidney Mintz, "is matched by a good-humoured but cruel unconcern about what happens to people, to their limbs, their brains, their children, if they are powerless and if they falter." Thus the poor are regarded as losers and an embarrassment; most Americans have little sympathy for them, and this is reflected in the lack of any real social safety net. We can rail at the French all we like, but it is not some misguided expression of knee-jerk anti-Americanism when Dominique Moïsi of the French Institute of Cultural Relations writes that a key feature of American culture is its "difficulty of empathizing with 'others.' " This seems hard to refute. I recall, in the wake of Abu Ghraib, an Iraqi mother appearing on television and directing a question to American mothers at large: "How would you feel if it was *your* sons who were being treated like this?" To the best of my knowledge, there was no response to this on the part of any women's organization in the United States. In general, Americans are simply not given to thinking empathically.[15]

The overall American reaction to the revelations regarding Abu Ghraib is very instructive, and a good example of how violence on an individual daily basis meshes with U.S. foreign policy. The sad truth is that there was not much of a reaction at all; as with every other story in America, it quickly sank into the background. The week after the story broke, a poll revealed that seven out of ten Americans felt that Secretary of Defense Donald Rumsfeld should not resign. (What would it take, one wonders: the DoD herding the Iraqis into gas chambers?) Rush Limbaugh, who broadcasts to twenty million mesmerized listeners ("dittoheads," as they like to call themselves), compared the whole thing to a fraternity prank, à la *Animal House* ("You heard of the need to blow some steam off?"). No independent investigation of Abu Ghraib was set up, and there was no groundswell in Congress or indeed anywhere to create one. Where were the sit-ins, the teach-ins, the demonstrations that were so much a part of the revulsion against what we were doing in Vietnam? Nonexistent, now. John Kerry never even mentioned Abu Ghraib in his presidential campaign, because he understood that it was a nonissue for Americans. All officers above the rank of colonel were absolved, and no political leader was ever held accountable. The general who set up the system of detention and interrogation at Guantánamo Bay is, as of this writing, in charge of prisons in Iraq, and the architect of the torture policy, Alberto Gonzales, is now head of the Department of Justice. In an editorial entitled "The System Endures," the *Washington Post* writes: "the worst aspect of the Abu Ghraib scandal is this: The system survived its public exposure. . . . Mr. Bush will perpetuate this systematic violation of human rights, and fundamental American values," while it prosecutes the grunts, "the lowly reservists depicted in the Abu Ghraib photos. . . ."[16]

Popular reaction to the grunts, it must be said, is a whole object lesson in itself. Consider, for example, the reaction to Specialist Joseph Darby, the courageous young soldier who slipped the photos of what was going on at Abu Ghraib under the door of the army's Criminal Investigation Division, on the part of his neighbors in Corriganville, Maryland, and the nearby towns in the Allegheny Mountains. These folks felt that he had "ratted them out," that he was a traitor, un-American. They vandalized Darby's home; the police refused to help. Meanwhile, a candlelight vigil was held in Cumberland, Maryland, to show support for the supposedly disgraced soldiers—"as if beating and sodomizing prisoners were some kind of patriotic duty," writes journalist Wil Hylton—and a sign was posted in nearby Hyndman, Pennsylvania, for one of the soldiers charged in the prisoner abuse scandal: JEREMY SIVITS, OUR HOMETOWN HERO.[17]

This "redneck" reaction, it must be said, went all the way to the top. Donald Rumsfeld showed no remorse at all, and subsequently blew the whole thing off as being nothing in comparison to the terrorists' practice of beheading their victims—as if this were now the standard by which our actions would be judged. It is fascinating to see how, up and down the scale in the United States, a lack of empathy, an almost congenital inability to imagine the pain or the reality of the Other, is bred in the bone. In his May 2004 congressional testimony about Abu Ghraib, when asked why he did not make all of this public that January, when he first heard about it, Rumsfeld said he hadn't imagined it would have the impact on the Arab world that it did; that it didn't seem like a big deal to him. At which point some senator—I believe it was John McCain, who had spent several years in a POW camp in Vietnam—said to this distinguished public servant: "Mr. Secretary, it doesn't take rocket science to figure out how Iraqis would respond to seeing other Iraqis being tortured and humiliated." But it *was* rocket science for Rumsfeld, and he was hardly alone. When Paul Wolfowitz was asked soon after, on 13 May, whether he thought putting a hood over someone's head for seventy-two hours constituted humane treatment (it is in fact a violation of the Geneva Convention), the deputy secretary of defense hemmed and hawed and finally managed to choke out the word "no," but only under unrelenting pressure from his questioner. Are these men sociopaths—or just mainstream Americans? (" 'Tis the time's plague when madmen lead the blind," writes Shakespeare in *King Lear*.) It's a scary question, and I don't mean it rhetorically. Back in the 1960s, when Yale University social psychologist Stanley Milgram was conducting his subsequently famous experiments on the willingness to inflict pain (published years later as *Obedience to Authority*), he remarked in a report to the National Science Foundation, which had funded the experiments:

> The results are terrifying and depressing. They suggest that human nature—or more specifically, the kind of character produced in American society—cannot be counted on to insulate its citizens from brutality and inhumane treatment at the direction of malevolent authority. In a naïve moment some time ago, I once wondered whether in all of the United States a vicious government could find enough moral imbeciles to meet the personnel requirements of a national system of death camps, of the sort that were maintained in (Nazi) Germany. I am now beginning to think that the full complement could be recruited in New Haven. A substantial proportion of people do what they are told to do, irrespective of the content of the act, and without pangs of conscience, so long as they perceive that the command comes from a legitimate authority.

Of course, as another social psychologist, Philip Zimbardo, discovered a few years later in the course of his notorious mock-prison experiments at Stanford, this kind of violence would seem to emerge from immediate context and situation rather than from moral character. Which seems right . . . but what if a nation such as ours creates a situation in which violence and lack of empathy *are* the immediate context and situation, and thereby, in effect, "manufactures" the "kind of character produced in American society"? What then?[18]

As it turns out, there is, in fact, a domestic correlate to the "American gulag," as Al Gore called it, and that is the torture that goes on in prisons right here in the United States. Americans don't know much about this, and it is doubtful that very many would care if they did. But occasionally, word does leak out, and there was some coverage of this after Abu Ghraib, because those who have spent their lives monitoring prisons and juvenile detention centers couldn't help but notice the obvious parallels. Detainees in America's immigration prisons (including political refugees seeking asylum), to start with, are routinely stripped, beaten, and sexually abused. Videotapes from a prison facility in Brooklyn, where Arab and Muslim detainees were incarcerated in the months after 9/11, show the guards slamming the inmates into walls and strip-searching them repeatedly. A video taken in 1996 at the Brazoria County Detention Center near Houston shows an attack dog mangling a prisoner, and another man with a broken ankle getting zapped with a stun gun while crawling along the floor. Brazoria is not unusual; this sort of thing happens all the time, although the evidence remains anecdotal. In April 2004, a videotape of abuse at a California youth prison became public, and it shows guards assaulting inmates who are lying defenseless on the floor. In 1980, Judge William Wayne Justice declared Texas' entire corrections system unconstitutional, in an effort to end the practice (among others) of deputized "guards" routinely raping, beating, and torturing their fellow prisoners. Guards at one prison in Arizona typically forced male prisoners to wear women's underwear (a practice that also, as with the use of attack dogs, occurred at Abu Ghraib). Lawyers and advocacy organizations have uncovered abuses in juvenile facilities in twenty-three states and the District of Columbia. As in the case of Abu Ghraib, it's the characteristic incapacity for empathy that is so striking here. "What makes all these trends possible," writes reporter Jonathan Cohn in an article entitled "America's Abu Ghraibs," is "vast public indifference . . . neither elected officials nor the public seem particularly worried that similar abuses [to those of Abu Ghraib] happen all the time right here at home." That the American public doesn't care is a recurrent theme in human rights groups' reports.[19]

Ignorance

Not caring and not knowing, of course, go hand in hand. Lack of the most basic knowledge is so extreme in the United States that one has to wonder if we are talking about ignorance or just outright stupidity. As in the case of alienation, the statistics, as astounding as they are, don't quite convey the quality of incredibility as effectively as the anecdotal information. Below are a few items from the latter category, randomly selected from my own experience.

✦ I occasionally listen to conservative radio talk shows, just to get an idea of what this audience, which constitutes a large segment of the American population, is thinking. One of the last times I tuned in, I learned from the host that (a) France was a socialist country; (b) the "noose of Islam" was tightening around American necks, poisoning our values; and (c) this latter development had already occurred in Canada, which is one reason "it is no longer a nation." (As Rush Limbaugh likes to say, I'm not making this up.)

✦ Some TV program—not Jay Leno—is interviewing high school seniors about American history. "Who won the Civil War?" asks the moderator, addressing a young man of about seventeen or eighteen years of age. "I don't know and I don't care!" he shouts at the interviewer. (Clearly, we have a possible future president on our hands.)

✦ Occasionally, I tune into the "courtroom" shows, such as *Judge Judy* or *Judge Mathis*. More often than not, the plaintiffs and defendants, even when their first language is English, are unable to utter a grammatically correct sentence. They also don't understand what evidence is, or how a trial or court hearing actually works. A landlord, for example, might be suing a tenant for nonpayment of rent, and fail to bring in a copy of the lease. When Judge Judy (Judith Scheindlin) pointedly (and rhetorically) asks them, "Weren't you aware that you were coming to court today?," they just shrug. On the *Judge Mathis* program, the participants often seem to think that evidence consists of yelling louder than their opponents; the show is more a carnival than a legal proceeding.

✦ I go to the circulation desk of the library of a major university on the East Coast and ask the librarian behind the desk (a woman in her thirties) where I might find books beginning with a certain call number. It turns out she doesn't know what a call number is.

✦ I'm in a delicatessen in downtown D.C. and buy a piece of fish. The clerk puts the fish on a digital scale, which then flashes ".33" in red numbers on the screen. The clerk says to me, "It's thirty-three ounces." As tactfully as I can, I say, "Well, uh, no, actually . . . that's the fraction of a pound that the scale is showing, in other words, about a third of a pound. Roughly five ounces." The clerk stares at me with an uncomprehending look; I realize she has no interest whatever in having this information, even though she can't really perform her job without it.

✦ In September and October of 2004, on the eve of the presidential election, I sit in bars and luncheonettes in Maryland and Virginia trying to get a sense of what the electorate is thinking. What I hear, in lieu of any real political or historical analysis, are recycled slogans from TV: "Well, the thing is that Bush is courageous, while Kerry is a flip-flopper." In fact, the newspapers around this time report that even in the foothills of the Appalachians, where thousands of people have been thrown out of work due to the administration's economic policies, people interviewed said that Kerry was a "tree-hugger," that he would tax them to death (based on what income, one might ask), that he had falsified his military record, and so on.[20]

✦ In 2002, the *New York Times* reported that in high school classes across the nation, cell phones go off and students simply take the calls; or they play video games or watch movies they've downloaded onto their laptops. At one high school in Hampton, Virginia, one student had a pizza delivered to himself in class, and couldn't understand why the teacher objected to this. In January 2004, the Nashville school system stopped posting the honor roll of A students, because it had become a source of embarrassment for underachievers. School lawyers also advised the school system to ban the practice of hanging samples of good work in the halls.[21]

✦ In October 2004, a public library in California unveiled a $40,000 ceramic mural on which the names of Einstein, Shakespeare, van Gogh, Michelangelo, and seven other major historical figures were misspelled. Upon being confronted with these errors by the library director, the artist made no apology for her mistakes, but instead told the Associated Press that the library was denigrating her work. "The people that are into [the] humanities, and are into Blake's concept of enlightenment, they are not looking at the words," she said. "In their mind [*sic*] the words register correctly."[22]

I'm assuming the reader gets the idea by now; I could fill dozens of pages with these types of stories, ones that were relatively rare thirty years ago, and that are fairly commonplace today. As for the statistics, read them and weep: 70 percent of American adults cannot name their senators or congressmen; more than half don't know the actual number of senators, and nearly a quarter cannot name a single right guaranteed by the First Amendment. Sixty-three percent cannot name the three branches of government. Other studies reveal that uninformed or undecided voters often vote for the candidate whose name and packaging (e.g., logo) are the most powerful; color is apparently a major factor in their decision. Only 21 percent of college-age Americans today read a daily newspaper, as compared with 46 percent in 1972. A 2002 study of college students in California found that most freshmen were not able to analyze arguments, synthesize information, or write papers that were free of major language errors. Over the past twenty years, the fraction of Americans age eighteen to twenty-four engaged in literary reading dropped 28 percent, and in general nonreaders now constitute more than half of the American population. All in all, the great mass of our countrymen talk, act, and "reason" as though their crania contained chopped liver rather than gray matter. Cicero wrote that "Not to know what happened before one was born is always to be a child." Most Americans don't seem to know what's happening during their own lifetimes.[23]

In fact, compared to their European counterparts in terms of being informed about the outside world, Americans come off looking like a collection of buffoons. Talk about living in a "terrarium," as Nicholas von Hoffman puts it: their insularity is the stuff of legend. Again, I'll do the anecdotal evidence first.

✦ I meet a couple from eastern Europe who, through an unexpected set of circumstances, wound up living on Long Island. They seem completely like fish out of water. "How is it for you out here?" I ask. The man shrugs his shoulders. "All right," he says sort of grudgingly, "except . . . well, when I tell Americans I'm from Europe, they draw a blank, and then ask me how long it takes to drive there from here."

✦ I'm staying at a small hotel in northern Italy. Every morning I borrow the desk copy of *Corriere della Sera* (the newspaper is published in Milan, with a daily circulation of 700,000), and over breakfast I slowly work my way through the "Culture" section—typically two or three pages of cultural analysis that are both dense and fascinating. Other European papers such as *Die Zeit* and *Le Monde* do something similar, and the essays in all of these papers are written at a level comparable to what one might find in specialized academic journals in the United States, never in a regular daily newspaper. I am aware that if, say, the *Washington Post* attempted anything on this order, it would probably go broke in three months for lack of readers. Because of their social and economic arrangements, European Union countries have a vibrant, literary, and growing middle class. Because of our social and economic arrangements, we have a besieged, anxiety-ridden, shrinking one.

✦ Thus it should not surprise us that the market for foreign books in English translation, which did a brisk trade in this country from the 1940s to the end of the 1970s, has now dried up. Laurie Brown, senior vice president for marketing and sales at Harcourt publishers, comments that Americans are not interested in foreign literature because it tends to be philosophical and reflective. Americans, she says, "want more immediate gratification." They have little understanding of nuance, and not much ability, or patience, to read between the lines.[24]

✦ I go to see Patrice Leconte's 2004 film, *Confidences trop intimes* (translated as *Intimate Strangers* for the English-speaking market). It is a masterpiece of indirect statement, about a relationship between a man and a woman, and it takes shape very gradually. Even at the end, the outcome is not certain. Its brilliance lies precisely in its nuance, its ambiguity. Typical reviews of the film in the United States complained that it moved too slowly, was somewhat boring, and "didn't go anywhere." The next evening on TV, I watch part of *The Peacemakers*, a 1997 George Clooney–Nicole Kidman "romantic" antiterrorist film that is embarrassingly stupid. From the outset, it is clear that the golden hero will defeat the "evildoers" and win the pretty girl. End of story.

✦ Writing in *The Nation*, Patricia Williams records an interaction she had with a twelve-year-old boy in rural France, who discussed John Kerry's foreign policy with her in detail and compared it to Bill Clinton's—something, she says, that a lot of American news anchors would not be able to do. Her general impression, traveling abroad, is that foreign schoolchildren know more about our wars "than the 'security moms' whose sons are marching off to fight them" and that "almost anyone I run into [abroad] has a better sense of our political system and its carryings-on than any given audience member of *The Tonight Show*."[25]

✦ The Palestinians have a joke about a U.N. world survey that asked, "What is your opinion about the food shortage in the rest of the world?" In the United States, goes the joke, no one could answer the question because they couldn't understand the phrase "the rest of the world."[26]

As for the corresponding statistics, there is no need to go on at any length here, inasmuch as I already cited data characteristic of this in the introduction. Data of this sort are massive, and they all corroborate the observation of Gerald Celente, director of the Trends Research Institute: "you are dealing here with people who are almost childlike in their understanding of what is going on in the world." They also, it must be added, don't really give a damn. Commenting on our cultural situation in an online review of Bill McKibben's book *The Age of Missing Information*, a critic writes: "If the populace of the future is made up mostly of ignorant, ahistorical, consumer drones with no concept of how a civilization is made possible and what it takes in order to maintain the precious gains of civilization, th-- aren't we looking into the abyss?" I'm not sure why this reviewer "of the future," but I am quite sure that we are looking into the aby

Nor is it of any use to point out that the United States still wins the most Nobel Prizes in the sciences, or that it currently has some of the world's most talented novelists alive on the planet today. All that is true (although, in fact, we are losing our edge in science); but a few islands of brilliance do not change the overall equation. As Charles Murray put it in a *Wall Street Journal* op-ed piece, "bean-counting doesn't work. . . . Whether a culture turns out bits and pieces of the admirable is irrelevant to understanding where it stands on the trajectory of history."[28]

And who has been the perfect icon of all this, presiding over the country as it transits into its dark age? Bush, writes *Washington Post* book critic Jonathan Yardley, "is a representative figure, who embodies, at this peculiar and scary moment in our history, aspects of the American state of mind and heart that cannot be dismissed as merely his own idiosyncracies." Several decades ago, playwright Arthur Miller remarked that "Richard Nixon's character is our history," which was true when he said it. Now it is Bush who holds that particular distinction, and it will remain true long after his presidency is over. If the man wound up in the White House by accident or theft in 2000, the same cannot be said of him in 2004. The basic perception of Americans from the outside is that we are children, adolescents at best, and Bush is just such a person. He is an alcoholic who never actually did the spiritual work that Alcoholics Anonymous asks of its members, and as a result no emotional growth ever took place. Switching from alcohol to religion, Bush remains essentially an adolescent, what AA refers to as a "dry drunk." His excitement over being able to wield power, to kill people, as a substitute for dealing with his considerable "inner demons" is quite palpable. Philosopher Peter Singer has mapped his simplistic, Manichaean worldview; psychiatrist Justin Frank shows how early damage left the man-boy unable to empathize, to feel the pain of other human beings. Indeed, says Frank, it left him with a "lifelong streak of sadism," and Christian fundamentalist sadism at that. But the real horror is that the majority of Americans do not see through this, and so mistake what is actually massive dysfunction and insecurity— including emptiness, alienation, violence, and ignorance—for strength. This man is no historical accident, and future presidents, I suspect, are going to be variations on this theme, which is grounded in a widespread cultural pattern.[29]

It is this, above all, that acts as a brake on any possible recovery for American civilization. The day after the 2004 election, a colleague of mine from Ohio, which was the state that put Bush over the top, said to me, after I remarked that Kerry had clearly won the three debates: "You are missing the point. Most folks in Ohio are pretty basic, not very successful, and not particularly happy with their lives. Believe me, I know; I was born and raised there. When they see Bush getting emotional and stumbling over elementary English words, they identify with him, whereas they find Kerry cool and intelligent, and they experience this as threatening, above their heads. To them, Kerry's wife, who speaks several languages, comes off as un-American, a kind of alien being; and his kids, en route to professional careers, make them feel uncomfortable about their own kids, who are in dead-end jobs and perhaps, like the Bush daughters, getting pulled over for drunk driving. In short, Kerry stirs deep anxieties about their selves, whereas Bush, *because* he is a bungler, soothes those anxieties, reassures these folks that their failure and anti-intellectualism is more 'genuine,' 'down to earth.'" Bush also, it seems to me, validates their rigidity, their insistence on having simple answers, and their repressed violence. Finally, he tells them that the American Dream is alive and well, and so keeps their undercurrent of panic at arm's length. In a word, Bush is us—or at least, a whole lot of us—and the scariness of this is not easy to digest. Given a population that embraces the collection of ideas, values, and policies that George W. Bush represents, how can a decline be avoided, or arrested? Where will a sane foreign policy come from, given the fact that neither he, nor the American people, as the Los Angeles journalist John Powers observes, are able to grasp the perfectly obvious bottom line, that "they hate us because we don't even know why they hate us"? All in all, when we contemplate America's downward trajectory, it's rather difficult to imagine the nation's suddenly reversing course.[30]

This is not a happy conclusion for me to come to, and in some ways, this has been a painful book to write. After all, I wouldn't be here today without the largesse of America; and when, in 1920, my family steamed past the Statue of Liberty and on toward Ellis Island, it was the most dramatic moment of their lives. My mother used to tell the story of her father, who, at some point after World War II, upon finding a small American flag on the ground, picked it up, dusted it off, and brought it home to put on the mantelpiece, saying, "If not for this, we would all have perished in Auschwitz." I agree with Walter McDougall when he writes that "no large nation on earth has provided more stability, prosperity, security, and liberty to more people than has the United States."[31] This was the glory of America: to be a land of great promise, a refuge from political tyranny, a place of immense creative energy, and the world locus of political freedom. But the glory had a shadow, a set of structural problems that were present quite early on and that eventually landed us in a very different, and inglorious, place. Those of us who now have different values from the country may have to look elsewhere for hope, quality, humanism, and—possibly—freedom, which is not exactly what we had in mind when we were growing up. And although it would be a fabulous turn of events, it is nevertheless very unlikely that the solution to the American dilemma can come from within America itself. The *zeitgeist*, it would seem, is moving on.

~ 9 ~

Empire Falls

There is the moral of all human tales;
'Tis but the same rehearsal of the past.
First freedom and then Glory—when that fails,
Wealth, vice, corruption,—barbarism at last.

—Lord Byron,
"Childe Harold's Pilgrimage"

This time . . . the barbarians are not waiting beyond the
frontiers; they have already been governing for quite some time.

—Alasdair MacIntyre,
After Virtue

THERE IS A SCHOOL of thought that argues that the solution to the current situation in America can come from within America itself. Sometimes known as the "pendulum theory" of American history, its
proponents include sophisticated scholars such as Anatol Lieven of the
New America Foundation and Geoffrey Stone of the University of
Chicago. What they argue for is the existence of self-corrective cycles,
and the notion that the rhythm of American history is one of
action/reaction, or thesis/antithesis.[1] Yes, we do get ourselves into a bit of
a mess from time to time is the idea here, but then countervailing forces

are unleashed and we manage to pull back from the edge. Lieven, for example, in *America Right or Wrong*, argues for the existence of an alternating pattern of tolerant pluralism and militant nationalism in U.S. foreign policy. If there is a messianic-idealistic tradition, there is also a pragmatic-realistic one, and we go back and forth. On that basis, he is optimistic that the United States will eventually correct its current excesses, and pull back from the present militant nationalist path it is on. Similarly, in *Perilous Times*, Stone turns his attention to the domestic arena, specifically the matter of constitutionality and civil liberties, and observes that loss of the latter typically occurs during time of war, but that the repression is lifted and liberty restored after the war is over.

Clearly, these arguments do not constitute a species of wishful thinking; no "magical" solutions are being proposed here. Lieven and Stone are merely reviewing the historical record. To refute the pendulum theory, then, one would have to show that there is reason to believe that things have changed to such a degree that what worked in the past will not work in the future; that, in effect, a Rubicon has been crossed, and that there are a number of crucial elements that are no longer reversible. Since I do find the arguments of the "pendulum school" unconvincing, let me just briefly indicate why I believe "that was then, this is now."[2]

It would seem that most of the refutation of the pendulum theory is already contained within the pages of this book. To summarize some of the things already stated:

◆ We are in a state of advanced cultural disintegration, or what might be termed spiritual death. Given the emptiness, alienation, violence, and ignorance that are now pervasive in this country, it is hard to imagine where a recovery would come from. The self-correction theory is at least partly based on the popular reaction of an informed citizenry. In this regard, the nature of the American populace today is not a source of inspiration or hope.

◆ As far as civil liberties go, the development and proliferation of extremely sophisticated surveillance technologies changes the picture considerably. These compromise the privacy of the individual out of existence, and the technology is clearly here to stay. Once in practice, it is very difficult to pull back from its employment; close governmental and even corporate observation of the citizenry, along with the massive collection of data, has now become the norm. All of this makes repression easy and change difficult.

+ We seem to have passed, in significant ways, from a nation of laws to a nation of men. This is the first time in our history, for example, that we rewrote the law to make torture legal, or seriously contemplated canceling a presidential election. Nor has there been any widespread objection on the part of the American people to these developments. Indeed, the dust settled on them fairly quickly; they too just became part of the "natural" political landscape.

+ As both Lieven and Stone themselves admit, 9/11 may well have damaged the cyclical or self-correcting pattern for good. After all, the "war on terror" is really a permanent state of war, without a clear objective and without a specific enemy. The risk, says Stone, is that so-called emergency restrictions will become a "permanent fixture of American life." It is also very likely that we shall eventually be attacked again, probably with nuclear weapons—in which case, all bets are off. "Tolerant pluralism" will definitely not be the order of the day.

+ Changes in quantity eventually turn into changes in quality. Past cyclical alternations may have finally taken their toll and exhausted our ability to rebound. Democrat friends try to reassure me: "Listen, we recovered from right-wing setbacks in the past." Did we? Repression in World War I, as historian Eric Foner observes, destroyed the Industrial Workers of the World, the Socialist party, and much of the labor movement.[3] Personally, I don't believe this country ever really recovered from McCarthyism, which dealt a severe blow to movements for social change, or from Ronald Reagan, whose spirit strongly animates the forces dismantling what's left of the New Deal. We didn't survive Vietnam; we didn't survive the repeal of Bretton Woods. The point is that when you look at the larger picture or the long waves, the short-term cycles seem far less impressive. Thus Arnold Toynbee noted that in the process of decline a civilization may, from time to time, rally for a while; but it is the overall trajectory, the structural properties of the situation, that ultimately determine the outcome.

❖ Immanuel Wallerstein remarks that Europe and Asia see us as much less important on the international scene, that the dollar is weaker, that nuclear proliferation is probably unstoppable, that the U.S. military is stretched to the limit, and that our national and trade debts are enormous. Our days of hegemony, and probably even leadership, would thus seem to be over. Can America rebound from all this? It depends, he points out, on how one defines "rebound." A genuine rebound would require an internal assessment of values and social structure, and a reversal of the deep social, economic, and political polarization of the last thirty years.[4] It would also require changing basic American habits and values, the minute particulars of daily life, and this simply isn't going to happen. Jimmy Carter tried something like this and was booted out of office for his efforts, inasmuch as the American people much prefer fantasy to reality. In addition, large-scale foreign and domestic policy is grounded in these minute particulars, making substantive changes terribly unlikely. So while I agree with Wallerstein that there is no hope without an "internal assessment," I very much doubt that such an assessment will come to pass.

The upshot of all this, it seems to me, is that the decline of Rome (for example), and not the self-corrective cycles of American history, may be a more reliable guide to our future. It was, of course, a process rather than an event; it occurred in stages. Caesar's move across the Rubicon in 49 B.C. marked a major discontinuity, signaling as it did the death of the Republic and the emergence of the Empire. "By crossing it," writes the British historian Tom Holland, Julius Caesar "engulf[ed] the world in war . . . [and] also helped to bring about the ruin of Rome's ancient freedoms, and the establishment, upon their wreckage, of a monarchy. . . ." De facto, the new government was an autocracy, an oligarchy, but it was dressed up in the form of a restored republic. Everybody continued to talk of "Senatus Populusque Romanus" (the Senate and the Roman people), but the phrase no longer had any basis in reality. In an eerie parallel to today, Holland summarizes that first shift as follows:

Something was changing in the mood of the Republic. Globalising fantasies were much in the air. . . . The old suspicion of empire was fading fast. Overseas commitments, it appeared, could be made to work. . . .

Assumptions that would have been unthinkable even a few decades previously were becoming commonplace. Enthusiasts for empire argued that Rome had a civilising mission; that because her values and institutions were self-evidently superior to those of barbarians, she had a duty to propagate them; that only once the whole globe had been subjected to her rule could there be a universal peace. Morality had not merely caught up with the brute fact of imperial expansion, but wanted more.[5]

As we progress through the centuries, the parallels between contemporary America and late-empire Rome, and the subsequent slide into the Dark Ages, become increasingly suggestive. The third century A.D. was characterized by near continuous warfare, combined with a collapse of the currency and the rise of a military monarchy. Some historians argue that the fourth century was a repressive reaction to the chaos of the third century, leading to the collapse of the empire in the fifth century. Thus by the time of Constantine's death in 337, according to the British historian and archaeologist Chris Scarre, "Rome had lost its pre-eminence, the old gods had gone, civic values and political life had been transformed. There [were] . . . new policies and strategies of power." What Constantine left behind him was a "theocratic-autocratic state." Writing in the early fourth century, the Christian author Lactantius asked: "What purpose does knowledge serve . . . what blessing is there for me if I should know where the Nile rises, or whatever else under the heavens the 'scientists' rave about?" A hundred years later, St. Augustine spoke contemptuously of "the disease of curiosity . . . which drives us to try and discover the secrets of nature." And commenting on the centuries that followed, Anthony Gottlieb, an editor for the *Economist*, reminds us of "the colossal ignorance of the Christian West in the second half of the first millennium. By the year 1000," says Gottlieb, "all branches of science, and indeed all kinds of theoretical knowledge except theology, had pretty much disintegrated. Most classical literature was largely unknown. The best educated people . . . knew strikingly less than many Greeks 800 years earlier."[6]

Of course, decay doesn't occur in a strictly linear way. For example, a brief deviation occurred during the reign of the emperor Julian "the Apostate" (361–63), celebrated by Gore Vidal in his superb biographical novel of the man. Julian struggled during his short lifetime to preserve the teachings of the Greeks, the vital intellectual legacy of the ancient world. He failed. Vidal writes:

The world Julian wanted to preserve and restore is gone . . . the barbarians are at the gate. Yet when they breach the wall, they will find nothing of value to seize, only empty relics. The spirit of what we were has fled. . . . With Julian, the light went, and now nothing remains but to let the darkness come, and hope for a new sun and another day, born of time's mystery and man's love of light.[7]

I believe Vidal is right: what we *can* count on are "time's mystery and man's love of light"; and in this larger, more ethereal sense I suppose I am an optimist, for I believe that the human spirit does ultimately manage to prevail. To shift back from Rome to the present time, then, two questions need to be asked: Would it have been different if John Kerry had won the presidential election of 2004, and if not, where is the *weltgeist* (metaphorically speaking, of course) migrating to? As the sun finally sets on the Anglo-American empire, who—if anybody—will live in the light of a new sun, another day?

Democrats versus Republicans

Although it might not seem so at first glance, the two questions I just raised are closely related. Since the late 1940s, the United States has been deliberately engaged in an imperial project, and anyone who would hold the office of the presidency has to be willing to serve that end. All presidents have to promote the national security state, both domestically and in American foreign policy, if they wish to attain and hold on to power. This is why nothing really changed after the end of the Cold War, militarily speaking. Our empire *expanded* after the USSR collapsed, which would suggest that the move toward empire in the decades after World War II was not the result of any external threat. In the post–Cold War era, President Clinton effectively picked up the imperial thread, but from an economic vantage point. NAFTA got passed; American enterprise would, he insisted, have to start operating on a global scale. On the domestic front, the gulf between rich and poor widened dramatically, as Clinton deregulated telecommunications and finance, cut the capital gains tax, and "reformed" welfare. As Chalmers Johnson notes, the rationales of free trade and open markets were used to disguise our hegemonic power during the 1990s, and to make that power seem benign and "natural." The upshot was that the United States would rule the world, but under camouflage—a kinder, gentler imperialism, if you will. But the bottom line is that it, and it alone, would rule.[8]

All of this makes one wonder about the rage that conservatives had for Clinton, who was in effect carrying out their agenda, but with a lot more panache than they could ever hope to muster. Indeed, in a way similar to FDR, Clinton was the ideal capitalist, smoothing over the rough edges, containing the contradictions as best he could, and generally seeing to it that the basic formula was left intact. The result, writes Alexander Cockburn, was that the Democrats and their associated public interest groups rallied around their leader

> and marched into the late 1990s arm in arm along the path sign-posted toward the greatest orgy of corporate theft in the history of the planet, deregulation of banking and food safety, NAFTA and the WTO [World Trade Organization], rates of logging six times those achieved in the subsequent Bush years, oil drilling in the Arctic, a war on Yugoslavia . . . a vast expansion of the death penalty, reaffirmation of racist drug laws, [and] the foundations of the Patriot Act.[9]

Cockburn could also have added that Clinton saw to it that the cruel and murderous sanctions against Iraq were kept in place, and that in June 2004 he declared his support for the U.S. invasion of that country. Not surprisingly, the objection to the new world order finally materialized in the streets of Seattle in 1999, not from within the ranks of the Democratic party.

As for Clinton's anticipation of the USA Patriot Act, I have already referred to the 1996 passage of the Effective Death Penalty and Anti-terrorism Act, which contained a lot of similar provisions. Concerned citizens can rail against John Ashcroft and Alberto Gonzales all they like, and with good reason; but the fact remains that Janet Reno paved the way.

Finally, it is difficult to make a partisan case against the Bush Jr. administration for its use of the military for diplomatic purposes when Clinton was doing much the same thing, albeit in a subtler way. As already noted, Clinton relied on the Pentagon to do much of his foreign policy, whether it was sending General Anthony Zinni to India and Pakistan, having the military carry out tasks such as disaster relief, or asking soldiers to help build pluralistic societies in countries that had no tradition of same. Bush Jr.'s assignment of the rebuilding of Iraq to the U.S. armed forces, a disaster in the making, was really the continuation of a pattern that goes back to Clinton and before.

And this, really, is a big part of the answer to our first question, Would it have been different if John Kerry were now sitting in the Oval Office? The point is that if you don't act as steward and promoter of the national security state, your chances of occupying the White House are less than zero. Even the preelection "debates" of 2004 made this quite clear. It was not permitted, for example, to analyze the invasion of Iraq in terms of neocon influence, to mention the Project for the New American Century, or to state that the war had been in the pipeline for a number of years. You could talk about Israeli suffering, as John Edwards did; but the occupation of Gaza and the West Bank, which is ultimately the source of the suffering, was somehow off limits. It was perfectly fine to say Iraq was a *strategic* error or that it was "mismanaged," but under no circumstances could you point out that it was an illegal and immoral neocolonial adventure, an intervention in someone else's civil war. And of course, absolutely verboten was the one thing everybody in the world seems to understand but us: that 9/11 was the blowback from an interventionist foreign policy. These were debates with 95 percent of the political reality screened out in advance. There was no anti-empire candidate on the podium (nor will there ever be); so what really was being debated? An imperialist rubric mandates a phony discussion, in which the two candidates energetically duke it out over a soft versus hard version of the same agenda, while a compliant press (ever mindful of their careers) reports on the "contrast" to an ignorant and gullible American public, who thinks it is getting the real McCoy. This is part of the deep structure of our decline: the truth of our situation won't fly politically, so perforce it must remain invisible.

As for the particulars of a hypothetical Kerry presidency, let's look at the record, as the pols like to say. Kerry is a strong proponent of free trade, and reportedly once called himself "Davos man." He voted with Clinton and the GOP for welfare reform; he not only supported the Patriot Act, but wrote some of the language for it. For all his talk about working with our allies and submitting major decisions to a "global test," Kerry made it quite clear that on his watch preemptive unilateral war would be a perfectly viable option, if he saw fit; and of course, he voted for the American invasion of Iraq without the approval of the U.N. Security Council. Kerry even said in August 2004 that he would have done so even had he known back then that Iraq had no weapons of mass destruction (he later retracted that statement). He also promised to send more troops to Iraq, so that America would be able to "get the job done" (and exactly what job is *that*, John?). (Howard Dean also said he wanted to win the war, even though he thought it was a mistake for us to have started it. This is the kind of "alternative" the American people are offered.) When, during the election campaign, in a rare moment of accidental clarity, Bush told an NBC interviewer that we could probably never really win the war on terror, Kerry did not seize the opportunity to say, "Finally, a glimmer of reality! Now let's have an honest discussion of our situation"—not at all. Instead, the Kerry camp immediately attacked the president for "defeatism" and declared the war "absolutely winnable." Indeed, from his opening mock salute at the Democratic National Convention ("reporting for duty!"), Kerry chose to cast his candidacy in the militaristic terms laid out by the Republicans, effectively telling the nation that he could out-macho his opponent (riding onto the set of *The Tonight Show* on a Harley-Davidson had to be the high point of kitsch here). Rather than emphasizing his courageous antiwar stance of 1971, when Kerry testified before the Senate Foreign Relations Committee that Vietnam had been a mistake and that we were guilty of committing atrocities, Democratic campaign headquarters glorified his valor in that war—a genocidal venture in which we murdered three million peasants. From a broad perspective, Kerry's foreign policies were merely softer versions of those held by the president.[10]

Nevertheless, let's not deceive ourselves: differences in style can sometimes amount to differences in substance, and I do think the reelection of Bush is an integral part of America's decline, especially since Kerry's disagreements with Bush were greatest on the domestic front. Several months before the election, Robert Reich prophesied that a Republican victory would mean that the constraint of another Bush election campaign would be lifted, and that therefore the gloves would come off the Bush administration's project to remake America. Specifically, Reich predicted the following: Patriot Act II will give the Department of Justice even greater powers to eviscerate the Constitution. The Christian right will solidify its control over the Justice, Education, and Health and Human Services Departments, and we can expect prayer in the public schools, the elimination of evolution from the curriculum, and perhaps the end of legalized abortion. Larger tax benefits will continue to widen the gap between rich and poor; domestic spending (except for defense) will essentially come to an end, and Social Security will be privatized. Right-wing justices will be nominated to the bench, including the Supreme Court. The assault on the environment will continue apace, and the push to turn America into a one-party nation will move into high gear. Finally, the Federal Communications Commission will stand by as the handful of giant media empires consolidate their ownership over the airwaves.[11]

Rather depressing, all this, and if you are reading these words in 2009 or after, you can check off the items on Reich's list and see how many of his predictions came true. It may well be that the real agenda of the Bush administration is to create a kind of soft fascism, a presidential dictatorship or one-party system that presides over a de facto Christian plutocracy, and that has managed to squelch all opposing voices. If so, it seems clear enough that this is light-years from anything Kerry had in mind. Writing in *Newsweek* in April 2004, for example, Jennifer Barrett pointed to Kerry's disagreement with the sections of the Patriot Act that he found too invasive: increased ease in obtaining wiretaps, search warrants, and access to personal information; the Justice Department's use of extended police powers to monitor church meetings and political rallies; and so on.[12] This is no small difference, in my opinion; indeed, it could be the difference between liberty and tyranny. We are knee-deep in Orwellian waters, my friends; I don't think the future bodes well for our much transformed experiment in democracy.

The name of Orwell, of course, brings up one other major difference between Kerry and Bush, one that lies at the heart of a free society: the matter of truth and evidence. That Kerry lives within a scientific and rational mind-set and that Bush lives within an evangelical-fundamentalist one is no mere difference in style. One might accuse John Kerry of lies of omission, of waffling on the issues, or of being as much a militarist in foreign policy as George W. Bush, but I don't think he can justly be accused of trying to persuade the American people that black is white, or that 2 + 2 = 5. Thus we have had "No Child Left Behind," which has been an educational failure; the "Clear Skies Bill," which permits the collapse of existing air-quality regulations; "sound science," which blocks all kinds of research from the standpoint of a thinly veiled religious bias; "democracy (or victory) in Iraq," which is contradicted by the daily reports of violence and instability; "tax cuts for small businesses," which in reality benefit the wealthiest 1 percent of the nation. The record on employment, which has been quite awful, is extolled as a great success. When the CIA's Duelfer Report of early October 2004 showed that Iraq had dismantled its WMD programs after the Gulf war and never tried to reconstitute them, Dick Cheney hit the airwaves to say that the report proved that waiting "wasn't an option," and this sort of deception is quite effective. Shortly after that, a major survey conducted by the University of Maryland revealed that 72 percent of Bush supporters believed that Iraq had possessed WMD or active programs to produce them, and 75 percent that Saddam Hussein had provided "substantial support" to Al Qaeda. Nearly 60 percent believed that this was also the consensus of the experts on the subject. And as for economic misperceptions, five out of nine Americans surveyed in election exit polls in 2004 said they believed the job situation was as good as, or better than, it was in 2000—something no economist of any political persuasion would argue. Politically speaking, then, Americans are ensconced in a world of fantasy that was deliberately and successfully promoted by the Bush administration.[13]

This is one reason that it is not likely that the United States will be able to recover from eight years of a fundamentalist boy emperor and a cynical, Dr. Strangelove–like vice president who have successfully persuaded the majority of the American people that up is down; and who, in a country in which an elementary understanding of thesis and proof, evidence and logical argumentation, are no longer part of the culture, have been able to get away with it. The loss of such understanding, however, certainly antedates the Bush Jr. administration: Todd Gitlin, in his memoir *The Twilight of Common Dreams*, notes that in twenty-five years of teaching the upper echelon of University of California students at Berkeley, he found that a large percentage of them didn't know the difference between an argument and an assertion, and were unable to make a case for or against a historical, philosophical, or sociological proposition. When comedian and political pundit Bill Maher remarked of George W. Bush that no other president had relied so heavily on the "intellectual sluggishness of the American people," he may have been unaware of the long-term collapse of American critical faculties that made Bush Jr. possible. Given the reality of this, the administration was free to engage in what Orwell called "reality control" and "newspeak," according to which, if the facts don't fit the mythology, you just deny the facts. Bush's "attitude toward the factual world in general," write the editors of *The Nation*, "is one of hostility and rejection. He has made fraud and fantasy foundations of his Administration. His own belief in something . . . appears to be evidence enough for him that it is true." Of this confusion between faith and empirical evidence, or propaganda and truth, Kerry is definitely not guilty; and on this crucial point, the difference between the two men is one of night and day.[14]

On the eve of the 2004 election, *The Nation* listed some of the dangers represented by the Bush Jr. administration, including the secret rewriting of the law, the removal of any checks or balances on the president, suspension of fundamental human rights, torture hidden under a barrage of euphemisms, and the rejection of any accountability, and asked: "Are these not the main features we might expect to see writ large if a full-scale collapse of the Constitution of the United States were to come?"

One has to wonder how exaggerated comparisons between the Bush administration and the Third Reich, which at first glance seem preposterous, really are. Was it an accident that, in the fall of 2004, Philip Roth published *The Plot Against America*, a novel about fascism come to America that has eerie echoes with our present situation? Or that the eminent historian Fritz Stern referred to Bush's "mission accomplished" landing on the USS *Abraham Lincoln* in May 2003 as part of the "Leni Riefenstahl-ization of American politics"? Or that philanthropist and author George Soros could say that the statements of John Ashcroft reminded him of similar ones that he heard coming out of the German propaganda ministry when he was a teenager? The truth is that there *are* creepy parallels, and they may get creepier. All of the social analyses of the "It can happen here" variety, beginning with Erich Fromm's *Escape from Freedom* (1941), are tied to a critique of popular culture that points to the existence of a large mass of people who are unable to think for themselves, operate out of an emotive basis, confuse entertainment with education, and desperately want to be "filled" from the outside. The ascendancy of fascism might be a lot less inexplicable than we think, and its attraction a lot more plausible in certain contexts than we can imagine at this particular moment. Thus Fromm held that a big part of that attraction was the need for a father figure who acted with conviction—someone who, in uncertain times, was perceived (even if unconsciously) as being able to allay widespread anxiety. And what kind of "father" is George W. Bush? Fritz Stern remarked just prior to November 2004 that "if we re-elect Bush, it would be a judgment on all of us." What does it mean, after all, to have an anti-Enlightenment president, and an American majority so easily seduced by faith-driven discourse? Obviously, Roth et al. (and I) could be accused of paranoia here, but I can't help wondering if America may not be drifting toward an ominous situation, with all of it being "willed by God."[15]

The opposite of the Enlightenment, of course, is tribalism and groupthink. More and more, this is the direction in which the United States is going. In the world of groupthink, loyalty is everything; and it was just this kind of tribalism, I believe, that got Bush reelected. Harvard University's Simon Schama notes that although Kerry won the televised debates, the real victory "was one of body language rather than reasoned discourse." Thus Kerry's charge that the Iraq war had actually made America less, not more safe, and had served to recruit more terrorists to the Al Qaeda cause failed to register with the majority of voters. Why, asks Schama, would that be?

> Because, the president had "acted," meaning he had killed at least some Middle Eastern bad dudes in response to 9/11. That they might be the wrong ones, in the wrong place—as Kerry said over and over—was simply too complicated a truth to master. Forget the quiz in political geography, the electorate was saying . . . it's all sand and towel-heads anyway, right? Just smash "them . . . like a ripe cantaloupe." Who them? Who gives a shit? Just make the testosterone tingle all the way to the polls.[16]

But we would be missing the point if we were to conclude that ignorance or stupidity by themselves kept Bush in the White House. They were crucial to his reelection, to be sure, but tribalism is hardly the prerogative of the ignorant and the stupid. In fact, many intelligent people voted for Bush. It's a question of how one defines "intelligence," or perhaps what kind of intelligence one is referring to. This brings to mind the German expression *blut und boden* ("blood and soil")—the tribal way of relating to the world. When the limbic system takes over, it's about fear, testosterone, and the logic of "either you're with us or you're against us." In such circumstances, a high IQ counts for nothing. One sees this *blut und boden* reasoning in the writings of the neocons, for example, with their call for

"World War IV." Smart people, but not very far removed from the 29 percent of Americans who believe that Muslims teach their children to hate and are engaged in a worldwide conspiracy "to change the American way of life." There is, in short, more than one way of being dumb. The result is that the Enlightenment is now skating on very thin ice.[17]

It was perhaps out of these sorts of concerns that, on the eve of the 2004 election, the syndicated cartoonist Wiley Miller, creator of *Non Sequitur*, ran a strip that shows a little girl and a dinosaur watching a news discussion program ("Crosshairs") on TV. She is interested, she tells her father, because she wants to see if she can pick up some debating techniques from the pros. He asks her what she's learned, and she replies: "That it's more important to demean the opponent's integrity than to be right about anything . . . and never, *ever* admit you're wrong." Her father says, "You were *born* for this era," to which she responds, "I just hope some stupid 'age of reason' doesn't come along by the time I grow up." The dinosaur finally speaks up: "Oh," he says, "I don't see much chance of that. . . ."[18]

With the reelection of George W. Bush, and the prospect of long-term Republican hegemony over American politics, it seems likely that American civilization is now transiting from a twilight phase to an actual Dark Age. In *The Right Nation*, two British journalists assert that conservative ideas are now so pervasive in the United States that a Kerry administration would not have been able to arrest the nation's long-term drift to the right any more than Clinton was.[19] I think this is largely true. Future "pendulum" alternations in the national consciousness and mode of government (if they occur at all) are likely to be quite modest, I suspect. But the one thing Kerry *could* have done was to have bought us more time before the curtain falls. Again, on this point the distinction between the two men is huge; and even though, as Wiley Miller writes, there isn't much chance of derailing our present downward trajectory with a revived "age of reason," I am not one of those who can look at the coming Dark Age and say, "Bring it on." Reason is always worth fighting for because its opposite brings with it the end of freedom and a massive assault on the human spirit. On the political level, it is always self-destructive, compromising a nation's ability to function in the world in a realistic way. Those who are not so compromised have a clear advantage on the international stage—which is precisely what is starting to happen.

China versus Europe

Who then will inherit the mantle of world leadership, as American hegemony begins ("continues" would be more accurate) to fade? Whose day
in the sun will it now be, and what will that look like? The two most
popular contenders for the "throne" that are bandied about are China and
the European Union. But before we look at the relative strengths and
weaknesses of these two powers, a few remarks about America's economic and military situation might be in order.

To address our economic situation first, consider the turnaround in
trade since 1945. At the end of World War II, half the manufactured
goods in the world originated in the United States. Today, our trade
deficit is on the order of half-a-trillion dollars a year. The deficit first
appeared (with Japan) around the time of the Bretton Woods repeal and
has since spread to the entire globe, according to Emmanuel Todd,
becoming "a basic structural element of the world economy." Here is a
list of our major trade deficits as of 2001:

China	$86.0 billion
Japan	68.0 billion
European Union countries	60.0 billion
Mexico	30.0 billion
South Korea	13.0 billion
Israel	4.5 billion
Russia	3.5 billion

The real money, says Todd, has piled up in Europe and Asia, whereas
America has become "the planet's glorious beggar." The imbalance of
trade reveals a nation that is industrially weak. Basically, the United States
is no longer able to subsist on its own production, and it needs an equivalent inflow of foreign capital in order to balance its accounts. Starting
around 1987, we have managed to accumulate nearly $3 trillion in for-
eign debt, a figure that economists predict will double by 2007–9. Lester
Thurow argues that this situation constitutes a severe threat to the United
States, because our standard of living now depends on borrowing from
abroad. At some point, he and many other economists believe, foreign

countries will pull the plug: they will not want to continue investing in American stocks, bonds, and dollars, and will buy euros instead— which means the dollar will crash. (Thus many financiers, such as billionaire investor Warren Buffett, have shifted large amounts of capital into foreign currencies.) In essence, the U.S. economy is propped up by huge foreign loans, enabling American consumers to keep buying even more foreign products. (The overall consumption of goods by Americans as of April 2003 was $1.4 billion a day.) This will come to an end when the countries on the above list (in particular, China, Japan, and those comprising the EU) decide we are an unsafe bet, an event that may be further abetted by a decision of the oil-producing nations to begin selling oil in euros. If that happens, the oil-importing nations will no longer need dollar reserves to purchase oil, which would lead to a serious decline in the demand for dollars. All of this does not bode well for the U.S. economy. As political journalist William Greider notes, "no nation can borrow endlessly from others without sooner or later forfeiting control of its destiny, and also losing the economic foundations of its general prosperity." The crunch—a huge stock market crash and the meltdown of the dollar—may not be very far off.[20]

Meanwhile, the myth of American economic superiority continues to be trumpeted by the American news media even while the data tell another story: Ford and GM are lagging behind Volkswagen; Nokia has more than two times the cell phone market as does Motorola; Airbus has overtaken Boeing, and now controls 76 percent of the global airplane market; Bertelsmann is the largest book publisher in the world; and the EU leads the United States in the number of science and engineering grads, public research and development expenditures, and new capital raised. After expanding to twenty-five members, the EU accounts for nearly half the world's foreign investment, and exerts greater leverage than America over key countries such as Russia and Brazil. Although there has been a lot of fluctuation in the euro-to-dollar exchange rate since the euro was first introduced, as of late 2005 the euro was still ahead of the game. As noted in the introduction, in 2003, for the first time ever, China supplanted the United States as the number one destination for worldwide foreign investment, while France was number two. Factor in the statistic that from 2001 to 2004 the United States went from a $5 trillion budget surplus to a $4 trillion budget deficit, and it's not exactly a rosy future we are looking at.[21]

As for our military situation, once again, appearance and reality are two different things. Despite all of our vast military resources and our cutting-edge technologies, they are in large part inadequate for fighting a war—a real one, that is. With our decision to act as world policeman, we have, says Chalmers Johnson, bought into a "domino theory" that leads to an endless number of places and commitments to protect, "resulting inevitably in imperial overstretch, bankruptcy, and popular disaffection, precisely the maladies that plagued Edwardian Britain." Note that since World War II, we have avoided taking on an equal power. Our engagement with the Soviet Union itself was a balancing act involving the (often judicious) use of diplomacy. When we actually attacked, it was at the periphery: Korea (a stalemate); Vietnam (a defeat). Otherwise, the engagement consisted of covert operations against virtually defenseless nations or massive attacks on puny countries or tinpot dictators (Grenada, Panama, Iraq, and so on). In situations that really matter, there is a huge gap between America's military power and its ability to shape events according to its will. "Preponderance," says Zbigniew Brzezinski, "should not be confused with omnipotence." By the summer of 2003 it had become clear that the waging of two small "wars" and the occupation of two weak nations—Afghanistan and Iraq—had strained our manpower to the limit.[22]

Meanwhile, serious rivals have better things to do with their time. *New York Times* reporter Jane Perlez observes that "China has wasted little time in capitalizing on the U.S. preoccupation with the campaign on terror to greatly expand its influence in Asia." In fact, most Asians regard the American obsession with terrorism as tedious, while China, she says, "has the allure of the new." Japan, Australia, and South Korea are all rebounding because of the huge exports being devoured by the Chinese economy, a process the Indonesians call "feeding the dragon." Indeed, in the fall of 2003, former Australian prime minister Paul Keating asserted that the American century was ending and the Asian one dawning, and there is a good bit of data to support this prediction. During the first six months of 2003, the Chinese car manufacturing industry, for example, expanded at a rate of 32 percent. Shopping malls have sprung up along Beijing's Avenue of Everlasting Peace, where tanks once mowed down protesters. In fact, the Chinese economy has been doubling in size every ten years, which is astounding. Thus a 2004 study by the investment firm of Goldman Sachs predicted the Chinese economy would be the world's biggest by the early 2040s. How long before China leverages that economic power into political power? Already, Perlez continues, it is pushing for an East Asian Economic Community "that would cut out the United States and create a global bloc to rival the European Union." If China does manage to replace us, it will do so by *becoming* us, and by doing that more successfully.[23]

And yet, there's the rub: thinking in terms of quality, and not just geopolitically (that is, who's top banana), this is as much a disappointment as the American experiment finally proved to be, if not more so. Change is always different, but it isn't necessarily better. There is little in the way of an "inner frontier" in China, a concern about civic virtue, civil liberties, or the quality of life—except on the part of dissidents, who are ruthlessly crushed. Leaving its abysmal record on human rights aside, China is beginning to resemble the United States in Mandarin. It seems to have no larger vision, and there is absolutely no indication that its emergence as a superpower will herald a better world. One percent of the Chinese population owns 40 percent of the nation's wealth, while 18 percent lives on less than a dollar a day. In a single generation, the gap between rich and poor there has become one of the largest in the world, with all the attendant problems characteristic of the U.S.: widespread corruption, huge inequities in health care, gated suburban communities (with names such as Napa Valley, Palm Springs, and Park Avenue), luxury supermarkets, fleets of SUVs and stretch limos, millions of workers laid off, and a candid belief on the part of the new elite that, as Ross Terrill writes in *The New Chinese Empire*, "the world is a huge jungle of Darwinian competition, where . . . notions of fairness count for little." A "me first" psychology is very much in evidence in the People's Republic now, as the old socialist China of thirty years ago is being replaced by a new "money-centered cutthroat society." Meanwhile, the number of beggars on the streets of the major cities has risen dramatically, and in the countryside the number of farmers living in poverty went up by eight hundred thousand during 2003 alone.[24]

It is also the case that the kitsch and crap of American culture is fast-being reproduced in China as well. In *China Pop*, Jianying Zha reports on the culture of mass consumerism—from soap operas to pornography—that has swept over the old People's Republic, the commercialization of every aspect of life, and the media market that propagates this whole process. By 2003 Wal-Mart had thirty-one outlets in the country (complete with the firm's characteristic exploitation of labor). Instead of buy-ing pancakes from street vendors, young families now crowd into McDonald's and KFC, while the walls of metro stations are lined with ads for cell phones and stylish clothing. Bustling bazaars—the famous old chaotic "wet markets" that used to sell ducks and squid—are now getting pushed aside by huge Western supermarkets (Carrefour, Hymart), with everything antiseptically packaged in clear wrap and Styrofoam. Nor does the plastic end there. Cosmetic surgery clinics have sprung up like pim-ples, promising to give young women more rounded, Western eyes; and beauty pageants, once regarded as bourgeois "spiritual pollution," are now held across the country, as the beauty industry rakes in something like $24 billion a year. In general, said Paul Keating in 2003, the Chinese goal is to give everyone "a refrigerator, a television set and CD player, plenty of telephones and lots of toys for the kids." Meanwhile, as in the United States, it's the kids who will suffer: the Chinese are starting to work ungodly hours to pay for all of this, and their lives aren't necessarily bet-ter. Indeed, more and more, the culture of China seems to be awash in power, money, and bullshit.[25]

And speaking of quality of life, it continues to deteriorate. The Chi-nese have always put production ahead of the environment, and this seems to be getting worse. The air quality, for example, is appalling; and while private houses are very clean, the Chinese—for reasons different from our own, of course—have very little regard for public space, so that the cities tend to be polluted and dirty. It turns out that China has sixteen of the world's twenty most polluted cities.[26]

China might indeed replace the United States as the world's major power by midcentury or before, the more so if it is savvy enough to pull off the East Asian bloc maneuver referred to above. But to what end? I repeat: this is basically the United States in Mandarin, but without the tradition of democracy and civil liberties. I may be totally off base here, but all this just seems like old wine in new bottles: a consumer capitalist regime complete with kitsch, corruption, class divisions, and a question-able quality of life. An economic powerhouse, but possibly not much else.

Which brings us to Europe. Some have argued that it will be the European Union, rather than China, that will replace the United States as the world's dominant power. We have already discussed how well European companies are doing in comparison with their American counterparts, and it is noteworthy that when French president Jacques

Chirac visited China in October 2004, he waltzed away with $4 billion in industrial orders, Airbus accounting for the lion's share. European productivity grew 2.4 percent annually from 1973 to 2000 as compared with America's 1.37 percent. The GDP of the EU is nearly 30 percent of that of the world's, and more than six times that of China. If one looks at the 140 largest companies in the Global Fortune 500 ratings, 61 of them are European, while only 50 are American. Fourteen of the twenty largest commercial banks in the world are European, including three of the top four. All in all, the EU has emerged as a formidable entity, with roughly 450 million citizens and a $9 trillion economy.[27]

There is also the matter of European military power, surprisingly enough. The combined armies of the EU number more than 1.6 million soldiers. Despite opposition from the United States and Great Britain, the EU is moving in the direction of having a military force capable of operating autonomously—that is, without American or NATO interference—and the plan is to build a command headquarters near Brussels. Many European officials see this as necessary if the EU is to have a meaningful foreign policy—i.e., to have clout in world affairs. European countries already provide ten times as many U.N. peacekeepers as does the United States, and its sixty-thousand-troop Rapid Reaction Force can be deployed around the world whenever this is deemed necessary. In *The New World Disorder*, philosopher and social critic Tzvetan Todorov candidly urges Europe to abandon its pacifism and rearm. "You must be able to defend your values," he writes; Europe "need not be submissive to the United States."[28]

Finally, in a short essay in *Foreign Policy*, Parag Khanna of the Brookings Institution points out that America has made a great mistake in conceiving of power primarily in military terms. Presence and influence, he says, are hardly the same thing. Real power is "overall leverage," and this Europeans understand very well. This is why the EU is the world's largest bilateral aid donor (it gives twice as much aid to poor countries as does the United States) and is the largest importer of agricultural goods from the Third World, thus enhancing its influence in unstable regions. Its universities are now attracting students in large numbers from all over the world, ones who would have wound up at American institutions of higher learning in earlier days. The EU also makes itself attractive via environmental sustainability and the promotion of international law and social welfare. The American record in these three areas is of course quite poor by comparison, and so European views are more easily exported to the rest of the world. Mickey Mouse and Coca-Cola will continue to have their allure, to be sure, in terms of "soft power" (cultural influence), but in the end, the sheer sensibleness of the European approach, its savvy internationalism, and perhaps its more solid currency are going to look a lot better than American arrogance and violence.[29]

Impressive as all this is, however, it does not mean that the EU will manage to outweigh China in terms of geopolitical power as the United States continues on its downward course. Thus historian Niall Ferguson asserts that "the reality is that demography likely condemns the EU to decline in international influence and importance." Fertility rates are dropping in Western Europe, while life expectancy is rising. By 2050, one in every three Italians, Spaniards, and Greeks is expected to be sixty-five or older, even allowing for immigration. The EU can counter this by permitting even more immigration than it has—which would entail cultural changes that many Europeans oppose (witness the conflicts that already exist in France, Germany, and elsewhere)—or by becoming a "fortified retirement community." Richard Bernstein of the *New York Times* agrees, pointing out that the median age in Europe is expected to be 52.3 by 2050, and that at the present time only 49 percent of European men between fifty-five and sixty-five still work. Forecasts of possible long-term French and German economic stagnation periodically appear in major newspapers. The upshot of all this is that the jury is still out, and one can find a wide variety of opinions across the political and social science spectrum as to what the world's power arrangements will look like fifty years hence. But that America will be in a much weaker position relative to China and the EU by that time is, in the view of many informed observers, a foregone conclusion.[30]

Regarding the matter of quality of life, however, here the verdict seems to be a bit less ambiguous. In terms of the "inner frontier" we have talked about, Europe may come closest to offering its citizens the best lifestyle currently available on the planet. While Robert Kagan's assessment—"Americans are from Mars, Europeans are from Venus"—was drawn up as a condescending neocon put-down of the EU as a collection of wimps, he did nevertheless manage to capture a stereotypical difference that does have a ring of truth to it. To reverse his condescension, one might argue that while the American norm is to throw one's life away in a frantic, workaholic competition for money and power, Europeans take time to savor what life is really all about. With their social safety net, generous pension plans, "extended" holidays and maternity leaves, and concern for nature and the environment, these folks have created a way of life that should be the envy of the world. They work, obviously, but they also linger in non–Starbuckish cafés, reading and conversing; prepare and eat food that doesn't taste like cardboard; stroll, drink wine, and make love (something Americans don't spend a lot of time doing anymore, according to all the latest studies); listen to music; and take time with their kids. Their cities are beautiful and organic, designed for human beings, not for corporations or commuters. Ever cynical, Kagan argues that all this is the result of no longer having any "real" power. But perhaps centuries of war and violence wised them up, so that they finally recognize the stupidity of trying to control everything and everybody and have discovered that the world has greater pleasures than being king of the dunghill. As for us, says Nicholas von Hoffman, "America will not rest until it has turned the globe into replicas of itself."[31] No triumph, that.

Europe is certainly not perfect, but it is far more humane. There is a conscious effort afoot there to avoid the pattern of liquid modernity described in the first chapter of this book. The reader will remember the discussion of Città Lente (Slow Cities), which now has over sixty member towns in Italy and beyond. These communities have worked to increase pedestrian zones, foster a spirit of neighborliness, ban supermarket chains and neon signs, and reduce cell phone use. The idea, writes Canadian journalist Carl Honoré, is to create places where one has time to think, to reflect on the big existential questions, rather than simply get caught up in the fury of the modern world. The movement has as its ideal the late-medieval town, where people walk on cobbled streets and socialize in the *piazze*. In fact, many European cities are emulating this pattern, banning traffic from the town center, or holding occasional car-free days.[32]

There is also a conscious attempt, both official and unofficial, to work less. Germans now spend 12 percent less time on the job than they did in 1979 and frankly regard leisure as a right. In 1993, the EU declared forty-eight hours of work to be a weekly maximum, and France subsequently cut its workweek to thirty-five hours. A survey taken in 1999 revealed that 77 percent of temp workers in the EU had chosen to work fewer hours so as to have time for family, hobbies, and rest. One of the best-selling books in France in recent years is Corinne Maier's *Bonjour paresse* ("Hello Laziness," an ironic echo of Françoise Sagan's best-seller of fifty years earlier, *Bonjour tristesse*), a slacker's manual(!) that coaches French workers how to engage in calculated loafing on the job. Why slave away for corporate culture, writes Maier, when it is nothing more than the "crystallization of the stupidity of a group of people at a given moment"?[33]

Of course, some sociologists have argued that Americans have no choice, that they *have* to work like slaves, given the absence of generous pensions, subsidized college education, universal health care, long paid vacations and maternity leave, and the other benefits that Europeans take for granted. Perhaps; but who agreed to this, after all? I don't know how far one can push the "false consciousness" argument in this case. Having bought into a pernicious philosophy that everyone has to make it by themselves, that there is and should be no free lunch, that these sorts of benefits are "socialistic" and therefore evil, Americans have only them-selves to blame for a life riddled with pervasive insecurity, which leaves them without a moment to breathe. As reporter Katrin Bennhold writes, "the Atlantic . . . separates two radically different philosophies of life." For Europeans, states one European commissioner for economic affairs, eco-nomic growth is a means, not an end—something Americans literally cannot fathom. Numerous polls have shown that Europeans are only too happy to pay high taxes to get social services in return, and they under-stand that their lower rates of child poverty, incarceration, illiteracy, homi-cide, suicide, and the like are the result of this. It's even more ironic when we consider the fact that Europe may be pulling ahead of America on the economic front.[34]

So many Americans possess what might be called a kind of "life stu-pidity": they haven't a clue as to what the good life really is. Like Edward G. Robinson in *Key Largo*, they think it amounts to a single word: more. I was having lunch one day at the Holiday Inn near the Department of Agriculture in downtown Washington, where I used to teach writing workshops for government employees, and started talking to an older Indian woman at the next table, who was also a government worker. The TV was blaring, as usual; nobody else was around. I got up and, with a nod from her, turned it off. She thanked me and said, "I'm so tired of the endless noise in America. You know, when you first come here, it's very exciting, because the possibilities seem endless. Then you get embedded in the system, and begin to see how limited you really are." She went on:

"Everybody in America works constantly. They have no time to enjoy anything. Even the simple enjoyment of being alive escapes them."

I am aware of this "life stupidity" every time I leave the country. Walking around an ordinary, somewhat out-of-the-way middle-class district of Barcelona a couple of years ago, I was struck by the beauty of the physical design, the palpable atmosphere of relaxation and friendliness, and the quiet of it all, the graciousness; and I couldn't help thinking how brutal life in so many American cities tends to be, by comparison: harsh, solitary, high-pressured, antagonistic. Joan McQueeney Mitric, who is a freelance writer based in Washington, D.C., reports a similar reaction she had in Belgrade. "Coming from the West," she writes, "it takes a while to remember that not everyone in the world is on edge." Americans don't know how to stroll, she continues. Whereas in American parks you see "homeless people trying to catch some shuteye on a bench, their possessions wadded up under their heads for safekeeping," in the parks of Belgrade one finds elderly couples strolling hand in hand, or chess players hunched over their boards for hours on end, arguing politics, or (on Sundays) crowds gathering to do traditional Balkan dances, to the accompaniment of live violin music. Oh sure, you can find similar activities in Washington Square Park in New York; but in the United States this is the exception, whereas in Europe it tends to be the ethos.[35]

Nevertheless, it's not all that rosy, and the American-European differences are not all that stark. Downtown Barcelona is not quite as noisy as Miami, but it is definitely moving in that direction. We are still talking about consumer societies, after all; and in addition, the European culture of leisure is being seriously threatened, in large part because of American economic pressure. German shopkeepers have had to extend their hours; the government of Gerhard Schröder pushed through tax cuts and reduced social benefits while it increased health costs (the "Agenda 2010" reform package); German workers have—like their French counterparts—been forced to give up the thirty-five-hour work week, and work forty to forty-two hours a week without extra pay; and so on. As of this writing, there have been huge protests across Germany, but it is unlikely they will succeed. Similar developments are taking place across the EU.[36]

Furthermore, writes Canadian journalist Doug Saunders, the basis of the European "paradise" may be loosely analogous to that of ancient Athens, where a vibrant democracy rested on a huge slave population at work in the silver mines. The European equivalent of the Athenian slave population, he claims, is a large number of migrant workers who constitute a shadow economy but who are themselves excluded from the good life. Beggars in Seville, he discovered, are rounded up at night and trucked out to an internment camp at the edge of town. Anywhere from 5 to 20 percent of Europe's economy, he asserts, is derived from the work of those who live unprotected lives on the outskirts of the major cities. It is the *ausländer* population, in other words, that enables the middle class to enjoy the life that it does.[37]

What about the sense of community in the EU countries? I have no idea how representative this is, but I was rather depressed by the story of Giorgio Angelozzi, a retired classics professor living in Rome, who was so lonely that he finally placed an ad offering five hundred euros to any family willing to adopt him as their grandfather(!). To Italy's credit, he was deluged with letters from his fellow countrymen willing to take him up on his offer, but I can't help wondering how many others there are across Europe in the same position.[38]

And are Europeans still on the cutting edge, intellectually speaking? "Don't have too many illusions about France," a French friend wrote me recently; "a lot of what you deplore about American culture . . . is more and more true in France too." She goes on to describe the "vacuum of thought" in French universities, the lock-step thinking that is prevalent there, the pervasive negativity and cynicism of the culture in general. "It's the twilight of France as well," she concludes. *New York Times* Paris correspondent Alan Riding corroborates this, noting that the tradition of the public intellectual is pretty much dead, replaced by a handful of media celebrities (Bernard-Henri Lévy being the most famous). Newspapers that serve as intellectual vehicles are starting to lose circulation, and the tradition of knowledge as an end, rather than a means, is starting to die out.[39]

Finally, are the villages of Europe still the epitome of medieval rural life? When I first visited Provence in 1973, this did seem to be the case. Upon my return in 1988, I discovered that entire towns had been "boutiqued." Everything had the feel of being on display, wrapped in plastic. In 2004, the village of Charence, an hour west of Paris (population 146), made a deal with France Télécom: FT would spend $150,000 to restore the town's eleventh-century Romanesque church, and in return the town agreed to let FT install an antenna in the steeple to allow for cell phone reception. America has come to Charence, then: inhabitants shop at a supermarket, and in nearby towns the butcher and baker have shut their doors. Village camaraderie, if not a thing of the past, has dropped off dramatically.[40]

In Benoît Duteurtre's prizewinning novel, *Le voyage en France*, the author offers his readers a send-up of the American view of Europe as some sort of paradise. David, the central character, lives in New York and dreams of the France of Monet and the *cafés des artistes*. Wearing a straw hat, he arrives in the old country, ready to embrace the nineteenth century. Instead, he finds that consumers in shopping malls dress like adolescents in Brooklyn; visits a medieval abbey where the monks are all on cell phones, make a living assembling personal computers, and shop in the nearby supermarket; and generally keeps meeting people who dream of living like Americans! He realizes that provincial America has been grafted onto a provincial Europe, in which beauty is preserved as a "cultural product." He finally has an imaginary encounter with Charles de Gaulle, who tells him, "You are chasing after chimeras, *mon vieux;* go back to New York." Which he does; whereupon he is caught up in the "vertical intoxication" of the place. He revels in the chaos, the uncertainty, the free-floating energy, sees "a population gathered by the urgency of being at the center of the world." In Manhattan, "everything is mixed in an urgent tumult"; the place crackles, this city of day and night. On the roof of his hotel, he feels like he is embracing all of space, all of history. Below, he tells himself, is an existence that endlessly destroys and reconstructs itself.[41]

I too have felt this energy; as the T-shirt says, I Heart New York. In fact, I adore New York. But we have to be careful about the meaning of this energy. David reflects that the world of towns and countrysides, voyages and lost time, new fashions in art, quality and elegance—all of this has been overwhelmed by America, occupied as it is with the rational and the technical, with profit and production. In this sense, David muses,

> America truly constituted the center of the world, since it had spread this mode of thinking everywhere. Like the Europe of yesterday, it invented its own history, becoming the history of the world . . . for which it wound up serving as a model. . . . This is the beauty of the American shambles: its narrow-minded pretension, but especially its inability to control itself. . . .[42]

And this is the heart of it, *n'est-ce pas?* The problem with the "vertical intoxication" Duteurtre describes is that *it has no particular purpose*. The world of infinite possibilities is a universal solvent, in effect—100 percent negative freedom. But *then* what? Endless shopping, endless novelty, and ruling the world in the name of democracy just don't cut it, finally. The central question remains: Under which way of life are human needs best served? Clearly, some of them—individualism, negative freedom, material acquisition—are best served by the American one . . . but at what cost? Europe is no paradise, but its value system and the EU experiment do point in a different direction, one that at least is aware of the neglected "inner frontier." Ultimately, that dimension of life is not just a luxury for a privileged few; without it, we all become variations on a theme by Bush—stuffed dolls, morons in denial, people living lives of substitute satisfaction while much of what we are doing is destructive. The *New York Times'* Bob Herbert writes of the situation in America:

> I look at the catastrophe in Iraq, the fiscal debacle at home, the extent to which loyalty trumps competence at the highest levels of government, the absence of a coherent vision of the future for the United States and the world, and I wonder, with a sense of deep sadness, where the adults have gone.[43]

As the American empire rolls mindlessly on, attempting to convert the entire world to its way of life, the loss of what is truly human is going to be pretty heavy. I would like to say that things can be turned around, that the nation will wake up, but all the signs indicate just the reverse. Europe may indeed be the likely candidate to replace us, but it is too soon to tell; nor will this renaissance be one of perfection, if and when it arrives. We'll never have a truly "inner frontier" society, so to speak; Lewis Mumford, with his insistence that technology be servant rather than master, and his understanding that relationship and reflection lie at the heart of being human, will always be an oddball in the modern industrial world. The issue, in any case, is not utopia, but something that supports a more authentic way of life.

Liberal versus Radical

Tikkun olam: the repair of the world. It may be the case that in order for the world to be healed or restored, the United States may have to be pushed off center stage; and this may be a good thing, from the viewpoint of the entire world. Of course, there will be a downside to this; of that, I have no doubt. But the upside is that too many of America's values in the early twenty-first century are corrosive, and unless the nation can do some rather elaborate soul searching, it needs to lose influence in the rest of the world. A world awash in suburbs and shopping malls, television and sensationalism, cell phones and Burger King, Prozac and violence, fundamentalist Christianity and sink-or-swim ethics, is no vision for the future. In addition, our foreign policy, the Cold War mentality that ran parallel to these developments, was a big mistake—even George Kennan saw that pretty soon after penning his famous "X" article. That we now persist in it goes back to the Hegelian theme of negative identity; and as aberrant as this Manichaean-imperial framework is, it has penetrated far too deeply into the American psyche for us to be able to suddenly (or even gradually) shift gears. Not only economically, but also psychologically, domestic and foreign policy reflect and reinforce each other, and this is a big part of why we cannot escape our fate. Thus former *Wall Street Journal* reporter Michael Ybarra, in *Washington Gone Crazy*, demonstrates quite clearly that the anti-Communist hysteria of the late 1940s and 1950s was not really a response to espionage or an external threat, but more fundamentally "a conservative reaction to the New Deal," a long-standing series of resentments that included "rural rancor toward urban elites, nativist dread of encroaching minorities, fundamentalist anxieties over the spread of secular values," and the like.[44] When you add to these the contemporary hatred of knowledge and Enlightenment thinking, and the subliminal awareness that we have become unmoored and are basically failing as a nation, you have a rather potent brew on your hands.

So "terrorism" now replaces communism as the enemy, since this involves only a change of content, not of form, and we are now set to rerun the old scenario at higher stakes—that is, at a rather precarious point in our history. This will mean vastly exaggerating the threat, never looking within ourselves or at our role in the overall scheme of things, persecuting many people at home and probably killing huge numbers abroad, living in an illusion, and in general doing ourselves irreparable harm. "The whole aim of practical politics," wrote H. L. Mencken many decades ago, "is to keep the populace alarmed (and hence clamorous to be led to safety) by menacing it with an endless series of hobgoblins, all of them imaginary." It's a pretty foolish way to live, but because it endows our lives with "meaning," it's not something we are going to be able to give up. As the saying goes, some alcoholics "hit bottom" the other side of death.

And what about the very small percentage of Americans who see through this charade? I'm referring to those of us who feel, along with (say) Dennis Kucinich, or Albert Borgmann, or perhaps the readership of *The Nation* (with a circulation of 150,000 at best), that we are strangers in a strange land? From our vantage point, the distinction between red and blue states doesn't mean very much, because John Kerry's election would not have altered the nation's course. Clearly, the support for a non-frontier-chasing, nonimperialist America is quite minuscule in this country. But if the United States at large isn't going to be doing any soul searching, writes Thomas de Zengotita, perhaps it is time that *we* did, in lieu of being able to alter the imperial trajectory. It may be, he points out, that our pretensions to radicalism, all along, were not real; that our political efforts were really about reform, never intending to go beyond bourgeois democracy. If your politics is "global new deal meets respect for diversity," then you are a liberal, he says, and "that means you basically accept a world system of private enterprise and technological innovation and consumer culture, and you want to see it managed so that no one is excluded, the environment is protected, free expression flourishes, and so on." If you really are a radical, on the other hand, you are aiming for something else—but what? Time, perhaps, to find out. My own belief is that there is no warding off the Dark Age; all the evidence points in that direction. But you can certainly do your best to keep it out of your head, which is a contribution of a sort. What is thus called for is long-term study and thought, in an effort to come up with a serious alternative to global bourgeois democracy—blueprints for a better time, perhaps, and for another place. "What radicals need right now," says de Zengotita, "isn't action but theory."[45]

That may indeed be the place to start, the more so in that sometimes theory constitutes a type of action (one can never be sure). Garrison Keillor tells the story of a town situated on a river that was rising, threatening to overflow its banks and destroy the town. One man began hauling sandbags down to the river, hoping to hold it back. It was slow work, and it seemed pretty futile. Keillor's comment on this effort is that when you're dealing with a river, there's only so much you can do. But, he adds, *you do that much*. Speaking for myself, at this point in time this book is the "that much" I can do, whether it counts for a little or a lot. I don't know exactly who's out there, but as they say on late-night radio: thanks for listening.

Notes

For any serious writer researching contemporary affairs, there is a "virtual" problem in terms of scholarly authenticity that is somewhat difficult to solve. References to Web sites are often unstable over time, and can thus be unavailable to the interested reader. In the notes below, I've listed the URL as it was posted during 2002–4. The problem is that the site may no longer exist, or the information may no longer be posted on the site. In addition, in a number of cases my citations from newspapers and journals are from the online edition (which can typically be recognized by an absence of page references), which may not exactly correspond to the date of hard-copy publication. All I can do, then, is assure the reader that all of the citations and quotations in this book are fully reliable: they were taken from actual documents, virtual or otherwise.

The following abbreviations are used throughout the notes:

CHE *Chronicle of Higher Education*
GW *Guardian Weekly*
IHT *International Herald Tribune*
NY *The New Yorker*
NYT *New York Times*
TLS *Times Literary Supplement* (London)
WSJ *Wall Street Journal*
WP *Washington Post*

Introduction

1. Shmuel Feiner, *The Jewish Enlightenment*, trans. Chaya Naor (Philadelphia: University of Pennsylvania Press, 2004), p. 3.
2. Morris Berman, *The Twilight of American Culture* (New York: W. W. Norton, 2000); Charles Freeman, *The Closing of the Western Mind* (London: William Heinemann, 2002); and Ron Suskind, "Without a Doubt," *NYT Magazine*, 17 October 2004.
3. Cornelia Dean, "Evolution Takes a Back Seat In U.S. Classes," *NYT*, 1 February 2005, pp. D1 and 6.

4. Results of *Time* magazine poll cited by John Sutherland in "America Gets Lost in Search for Certainty," *GW*, 13–19 May 2004, p. 18. For this and the following paragraph, see David Gates, "The Pop Prophets," *Newsweek*, 24 May 2004, pp. 45–50; and Christopher Taylor, "Rapt Attention," *TLS*, 7 May 2004, p. 36.

5. Anthony Lewis, "One Liberty at a Time," *Mother Jones*, May–June 2004, pp. 73–78.

6. Patrick O'Gilfoil Healy, "Sobriety Tests Becoming Part of School Day," *NYT*, 3 March 2005, pp. A1 and 25; Anne Cronin, "America's Grade on Twentieth-Century European Wars: F," *NYT*, 3 December 1995, sect. 4, p. 5; National Public Radio, 13 December 2003; Michael Mann, *Incoherent Empire* (London: Verso, 2003), pp. 102–3 (from a 2000 *Popular Science* survey, and a 2002 National Geographic Society/Roper Poll survey); David Mindich, "Dude, Where's Your Newspaper?," *CHE/Chronicle Review*, 8 October 2004, p. B5 (from a Roper survey); Tamar Lewin, "Writing in Schools Is Found Both Dismal and Neglected," *NYT*, 26 April 2003, p. A13; Stefan Halper and Jonathan Clarke, *America Alone* (Cambridge: Cambridge University Press, 2004), p. 303, and passport statistics posted at http://travel.state.gov/passport/other_stats.html; Andrew Gumbel, "What Americans Know," *The Independent* (London), 8 September 2003, posted at http://news.independent .co.uk/world/americas/story.jsp?story=441456 (on ignorance of postwar division of Germany); and "Still Misinformed," *Kansas City Star*, 6 October 2004, p. A2, reporting on a *USA Today*/Gallup poll (on Saddam Hussein and 9/11).

7. John Powers, *Sore Winners* (New York: Doubleday, 2004), pp. 8–9, 14, 20, 22, 42, 95, 124, and 345.

8. Quote from Gore in David Remnick, "The Wilderness Campaign," *NY*, 13 September 2004, p. 57; Dana Priest and Barton Gellman, "U.S. Decries Abuse but Defends Interrogation," *WP*, 26 December 2002, p. A1; Douglas Jehl et al., "Abuse of Captives More Widespread, Says Army Survey," *NYT*, 26 May 2004, pp. A1 and 11; R. Jeffrey Smith and Dan Eggen, "New Papers Suggest Detainee Abuse Was Widespread," *WP*, 22 December 2004, p. A1; James Risen and Thom Shanker, "Secret Universe Holds U.S. Terror Suspects," *IHT*, 19 December 2003, p. 5; Reed Brody, "What About the Other Secret U.S. Prisons?," *IHT*, 4 May 2004; "The U.S. Military Archipelago," *IHT*, 8–9 May 2004, p. 4; and Dana Priest and Joe Stephens, "Secret World of U.S. Interrogations," *WP*, 11 May 2004, pp. A1 and 12.

9. Mark Danner, "Will All Americans Become Torturers?," *IHT*, 7 January 2005, p. 6.

10. Andrew Moravcsik, "Dream on America," *Newsweek International*, 31 January 2005; Emmanuel Todd, *After the Empire*, trans. C. Jon Delogu (New York: Columbia University Press, 2003); Neil Henderson, "Economists Warn of Dollar Slump as U.S. Trade Gap Widens by $55 Billion," *GW*, 20–26 August 2004, p. 7; William Greider, "The Serpent That Ate America's Lunch," *The Nation*, 10 May 2004, pp. 11–18; Will Hutton, "The American Prosperity Myth," *The Nation*, 1–8 September 2003, pp. 20–24; "America's Deficit Time Bomb," *IHT*, 1 October 2004, p. 8 (from the *Boston Globe*, and including the quote from the IMF report); and David J. Rothkopf, "Just as Scary as Terror," *WP*, 25 July 2004, pp. B1 and 3.

1. Liquid Modernity

1. On the 1995 wealth distribution, see Robert Reich, "My Dinner with Bill," *American Prospect*, no. 38 (May–June 1998), pp. 6–9. This figure, which excludes the value of homes, represents $4 trillion in assets. At the same time, the upper quintile in America owned 93 percent of the wealth. The reference to the 400 richest individuals comes from a U.N. Development Program report of 1998 discussed in "The Other Davos in Action," in

François Houtart and François Polet, eds., *The Other Davos* (London: Zed Books, 2001), p. 85. The wealth of 85 of the 400 exceeds the annual output of China. If the 400 were taxed 4 percent, it would eliminate all poverty and health problems in the entire world. On the significance of the Bretton Woods repeal, see, for example, Will Hutton, *The World We're In* (London: Little, Brown, 2002), p. 187.

2. Will Hutton and Anthony Giddens, eds., preface to *Global Capitalism* (New York: The New Press, 2000), p. vii.

3. Hutton, *World We're In*, p. 7; Zygmunt Bauman, *Liquid Modernity* (Cambridge: Polity Press, 2000), pp. 5, 7, 28–29, 33, and 36.

4. Ian Buruma, "What We Think of America," *Granta*, no. 77 (Spring 2002), p. 19; and Bauman, *Liquid Modernity*, pp. 20–21, 32, 34, and 126.

5. Bauman, *Liquid Modernity*, pp. 5, 147, 151–53, 162, 164, and 192.

6. Clare Ansberry, "In the New Workplace, Jobs Morph to Suit Rapid Pace of Change," *WSJ*, 22 March 2002.

7. Ellen Ullman, *Close to the Machine* (San Francisco: City Lights Books, 1997), pp. 12, 19–20, 96, 123–27, 129, 131, and 146.

8. Richard Sennett, *The Corrosion of Character* (New York: W.W. Norton, 1998), pp. 11, 20, 22, 51, 62, 66, 68, 116, 118–19, 122, 146, and 168.

9. Robert Reich speaking at Politics and Prose Bookstore, Washington, D.C., 22 January 2001; Reich, *The Future of Success* (New York: Alfred A. Knopf, 2001), pp. 4–6, 98–100, 111–12, and 117–19; and Reich, "The Thought Leader Interview," *Strategy + Business*, no. 21 (4 2000), p. 98.

10. Gwyn Williams, "The Concept of 'Egemonia' in the Thought of Antonio Gramsci: Some Notes on Interpretation," *Journal of the History of Ideas* 21 (1960), 586–99.

11. For this and the section below, see Thomas Frank, *One Market Under God* (New York: Anchor, 2001), pp. xii–xv, 3, 9, 11–12, 65–69, 85–87, 94, 96–97, 103, 175, 179–80, 190–92, 196–200, 203, 226–28, 245, 247, 380, and 405.

12. "Rise in Joblessness Delights U.S. Markets," *IHT*, 3–4 June 2000, p. 1.

13. Reich, *Future of Success*, pp. 31 and 66–68; and Bauman, *Liquid Modernity*, pp. 214–15.

14. Alan Lightman, *The Diagnosis* (New York: Pantheon, 2000); and review of Lightman by Abraham Verghese in *NYT Book Review*, 24 September 2000, p. 26. On the addictive aspect of electronic devices, see Matt Richtel, "Wired to an Addiction," *IHT*, 7 July 2003, pp. 1 and 4.

15. David J. Lynch, "In Italy, Thirty-three Towns Known as Città Lente Make a Conscious Decision to Take it Slow," *USA Today*, 13 October 2000, pp. D1–2.

16. Thomas de Zengotita, "The Numbing of the American Mind," *Harper's Magazine*, April 2002, pp. 33–34 and 38–39.

17. For this and the section below, see Todd Gitlin, *Media Unlimited* (New York: Metropolitan/Henry Holt, 2002), pp. 6–7, 9, 15, 18, 38–39, 63–65, 87–88, 91, 94, 96, 98–99, 110, and 121.

18. Ibid., pp. 164–65; and review of Gitlin by Jonathan V. Last, in *WSJ*, 6 April 2002, p. A14. The argument about nihilism is from Thomas S. Hibbs, *Shows About Nothing* (Dallas: Spence, 1999).

19. Gitlin, *Media Unlimited*, pp. 56 and 58; Stephen L. Carter, *Civility* (New York: Harper Perennial, 1998), pp. 91 and 199. Huxley's comment is from his extremely popular *Ends and Means*. For data on cell phone ownership, see item no. 1144 under www.census .gov/prod/2004pubs/04statab/infocomm.pdf.

. I wrote the American Museum of Natural History in 2003 about the cell phone problem —patrons even talk on them in the live butterfly room, for example—and was given a bureaucratic brushoff that oddly went on and on about the "prestige" of the AMNH (a subsequent follow-up elicited no response). I also wrote the Metropolitan Museum of Art in 2004, noting that some of the guards did not enforce the no-cell phone rule, and patrons paid no attention to them when they tried to. Hence, I suggested that the only way the rule could be enforced was to ask patrons to check their phones at the front desk upon entering the building. The reply I received duly reiterated that cell phone usage was not permitted in the MMA galleries, and that all of the guards were trained to enforce this. Since my original letter made it clear that current "enforcement" was not working, this was basically another bureaucratic brush-off. When I went to the Cloisters, the medieval section of the Met located in Upper Manhattan, I sat in the thirteenth-century Cuxa Cloister while two patrons loudly chatted on cell phones, discussing their dinner plans and reviewing their stock options. So much for the *via contemplativa*.

20. Gitlin, *Media Unlimited*, pp. 179, 185, 198–200, and 205–8. For the Zogby poll, see *WSJ*, 11 April 2002, p. A15.

21. Some sources include: *WP*, 30 November 2000, p. A1; *San Francisco Examiner*, 16 October 2000, p. A15; Fox News report of 9 July 2001 (on children home alone); and Peter J. Boyer, "Two Mothers," *NY*, 3 July 2000, pp. 38–53. On the use of stun guns, see "Police Are Urged Not to Stun Young Children," *WP*, 21 November 2004, p. A10.

22. *US News & World Report*, 23 November 1998; Arthur Allen, "The Trouble with ADHD," *WP Magazine*, 18 March 2001, pp. 8–13 and 21–23; Francis Fukuyama, *Our Posthuman Future* (New York: Farrar, Straus and Giroux, 2002), pp. 47 and 51; Shankar Vedantam, "Antidepressant Use Among Children Soars," *GW*, 22–28 April 2004, p. 31; Judith Warner, "Where's Mommy?," *WP Book World*, 21 November 2004, p. 10; Richard DeGrandpre, *Ritalin Nation* (New York: W.W. Norton, 2000); and "Medicating Kids," *Frontline*, 26 February 2003 (available at www.pbs.org). FDA approval of Prozac for children was reported on the CBS Evening News, 3 January 2003.

In what follows in the text I focus on the impact liquid modernity has on children, but I am assuming the reader is aware of the relationship between it and the colossal increase in the incidence of depression, psychosis, and anxiety among the American population as a whole, all of which most of the medical profession (with the strong encouragement of the health insurance companies) treats with drugs. Thus the number of doctor visits for depression in the U.S. rose from 14 million in 1987 to nearly 25 million in 2001, and medication was prescribed in 90 percent of all these cases. Prozac and its spin-offs, such as Zoloft and Paxil, have been taken by 28 million Americans, or 10 percent of the entire population. A 2001–2 study by the National Epidemiologic Survey on Alcohol and Related Conditions (NESARC) found that nearly 15 percent of American adults (more than 30 million people) have a serious personality disorder. Yet the notion that the statistics of mental illness reflect a serious disturbance in the American soul, that many or even most of these patients are being made sick by the way we are forced to live, is barely up for discussion. See Shankar Vedantam, "Down in the Dumps? Chill with a Sugar Pill," *IHT*, 8 May 2002, pp. 1 and 4; Fukuyama, *Our Posthuman Future*, p. 43; and T. M. Luhrmann, *Of Two Minds: The Growing Disorder in American Psychiatry* (New York: Alfred A. Knopf, 2000). The NESARC study was discussed at www.niaah.nih.gov on 2 August 2004, and published in the *Journal of Clinical Psychiatry* 65 (2004), 948–58.

23. For this and the following section, see Gary Cross, *Kids' Stuff: Toys and the Changing World of American Childhood* (Cambridge, Mass.: Harvard University Press, 1997), pp. 4, 6–7, 10, 81, 106–7, 115, 148, 164–65, 173, 175, 188–89, 193, 195, 227, 229, 235, and 237. For an extended discussion of attachment theory and the "transitional object," see my *Coming to Our Senses* (New York: Simon and Schuster, 1989), especially ch. 1.

24. Data for 2002 cited in *Statistical Abstract of the United States: 2003*, published by the U.S. Census Bureau, available at www.census.gov.

25. See Eric Schlosser, *Fast Food Nation: The Dark Side of the All-American Meal* (Boston: Houghton Mifflin, 2001); and also Greg Critser, *Fat Land* (Boston: Houghton Mifflin, 2002).

26. For this and the section below, see Gary Ruskin, "Why They Whine: How Corporations Prey on Our Children," *Mothering*, November–December 1999, pp. 41–50. Also see George Will, "Consumer Cadets," *WP*, 6 May 2001, p. B7. There are a few books on this important subject, such as Shirley R. Steinberg and Joe L. Kincheloe, eds., *Kinderculture: The Corporate Construction of Childhood* (Boulder, Colo.: Westview Press, 1997); and Alex Molnar, *Giving Kids the Business* (Boulder, Colo.: Westview Press, 1996).

27. Will, "Consumer Cadets," p. B7.

28. From a review by Kenneth Anderson in the *TLS*, 4 February 2000, p. 3 (also the source for the two quotes below).

29. Alex Marshall, *How Cities Work* (Austin: University of Texas Press, 2000), pp. 189–90; and Hutton, *World We're In*, p. 7.

30. David A. Fahrenthold, "As D.C. Man Lay Dying, Witnesses Turned Away," *WP*, 15 February 2003, pp. A1 and 13.

31. Colin M. Turnbull, *The Mountain People* (1972; repr., New York: Simon and Schuster, 1987), especially pp. 124, 197, and 290–92.

32. "Woman Leaps Off Bridge as Drivers Urge Her On," *WP*, 29 August 2001, p. A9; and Yi-Fu Tuan, *Who Am I?* (Madison: University of Wisconsin Press, 1999), p. 123.

33. Louis Menand, "Alone Together," *NY*, 2 July 2001, pp. 21 and 24.

34. David Blum, "Maybe We're the Desperate Ones," *WP*, 19 December 2004, p. B3.

35. Rebecca Mead, "Love for Sale," *NY*, 24 November 2003, pp. 104–7.

36. Jeffrey Rosen, "In Lieu of Manners," *NYT Magazine*, 4 February 2001; Jonathan Rauch, "Law and Disorder," *New Republic*, 30 April 2001; Hutton, *World We're In*, p. 160; Patrick Garry, *A Nation of Adversaries* (New York: Insight Books, 1997); and George Will, "A Gross-Out Culture," *WP*, 18 June 2000, p. B7 (Will's article also cites Nancy Jeffrey).

37. For this and the section below, see Carter, *Civility*, pp. xi, 4, 6, 10, 13, 53, and 168.

38. For this and the following, see Alan Ehrenhalt, *The Lost City* (New York: Basic Books, 1996), pp. 14–16, 21–25, 28, 32, 57, 258, 266–67, and 271.

39. Sally Pfoutz, "Signs of the Time," *WP*, 31 October 2004, p. B8.

40. Material from Putnam is taken from "Bowling Alone: America's Declining Social Capital," *Journal of Democracy* 6, no. 1 (January 1995), 66–78, and from his *Bowling Alone* (New York: Simon and Schuster, 2000), pp. 16–21, 41–46, 86, 93 (and n.), 98, 100, 104–5, 140, 142, 146, and 211.

41. Bettina Drew, *Crossing the Expendable Landscape* (St. Paul: Graywolf Press, 1998), pp. 4–7, 22–25, 63, 94, 100, 108, and 160. Quote from Kenneth Jackson is in Putnam, *Bowling Alone*, p. 211.

42. Drew, *Crossing the Expendable Landscape*, p. 31.

43. David Denby, "Women and Children," *NY*, 11 February 2002, p. 93.

2. Economy, Technology

1. George Modelski, *Long Cycles in World Politics* (Seattle: University of Washington Press, 1987), pp. 97–98. Modelski identifies four phases of any "long cycle" of world leadership —global war, or intense political conflict; world power; delegitimation; and deconcentration—and argues that the United States ended its world power phase at some point

between 1971 (end of dollar convertibility) and 1975 (end of Vietnam war). At a systemic level, he says, America entered the phase of delegitimation, in which the constitutional center of a system begins to falter (what I have called the "twilight" phase). Here, he says, the legitimacy of various aspects of American hegemony, such as its international currency arrangements or its pattern of military intervention, got called into question. In the fourth phase, deconcentration, that which was holding the system together fractures and disintegrates. (See ibid., pp. 30–31 and 118–19 for elaboration of these themes.)

2. Barry Eichengreen, *Globalizing Capital* (Princeton: Princeton University Press, 1998), especially pp. 93–96 (quote from Keynes is on p. 93); and Herman Schwartz, *States Versus Markets*, 2d ed. (New York: St. Martin's, 2000), especially pp. xii, 2, and 317–18.

3. Robert Skidelsky, *Keynes* (New York: Oxford University Press, 1996), pp. 1, 28, 32, 47, 90, and 108.

4. David Felix, "Repairing the Global Financial Architecture," 1999, online at www .foreignpolicy-infocus.org/papers/gfa/index_body.html. "Adjustable peg" exchange rates were fixed for long periods of time, but were supposed to be changed as needed to eliminate disequilibrium in countries' balance of payments.

5. Ibid.

6. Skidelsky, *Keynes*, pp. 95, 112–13; Chalmers Johnson, *Blowback: The Costs and Consequences of American Empire* (New York: Metropolitan/Henry Holt, 2000), pp. 200–201; and Robert Blecker, *Taming Global Finance* (Washington: Economic Policy Institute, 1999), p. 162.

7. Eric Helleiner, *States and the Reemergence of Global Finance* (Ithaca, N.Y.: Cornell University Press, 1994), pp. 2–5.

8. Ibid., pp. 33–49. The final version of the agreement was a little more complicated than this, because the banking establishment wanted to dilute Bretton Woods. Governments would be *permitted* to cooperate in controlling capital movements, and they were required to provide the IMF with information on these only on request, excepting when such information would disclose the affairs of individuals or companies. The bankers also tried to dilute the bit about cooperation at both ends. The result was a somewhat weaker version of the articles than Keynes and White had in mind, but nevertheless the overriding principle was one of restriction (states could control capital movements).

9. Felix, "Repairing the Global Financial Architecture"; Skidelsky, *Keynes*, p. 113; and James Chase, "1945, Year Zero," *World Policy Journal* 12, no. 4 (Winter 1995–96), p. 63. On median wage figures see Harry Throssell, "Globalisation Fails the Poor," available at www.geocities .com/youngmick/levellers/. For a dissenting opinion, see Anna J. Schwartz, "Do We Need a New Bretton Woods?," *Cato Journal* 20, no. 1 (Spring–Summer 2000), 21–25.

10. Sheng is cited in Felix, "Repairing the Global Financial Architecture."

11. The pressure of capitalism for markets is probably the most obvious cause of the repeal of Bretton Woods, but it is also the most complicated one. In what follows I shall present the "streamlined" version of these events so as not to bog the reader down in a lot of abstruse economic detail, but those seeking (some of) that detail may find it below, in n. 13.

12. Eichengreen, *Globalizing Capital*, pp. 135–36; and Schwartz, *States Versus Markets*, pp. 198–99 and 205–6.

13. Helleiner, *States and the Reemergence*, pp. 12–13, 21, and 82; and Will Hutton, *The World We're In* (London: Little, Brown, 2002), p. 189.

It must be said, however, that the undermining of Bretton Woods had already begun in the late 1950s. The first loophole in the system occurred in 1958–59, when there was a return to what is known as current-account convertibility, thereby weakening the effectiveness of exchange controls. The current account is the part of the international balance of payments that reflects transactions in goods and services, whereas the capital account is the part that reflects foreign investment. Current-account convertibility means that if you want to import something, you don't need a permit for the foreign currency exchange involved. Convertibility constituted a loophole in that it enabled capital transactions (including the purchase of stocks and speculation in currency) to be channeled through the current account. Without labels, it became difficult to distinguish between purchases or sales of foreign currency related to transactions on the two types of accounts. Capital transactions could be disguised as current ones, and governments were not easily able to verify that a particular bit of foreign exchange had been undertaken for purposes of trade rather than currency speculation. Hence, lots of speculative capital leaked around the edges. This was a major factor in the increasing move toward a liberal financial order.

Equally important to this drift toward liberalization was a competitive deregulation dynamic promoted by the United States and the United Kingdom that other nations were forced to follow. These two countries had the power to undermine the system unilaterally by offering financial traders a place to operate without regulation. Other countries could watch business and capital migrate to Great Britain and the United States, or they could get on the bandwagon. It wasn't much of a choice. Thus in the late fifties as well, the Euromarket was created, operating outside the control of any national government. It was strongly supported by America and Britain and based in the latter during the sixties. It constituted a decisive shift away from Bretton Woods—really, the beginning of the end of it—and drew major support from the Wall Street and multinational industrial firms, which demanded access to the Euromarket as compensation for "freedom" lost due to capital controls.

During the 1960s, then, the growth of private international financial activity led to large speculative capital flows that were disruptive of Bretton Woods by the end of the decade. Europe, for its part, was opposed to these trends. Belgium's finance minister, for example, argued that these speculative flows would hurt the lives of millions of people. Nor did Europe and Japan wish to finance growing U.S. deficits. But as noted in the text, the United States could not be stopped; its strategy was to use these speculative flows to force foreign governments to revalue their currencies, thereby absorbing the adjustment burden required to correct America's large current-account deficits. (In fact, the government indirectly encouraged private financial operators to speculate against the dollar in favor of other currencies.) During 1971–73, Europe tightened capital controls in an effort to prevent this, but market pressures—including the loopholes discussed above—now made it extremely difficult to control capital movements. So Europe and Japan finally had to float their currencies. By 1973, the U.S. current-account deficit had been nearly eliminated, by transferring to foreigners the bulk of the adjustment burden. By 1976, in any case, the articles of agreement were amended to read that the purpose of the international monetary system was to facilitate the exchange of goods and services—and capital.

See Eichengreen, *Globalizing Capital*, pp. 94–96, 136, and 194; and Helleiner, *States and the Reemergence*, pp. 12–13, 21, 82, and 99–115. I am grateful to Paul Krugman for helping me pick my way through the intricacies of financial convertibility (personal communications of April 2002).

14. Johnson, *Blowback,* pp. 201–2 and 206. The data on circulation of speculative money come from a speech by German president Johannes Rau, given in Berlin on 13 May 2002, and reported in "Steering of Globalization Urged," *Frankfurter Allgemeine Zeitung* (English ed.), 14 May 2002, p. 2.

15. Schwartz, *States Versus Markets*, p. 205; Skidelsky, *Keynes*, pp. 114 and 116; Daniel

Mitchell, "Dismantling the Cross of Gold: Economic Crises and U.S. Monetary Policy," *North American Journal of Economics and Finance* 11, no. 1 (August 2000), 77–104; J. Bradford DeLong, "Slouching Towards Utopia: The Economic History of the Twentieth Century," 2000, online at http://www.j-bradford-delong.net/TCEH/Slouch_Old.html.

Thanks to the Great Society programs, the number of Americans living below the poverty line dropped from 22 percent in 1959 to 11 percent in 1979. The programs were especially beneficial to senior citizens (see Serge Halimi, "How Neo-Liberalism Took over the World," *Le Monde diplomatique* online, English edition, at http://MondeDiplo.com/2002/01/11alternative).

16. F. A. Hayek, *The Road to Serfdom* (1994; repr., Chicago: University of Chicago Press, 1956). The quotation from Keynes is in John Cassidy, "The Price Prophet," *NY*, 7 February 2000, p. 46. In fact, Hayek's book is quite confusing, because while he espouses a completely black-and-white theory, he then compromises the argument in practical terms by talking about the need for state intervention in areas such as pollution, price regulation, and social insurance (compare, for example, pp. 37–39 and 120–22 with 42 and 199).

17. Helleiner, *States and the Reemergence*, pp. 15–16, 66, 77, and 115–19. For additional discussion of the ideological factor, see Hutton, *World We're In*, pp. 56, 68–69, 94–99, and 103–4. There was actually a fourth factor that was operative: domestic American politics. Nixon was coming up for reelection in 1972, and he and John Connally, his treasury secretary, saw Bretton Woods as an obstacle because they wanted to reduce unemployment and thus increase Nixon's chances at the polls. They proposed to do this via devaluation, but as already noted, Bretton Woods rules did not permit this. For more detail, see DeLong, "Slouching Towards Utopia"; Mitchell, "Dismantling the Cross of Gold"; and Chase, "1945, Year Zero," p. 63.

18. Helleiner, *States and the Reemergence*, pp. 123–24; Duncan Green, "Capital Punishment," 1999, available at www.cafod.org.uk; Felix, "Repairing the Global Financial Architecture"; Robert Kuttner, "When the Free Market Is Too Free," *Business Week*, 12 October 1998, p. 24. On Argentina, see Paul Krugman, "Crying with Argentina," *NYT*, 1 January 2002, p. A21.

Productivity growth dropped off sharply in both the developing and the industrialized nations in the 1970s, and never recovered. Economist John Eatwell of Cambridge University notes that the falloff in global growth figures coincides with the abolition of Bretton Woods and fixed exchange rates, and that in every one of the (then) G-7 countries (the United States, Canada, France, Germany, Italy, Japan, and the United Kingdom) growth dropped to two-thirds of the rate it was at in the 1960s, and unemployment rose (cited in Green, "Capital Punishment").

19. On the comparison between 1968 and 1776, see Barry Coates, "Matters of Life and Debt" (review of Daniel Cohen, *The Wealth of the World and the Poverty of Nations*), *TLS*, 21 April 2000, p. 31. On Congressional Budget Office figures, see Paul Krugman, "The Death of Horatio Alger," *The Nation*, 5 January 2004, p. 16. On Gates, see Thomas Frank, "To Market" (review of Jeff Gates, *Democracy at Risk*), *WP Book World*, 1 October 2000, p. 6. On Citicorp, see Carol J. Loomis, "This Stuff Is Wrong," *Fortune*, 25 June 2001, p. 78 (this entire issue, remarkably enough, is devoted to an indictment of "the great CEO pay heist"). On gains for the upper 1 percent, see Robert Reich, "How Selective Colleges Heighten Inequality," *CHE*, 15 September 2000, p. B8. On poverty line and prison population, see Manuel Castells, "Information Technology and Global Capitalism," in *Global Capitalism*, ed. Will Hutton and Anthony Giddens (New York: New Press, 2000), p. 66; "U.S. Imprisoned Population May Hit 2 Million in 2000," *WP*, 1 January 2000, p. A4; and "Nation's Prison Population Climbs to Over 2 Million," *WP*, 10 August 2000, p. A4. On

the homeless, see Michael Powell, "Homeless Surge in N.Y. Symbol of New Crisis," *WP*, 23 December 2001, pp. A1 and 6. On Kevin Phillips, see Thomas Ferguson, "Following the Money," *WP Book World*, 19 May 2002, p. 7.

20. Barbara Ehrenreich, *Nickel and Dimed* (New York: Metropolitan/Henry Holt 2001), p. 200; and Heather Boushey et al., *Hardships in America* (Washington, D.C.: Economic Policy Institute, 2001), pp. 1–2, 20, 29, 31, and 35.

21. Ehrenreich, *Nickel and Dimed,* pp. 3, 6–7, 10, 25–28, 41–42, 173–75, and 185.

For a detailed look at how the Clinton administration made the rich richer (for instance, by deregulating telecommunications and finance, or cutting the capital gains tax), see Joseph Stiglitz, *The Roaring Nineties* (New York: W.W. Norton, 2003).

22. Lead articles in *NY* by Hendrik Hertzberg, 12 March 2001, 4 June 2001, and 12 November 2001. On the Senate bill and Mark Shields, see Throssell, "Globalisation Fails the Poor."

23. David Stout, "Bush Budget tilts Toward Military," *IHT*, 3 February 2004, pp. 1 and 4; "Skewed Priorities," *WP*, 8 February 2004, p. B6; Michelle Conlin and Aaron Bernstein, "Working . . . and Poor," posted 31 May 2004 at www.businessweek.com; Brian Knowlton, "Poverty in the U.S. Climbs for the Third Year," *IHT*, 27 August 2004, pp. 1 and 4; "Economic Reality Bites," *IHT*, 2 September 2004, p. 6.

Federal statistics for health insurance listed on the government Web site www.meps .ahrq.gov/CompendiumTables/TC_TOC.HTM (under "Household Health Insurance Tables") are a bit different from the stats in these articles. For the first half of 1999, it lists 42.8 million people as uninsured, or 15.8 percent of the population; for the first half of 2003, it lists 47.3 million as uninsured, or 16.6 percent of the population. The total increase over this period was 4.5 million people.

24. "As Budget Deficits Loom, Many Promises, Programs, Could Suffer," *WSJ*, 24 January 2002. Quote from Justice Brandeis in Lewis Lapham, "A Citizen in Full," *Harper's Magazine*, September 2000, p. 35.

25. These data (from "During the past fifteen to twenty years" to "than they did in the early 1980s") are from U.N. Development Program reports, as cited in François Polet, "Some Key Statistics," in *The Other Davos*, ed. François Houtart and François Polet (London: Zed Books, 2001), pp. 3–4. The figures on the size of emerging markets are in Castells, "Information Technology and Global Capitalism," p. 66. For three billion living on less than $2 a day, see John Cassidy, "Master of Disaster," *NY*, 15 July 2002, p. 84. For the U.N. Report of 2003, see John Vidal, "A Third of Humanity Will Be Slum Dwellers by 2003," *GW*, 9–15 October 2003, p. 7. The *IHT* editorial is "Showdown in Cancún," 12 September 2003, p. 6.

26. Blecker, *Taming Global Finance*, pp. 1, 4, 26, 33, 106, and 115–16; Kuttner, "When the Free Market Is Too Free"; and Wayne Ellwood, "Redesigning the Global Economy," section on "The Bretton Woods Trio," *New Internationalist*, no. 320 (January–February 2000).

The World Bank is starting to wake up to all this, however. At its annual meeting in 2003, World Bank president James Wolfensohn blasted the rich nations of the world for providing $56 billion to poor countries while they spent $300 billion on agricultural subsidies and $600 billion on their militaries. He also attacked them for preaching free trade and then maintaining high subsidies and barriers for goods in which poor countries could have a comparative advantage. (See "World Bank Faults the Rich Countries," *IHT*, 24 September 2003, p. 1.)

27. Joseph E. Stiglitz, *Globalization and Its Discontents* (New York: W.W. Norton, 2002), pp. xiv, 19–20, 24, 207, 210, 247, 252, and *passim*.

28. Chalmers Johnson, *The Sorrows of Empire* (New York: Metropolitan/Henry Holt,

2004), pp. 260–61. The dissenting advisory panel within the Pentagon referred to was the Defense Science Board, which issued a 102-page report late in 2004 on U.S. failures in the Muslim world ("Strategic Communication"). See Thom Shanker, "U.S. Failing to Persuade Muslims, Panel Says," *IHT*, 25 November 2004, pp. 1 and 7; and Neil Mackay, "US Admits the War for 'Hearts and Minds' in Iraq Is Now Lost," *Sunday Herald* (Scotland), 5 December 2004.

29. Wallace Shawn, *The Fever* (New York: Noonday Press, 1991), pp. 64–66.

30. Quoted in Green, "Capital Punishment."

31. For this and the discussion below, see Albert Borgmann, *Technology and the Character of Contemporary Life* [hereafter *TCCL*] (1984; repr., Chicago: University of Chicago Press, 1987), pp. 3–5, 11, 41–42, 44, and 47.

32. David Strong and Eric Higgs, "Borgmann's Philosophy of Technology," in *Technology and the Good Life?*, ed. Eric Higgs et al. (Chicago: University of Chicago Press, 2000), pp. 23–24.

33. Borgmann, *TCCL*, pp. 10–11 and 46; and Strong and Higgs, "Borgmann's Philosophy," p. 30.

34. Borgmann, *TCCL*, pp. 39, 48, 59, and 115; and Strong and Higgs, "Borgmann's Philosophy," pp. 20–21, 28, and 32.

35. For the following section, see Borgmann, *TCCL*, pp. 126–31.

36. For the following, see Isaiah Berlin, *Two Concepts of Liberty* (Oxford: Clarendon Press, 1958), especially pp. 7, 11, and 16–18; Michael Ignatieff, *Isaiah Berlin* (New York: Henry Holt, 1998), pp. 202–3 and 226–31; Michael Ignatieff, "First Loves," *NY*, 28 September 1998, p. 72; and Borgmann, *TCCL*, pp. 88–91. The point about negative freedom as an apology for a laissez-faire economy was made by the Canadian philosopher Charles Taylor.

37. John Ralston Saul, "The Collapse of Globalism," *Harper's Magazine*, March 2004, pp. 33–43; Johnson, *Sorrows of Empire*, p. 275.

38. Stiglitz, *Globalization and Its Discontents*, p. 73.

39. Hutton, *World We're In*, p. 80; for Sandel, see ibid., p. 81.

40. For this and the section below, see Borgmann, *TCCL*, pp. 52, 81–82, 92, 107, 112–13, and 133.

41. Ellen Goodman, "Real Men Don't Drive Hybrid Cars," *IHT*, 20 July 2004, p. 9.

42. Only 12 percent of high-income Americans believe the state should offer a basic income to all citizens, which is not surprising. But among low-income respondents to this survey, only 33 percent agreed with this, suggesting that in America rich and poor do indeed share the same mind-set. By contrast, in Britain, Germany, Holland, and Italy, 39 percent to 53 percent of high-income respondents said yes to this, and 58 percent to 80 percent of low-income respondents replied in the affirmative. See Hutton, *World We're In*, p. 70.

43. Ignatieff, *Isaiah Berlin*, p. 230.

44. Borgmann, *TCCL*, p. 231; Gordon G. Brittan Jr., "Technology and Nostalgia," in *Technology and the Good Life?*, ed. Higgs et al., p. 85.

45. Castells, "Information Technology and Global Capitalism," pp. 53–57.

46. Francis Fukuyama, *Our Posthuman Future* (New York: Farrar, Straus and Giroux, 2002).

47. Quoted in David Cesarani, *Arthur Koestler* (New York: Free Press, 1998), p. 388.

48. Zygmunt Bauman, *Liquid Modernity* (Cambridge: Polity Press, 2000), pp. 168 and 184; and Christopher Clausen, "Making Sense of America," *Virginia Quarterly Review* 78, no. 2 (Spring 2002), 278.

3. The Home and the World

1. Philip Slater, *Earthwalk* (New York: Bantam, 1975), pp. 26–27.

2. Ibid., p. 27.

3. On Durkheim, see Talcott Parsons, "Durkheim, Émile," in *International Encyclopedia of the Social Sciences*, ed. David Sills (New York: Macmillan, 1968), vol. 4, pp. 314–16; and Frank Parkin, *Durkheim* (Oxford: Oxford University Press, 1992), pp. 16–17. Also see Benjamin Barber, *Jihad vs. McWorld* (New York: Ballantine, 1996).

4. Benjamin Barber, talk at the University of Maryland, College Park, 24 September 2001 (recorded on C-SPAN2, *Book TV*); and Megan Rosenfeld, "Global Thinker," *WP*, 6 November 2001, pp. C1 and 8.

5. Muhammad Asad, *The Road to Mecca*, 4th ed. (Louisville, Ky.: Fons Vitae, 1993), pp. 23–24, 80, 89, 103, 141, 180, 294, and 347.

6. Karen Armstrong, *Islam* (New York: Modern Library, 2000), pp. xi–xii.

7. Ibid., pp. 154–55, 158, and 172.

8. Kenneth M. Pollack, "Faith and Terrorism in the Muslim World" (review of Lewis' *The Crisis of Islam*), *NYT Book Review*, 6 April 2003, p. 11. For trenchant critiques of *What Went Wrong?*, see Edward Said in *Harper's Magazine*, July 2002, pp. 69–74; and Francis Robinson in the *TLS*, 11 April 2003, p. 26. For more general commentary on Lewis, see Terry Eagleton, "Roots of Terror," *The Guardian*, 6 September 2003.

9. Kishore Mahbubani, "The Dangers of Decadence," in *The Clash of Civilizations? The Debate* (New York: Council on Foreign Relations, 1996), p. 40; James Carroll, "Articles of Faith" (review of *The Heart of Islam*, by S. H. Nasr), *NYT Book Review*, 8 September 2002, p. 13; and Robert Irwin, "Anti Occident," *WP Book World* 27 January 2002, p. 5. The quotation from Qutb is in J. G. Ballard, "Gone West" (review of *Dead Cities*, by Mike Davis), *GW*, 6–12 March 2003, p. 16. On Qutb, see also Malise Ruthven, *A Fury for God* (London: Granta, 2002), ch. 4, and Lawrence Wright, "The Man Behind Bin Laden," *NY*, 16 September 2002, pp. 56–85.

I am not sure where Mahbubani obtained his data, but they do seem to roughly conform with statistics available on the U.S. Census Bureau Web site: www.census.gov. For example, under table CH-1, "Living Arrangements of Children Under 18 Years Old: 1960 to Present," the number is 5,829,000 living with one parent in 1960, and 18,938,000 in 1995 (and then 20,093,000 in 2003); so the number more than tripled from 1960 to 1995. However, the U.S. population grew by 90 million during 1960–95, so it's not truly a 300 percent increase.

10. Raymond Tallis, "Dreamers of Paradise" (review of Roger Sandall, *The Culture Cult*), *TLS*, 16 August 2002, p. 6; and Judith Miller, "Naming the Evildoers," *NYT Book Review*, 29 September 2002, p. 12.

11. Bernard Lewis, "Islam and Liberal Democracy," *Atlantic Monthly*, February 1993.

12. Ruthven, *Fury for God*, pp. 252–59.

13. Ibid., pp. 21 and 260.

14. V. S. Naipaul, *Among the Believers* (New York: Vintage, 1982), pp. 318 and 328.

15. Quote from Bellah restated in his "Seventy-Five Years," in Stanley Hauerwas and Frank Lentricchia, eds., *Dissent from the Homeland: Essays After September 11,* special issue of *The South Atlantic Quarterly* 101, no. 2 (Spring 2002), 262.

16. Naipaul, *Among the Believers*, pp. 164–65; Ruthven, *Fury for God*, p. 144; and David Finkel, "Crime and Holy Punishment," *WP*, 24 November 2002, pp. A1, 24, and 25.

17. Kate Cooper, "In Debt to Islam" (review of Charles Freeman, *The Closing of the Western Mind*), *TLS*, 17 January 2003, p. 12.

18. Comments made by Milton Viorst and Akbar Es-Ahmed at a symposium on Islam

held at Politics and Prose Bookstore, Washington, D.C., 10 October 2001.

19. Ruthven, *Fury for God*, p. 39; and "Iran's Revolution Has Failed," *IHT*, 5 February 2003, p. 6. Ironically, Abbas Abdi was one of the students who led the takeover of the U.S. embassy in Tehran in 1979.

20. Aziz Al-Azmeh, *Islams and Modernities*, 2d ed. (London: Verso, 1996), pp. 43–44. On Aghajari, see "Iran Reformist Sentenced to Death," *IHT*, 8 November 2002, p. 5; "Iranian Court Lifts Critic's Death Sentence," *WP*, 15 February 2003, p. A29; and "Once Sentenced to Death, Iranian Activist Gets Five Years," *IHT*, 21 July 2004, p. 7. On the Zeid affair, see Ruthven, *Fury for God*, pp. 39–41; and Daniel del Castillo, "An Exiled Scholar of Islam," *CHE*, 8 February 2002, p. A48.

21. Asad, *Road to Mecca*, pp. 189–92.

22. Ruthven, *Fury for God*, p. 33; Jon Henley and Jeevan Vasagar, "Think Muslim, Drink Muslim, Says New Rival to Coke," *GW*, 16–22 January 2003, p. 3; Jim VandeHei, "Islam's Split-Screen View of the U.S.," *WSJ*, 11 April 2002, p. A15; and Tim Juday, "The Sullen Majority," *NYT Magazine*, 1 September 2002, pp. 42–47.

The Mecca-Cola phenomenon is not restricted to France; there is also Cola Turka in Turkey and Zam Zam Cola in Iran, both launched as Islamic alternatives to Coke and Pepsi, and regarded as expressions of anti-American sentiment (in reality, I suspect they reflect just the opposite). See "Made in Turkey: Mix Soda, a Star, Nationalism and Stir," *WP*, 10 August 2003, pp. B1 and 6.

23. Ruthven, *Fury for God*, pp. 261–64.

24. Samuel P. Huntington, "The Clash of Civilizations?" *Foreign Affairs* 72, no. 3 (Summer 1993), 22–49; and Huntington, *The Clash of Civilizations and the Remaking of the World Order* (New York: Touchstone, 1997).

25. For example, see Marc Champion, "Can Professor, Clerics Co-Exist at Forum?," *WSJ*, 31 January 2002, p. A14; Shahid Qadir, "Civilizational Clashes: Surveying the Fault-Lines," *Third World Quarterly* 19, no. 1 (March 1998), 149–53; and Z. A. Kader, review in *Arab Studies Quarterly*, 20, no. 1 (Winter 1998), 89–93.

It is worth noting, however, that there is continuity as well as difference between fundamentalist and mainstream attitudes. As John Raines points out, the Third World tends to regard the Western nations "as acting in a simple, powerful, and uniformly grandiose way. As a historical past and present, as a persisting source of dynamism, as a culture of commodities and sensate satisfactions, as images of success and beauty projected upon magazine covers and television screens worldwide, there does seem to be a 'West' that presents itself powerfully to all Muslims." See John C. Raines, "The Politics of Religious Connectedness: Islam and the West," *Cross Currents* 46, no. 1 (Spring 1996), 39–49.

26. Bernard Lewis, "The Roots of Muslim Rage," *Atlantic Monthly*, September 1990, pp. 47–60; and Lewis, "The Revolt of Islam," *NY*, 19 November 2001, pp. 50–63.

27. Huntington, "Clash of Civilizations?" The quotation about the treatment of minorities (from Huntington, *Clash of Civilizations*) is in William Pfaff, "The Reality of Human Affairs," *World Policy Journal* 14, no. 2 (Summer 1997), 89–97.

28. Huntington, "Clash of Civilizations?"; and Huntington, *Clash of Civilizations*, p. 312.

29. Huntington, *Clash of Civilizations*, p. 51.

30. This is one of the points against Huntington made by Stephen M. Walt in "Building Up New Bogeymen," *Foreign Policy*, no. 106 (Spring 1997), pp. 176–90. The "neglect of nationalism," Walt writes, "is the Achilles' heel of the civilizational paradigm."

31. Masoud Golsorkhi, personal communication, November 2001; quoted by permission.

Before we turn to postwar American foreign policy, however, there is one final aspect of the Lewis/Huntington argument I find problematic. Does it really make sense to talk about Judeo-Christian civilization as a unit, when the clash between the two—in partic-ular, the Christian persecution of the Jews—goes back at least a millennium and may hardly be a thing of the past? Let us not forget, writes my Iranian colleague, that the Jews who fled the Spanish Inquisition were taken in by the Ottoman Empire, and that histori-cally Arab societies have often been quite tolerant toward their Jewish populations. Mus-lim intellectuals in Iran, he points out, were originally fascinated by the kibbutz experiment; Iran houses a large Jewish population (many, however, left after 1979); and the name Cohen is Persian in origin. "Recently," he writes, "in a trial of some eighteen Iranian Jews accused of spying for Israel, by the conservative judiciary (as part of the con-tinuing political wrestling match for power between the moderates and the conserva-tives), some of the accused turned up at the court wearing medals they had won in the war against Iraq, for which they had volunteered. The result was a huge wave of sympathy, and a sense of national shame and I am glad to say conciliation."

32. Michael Scheuer ("Anonymous"), *Imperial Hubris: Why the West Is Losing the War on Terror* (Washington, D.C.: Brassey's, 2004).

33. Ibid., pp. 101, 154, and 160.

34. Ibid., pp. 101, 203, and 249.

35. Ibid, pp. 17, 129–31, 141, 153, 157, 210, and 253. On Indonesia, see below, p. 345, n. 14, as well as Chalmers Johnson, *The Sorrows of Empire* (New York: Metropolitan/Henry Holt, 2004), p. 69, and Ivan Eland, *The Empire Has No Clothes* (Oakland: Independent Insti-tute, 2004), p. 133. For an example of bin Laden's clarity (and eloquence) on these issues, see the full text of his 29 October 2004 address to the American people, posted at http:// english.aljazeera.net/NR/exeres/79C6AF22-98FB-4A1C-B21F-2BC36E87F61F.htm.

36. Scheuer, *Imperial Hubris*, pp. xi, 15, and 247.

37. Andrew J. Bacevich, *American Empire* (Cambridge, Mass.: Harvard University Press, 2002), pp. 14 and 17–18.

38. William Appleman Williams, *The Tragedy of American Diplomacy* (1959; repr., New York: W.W. Norton, 1972), pp. 9, 18, 21–22, 32, and 42; and Michael H. Hunt, *Ideology and U.S. Foreign Policy* (New Haven: Yale University Press, 1987), pp. 29–31 and 40. The Louisiana Purchase as the "greatest land grab" is from Jonathan Yardley's review of John Kukla, *A Wilderness So Immense, WP Book World*, 27 April 2003, p. 2.

39. Hunt, *Ideology*, pp. 32–34 (Greeley quoted on p. 34); and John S. D. Eisenhower, *So Far from God: The U.S. War with Mexico, 1846–1848* (New York: Random House, 1989).

40. Williams, *Tragedy*, pp. 23, 27, 45, 47, 52, and 71.

41. Thomas G. Paterson, "U.S. Intervention in Cuba, 1898: Interpreting the Spanish-American-Cuban-Filipino War," *OAH Magazine of History* 12, no. 3 (Spring 1998), 5–8.

42. David F. Trask, *The War with Spain in 1898* (New York: Macmillan, 1981). The Wilson quotation is in Hunt, *Ideology*, p. 129. On the role of Pulitzer and especially Hearst in the Spanish-American War, see Neil Gabler, *Life: The Movie* (New York: Vintage, 2000), pp. 67–69 and the accompanying references.

43. Paterson, "U.S. Intervention in Cuba," p. 6; Sumner quoted in Hunt, *Ideology*, p. 40; and Twain quoted on "Pax Americana," NPR (WBUR in Boston), available at www.insideout.org/documentaries/pax/twainpage.asp.

44. Williams, *Tragedy*, pp. 59 and 63; and Hunt, *Ideology*, p. 128.

45. Williams, *Tragedy*, pp. 13–15, 88, and 93–96; and Bradford Perkins, "The Tragedy of American Diplomacy: Twenty-Five Years After," *Reviews in American History* 12, no. 1 (March 1984), 9.

46. Williams, *Tragedy*, pp. 66–67, 74 and n., 82, 84, 129–30, and 165.

47. Hunt, *Ideology*, pp. 5 and 10–11; J. A. Thompson, "William Appleman Williams and the

'American Empire,'" *Journal of American Studies* 7, no. 1 (April 1973), 95–97; and Perkins, "Tragedy," p. 5.

One of the most telling criticisms made by Thompson (pp. 102–4) is that Williams never successfully distinguishes between Open Door imperialism and good old foreign trade. If any political action designed to promote foreign trade is imperialism, and "imperial expansion" means little more than successful economic competition, then the whole point becomes a tautology; almost any American policy can then be made to fit Williams' interpretation.

This argument, it seems to me, has some validity, except there is an issue of choice that I believe Thompson may be overlooking. In our dealings with smaller nations, do they really have a choice? Do we really allow them to disagree and go their own way? As Williams points out (*Tragedy*, p. 55), when an advanced industrial nation deals with a weaker one, the latter "makes its choices within limits set . . . by the powerful society." While it is true that, until recently, exports were only a small fraction of the national output, and that we do more business with (relative) economic equals than with economic inferiors, it does seem to be the case that beginning with the Spanish-American War, we attempted to police a good part of the globe, and that economic interests—real or perceived—were a major (if not exclusive) motivation behind that.

It is also the case, as Bradford Perkins points out (pp. 8–12), that if Williams' economic emphasis is too narrow, he nevertheless left an important legacy. His argument has been broadened and made more complex by a number of historians, such as Michael Hogan, N. Gordon Levin, and Bruce Kuklick (in addition to Gardner and LaFeber), showing that, for example, American leaders sought a stable world not only *for* economic growth but *through* economic growth, or that the American vision embraces both moral commitment and economic interest simultaneously.

48. Hunt, *Ideology*, pp. 12–14, 17–18, and 189.

49. Ibid., pp. 29–30, 42, and 129.

50. Ibid., pp. 48, 52, 58–77, 90-91, 140, 160, 162, and 176–77; and Ruthven, *Fury for God*, pp. 16–18.

51. Hunt, *Ideology*, pp. 116–17, 161, 165–66; Schumpter quote on p. 195.

4. Pax Americana

1. For an excellent review of the Courtois book see Michael Scammell, "The Price of an Idea," *New Republic*, 20 December 1999, pp. 32–42.

2. Chalmers Johnson, *The Sorrows of Empire* (New York: Metropolitan/Henry Holt, 2004), pp. 33–34; Ivan Eland, *The Empire Has No Clothes* (Oakland: The Independent Institute, 2004), pp. 12, 14–15, and 63; Vojtech Mastny, *The Cold War and Soviet Insecurity* (New York: Oxford University Press, 1996); and Vladislav Zubok and Constantine Pleshakov, *Inside the Kremlin's Cold War* (Cambridge, Mass.: Harvard University Press, 1996). Stereotypical approaches to the Cold War, which attempt to make it the exclusive product of Stalin's paranoia (which was real enough)—e.g., John Lewis Gaddis' *We Now Know* (New York: Oxford University Press, 1997)—simply don't hold up, as Melvin P. Leffler shows in "The Cold War: What Do 'We Now Know'?," *American Historical Review* 104, no. 2 (April 1999), 501–24. The 2002 "National Security Strategy" was written by Condoleezza Rice and is available at www.whitehouse.gov/nsc/nss.html.

3. Eland, *Empire*, pp. 230–31; John Lewis Gaddis, *Strategies of Containment* (Oxford: Oxford University Press, 1982), pp. 4, 14, 18–20, and 26; and "X" [George F. Kennan], "The Sources of Soviet Conduct," *Foreign Affairs* 25, no. 4 (July 1947), 566–82.

4. Gaddis, *Strategies*, pp. 4, 21, and 26; Walter LaFeber, *America, Russia, and the Cold War*, 7th ed. (New York: McGraw-Hill, 1993), p. 3; and H. W. Brands, *The Devil We Knew* (New York: Oxford University Press, 1993), p. vi.

5. Gaddis, *Strategies*, pp. 21 and 83; Kennan quoted in Sam Tanenhaus, "Foreign Policy's Big Moment Looks for a Big Idea," *NYT*, 23 February 2003, sect. 4, p. 12.

6. Gaddis, *Strategies*, pp. 28, 30–35, 41, 44, 47–48, and 56.

7. Ibid., pp. 55, 58–59, 64, 71, 79, and 88; Kennan quote on p. 83.

8. Ibid., pp. 84 and 91–92; and William Appleman Williams, *The Tragedy of American Diplomacy* (1959; repr., New York: W. W. Norton, 1972), pp. 260 and 269. Nitze quoted in Gaddis Smith, *Morality, Reason, and Power* (New York: Hill and Wang, 1986), p. 21.

9. Gaddis, *Strategies*, pp. 93–95, 98–99, 104, and 106. NSC-68 was not declassified until 1975, when it was published in the *Naval War College Review.*

10. Gaddis, *Strategies*, pp. 108–10, 114, and 117; and Williams, *Tragedy*, pp. 240 and 273.

11. Smith, *Morality, Reason, and Power*, p. 22. McCarthy's comment is paraphrased by William Pfaff in "Auditioning for McCarthy," *IHT*, 8 May 2003, p. 6.

12. Gaddis, *Strategies*, pp. 130 and 133–36.

13. Ibid., pp. 136–41, 144–46, and 168; Dulles is quoted on p. 141 ("vast monolithic system") and his remarks to *Life* are on p. 151.

14. Ibid., pp. 158–59 and 182. The 1965 "regime change" in Indonesia resulted in a bloodbath, in which the CIA played a significant role. The agency itself described these events as "one of the worst episodes of mass murder of the twentieth century, ranking with Germany's Holocaust against the Jews." See James Bamford, "Company Man" (review of Richard Helms, *A Look over My Shoulder*), *WP Book World* 27 April 2003, p. 7.

15. Louis Menand, "Ask Not, Tell Not," *NY*, 8 November 2004, pp. 110–13 and 119; and Gaddis, *Strategies*, pp. 211, 213–14, 218, 223–25, and 231.

16. Brands, *Devil We Knew*, pp. 90–92.

17. William Blum, *Killing Hope: U.S. Military and CIA Interventions Since World War II* (Monroe, Me.: Common Courage Press, 1995 [rev. and enl. ed. of *The CIA*, 1986]), pp. 122–24 and 131–33; Michael H. Hunt, *Ideology and U.S. Foreign Policy* (New Haven: Yale University Press, 1987), p. 173; Seymour M. Hersh, "Uncovered," *NY*, 10 November 2003, pp. 41 and 44; John Kifner, "Ex-G.I.'s Tell of Vietnam Brutality," *IHT*, 29 December 2003, pp. 1 and 7; and Scott Sherman, "The Other My Lai," *The Nation*, 1 March 2004, pp. 9 and 24. None of the four major TV networks picked *The Blade* story up, and most major newspapers ignored it. Very few American soldiers ever got charged for war crimes. The Tiger Force unit is still part of the army and, as of 2004, was serving in Mosul, Iraq.

18. Gaddis, *Strategies*, pp. 131, 237–43, 259–60, 263, 265–66, and 273; Melvin Gurtov and Ray Maghroori, *Roots of Failure: United States Policy in the Third World* (Westport, Conn.: Greenwood Press, 1984), p. 34; Joseph Persico, "Company Man" (review of Richard Helms, *A Look over My Shoulder*), *NYT Book Review*, 4 May 2003, p. 9; and Brands, *Devil We Knew*, pp. 58 and 103.

19. Gaddis, *Strategies*, pp. 276–85.

20. Ibid., pp. 287–88, 306, 338–41, and 356.

21. Blum, *Killing Hope*, pp. 73–74.

22. Ibid., pp. 75–80. Blum's primary source for this material is Stephen Schlesinger and Stephen Kinzer, *Bitter Fruit: The Untold Story of the American Coup in Guatemala* (New York: Doubleday, 1982), which in turn is based partly on documents obtained under the Freedom of Information Act from the State Department, Defense Department, CIA, National Archives, the U.S. Navy, FBI, and elsewhere. Schlesinger and Kinzer also used the Allen Dulles papers at Princeton University.

23. Blum, *Killing Hope,* pp. 80–83.

24. Ibid., pp. 206–15; and Peter Kornbluh, *The Pinochet File* (New York: New Press, 2003). In Senate hearings of 1973, CIA director Richard Helms lied to the Church Committee about agency involvement in these events and was subsequently sentenced to two years in prison (suspended) for it. In 1983, President Reagan awarded him the National Security Medal for "exceptional meritorious service," and when he died in 2002 he was buried with full honors in Arlington National Cemetery. See Bamford, "Company Man," p. 6, and Persico, "Company Man," p. 9.

25. Brands, *Devil We Knew,* pp. v, vii–viii, 21–22, 26, and 28. Truman is quoted in Gurtov and Maghroori, *Roots of Failure,* p. 22.

26. Brands, *Devil We Knew,* pp. 32–38.

27. Ibid., pp. 39, 41, and 55–56. To stem leaks coming from the CIA, President Eisenhower enlisted the help of General James Doolittle, who wrote of our campaign against the USSR, "Hitherto unacceptable norms of human conduct do not apply," and went on to assert that the American people would have to be educated to "support this fundamentally repugnant philosophy." Brands comments (pp. 61 and 66) that Ike rejected Doolittle's language but not his substantive recommendations, and gave covert CIA agents carte blanche to do whatever they felt was necessary. Doolittle later became an executive at Shell Oil.

28. Brands, *Devil We Knew,* pp. 163 and 169.

29. Ibid., pp. 218–19 and 224; LaFeber, *America, Russia, and the Cold War,* p. 1. On the specious nature of the argument that Reagan caused the collapse of communism, see also Johnson, *Sorrows of Empire,* pp. 17–19.

30. Smith, *Morality, Reason, and Power,* pp. 26, 28 and 49; Brands, *Devil We Knew,* p. 142; Robert A. Strong, *Working in the World* (Baton Rouge: Louisiana State University Press, 2000), p. 73; and Gaddis, *Strategies,* p. 345.

31. Smith, *Morality, Reason, and Power,* pp. 6–7 and 62.

32. Ibid., pp. 9, 48, and 242; and Brands, *Devil We Knew,* p. 156.

33. Smith, *Morality, Reason, and Power,* pp. 35, 37, and 41.

34. Ibid., pp. 55, 57, 223, 242, and 247.

35. Strong, *Working in the World,* pp. 7–8; and James Fallows, "The Passionless Presidency," *Atlantic Monthly,* May–June 1979.

36. Strong, *Working in the World,* pp. 117–18. The author notes that Fallows subsequently insisted that he saw Carter staple the two memos together and claimed that the speechwriting files at the presidential library were incomplete.

37. Ibid., pp. 119–20.

38. Ibid., pp. 73–74.

39. Ibid., pp. 75 and 82, and also see p. 86; and Brands, *Devil We Knew,* pp. 144–45.

40. Strong, *Working in the World,* pp. 120 and 265–70.

41. Ibid., pp. 121–22, 265, and 271–74.

42. Jeane Kirkpatrick, "Dictatorships and Double Standards," *Commentary,* November 1979, pp. 34–45; Smith, *Morality, Reason, and Power,* p. 55; and Brands, *Devil We Knew,* p. 157. For William Casey, see Nicholas D. Kristof, "Missing in Action: The Truth About Iraqi Arms," *IHT,* 7 May 2003, p. 6. The report of a CIA training manual that describes torture methods used in Honduras in the 1980s first appeared in the *Baltimore Sun* in 1995; see the *Seattle Post-Intelligencer,* 27 January 1997.

43. Christopher Hitchens, "Rogue Nation U.S.A.," *Mother Jones,* June 2001, pp. 32–36; Brands, *Devil We Knew,* pp. 97 and 147; and Smith, *Morality, Reason, and Power,* p. 254 (the 1980 prediction about the year 2000 occurs in *The Global 2000 Report to the President,* 3

vols. [Washington, D.C.: GPO, 1980–81]). Kennan's report is known as PPS/23, and appeared as "Review of Current Trends in U.S. Foreign Policy," 24 February 1948, in *Foreign Relations of the United States* (Washington, D.C.: GPO, 1948), vol. 1, pp. 509–29. This document is also posted on a number of Web sites, including www.geocities.com /Athens/Forum/2496/future/Kennan/pps23.html.

44. Bill Minutaglio, *First Son: George W. Bush and the Bush Family Dynasty* (New York: Times Books, 1999), p. 318.

45. Smith, *Morality, Reason, and Power*, pp. 3, 57 and 247.

46. John Cassidy, "Pump Dreams," *NY*, 11 October 2004, p. 45. Some of this is based on the analysis of Michael T. Klare, *Blood and Oil* (New York: Metropolitan/Henry Holt, 2004). On the Soviet invasion of Afghanistan, see Douglas Little, *American Orientalism* (Chapel Hill: University of North Carolina Press, 2002), pp. 150–52.

47. Eland, *Empire*, pp. 89–90; and Little, *American Orientalism*, pp. 150-52. Also see below, chapters 5 and 6.

48. Williams, *Tragedy*, pp. 310–12.

49. Helen Caldicott, *The New Nuclear Danger* (New York: New Press, 2002), pp. 119 and 121.

50. 2002 "National Security Strategy" (the identification of freedom with consumerism occurs on p. 18). On the national security state, see, for example, Blum, *Killing Hope*, pp. 2–3 and 13, as well as various essays by Gore Vidal.

51. Andrew J. Bacevich, *American Empire* (Cambridge, Mass.: Harvard University Press, 2002), pp. 3–4, 6, and 9.

52. Ibid., pp. 33, 95–96, and 102.

53. Herman Schwartz, *States Versus Markets*, 2d ed. (New York: St. Martin's, 2000), p. 183; Chalmers Johnson, *Blowback: The Costs and Consequences of American Empire* (New York: Metropolitan/Henry Holt, 2000), pp. 85–87; "Pax Americana with Michael Goldfarb," WBUR (Boston), 2002, available at www.insideout.org/documentaries/pax/radioprogram .asp; Bacevich, *American Empire*, p. 266, n. 35; Thom Shanker, "U.S. Again Leads World International Weapons Sales," *IHT*, 26 September 2003, p. 3; Seymour Melman, *After Capitalism* (New York: Alfred A. Knopf, 2001), p. 102; Caldicott, *New Nuclear Danger*, pp. viii and 185; and Eland, *Empire*, pp. 261–62. Discretionary spending refers to the part of the federal budget that is up to the discretion of Congress; the part that (at least up to now) cannot be touched, such as Social Security, is called nondiscretionary. So it is the discretionary budget that is the issue (rather than the GDP or the entire budget) because it is that that is up for grabs. For Vidal's calculations, see his *The Decline and Fall of the American Empire* (Berkeley: Odonian Press, 1992), p. 32; a more precise analysis can be found in the reports of the War Resisters League, posted at www.warresisters.org/piechart.htm.

On military expenditures in the wake of 9/11 and after, see Nicholas Lehmann, "Less than Zero," *NY*, 10 December 2001, pp. 50–54; Eric Planin, "Bush to Seek Deep Cuts in Domestic Programs," *WP*, 3 February 2002, pp. A1 and 6; *WSJ*, 5 February 2002, p. A1, and related stories pp. A2, 8, and 10; James Dao, "One Nation Plays the Great Game Alone," 7 July 2002, *NYT* sect. 4, pp. 1 and 5; and "A Pentagon Spending Spree," *IHT*, 11 February 2003, p. 6.

54. Melman, *After Capitalism*, pp. 32–33, 99, 102, 109, and 141–43. Also see Seymour Melman, *Pentagon Capitalism* (New York: McGraw-Hill, 1970).

55. Dana Priest, *The Mission* (New York: W.W. Norton, 2003), pp. 11, 32–33, 37, 42, and 45.

56. Bacevich, *American Empire*, pp. 74, 142-43, 167, and 181; and also Bacevich, "Policing Utopia: The Military Imperatives of Globalization," *The National Interest*, Summer 1999.

57. Gore Vidal, *Perpetual War for Perpetual Peace* (New York: Nation Books, 2002), pp. 158–59.

58. Some of this ground is covered by Bacevich (*American Empire*, pp. 2, 55–59, 63–64, 76–78, 88, and 90), although from a curious angle: he wants to say that we were not floundering after the Cold War, and that the fall of the Berlin Wall was historically a "mere blip," because our foreign policy had been constant since 1899: the Open Door. But such an interpretation finally depends on making economics the sole motivator for American foreign policy and, as we have seen, this is too narrow. As a result, Bacevich inadvertently provides evidence for the argument I am making. In fact, as noted below, Bill Clinton's attempt to fill the void with a refurbished Open Door policy really didn't work, or at least not for more than a few years. It was not enough of a "Big Idea," such as anticommunism or antiterrorism, in terms of mass appeal.

59. Ibid., p. 133. In addition to a number of books on the subject, including Alan Dershowitz's *Supreme Injustice*, David Kaplan's *The Accidental Presidency*, and Vincent Bugliosi et al.'s *The Betrayal of America*, the corruption involved in that election is very well documented in the film *Unprecedented: The 2000 Presidential Election*, directed by Richard R. Pérez and Joan Sekler. See also David Margolick et al., "The Path to Florida," *Vanity Fair*, October 2004, pp. 310–69.

60. Bacevich, *American Empire*, p. 43; Nicholas Lehmann, "The Next World Order," *NY*, 1 April 2002, pp. 42–43; Barton Gellman, "Keeping the U.S. First," *WP*, 11 March 1992, p. A1; Tom Barry and Jim Lobe, "The Man Who Stole the Show," Foreign Policy in Focus, special report no. 18, October 2002, available at www.fpif.org/papers/02men/index_body.html; and David Armstrong, "Dick Cheney's Song of America," *Harper's Magazine*, October 2002, pp. 76–79.

61. Armstrong, "Cheney's Song," pp. 78–79; Barry and Lobe, "Men Who Stole the Show"; and Bacevich, *American Empire*, p. 45.

62. Bacevich, *American Empire*, p. 45; Armstrong, "Cheney's Song," p. 79; Barry and Lobe, "Man Who Stole the Show"; and [Thomas Donnelly], *Rebuilding America's Defenses* (Washington, D.C.: Project for the New American Century, 2000), also available at http://www.newamericancentury.org.

63. Bacevich, *American Empire*, pp. 219 and 282, n. 50; John M. Collins, *Military Space Forces: The Next Fifty Years* (Washington, D.C.: Pergamon-Brassey's International Defense Publishers, 1989); and Caldicott, *New Nuclear Danger*, pp. 115–21.

64. *Rebuilding America's Defenses*, pp. i–ii, 2–4, 11, 14–15, 19, 23, 52, and 54–55.

65. Polly Toynbee quoted in Caldicott, *New Nuclear Danger*, p. 171.

66. Michael Lind, "The Weird Men Behind George W. Bush's War," *New Statesman*, 7 April 2003; and "Wondering About Bush," *IHT*, 22 July 2002, p. 8.

67. *Rebuilding America's Defenses*, p. 51; Lind, "Weird Men"; Barry and Lobe, "Man Who Stole the Show"; Lehmann, "Next World Order," p. 44; and Armstrong, "Cheney's Song," p. 81.

68. Mike Allen and Karen DeYoung, "Bush: U.S. Will Strike First at Enemies," *WP*, 2 June 2002, pp. A1 and 8; and Armstrong, "Cheney's Song," p. 81.

69. 2002 "National Security Strategy," sect. 3.

70. William Pfaff, "A Radical Rethink of International Relations," *IHT*, 3 October 2002, p. 4.

71. Hendrik Hertzberg, "Manifesto," *NY*, 14–21 October 2002, pp. 63–66.

72. Armstrong, "Cheney's Song," pp. 76–83.

73. Bacevich, *American Empire*, pp. 45–46; and William Pfaff, "Geopolitics Have Changed for the Worse," *IHT*, 11 September 2002, p. 8.

74. Barry and Lobe, "Man Who Stole the Show"; and Caldicott, *New Nuclear Danger*, pp. 162–64. On right-wing control of the media, see especially David Brock, *The Republican Noise Machine: Right-Wing Media and How It Corrupts Democracy* (New York: Crown, 2004); the phrase "seamless propaganda machine" is from the review of this book in *Publishers Weekly*. Research on tax records of right-wing nonprofit groups was done by Rob Stein, and reported on by Jane Mayer in "The Money Man," *NY*, 18 October 2004, p. 188. Lockheed Martin was the top defense contractor in 2000, receiving $15.1 billion in taxpayer funds.

75. Priest, *The Mission*, pp. 30 and 399, n. 3; Hertzberg, "Manifesto," p. 66; and Benjamin Schwarz and Christopher Layne, "A New Grand Strategy," *Atlantic Monthly*, January 2002, p. 36 and 42 (Kissinger quote on p. 38).

5. Axis of Resentment: Iran, Iraq, and Israel

1. Stephen Kinzer, *All the Shah's Men* (Hoboken N.J.: John Wiley and Sons, 2003), pp. 2, 39, 49–50, and 56. In what follows I shall be drawing on this and on an earlier work by Barry Rubin, *Paved with Good Intentions* (New York: Penguin, 1981), among other sources.

2. Kinzer, *All the Shah's Men*, pp. 51–53, 58–59, and 67–68; and Rubin, *Paved with Good Intentions*, p. 12.

3. Kinzer, *All the Shah's Men*, pp. 69–71, 76–77, 80, and 91; and Mark J. Gasiorowski, "The 1953 *Coup d'État* in Iran," *International Journal of Middle East Studies*, 19, no. 3 (August 1987), 262.

4. Kinzer, *All the Shah's Men*, pp. 92, 147–48, and 215; and Mostafa T. Zahrani, "The Coup That Changed the Middle East: Mossadeq v. the CIA in Retrospect," *World Policy Journal* 19, no. 2 (Summer 2002), 93–99.

5. Kinzer, *All the Shah's Men*, pp. 117–18, 120, 132, and 221; and Gasiorowski, "1953 Coup," p. 264.

6. Kinzer, *All the Shah's Men*, p. 208; Gasiorowski, "1953 Coup," p. 276; Rubin, *Paved with Good Intentions*, pp. 59, 63, and 76; William R. Corson, *The Armies of Ignorance* (New York: Dial Press, 1977), p. 352; Zahrani, "Coup That Changed the Middle East"; William Blum, *Killing Hope: U.S. Military and CIA Interventions Since World War II* (Monroe, Me.: Common Courage Press, 1995 [rev. and enl. ed. of *The CIA*, 1986]), p. 71.

Long after the coup, notes Kinzer (p. 206), the American diplomat who specialized in monitoring the Tudeh during the early 1950s and two CIA agents who had been posted with him at the U.S. embassy in Tehran admitted that the Tudeh was never very powerful, and that high-level U.S. officials during the Eisenhower administration routinely exaggerated its strength and Mossadegh's reliance on it.

7. Kinzer, *All the Shah's Men*, p. 131.

8. For this and the following paragraph, see ibid., pp. 3–4, 148, 151, and 155–58; Rubin, *Paved with Good Intentions*, pp. 56 and 77–78; Gasiorowski, "1953 Coup," p. 277; and Douglas Little, *American Orientalism* (Chapel Hill: University of North Carolina Press, 2002), p. 216.

9. On exaggerating the importance of the Tudeh, see above, n. 6.

10. Rubin, *Paved with Good Intentions*, pp. 56 and 80–81; and Kinzer, *All the Shah's Men*, pp. 156–63. Mossadegh offered to have the dispute with Great Britain mediated by Switzerland or Germany, but Britain and her American contacts ignored this. In fact, Iranians on the MI6 payroll were, at the same time, doing their best to create chaos in Iran, which further helped the Dulles brothers persuade the president that the country was nearing collapse. Eisenhower ratcheted up the crisis by refusing Mossadegh's desperate request (May 28) that the United States increase its aid to Iran or agree to buy Iranian oil.

11. Kinzer, *All the Shah's Men*, pp. 6, 142, 163, 173–76, 186, and 190–91; Rubin, *Paved with Good Intentions*, pp. 82–85; and Blum, *Killing Hope*, pp. 67–69. Some estimates have it that Operation Ajax cost as much as $20 million.

12. Kinzer, *All the Shah's Men*, pp. 193–96, 202, and 210; Rubin, *Paved with Good Intentions*, pp. 88–89, 92–95, and 103; Blum, *Killing Hope*, p. 71; and Gasiorowski, "1953 *Coup*," p. 279.

13. Kinzer, *All the Shah's Men*, pp. 208–9 (the quote from Roosevelt is on p. 209).

14. Ibid., pp. 203–4 and 215; Blum, *Killing Hope*, p. 72; Rubin, *Paved with Good Intentions*, pp. 177–81 and 205; John K. Cooley, *Payback: America's Long War in the Middle East* (McLean, Va.: Brassey's, 1991), pp. 30–31; Yossi Melman and Dan Raviv, *The Imperfect Spies: The History of Israeli Intelligence* (London: Sidgwick and Jackson, 1989), pp. 89–90; Melvin Gurtov and Ray Maghroori, *Roots of Failure: United States Policy in the Third World* (Westport, Conn.: Greenwood Press, 1984), pp. 85–87; and Seymour Hersh, "Ex-Analyst Says CIA Rejected Warning on Shah," *NYT*, 7 January 1979, p. 3.

15. Rubin, *Paved with Good Intentions*, pp. 113, 119–35, 158, and 160; Little, *American Orientalism*, pp. 221–22.

16. Rubin, *Paved with Good Intentions*, pp. 133, 142–44, 149, 186–87, 225, and 238; Little, *American Orientalism*, pp. 221–22 and 226.

17. Rubin, *Paved with Good Intentions*, pp. 260–61, 265, 267–68, 273, 279, and 320.

18. Ibid., pp. 249, 278, 303–4, 307, and 334.

For an excellent study of the hostage crisis, see David Harris, *The Crisis* (New York: Little, Brown, 2004). This book exposes the secret agreement Republicans made with Iran's clerical establishment not to release the hostages until the American presidential election of 1980 was over, so as to thwart the possibility of Jimmy Carter's reelection.

19. Kinzer, *All the Shah's Men*, p. 203; Little, *American Orientalism*, p. 314; and Peter Finn and Susan Schmidt, "Al Qaeda Plans a Front in Iraq," *WP*, 7 September 2003, p. A1. Note that on 4 August 2003 Iran indicated that it would not turn over the senior Al Qaeda captives it was holding to the United States (*IHT*, 5 August 2003, p. 8).

20. Little, *American Orientalism*, pp. 150–52; and Blum, *Killing Hope*, p. 345. Brzezinski is quoted in Stephen Zunes, *Tinderbox* (Monroe, Me.: Common Courage Press, 2003), p. 175; his *Nouvel Observateur* interview is in the issue of 15–21 January 1998.

21. Little, *American Orientalism,* pp. 152–54; Blum, *Killing Hope*, p. 348; Zunes, *Tinderbox*, p. 176; Lawrence Wright, "The Man Behind Bin Laden," *NY*, 16 September 2002, p. 77; and Michael Meacher, "This War on Terrorism Is Bogus," *The Guardian*, 6 September 2003 (this article cites the BBC report of 6 November 2001 and the *Newsweek* article of 15 September 2001).

I have avoided using John Cooley's well-known *Unholy Wars* in this sketch because, although he has the basic picture correct, there is too much in the text that is unreliable or unverified. For a critique of his work, see the review by Barnett Rubin in *International Affairs* 75, no. 4 (October 1999), 870–71.

Figures of Afghani casualties are given in Blum, *Killing Hope*, p. 351, and the data on civilian deaths are corroborated in various sources, including *Britannica Annual,* a Gallup poll, and several major American newspapers (for a complete list of sources, see http://users.erols.com/mwhite28/warstat2.htm#Afghanistan).

22. Little, *American Orientalism*, pp. 155 and 316–17.

23. For this and the following paragraph, see Dilip Hiro, *Iraq: In the Eye of the Storm* (New York: Nation Books, 2002), pp. 22 and 25; Little, *American Orientalism*, pp. 62–63,

203, and 206; and Bruce W. Jentleson, *With Friends Like These* (New York: W. W. Norton, 1994), p. 32.

24. Hiro, *Iraq*, pp. 158–59; and Jentleson, *With Friends Like These*, p. 39.

25. Hiro, *Iraq*, pp. 237 and 240; Jentleson, *With Friends Like These*, pp. 15 and 35; Salim Lone, "Iraq Is Now Another Palestine," *The Guardian*, 7 July 2004, p. 22; and Fawaz A. Gergez, *America and Political Islam* (Cambridge: Cambridge University Press, 1999), p. 102.

26. For the information contained in the following bulleted paragraphs, see Jentleson, *With Friends Like These*, pp. 16, 33, 40–42, 44, 46, 48–52, 54, 61–63, 68–69, 75, 78–79, 88, 92, 110, 138–39, 141, 145–50, 154–55, 159, 172, and 221–26; *The Hidden Wars of Desert Storm*, documentary directed by Audrey Brohy and Gerard Ungerman, 2000; Little, *American Orientalism*, pp. 249, 251, and 254; Zunes, *Tinderbox*, p. 54; Hiro, *Iraq*, pp. 30–31, 74–75, and 238; Noam Chomsky, "U.S. Iraq Policy," in *Iraq Under Siege*, ed. Anthony Arnove (Cambridge, Mass.: South End Press, 2000), pp. 48–49; Charles Glass, "The Emperors of Enforcement," *New Statesman*, 20 February 1998, pp. 14–15; Patrick E. Tyler, "U.S. Aided Iraq in '80s Despite Gas Use, Officials Say," *IHT*, 19 August 2002, p. 3; Joost R. Hiltermann, "Who Minded Iraqi Mustard Gas in 1983?," *IHT*, 29 November 2002, p. 6; Joost R. Hiltermann, "America Didn't Seem to Mind Poison Gas," *IHT*, 17 January 2003, p. 8; Michael Dobbs, "Not So Long Ago, Washington Made Iraq a Valued Ally," *IHT*, 31 December 2002–1 January 2003, p. 2; and Philip Shenon, "Iraq Says Virginia and French Labs Supplied All Its Germs," *IHT*, 17 March 2003, p. 5.

Stephen C. Pelletiere, who was a CIA analyst during the Reagan-Bush years, claims that it was in fact Iranian gas that killed the Kurds at Halabjah, but this seems to me to be rather speculative at this point (Pelletiere, "A War Crime or an Act of War?," *NYT*, 31 January 2003).

27. Jentleson, *With Friends Like These*, pp. 95 and 191. For the conspiracy theory of the Gulf war, see Blum, *Killing Hope*, pp. 322–24; and *Hidden Wars of Desert Storm*.

28. Hiro, *Iraq*, pp. 33 and 161; Blum, *Killing Hope*, p. 321; and Scott Peterson, "In War, Some Facts Less Factual," *Christian Science Monitor*, 6 September 2002.

29. Little, *American Orientalism*, pp. 255 and 257; Douglas Kellner, *The Persian Gulf TV War* (Boulder, Colo.: Westview Press, 1992), pp. 27–28; and Peterson, "In War, Some Facts Less Factual."

30. Little, *American Orientalism*, p. 257; Blum, *Killing Hope*, p. 331; Kellner, *Persian Gulf TV War*, pp. 26 and 30; and "The Gulf War," *Frontline*, 9 January 1996, updated July 2002 (available at www.pbs.org).

31. Kellner, *Persian Gulf TV War*, pp. 13–15.

32. Jentleson, *With Friends Like These*, pp. 19, 169–71, 197–99, and 201–2; Little, *American Orientalism*, pp. 254–55; Blum, *Killing Hope*, p. 322.

For documentation of the Glaspie-Hussein meeting, see the references listed by Jentleson, pp. 280–81, n. 98. Jentleson's references include the crucial transcript of the discussion: "Confrontation in the Gulf; Excerpts from Iraqi Document on Meeting with U.S. Envoy," *NYT*, 23 September 1990, sect. 1, p. 19; an article in the *WP* (21 October 1992, p. A17); and congressional testimony. The transcript is also reprinted in Phyllis Bennis and Michel Moushabeck, eds., *Beyond the Storm* (New York: Olive Branch Press, 1991), pp. 391–96.

33. Jentleson, *With Friends Like These*, pp. 26, 93, 194, and 196.

34. Kellner, *Persian Gulf TV War*, pp. 31–37; "The Gulf War," *Frontline*; Hiro, *Iraq*, p. 38; and Zunes, *Tinderbox*, p. 78. The newspaper reports include an editorial in the *Financial Times*, 13 August 1990, as well as the *Mideast Mirror* (London), 15 August 1990, and *Newsday*, 29 August 1990.

Saddam Hussein wrote George H. W. Bush in early August 1990 and received no reply; then, on August 9, he made a back-channel offer to withdraw from Kuwait in return for the settlement of some border disputes, which the National Security Council rejected as "already moving against policy." (Richard Helms, the former CIA director, tried to move forward on this initiative and failed.) On August 12 he proposed another settlement of the conflict, which was dismissed with derision by the United States. King Hussein of Jordan brought Bush a peace proposal from Iraq on August 15, which went unanswered. Tariq Aziz appeared on television on August 21 and indicated a willingness to talk. Another offer was made on August 23 and was described by one Middle Eastern specialist as "serious" and "negotiable," but ridiculed by U.S. government spokesmen as "baloney." There were some Jordanian and PLO proposals made in December, again immediately dismissed by the Bush administration, and one made by France on 14 January 1991.

35. Blum, *Killing Hope*, pp. 326–27; Kellner, *Persian Gulf TV War*, p. 31; "The Gulf War," *Frontline*; and Christopher Layne, "Why the Gulf War Was Not in the National Interest," *Atlantic Monthly*, July 1991.

36. Hiro, *Iraq*, pp. 38–39 (quote from Tony Clifton on p. 39); David C. Hendrickson, "Toward Universal Empire," *World Policy Journal* 19, no. 3 (Fall 2002), 8; *Hidden Wars of Desert Storm*; Phyllis Bennis and Denis J. Halliday, "Iraq: The Impact of Sanctions and U.S. Policy," in Arnove, ed., *Iraq Under Siege*, p. 35; Barton Gellman, "Allied Air War Struck Broadly in Iraq; Officials Acknowledge Strategy Went Beyond Purely Military Targets," *WP*, 23 June 1991, p. A1; Zunes, *Tinderbox*, pp. 64–65 and 82–85; Blum, *Killing Hope*, pp. 335–36; and Kellner, *Persian Gulf TV War*, pp. 377–83 and 404–10. The key article about the massacre of retreating forces, authorized by General Barry McCaffrey, didn't appear until years later: Seymour M. Hersh, "Overwhelming Force," *NY*, 22 May 2000, pp. 48–82.

37. International Committee of the Red Cross, "Iraq: A Decade of Sanctions" (Geneva, December 1999), available at www.icrc.org; John Mueller and Karl Mueller, "Sanctions of Mass Destruction," *Foreign Affairs* 78, no. 3 (May–June 1999), 43–53; Joy Gordon, "Cool War," *Harper's Magazine*, November 2002, pp. 43–49; *Hidden Wars of Desert Storm*; Hiro, *Iraq*, pp. 4–17; and the following articles from Arnove, ed., *Iraq Under Siege*: Bennis and Halliday, "Impact of Sanctions," p. 45; John Pilger, "Collateral Damage," pp. 60–61; and Kathy Kelly, "Raising Voices," p. 111.

Madeleine Albright has since labeled her remark "a stupid comment" even while insisting that the deaths of Iraqi children were caused by Saddam Hussein and not the United States, and claiming that the sanctions never applied to food and medicine. Apparently, her "remorse" is for her faux pas, not for the half million dead Iraqi children. See interview by Barbara Spindel, "A Woman's Place," *Time Out (New York)*, 18–25 September 2003, pp. 62–63.

38. Gordon, "Cool War," p. 49.

39. Interview with Emmanuel Todd appeared in the *Neue Zürcher Zeitung* on 20 July 2003 and was translated as "The Conceited Empire" for *The Dominion* (Halifax), 26 July 2003 (available online at http://dominionpaper.ca/features/2003/the_conceited_empire .html). See also Little, *American Orientalism*, p. 252; "The Gulf War," *Frontline*; and Zunes, *Tinderbox*, p. 103.

40. Blum, *Killing Hope*, pp. 326 and 328.

41. Naseer Aruri, "America's War Against Iraq: 1990–1999," in Arnove, ed., *Iraq Under Siege*, p. 23; Kellner, *Persian Gulf TV War*, pp. 37, 39, and 41; Layne, "Gulf War Not in National Interest"; and Immanuel Wallerstein, "The Eagle Has Crash Landed," *Foreign Policy*, no. 131 (July–August 2002), pp. 60–68.

42. Ibrahim Abu-Lughod, "The War of 1948: Disputed Perspectives and Outcomes," *Journal of Palestine Studies* 18, no. 2 (Winter 1989), 119–27; and Ethan Bronner, "What Led to the Flight of the Palestinians?," *IHT*, 21–22 February 2004, p. 5.

43. Zachary Lockman, "Original Sin," *Middle East Report*, May–June 1988, pp. 57–64.

44. Ibid.; Little, *American Orientalism*, p. 269; Bronner, "What Led to the Flight," p. 5; Benny Morris, *The Birth of the Palestinian Refugee Problem Revisited* (Cambridge: Cambridge University Press, 2004), pp. 1, 5, 592, 597, and *passim*.

45. For this and the following paragraph, see Morris, *Birth*, pp. 5, 7, 10–13, 34, 588–91, and 597–99; Michael J. Cohen, review of *The Birth of the Palestinian Refugee Problem, 1947–1949*, by Benny Morris, *American Historical Review* 95, no. 1 (February 1990), 219–20; A. Orr, review of *The Birth of the Palestinian Refugee Problem, 1947–1949*, by Benny Morris, *International Affairs (Royal Institute of International Affairs 1944–)* 65, no. 2 (Spring 1989), 365–66; and Lockman, "Original Sin," pp. 57–64.

46. Gerd Nonneman, review of *The Birth of the Palestinian Refugee Problem, 1947–1949*, by Benny Morris, *Bulletin (British Society for Middle Eastern Studies)* 16 (1989), 198–99; and Little, *American Orientalism*, pp. 270–72.

47. Phillip J. Baram, *The Department of State in the Middle East, 1919–1945* (Philadelphia: University of Pennsylvania Press, 1978). Other authors, such as Arthur Morse and Henry Feingold, have also argued that State consistently opposed Zionist aspirations.

48. Ibid.; and David S. Wyman, *The Abandonment of the Jews* (New York: Pantheon, 1984). As is well-known, Roosevelt was unwilling to bomb the death camps or even the rail lines leading up to them. As for the State and the War Departments, they kept the lid on the news of the death camps as long as they could, rejected Romania's offer to free seventy thousand Jews, tightened immigration procedures, and dissuaded Latin American countries from taking Jewish refugees.

49. For this and the following paragraph, see Little, *American Orientalism*, pp. 5, 10–11, 15–20, 25–32, 35, 38, and 41–42.

50. Ibid., pp. 11, 34, 268, and 280–84; and "Israeli Settlements in the Occupied Territories: A Guide," special report published by the Foundation for Middle East Peace (FMEP), March 2002 (see www.fmep.org/reports/2002/sr0203.html). Ben-Yair's article appeared in the Israeli newspaper *Ha'aretz* on 3 March 2002.

An important dissenting interpretation of these events is that of Michael Oren in his widely acclaimed *Six Days of War* (New York: Oxford University Press, 2002). Oren is a senior fellow at the Shalem Center in Jerusalem, a Zionist research organization that is staunchly opposed to revisionists such as Benny Morris (who, it should be noted, shifted his position from dove to hawk after the second intifada). Unlike the revisionists, who point to Israeli aggression against the Arabs, Oren's own bias is the reverse. As I said above, both are true; the question is where the balance is to be struck. What is unconvincing about Oren's narrative is that it strikes the balance very much in favor of Israel by omitting a number of crucial issues, as his critics have pointed out. Thus Yoram Meital of Ben-Gurion University notes that Oren makes no reference to the project that was initiated, shortly after the Six Day War, of establishing settlements in the territories newly occupied by the Israel Defense Forces, and the contribution of that policy to subsequent strife. Professor Meital and others also observe that the language Oren uses to describe central events is very "clean" ("exodus" and "flight," for example, but never "expulsion"). The real agenda here, says Meital, is to suggest that throughout the years of conflict between Arabs and Jews, the latter wanted peace while the former wanted war. And yet we have the Camp David agreement of 1978, the Egyptian-Israeli peace treaty of 1979, as well as the early efforts of Nasser, Anwar Sadat, and Syrian president Hafez Assad to reach a political settlement with Israel. There is also no mention of the closer relationship between the

United States and Israel that developed in the wake of the war, and the increasingly large amounts of military aid that Washington shipped to Tel Aviv as a result. The problem with these omissions is that one can finally lose sight of who is the occupier, and who the occupied.

See reviews by Yoram Meital in *Shofar: An Interdisciplinary Journal of Jewish Studies* 22, no. 4 (Summer 2004), 179–81; Jerome Slater in *Political Science Quarterly* 118, no. 2 (Summer 2003), 363–64; and Michael Rubner in *Middle East Policy* 9, no. 4 (December 2002), 172–75.

51. Henry Siegman, "Has Sharon Set a Trap for Bush?," *IHT,* 3 June 2003, p. 8; Little, *American Orientalism,* pp. 291–98; "Israeli Settlements in the Occupied Territories"; and Zunes, *Tinderbox,* p. 130. On Sabra and Shatila, and the possible role played by the United States, see Zeev Schiff, "America and Israel: Green Light, Lebanon," *Foreign Policy,* Spring 1983, pp. 73–85.

52. Little, *American Orientalism,* pp. 5, 78, 105, 127, and 309; and Naseer Aruri, "The U.S. and the Arabs: A Woeful History," *Arab Studies Quarterly* 12, no. 3 (Summer 1997), pp. 29–46. The latter is the source for the *New York Times* and Eshkol quotations.

53. Thomas W. Lippman, "Holy Ground" (review of Anton La Guardia's *War Without End*), *WP Book World,* 30 June 2002, pp. 4–5; Rashid I. Khalidi, "Road Map or Road Kill?," *The Nation,* 9 June 2003, pp. 29–30; Zunes, *Tinderbox,* pp. 149 (source for Ben-Eliezer quotation) and 152; and Steven Erlanger, "Israel's General Eitan Drowns," *IHT,* 24 November 2004, p. 4. Like Ariel Sharon, Eitan was implicated in the 1982 Sabra and Shatila massacres and "allowed to retire" after thirty-seven years in the military.

54. Stephen Zunes notes (*Tinderbox,* pp. 161–63) that Israel has acted to prevent victories by radical nationalist movements in Palestine, Lebanon, Jordan, and Syria, where such victories could have threatened U.S. control of oil and other strategic interests. During the Iran-contra scandal, in which Israel played a crucial intermediary role, one Israeli analyst commented that Israel had become like another federal agency, one convenient to use when the United States wanted something done quietly. Zunes also cites the late Yeshayahu Liebovitz, a leading Israeli intellectual, who commented in the 1980s that the Israelis had become America's mercenaries, defending what the American ruling class considered to be America's interests. The Israeli press, adds Zunes, has sometimes described Israel as "the Godfather's messenger."

U.S. votes at the United Nations are cited by Zunes on pp. 26, 32–33, 115, 129, and 184–85, but complete lists can be obtained as follows: for a list of U.N. resolutions critical of Israel, 1955–92, see www.middleeastnews.com/unresolutionslist.html; for U.N. resolutions pertaining to Israel during the period 1993–95, see www.undp.org/missions/israel/un2.htm; and for U.S. vetoes of U.N. resolutions critical of Israel during 1972–2002, see www.us-israel.org/jsource/UN/usvetoes.html.

For the Pew Research Center data, see Meg Bortin, "Muslims Lament Israel's Existence," *IHT,* 4 June 2003, pp. 1 and 6. The events of 2004 were reported on in Chris McGreal, "Israel Shocked by Image of Soldiers Forcing Palestinian Violinist to Play at Roadblock," *GW,* 3–9 December 2004, p. 10.

55. Avraham Burg, "A Failed Israeli Society Is Collapsing," *IHT,* 6–7 September 2003, p. 4.

6. The Meaning of 9/11

1. Rebecca Mead, "The Marx Brother," *NY,* 5 May 2003, p. 47; and George Monbiot, "The Logic of Empire," *GW,* 15–21 August 2002, p. 13. The statement by Bush and Blair from the Azores was reported by Michael Gordon in the *NYT,* 18 March 2003. For two

particularly insightful discussions of these issues, see Jay Bookman, "The President's Real Goal in Iraq," *Atlanta Journal-Constitution*, 29 September 2002, and Anatol Lieven, "The Push for War," *London Review of Books* 24, no. 19 (3 October 2002).

2. David Stout, "White House Launches Counterattack on Critic," *IHT*, 23 March 2004, pp. 1 and 4; Hendrik Hertzberg, "In the Soup," *NY*, 10 May 2004, pp. 98–102; and Paul Krugman, "A Pattern of Corruption in U.S. Intelligence," *IHT*, 16 July 2003, p. 8. A report posted on CBS.com during September 2002 revealed Rumsfeld's intent to "sweep" everything together.

The comprehensive sources on the run-up to war are Stefan Halper and Jonathan Clarke, *America Alone* (Cambridge: Cambridge University Press, 2004); and Bryan Burrough et al., "The Path to War, *Vanity Fair*, May 2004, pp. 228–44 and 281–94. Other valuable exposés of the 2003 war are James Bamford, *A Pretext for War* (New York: Doubleday, 2004); Joseph Wilson, *The Politics of Truth* (New York: Carroll & Graf, 2004); Richard Clarke, *Against All Enemies* (New York: Free Press, 2004); Bob Woodward, *Plan of Attack* (New York: Simon and Schuster, 2004); Ron Suskind, *The Price of Loyalty* (New York: Simon and Schuster, 2004); Patrick Buchanan, *Where the Right Went Wrong* (New York: St. Martin's, 2004); Hans Blix, *Disarming Iraq* (New York: Pantheon, 2004); John Prados, *Hoodwinked* (New York: New Press, 2004); and James Mann, *Rise of the Vulcans* (New York: Viking, 2004). These monographs were valuable sources for much of what follows.

3. Glenn Kessler, "U.S. Decision on Iraq Has Puzzling Past," *WP*, 12 January 2003, p. A1.

4. Ibid.; John B. Judis and Spencer Ackerman, "The Selling of the Iraq War," *New Republic*, 30 June 2003 (I used the online version, which incorporated corrections to the print version: www.tnr.com, posted 19 June 2003); and Nicholas Lemann, "How It Came to War," *NY*, 31 March 2003, pp. 34–40.

5. Judis and Ackerman, "Selling of the Iraq War"; Dilip Hiro, *Iraq: In the Eye of the Storm* (New York: Nation Books, 2002), p. 98; and Todd S. Purdum and Patrick E. Tyler, "Republicans Break Ranks over Bush's Iraq Policy," *IHT*, 17–18 August 2002, pp. 1 and 5. The Scowcroft op-ed piece appeared in *WSJ*, 15 August 2002.

6. Hiro, *Iraq*, p. 213; Judis and Ackerman, "Selling of the Iraq War"; Michael R. Gordon, "CIA Letter Shows Split over Iraq," *IHT*, 11 October 2002, pp. 1 and 8; Paul Krugman, "The War on Truth Is Not over Yet," *IHT*, 11 June 2003, p. 8; Suzanne Goldenberg, "CIA Had Doubts on Iraq Link to al-Qaeda," *GW*, 12–18 June 2003, p. 1; Bill Keller, "Corrupted Intelligence Weakens America," *IHT*, 14–15 June 2003, p. 10; Walter Pincus, "Report Cast Doubt on Iraq–Al Qaeda Connection," *WP*, 22 June 2003, pp. A1 and 19; Seymour M. Hersh, "Selective Intelligence," *NY*, 12 May 2003, pp. 44–51; and Burrough et al., "Path to War," p. 238.

7. Barton Gellman and Walter Pincus, "Depiction of Threat Outgrew Supporting Evidence," *WP*, 10 August 2003, p. A9. The story about *Newsweek* was posted by Fairness and Accuracy in Reporting on 27 February 2003 as "Star Witness on Iraq Said Weapons Were Destroyed," at www.fair.org/press-releases/kamel.html; see also John Barry, "Exclusive: The Defector's Secrets," *Newsweek*, 3 March 2003, p. 6 (for transcript of Kamel interview, see http://middleeastreference.org.uk/kamel.html). The Gellman and Pincus article does say that Kamel's testimony was "the reverse of Cheney's description."

8. Paul Krugman, "The Bush Administration's Weapons of Mass Deceit," *IHT*, 30 April 2003, p. 8.

9. Judis and Ackerman, "Selling of the Iraq War"; Gellman and Pincus, "Depiction of Threat," p. A9; Joby Warrick, "Some Evidence on Iraq Called Fake," *WP*, 8 March 2003, pp. A1 and 18; Seymour M. Hersh, "Who Lied to Whom?," *NY*, 31 March 2003, pp. 41–43; Sarah Lyall, "Britain Admits That Much of Its Report on Iraq Came from Maga-

zines," *NYT*, 8 February 2003; and Brian Whitaker and Michael White, "War Dossier Branded a 'Sham,'" *GW*, 13–19 February 2003, p. 7.

10. Hersh, "Who Lied"; Judis and Ackerman, "Selling of the Iraq War"; Nicholas D. Kristof, "Missing in Action: The Truth About Iraqi Arms," *IHT*, 7 May 2003, p. 6; Richard Leiby and Walter Pincus, "Retired Envoy: Nuclear Report Ignored," *WP*, 6 July 2003, p. A13; Dana Milbank and Walter Pincus, "Bush Aides Disclose Warnings from CIA," *WP*, 23 July 2003, pp. A1 and 14; and Walter Pincus, "Bush Team Kept Airing Doubtful Iraq Allegation," *GW*, 14–20 August 2003, p. 31. Joseph Wilson's op-ed piece on the whole affair was published in the *NYT* on 6 July 2003.

11. Bill Keller, "Corrupted Intelligence Weakens America," *IHT*, 14–15 June 2003, p. 10; James Risen and Douglas Jehl, "Expert Said to Tell Legislators He Was Pressed to Distort Some Evidence," *NYT*, 25 June 2003, p. 11; Burrough et al., "Path to War," p. 242; Kristof, "Missing in Action"; Philip Gourevitch, "Might and Right," *NY*, 16–23 June 2003, pp. 69–70; Judis and Ackerman, "Selling of the Iraq War"; and Halper and Clarke, *America Alone*, p. 224. A 2003 report by the Carnegie Endowment for International Peace also notes the intense pressure put on intelligence experts to conform to administration views (see "How Was the U.S. So Misled?," *IHT*, 12 January 2004, p. 8). On the de facto inevitability of the war, and the diplomatic debacle involved, see James P. Rubin, "Stumbling into War," *Foreign Affairs* 82, no. 5 (September–October 2003), 46–66.

12. Scott Ritter, "Not Everyone Got It Wrong on Iraq's Weapons," *IHT*, 6 February 2004, p. 7; Sidney Blumenthal, "US Spies Were Ignored, or Worse, If They Failed to Make the Case for War," *The Guardian*, 5 February 2004; Jim Lobe, "Diversion and Delay: When in Trouble, Blame the CIA," posted 2 February 2004 at www.commondreams.org; and Burrough et al., "Path to War," p. 294.

13. Burrough et al., "Path to War"; Brian Knowlton, "UN Speech Turned Heads but Probably Didn't Change Minds," *IHT*, 6 February 2003, p. 4; Lyall, "Britain Admits That Much of Its Report"; Whitaker and White, "War Dossier Branded a 'Sham'"; Peter Slevin and Colum Lynch, "U.S. Meets New Resistance at U.N.," *WP*, 15 February 2003, pp. A1 and 27; Judis and Ackerman, "Selling of the Iraq War"; Gourevitch, "Might and Right"; Maureen Dowd, "When the Truth Got in the Way of a War," *IHT*, 5 June 2003, p. 7; Dan Plesch and Richard Norton Taylor, "Straw and Powell had Serious Doubts over Weapons Claims," *GW*, 5–11 June 2003, p. 1; and Krugman, "War on Truth." The text of Powell's 2001 remarks in Cairo can be found at www.state.gov/secretary/rm/2001/933.htm; see also Michael Getler, "More on the War," *WP*, 31 October 2004, p. B6.

14. Hertzberg, "In the Soup," p. 100; Bamford, *A Pretext for War*; Blumenthal, "US Spies Were Ignored"; Plesch and Taylor, "Straw and Powell Had Serious Doubts"; Judis and Ackerman, "Selling of the Iraq War"; "How the Bush Crowd Twisted Intelligence," *IHT*, 25 October 2004, p. 8; "With Friends Like This," *IHT*, 22–23 May 2004, p. 4; Julian Borger, "US intelligence Fears Iran Duped Hawks into Iraq War," *GW*, 28 May–3 June 2004, p. 1; Jane Mayer, "The Manipulator," *NY*, 7 June 2004, pp. 58–72; and Hersh, "Selective Intelligence." Judith Miller's article was "A Nation Challenged: Secret Sites," *NYT*, 20 December 2001, p. A1.

15. David Corn, "Now They Tell Us," *The Nation*, 19 May 2003, pp. 11–13; Sam Tanenhaus, "Bush's Brain Trust," *Vanity Fair*, May 2003; Dana Milbank, "Bush Remarks Confirm Shift in Justification for War," *WP*, 1 June 2003, p. A18; Paul Krugman, "Bush Follows a Hollywood Script," *IHT*, 2 June 2003, p. 6; George Wright, "Wolfowitz: Iraq War Was About Oil," *The Guardian*, 4 June 2003; Harper and Clarke, *America Alone*, pp. 201 and 303; Judis and Ackerman, "Selling of the Iraq War"; Jules Witcover, "Look Who's Rewriting History Now," *Baltimore Sun*, 18 July 2003; and "Sidestepping on Iraq," *NYT*, 31 July 2003.

16. Mann, *Rise of the Vulcans*; and Stephen Holmes, "The National Insecurity State," *The Nation*, 10 May 2004, pp. 25–30.

17. Halper and Clarke, *America Alone*, pp. 202–3, 217, and 230–31.

18. Newspaper quote is from Joseph Fitchett, "Speed Is Core Element of U.S. Battle Strategy," *IHT*, 21 March 2003, p. 1. The standard text reference on "shock and awe" is Harlan K. Ullman et al., *Shock and Awe* (Washington, D.C.: NDU Press, 1996) (Ullman was Colin Powell's teacher at the National War College). To see what shock and awe looks like on the human level, the reader might wish to look at the Web site www.marchforjustice.com/shock&awe.php.

19. Karl Vick, "Children Pay Cost of Iraq's Chaos," *WP*, 21 November 2004, pp. A1 and 31. On the Johns Hopkins study, see Elisabeth Rosenthal, "Iraqi Toll Is Put at 100,000," *IHT*, 29 October 2004, pp. 1 and 8; and Les Roberts et al., "Mortality Before and After the 2003 Invasion of Iraq: Cluster Sample Survey," *The Lancet* 364, no. 9445 (30 October 2004), posted at www.thelancet.com on 29 October 2004. Civilian casualty and mortality figures are also available at www.iraqbodycount.net.

20. The statue is discussed by Alexander Cockburn in "The Decline and Fall of American Journalism," *The Nation*, 12 May 2003, p. 9. The Internet photo I refer to was posted at www.counterpunch.org/statue.html.

21. "The Wrong Message in Iraq," *IHT*, 31 March 2004, p. 8; "Mission Accomplished II?," *The Nation*, 19–26 July 2004, p. 3; "Banning Bad News in Iraq," *IHT*, 11 August 2004, p. 6; "Allawi Shows the Face of Iraqi Democracy," *IHT*, 25–26 September 2004, p. 6; and Scott Ritter, "Saddam's People Are Winning the War," *IHT*, 23 July 2004, p. 7.

22. Ben Okri, "The New Dark Age," *The Guardian*, 19 April 2003; Edmund L. Andrews, "Looters Sack Ancient Sites in Iraq," *IHT*, 24–25 May 2003, pp. 1 and 4; and Frank Rich, "A Damning Jigsaw Puzzle in Baghdad," *IHT*, 26–27 April 2003, p. 20. See also Ernest Beck, "What Was Taken and When," *ARTnews*, June 2003, pp. 44–48, for a longer discussion of lost treasures. On Marines defacing sites at Ur, see Chalmers Johnson, *The Sorrows of Empire* (New York: Metropolitan/Henry Holt, 2004), p. 234.

23. Okri, "New Dark Age."

24. Paul Reidinger, "Chronicle of a Slide Foretold," *San Francisco Bay Guardian*, *Guardian Literary Supplement*, November 2001, pp. 4–5.

25. "Liberté, Egalité . . . Stupidité," *WP*, 15 March 2003, p. A22. For psychological profiles of Bush Jr., see Justin A. Frank, *Bush on the Couch* (New York: Regan Books, 2004); and Mark Crispin Miller, *The Bush Dyslexicon* (New York: W.W. Norton, 2002). Significantly, these authors see the man as more sadistic than robotic.

26. For an article on the event plus the transcript of Hedges' speech, see www .commondreams.org/headlines03/0520-12.htm.

27. Jonetta Rose Barras, "Many Blacks Have Doubts. Here's Why," *WP*, 28 October 2001, p. B3.

28. For this and the following paragraph, see Elizabeth Becker, "U.S. Business Will Get Role in Rebuilding Occupied Iraq," *NYT*, 18 March 2003, p. A18, and her "Questions on Iraq Contract," *IHT*, 12–13 April 2003, p. 11; Bob Herbert, "The War May Be Quick but Still Not Wise," *IHT*, 21 March 2003, p. 11, his "Who Will Profit from This War?," *IHT*, 11 April 2003, p. 6, and his "Ask Bechtel What War Is Good For," *IHT*, 22 April 2003, p. 6; Diane B. Henriques, "First Bids to Rebuild Iraq to Go Only to Americans," *IHT*, 24 March 2003, p. 12; Oliver Morgan and Ed Vulliamy, "Chasing Riches in the Ruins of Iraq," *GW*, 10–16 April 2003, p. 12; "Profiting from the War," *IHT*, 21 April 2003, p. 8; Suzanne Goldenberg, "Bush Election Donors Share $8 Billion Bonanza," *GW*, 6–12 November 2003, p. 5; Rajiv Chandrasekaran, "U.S. Funds for Iraq Are Largely Unspent,"

WP, 4 July 2004, p. A1; Jacob Levich, "Kick Their Ass and Take Their Gas: Democracy Comes to Iraq," posted 13 May 2003 on www.commondreams.org; Naomi Klein, "Downsizing in Disguise," *The Nation*, 23 June 2003, p. 10; and Seumas Milne, "Asserting the Right to Resist," *GW*, 26 June–2 July 2003, p. 13.

29. Danny Schechter, *Embedded: Weapons of Mass Deception* (Amherst, N.Y.: Prometheus, 2003); Scott Sherman, "Floating with the Tide," *The Nation*, 15 March 2004, pp. 4–5 (the two studies of articles and editorials are Michael Massing's essay in the *New York Review of Books*, 26 February 2004, and the one by Chris Mooney in the March–April 2004 issue of the *Columbia Journalism Review*); Howard Kurtz, "N.Y. Times Cites Defects in Its Reports on Iraq," *WP*, 26 May 2004, p. C1; "The Times and Iraq," *NYT*, 26 May 2004, p. A10; Wallace Shawn, "Fragments from a Diary," *The Nation*, 31 March 2003; and Howard Kurtz, "The Post on WMDs: An Inside Story," *WP*, 12 August 2004, p. A1.

30. Eric Alterman, *What Liberal Media?* (New York: Basic Books, 2003); Michael Mann, *Incoherent Empire* (London: Verso, 2003), p. 101; Antonia Zabisias, "CNN's Hatchet Job on Scott Ritter," *Toronto Star*, 12 September 2002; David K. Kirkpatrick, "War Spotlights Power of Murdoch's Press," *IHT*, 9 April 2003, p. 2; Harper and Clarke, *America Alone*, pp. 192–96; Matt Taibbi, "Cleaning the Pool: The White House Press Corps Politely Grabs its Ankles," *New York Press*, 12–18 March 2003, posted on www.nypress.com.

31. Nicholas von Hoffman, *Hoax* (New York: Nation Books, 2004), pp. 101–6.

32. Walter Pincus, "Iraq Tactics Have Long History with U.S. Interrogators," *WP*, 13 June 2004, p. A8. The CIA manual is called "KUBARK Counterintelligence Interrogation." On "the Vietnam," see Mark Hosenball et al., "The Roots of Torture," *Newsweek*, 24 May 2004, pp. 25–34. See also James Risen, "Sex Abuse Alleged at Iraqi Prison," *IHT*, 30 April–2 May 2004, p. 5; Philip Kennicott, "A Wretched New Picture of America," *WP*, 5 May 2004, pp. C1 and 11; Seymour M. Hersh, "Torture at Abu Ghraib," *NY*, 10 May 2004, pp. 42–47; Scott Higham and Joe Stephens, "New Details of Prison Abuse Emerge," *WP*, 21 May 2004, pp. A1 and 17, and their "Punishment and Amusement," *WP*, 22 May 2004, pp. A1 and 17; Josh White et al., "Videos Amplify Picture of Violence," *WP*, 21 May 2004, pp. A1 and 16; Josh White and Christian Davenport, "Soldiers and Detainees Tell Stories Behind the Pictures," *WP*, 22 May 2004, pp. A1 and 16; and Julie Scelfo and Rod Nordland, "Beneath the Hoods," *Newsweek*, 19 July 2004, pp. 26–28.

33. Kennicott, "Wretched New Picture of America"; "The Images of Torture," *IHT*, 6 May 2004, p. 8; and Alan Cowell, "No Letup in Anger Worldwide," *IHT*, 7 May 2004, pp. 1 and 4.

34. Hersh, "Torture at Abu Ghraib"; Seymour M. Hersh, "The Gray Zone," *NY*, 24 May 2004, pp. 38–44; Seymour M. Hersh, *Chain of Command* (New York: HarperCollins, 2004); "Red Cross Describes Systematic Abuse in Iraq," *IHT*, 8–9 May 2004, p. 2; "Red Cross Reported Systemic Iraqi Abuse," *IHT*, 11 May 2004, p. 5; Gary Younge, "Blame the White Trash," *GW*, 20–26 May 2004, p. 11; "Doctors Linked to Abuse," *IHT*, 20 August 2004, p. 4; Jane Mayer, "The Experiment," *NY*, 11–18 July 2005, pp. 60–71; "Doctors and Detention," *WP*, 13 July 2005, p. A20; "Torturous Methods," *GW*, 10–16 December 2004, p. 3; and "Abu Ghraib, Caribbean Style," *IHT*, 2 December 2004, p. 8.

35. Karen J. Greenberg and Joshua L. Dratel, eds., *The Torture Papers* (Cambridge: Cambridge University Press, 2005); Anthony Lewis, "Making Torture Legal," *New York Review of Books* 51, no. 12 (15 July 2004); Hosenball, "Roots of Torture"; Jess Bravin, "Pentagon Report Set Framework for Use of Torture," *WSJ*, 7 June 2004, pp. A1 and 17; Dana Priest and R. Jeffrey Smith, "Memo Offered Justification for Use of Torture," *WP*, 8 June 2004; David Johnston and James Risen, "U.S. Memo Provided Basis for CIA Coercion," *IHT*, 28 June 2004, p. 6; and Suzanne Goldenberg, "Bush Memos Reveal Stance on Torture," *GW*, 2–8 July 2004, p. 7.

36. Michael Isikoff, "Election Day Worries," *Newsweek*, 19 July 2004; "Bush May Use Terrorism Excuse to Delay Elections," posted 12 July 2004 at www.capitolhillblue .com/artman/publish/article_4823.shtml; Julian Borger, "Terror Attack 'Could Delay US Election,'" *The Guardian*, 13 July 2004, p. 11; "A Threat to the U.S. Election," *IHT*, 19 July 2004, p. 8.

37. "Answers About Torture," *WP*, 16 March 2003, p. B6.

38. Information on the 1996 Effective Death Penalty and Anti-terrorism Act is posted at www.geocities.com/WestHollywood/Heights/3335/aliens.html and at www.certip.org/ resources/wmd/legislation.html. CERTIP (the Center for Emergency Response Technology, Instruction, and Policy)—is a public/private enterprise that fosters research to enhance emergency response for natural and man-made disasters.

39. Richard Falk and David Krieger, "Congress Has Marginalized Itself," posted on 22 February 2003 at www.counterpunch.org/krieger02222003.html; Cynthia Brown, ed., *Lost Liberties: Ashcroft and the Assault on Personal Freedom* (New York: New Press, 2003); Frank Davies, "Secrecy Cloaks Patriot Act," *Seattle Times*, 9 September 2002; Jay Stanley and Barry Steinhardt, "Bigger Monster, Weaker Chains: The Growth of an American Surveillance Society," posted by the American Civil Liberties Union, January 2003, at www.aclu.org; Dan Eggen and Robert O'Harrow Jr., "U.S. Steps Up Secret Surveillance," *WP*, 24 March 2003, pp. A1 and 7; "A Voice of Reason," *WP*, 11 December 2002, p. A32; Charles Lane, "In Terror War, Second Track for Suspects," *WP*, 1 December 2002, p. A1; "An Unpatriotic Act," *IHT*, 26 August 2003, p. 6; and Eric Lichtblau, "U.S. Patriot Act Being Used in Many Nonterrorism Cases," *IHT*, 29 September 2003, p. 5. The full text of the USA Patriot Act is available at www.epic.org/privacy/terrorism/hr3162.html.

40. "A nation of spies?," *IHT*, 25 July 2002, p. 6; Will Doherty, "Big Brother Is No Longer Fiction," *MIT Alumni Association Newsletter*, January 2003, posted at http:// alumweb.mit.edu/whatmatters/200301; "Big Brother Is No Longer a Fiction," posted on 15 January 2003 at www.aclu.org; Maureen Dowd, "Better Watch Your Step—Or the Pentagon Will," *IHT*, 22 May 2003, p. 7; interview with Chuck Lewis on *NOW with Bill Moyers*, PBS, 7 February 2003 (posted at www.pbs.org); "ACLU Says New Ashcroft Bill Erodes Checks and Balances on Presidential Power," posted on 12 February 2003 at www.aclu.org; "A Threat to Freedom," *IHT*, 23 September 2003, p. 8; and Stephen R. Shalom, "After Two Years," posted at www.zmag.org/znet.htm on 11 September 2003.

In February 2003, House and Senate negotiators agreed that Total Information Awareness could not be used against Americans, something that may change as the war on terrorism intensifies (Adam Clymer, "Congress Restricts Surveillance Plan," *IHT*, 13 February 2003, p. 3). In addition, de facto "progress" toward Patriot Act II got sneaked in during December 2004 as part of the legislation to create a new director of intelligence. This includes easier provisions for denying bail and obtaining surveillance warrants, gutting the proposal for a watchdog panel to prevent abuses by the government, and leeway to track and harass lone individuals not connected to terrorist groups ("Intelligence and Civil Rights," *IHT*, 14 December 2004, p. 8).

41. David S. Broder, "If the Economy Mattered," *WP*, 13 October 2002, p. B7; Robert Kuttner, "A Presidency at the Brink," *Boston Globe*, 29 January 2003; Amy Goldstein and Mike Allen, "Budget Sharply Boosts Defense," *WP*, 4 February 2003, pp. A1 and 6; Jonathan Weisman, "In 2003, It's Reagan Revolution Redux," *WP*, 4 February 2003, p. A6; Amy Goldstein and Jonathan Weisman, "Bush Seeks to Recast Federal Ties to the Poor," *WP*, 9 February 2003, pp. A1 and 6–7; Gary Younge, "Bush Needs His Next Fix," *GW*, 24–30 April 2003, p. 13; Michael Powell, "Rescue's Just Not Part of the Plan," *WP*, 4 May 2003, pp. B1 and 5; Alan Fram, "Tab for Rebuilding Iraq Could Reach $600 Billion," *IHT*, 13 August 2003, p. 3; Dave Moniz, "Monthly Costs of Iraq, Afghan Wars

Approach That of Vietnam," *USA Today*, 8 September 2003; "A Pentagon Spending Spree," *IHT*, 11 February 2003, p. 6; Stephen Kinzer, "Some States Propose End to Arts Spending," *NYT*, 20 February 2003; Suzanne McGee, "Arts Funding Under Fire," *ARTnews*, April 2003, p. 41; Elizabeth Maupin, "Cutbacks Nationwide," *Orlando Sentinel*, 26 April 2003; "Orchestras in Trouble," *Fort Lauderdale Sun-Sentinel*, 11 May 2003; and Peronet Despeignes, "White House Shelved Deficit Report," *Financial Times* (London), 29 May 2003.

For data on health insurance, see above, p. 339, n. 23. The government Web site indicates 45.9 million Americans without coverage as of mid-2001, and 48.2 million without it as of mid-2004, or an increase of 2.3 million people.

42. Paul Krugman, "Bush's 'War on Terror' Is All Smoke and Mirrors," *IHT*, 18 June 2003, p. 8, and his "Security Funds Favor Bush States," *IHT*, 2 April 2003, p. 12; Jo Becker et al., "Anti-Terrorism Funds Buy Wide Array of Pet Projects," *WP*, 23 November 2003, pp. A1 and 16–17; "Operation Atlas, Shrugged Off," *NYT*, 19 March 2003, p. A28; Hiro, *Iraq*, p. 182; Bob Herbert, "While the Lights Are On, America Shuts Its Eyes," *IHT*, 19 August 2003, p. 7; and Shalom, "After Two Years." See also the very disturbing article by Mark Hertsgaard, "Nuclear Insecurity," *Vanity Fair*, November 2003.

43. Robert Baer, *Sleeping with the Devil* (New York: Crown, 2003); and Craig Unger, *House of Bush, House of Saud* (New York: Scribner, 2004). See also Julian Borger, "U.S. Still Hooked on Saudi Connection," *GW*, 7–13 August 2003, p. 6; and Eric Lichtblau, "White House Agreed to Whisk Saudis Away," *IHT*, 5 September 2003, p. 4.

44. Emily Wax, "Outrage Spreads in Arab World," *WP*, 30 March 2003, pp. A19 and 26 (see also articles on p. A26 by Carol Morello and by Michael Dobbs and Mike Allen); Susan Sachs, "Arab Media Portray War as Killing Field," *NYT*, 4 April 2003; Meg Bortin, "In War's Wake, Hostility and Mistrust," and her "Muslims Lament Israel's Existence," both in *IHT*, 4 June 2003, pp. 1 and 6, respectively; Amy Waldman and Dexter Filkins, "Two U.S. Fronts: Quick Wars, but Bloody Peace," *NYT*, 19 September 2003, pp. A1 and 12; Neil Mackay, "US Admits the War for 'Hearts and Minds' in Iraq Is Now Lost," *Sunday Herald* (Scotland), 5 December 2004.

45. Chalmers Johnson's interview with *In These Times* is available at www.inthesetimes .com/issue/25/24/shaw2524.html; William Raspberry, "Bush Mistakes Saddam for Osama bin Laden," *IHT*, 10 September 2002, p. 7; and Buchanan, *Where the Right Went Wrong*.

46. Graham Allison, *Nuclear Terrorism* (New York: Times Books/Henry Holt, 2004); see also his Web site, www.nuclearterror.org. Matthew Bunn, also at the Belfer Center, has written a number of publications on the subject, which are available at http:// bcsia.ksg.harvard.edu/publication_list_by_person.cfm?item_id=405. I am grateful to Kelly Gerling for these references and for his observations on this terrifying possibility.

47. Joseph Nye, "The New Rome Meets the New Barbarians: How America Should Wield Its Power," *The Economist*, 23 March 2002.

48. C. P. Cavafy, *Collected Poems*, trans. Edmund Keeley and Philip Sherrard (Princeton: Princeton University Press, 1975), p. 18.

49. Robert Lowell, *Collected Poems*, ed. Frank Bidart and David Gewanter (New York: Farrar, Straus and Giroux, 2003), p. 386. Quote from Tom Paulin is in "The Voice of America," *The Observer* (London), 3 August 2003.

7. The Roads Not Taken

1. Mary Pipher, *Letters to a Young Therapist* (New York: Basic Books, 2003), p. 170. Fareed Zakaria quoted in Marion Maneker, "Man of the World," *New York*, 21 April 2003, p. 38.

2. "Florida Woman Trampled by Shoppers," Newsday.com, 30 November 2003; "Bar-

gains and Broken Bones," Provo (Utah) *Daily Herald*, 4 December 2003 (reprinting *Chicago Tribune* report of 1 December 2003).

The incident may have been murkier than it originally appeared, however, inasmuch as—according to Wal-Mart—the woman, Patricia VanLester, was a former company employee, and had filed a number of claims against Wal-Mart for falling down in its stores. This does not, of course, make the behavior of the shoppers who trampled her any less reprehensible, but it does perhaps point to another facet of the American shadow. See John Sutherland, "Frequent Filer Miles," *GW*, 18–24 December 2003, p. 13.

3. Alex Marshall, *How Cities Work* (Austin: University of Texas Press, 2000), p. xxii.

4. For a poignant example of two Native American tribes taking very different paths, see Debbie S. Miller, "Clinging to an Arctic Homeland," in *Arctic National Wildlife Refuge: Seasons of Life and Land*, ed. Subhankar Banerjee (Seattle: Mountaineers Books, 2003), pp. 132–41. The ANWR is the homeland of the Inupiats as well as the Gwich'in Athabascans. For the latter, the coastal plain is sacred ground, the home of the porcupine caribou, which they wish to see left undisturbed. Meanwhile, the corporate world has convinced the Inupiat that if they opt for "development," a storehouse of oil beneath the tundra will bring them jobs and millions of dollars. While the salary of Inupiat maintenance workers is now $41 an hour as a result, that of maintentance workers in the Gwich'in villages—who refused the deal (they formed a steering committee in 1988 to protect their land and way of life from corporate development)—is at most $19 an hour. The Inupiat have entered the world of an oil-rich economy, watching the industrial development of the coastal plain, whereas the Gwich'in own title to 1.8 million acres of tribal lands, call themselves the "caribou people," and continue to make clothing from hides and perform caribou songs and dances. They refer to the coastal plain as "the sacred place where life begins."

5. David M. Potter, *People of Plenty* (1954; repr., Chicago: Phoenix Books, 1958). See also reviews by Geoffrey Gorer in *American Quarterly* 7, no. 2 (Summer 1955), 182 and 184–86; and Robert M. Collins in *Reviews in American History* 16, no. 2 (June 1988), 321–35.

6. Walter M. McDougall, *Freedom Just Around the Corner* (New York: HarperCollins, 2004). See also the review by Gordon Wood in the *NYT Book Review*, 28 March 2004, p. 7.

7. David E. Shi, *The Simple Life* (New York: Oxford University Press, 1985), pp. 4, 8, 12, and 15–17; William Grimes, review of John Steele Gordon, *The Empire of Wealth*, in *IHT*, 14 December 2004, p. 12; and Michael Hotz, ed., *Holding the Lotus to the Rock* (New York: Four Walls Eight Windows, 2003), p. 1. Classic studies of the Puritans include Perry Miller, *The New England Mind: The Seventeenth Century* (New York: Macmillan, 1939); and Edmund Morgan, *Visible Saints: The History of a Puritan Idea* (New York: New York University Press, 1963).

8. Joyce Appleby, *Capitalism and a New Social Order* (New York: New York University Press, 1984), pp. 9 and 14–16.

9. Ibid., pp. 21–22, 25–27, and 31–33.

10. Ibid., pp. 36, 43–44, 46, 49, 53, and 87–89. The 2002 "National Security Strategy" is available at www.whitehouse.gov/nsc/nss.html.

11. Appleby, *Capitalism*, pp. 96 and 104–5.

12. Gordon S. Wood, *The Radicalism of the American Revolution* (New York: Vintage, 1993), p. ix.

13. Ibid., pp. 4–8 and 19.

14. Ibid., pp. 96, 104, 109, 113, 116, 120, 124, 178–80, 187, 189–90, and 219.

15. Ibid., pp. 229–30, 250, 252, 255, 261, 305, 326–27, and 365–66.

16. Seymour Martin Lipset, *American Exceptionalism* (New York: W. W. Norton, 1997), pp. 20–21, 24, 31, 49, 64, 71, 73, 76 (reference to highest level of poverty), 109 (quote from Burnham), and 267.

17. Wood, *Radicalism of the American Revolution*, pp. 32–33.

18. Fareed Zakaria, *The Future of Freedom* (New York: W.W. Norton, 2003), pp. 200–255.

19. Wood, *Radicalism of the American Revolution*, pp. 329–31, 333, and 336; Hofstadter quoted in Lipset, *American Exceptionalism*, p. 18.

20. Robert N. Bellah, "Civil Religion in America," *Daedalus*, no. 96 (1967), pp. 1–21; and Sidney E. Mead, *The Nation with the Soul of a Church* (New York: Harper and Row, 1975), pp. 64 and 71–73 (quote from Beecher on p. 73).

21. Lipset, *American Exceptionalism*, pp. 31 and 63–65.

22. Sidney E. Mead. *The Lively Experiment* (New York: Harper and Row, 1963), pp. 5 and 8.

23. Ibid., pp. 5–6 and 12; and Jane Holtz Kay, *Asphalt Nation* (Berkeley: University of California Press, 1998), p. 8 (quote from Studebaker president is on p. 219).

24. Clay McShane, *Down the Asphalt Path* (New York: Columbia University Press, 1994), pp. ix–x, 57, and 79–80; and William Leach, *Land of Desire* (New York: Pantheon, 1993). Kroeber is quoted in James J. Flink, "Three Stages of American Automobile Consciousness," *American Quarterly* 24, no. 4 (October 1972), 455n.

25. I am drawing here on Flink, "Three Stages," pp. 454, 455 and 455n. This article was later expanded into *The Car Culture* (Cambridge, Mass.: MIT Press, 1976).

26. Flink, "Three Stages," pp. 456–57; and McShane, *Down the Asphalt Path*, p. 123.

27. Flink, "Three Stages," pp. 453–54, 458, and 460; Flink, *Car Culture*, pp. 140, 151, 187, and 214; and Kay, *Asphalt Nation*, pp. 197–98.

28. Flink, *Car Culture*, pp. 141 and 220–21; Kay, *Asphalt Nation*, p. 213; and McShane, *Down the Asphalt Path*, p. 115.

29. Flink, "Three Stages," p. 467; Kay, *Asphalt Nation*, pp. 232–33, 254, 256, 261–62, and 270 (Mumford quoted on p. 265); and Anne Mackin, "The Driven Society: Why Americans Don't Listen to Car Critics," *The Responsive Community* 9, no. 2 (Spring 1999), 47.

30. McShane, *Down the Asphalt Path*, pp. 125, 130, 136, and 142–44.

31. Flink, "Three Stages," pp. 458–59 and 466; and Flink, *Car Culture*, pp. 214–15.

32. Malcolm Gladwell, "Big and Bad," *NY*, 12 January 2004, pp. 28–33. If every SUV owner in the United States traded in his or her vehicle for a passenger sedan, we would be free to ditch the 2.3 million barrels of oil per day we import from the Middle East. See Jonathan Weisman, "No Guzzle, No Glory," *WP*, 13 June 2004, pp. F1 and 14.

33. Mackin, "Driven Society," 49 and 52–53.

34. Eric H. Monkkonen, *America Becomes Urban* (Berkeley: University of California Press, 1988), pp. xiv, 34, 37, 40, 42, and 54–55; Donald L. Miller, *Lewis Mumford* (New York: Weidenfeld and Nicolson, 1989), pp. 356–57; and Witold Rybczynski, *City Life* (New York: Scribner, 1995), pp. 33 and 79.

35. Monkkonen, *America Becomes Urban*, pp. 2, 40, and 52; and Rybczynski, *City Life*, pp. 24–25 and 114.

36. Rybczynski, *City Life*, p. 32; James Howard Kunstler, *The Geography of Nowhere* (New York: Touchstone Books, 1994), pp. 25 and 33, and *The City in Mind* (New York: Free Press, 2001), p. 25; Robert Fishman, *Bourgeois Utopias* (New York: Basic Books, 1987), pp. 12, 111–14, 116, and 194; and David P. Jordan, *Transforming Paris* (Chicago: University of Chicago Press, 1996), chs. 7 and 10.

37. Rybczynski, *City Life*, pp. 124 and 148; Frederick Law Olmsted, "Public Parks and the Enlargement of Towns," in *The City Reader*, ed. Richard T. LeGates and Frederick Stout (New York: Routledge, 1996), p. 338 (see also pp. 334–37, remarks by the editors); Robert Fishman, "The American Planning Tradition: An Introduction and Interpretation," in *The American Planning Tradition*, ed. Robert Fishman (Washington, D.C.: Woodrow Wilson Center Press, 2000), p. 10; Geoffrey Blodgett, "Frederick Law Olmsted:

Landscape Architecture as Conservative Reform," *Journal of American History* 62, no. 4 (March 1976), 869–89; and Witold Rybczynski, *Frederick Law Olmsted and America in the Nineteenth Century* (New York: Scribner, 1999), pp. 417–18.

38. Lewis Mumford, *The Highway and the City* (New York: Harcourt, Brace, & World, 1963), p. 244; Kunstler, *City in Mind*, pp. xiv–xv; Allan B. Jacobs, *Great Streets* (Cambridge, Mass.: MIT Press, 1993); Miller, *Lewis Mumford*, p. 483; Thomas Bender, "Medieval New York," review of *Around Washington Square,* by Luther S. Harris, in the *TLS,* 5 March 2004, p. 26; and Joel Kotkin, "A Bit of a Chill for Hot Times in the Big City," *WP,* 24 March 2002, pp. B1 and 3. On Robert Moses, see Robert A. Caro, *The Power Broker* (New York: Vintage, 1975).

Robert Putnam and Lewis Feldstein, in *Better Together* (New York: Simon and Schuster, 2003), provide a few examples of city neighborhoods and towns they regard as exceptional, but admit that the evidence is anecdotal, and that it doesn't really manage to refute the data on collapse of community in America that is so well documented in Putnam's *Bowling Alone.*

39. Le Corbusier, "A Contemporary City," in LeGates and Stout, eds., *City Reader,* pp. 366–75; Richard Sennett, *The Conscience of the Eye* (New York: W.W. Norton, 1992), pp. 170–71; Robert Fishman, *Urban Utopias in the Twentieth Century* (Cambridge, Mass.: MIT Press, 1982), pp. 164, 190, 206–7, 230, 240, and 244; Rybczynski, *City Life*, pp. 162–64; Kunstler, *Geography of Nowhere*, pp. 59, 67, and 76–81; and Robert Twombly, *Power and Style* (New York: Hill and Wang, 1995), pp. 76–95.

40. Kunstler, *Geography of Nowhere*, pp. 67, 274, and back cover; and Sennett, *Conscience*, pp. xi and 46.

41. Mies quote in Louis Hellman, *Architecture for Beginners* (New York: Writers and Readers, 1988), p. 1; Mumford quote in Marshall, *How Cities Work*, p. 102.

42. Fishman, *Bourgeois Utopias*, pp. x, 4–5, and 12.

43. Ibid., pp. 175–77 and 182; and Kunstler, *Geography of Nowhere*, pp. 102–5.

44. Fishman, *Bourgeois Utopias*, pp. 15–16, 155–57, 160–66, 170–73, and 178–81.

45. Kunstler, *Geography of Nowhere*, pp. 113, 118–19, and 273; Barry James, "Learning to Manage Urban Sprawl," *IHT,* 12 August 2002, pp. 1 and 6; Ray Oldenburg, *The Great Good Place*, 2d ed. (New York: Marlowe and Company, 1999); and Sennett, *Conscience*, p. xii. For Mother Teresa, see Pipher, *Letters to a Young Therapist.* See also Ian Roberts, "We Are Driving as to War," *GW,* 23–29 January 2003, p. 11.

46. Setha Low, *Behind the Gates* (New York: Routledge, 2003), pp. 10, 15, 21–23, and 143; and Joseph Rykwert, *The Seduction of Place* (New York: Pantheon, 2000), p. 218.

47. Fishman, *Urban Utopias*, pp. 5, 8, 23–25, 37, and 39–41; LeGates and Stout, eds., *City Reader*, pp. 334–35 (editors' comments); Ebenezer Howard, "Author's Introduction" and "The Town-Country Magnet," from *Garden Cities of To-morrow*, in LeGates and Stout, eds., *City Reader*, pp. 345–53 (including editors' comments). Howard's book originally appeared in 1898 under the title *To-morrow: a Peaceful Path to Real Reform.*

48. LeGates and Stout, eds., *City Reader*, pp. 345–46 (editors' comments); Miller, *Lewis Mumford*, pp. 85–86; and Fishman, *Urban Utopias*, pp. 23–24.

49. Fishman, "American Planning Tradition," p. 83.

50. Fishman, *Urban Utopias*, pp. 41, 61–62, 65–66, and 80; and LeGates and Stout, eds., *City Reader*, pp. 334–35 (editors' comments).

51. Miller, *Lewis Mumford*, pp. 191, 196, and 202–3; Ada Louise Huxtable, "Stein's 'Sunnyside' Left a Permanent Imprint," *NYT,* 25 June 1972; and "Sunnyside Gardens: A Walking Tour," brochure kindly provided to me by Carmela Massimo at Welcome Home Real Estate, Queens, New York.

52. Miller, *Lewis Mumford*, p. 206; Paul and Percival Goodman, *Communitas*, 2d ed. (New

York: Vintage, 1960), pp. 4 and 8; and Greenbelt data located at www.ci.greenbelt.md.us (click on "Census 2000").

53. Fishman, *Bourgeois Utopias*, p. 177; and Robert Fishman, "The Mumford-Jacobs Debate," *Planning History Studies* 10, no 1–2 (1996), 5–6.

54. Marshall, *How Cities Work*, pp. 148–49. Demographics for Columbia are located at www.columbia-md.com and also http://factfinder.census.gov (data from 2000).

55. Miller, *Lewis Mumford*, p. 472. Demographics for Reston are located at http://factfinder.census.gov (data from 2000).

56. Kunstler, *Geography of Nowhere*, pp. 200–205; Fishman, "American Planning Tradition," pp. 21–22; Marshall, *How Cities Work*, p. 158; and Carl J. Abbott, "The Capital of Good Planning," in Fishman, ed., *American Planning Tradition*, pp. 241–43 and 249.

57. Abbott, "Capital of Good Planning," p. 244.

58. Ibid., pp. 245 and 248–53; Marshall, *How Cities Work*, p. 169; R. Bruce Stephenson, "A Vision of Green: Lewis Mumford's Legacy in Portland, Oregon," *Journal of the American Planning Association* 65, no. 3 (Summer 1999), 264; Fishman, "American Planning Tradition," pp. 21–22; and Kunstler, *Geography of Nowhere*, p. 204.

A fourth factor in Portland's success was the long-range influence of Mumford and Olmsted. The city's environmental and urban-planning orientation drew explicitly on their ideas, especially the garden city concept. As early as 1903, Olmsted's son, John, visited Portland to prepare a plan for city parks, and Mumford delivered a speech to the City Club in 1938. Mumford also left a memo with the city, "Regional Planning in the Northwest," which regional advocates in Portland still quote. The memo recommends constructing a series of "urban inter-regions," greening the city core, and connecting the greenbelt towns in order to ease congestion. To implement this, said Mumford, Portland would need a regional authority to plan and zone the city—he called it "collective democratic controls." While the immediate impact of all this was nil, Neil Goldschmidt brought a number of these proposals into his administration when he became mayor in 1972. During the 1970s, the Mumford-Olmsted vision became widely known in Portland, and given the new political context, it had a significant impact. Thus when Mike Houck of the Portland Audubon Society was awarded a grant in the early 1980s to set up a Metropolitan Wildlife Refuge System, he appealed to the legacy of Mumford and Olmsted in his plan to design an interconnected system of natural landscapes, and to have "greenways" that would bring people together. In a publication of 1991, the Metropolitan Service District, the agency set up to enforce the UGB, specifically cites the two planners as having influenced its proposal for a system of interconnected parks. The next year, it published *A Guidebook for Maintaining and Enhancing Greater Portland's Special Sense of Place*, which reprints Mumford's 1938 lecture to the City Club. (See Abbott, "Capital of Good Planning," pp. 242 and 253; Miller, *Mumford*, p. 482; and Stephenson, "Vision of Green," pp. 262–66.)

59. Malcolm Gladwell, "The Vanishing," *NY*, 3 January 2005, pp. 72–73.

60. Abbott, "Capital of Good Planning," pp. 245 and 247; Marshall, *How Cities Work*, p. 169; and Fishman, "American Planning Tradition," pp. 21–22.

61. Michael Leccese and Kathleen McCormick, eds., *Charter of the New Urbanism* (New York: McGraw-Hill, 2000), p. v; Todd W. Bressi, "Planning the American Dream," in *The New Urbanism*, ed. Peter Katz (New York: McGraw-Hill, 1994), p. xxx.

62. William Fulton, *The New Urbanism: Hope or Hype for American Communities?* (Cambridge, Mass.: Lincoln Institute of Land Policy, 1996), pp. 10–11; Katz, *New Urbanism*, pp. 3–17; Richard Sexton, *Parallel Utopias* (San Francisco: Chronicle Books, 1995), p. 114; Christina Binkley, "Despite Acclaim, Town of Seaside Fails to Become a Cozy Commu-

nity," *WSJ*, 7 June 1995, p. F1; Abby Goodnough, "The Mouse Moves Out of Disney's Hometown," *IHT*, 17–18 June 2004, p. 11; and Andrew Ross, *The Celebration Chronicles* (New York: Ballantine, 1999).

I observed something similar when I visited Kentlands, which is part of the township of Gaithersburg, Maryland. It's a very upscale town; the median household income is $60,000. The "local" coffee shop is Starbucks; "Market Square" consists of boutiques—a cashmere shop, for example, but no bookstore. The town has no real center, no point of convergence. I visited on a Saturday; there were very few people on the streets, and the place felt soulless. The purported "community center," Tschiffely Square, was empty; and the Kentlands Clubhouse, located in the square, essentially consists of recreational facilities (gym, squash courts) for which residents of the town pay a mandatory $86 per month (as of 2004). It is, in short, not a place to gather or hang out. Very few people actually work in Kentlands: 82 percent commute to work, mostly to Baltimore or Washington. At root, it doesn't seem to be very different from the conventional suburban development, with a large component of "soccer moms" who stay at home. (See Katz, *New Urbanism*, pp. 31–45; and "New Urbanism," *Harvard Design Magazine*, Winter–Spring 1997, pp. 50 and 55.)

63. Bressi, "Planning the American Dream," p. xlii; Alex Marshall, personal communication, April 2004; Michael Sorkin, "Acting Urban," *Metropolis* 18, no. 1 (August–September 1998), 39; and "New Urbanism," p. 53.

64. Fishman, *Bourgeois Utopias*, pp. xi, 17, and 197–98; Robert Fishman, "Beyond Suburbia: The Rise of the Technoburb," in LeGates and Stout, eds., *City Reader*, pp, 485 and 490; Joel Garreau, *Edge City* (New York: Doubleday, 1991); and William Sharpe and Leonard Wallock, "Bold New City or Built-Up 'Burb? Redefining Contemporary Suburbia," *American Quarterly* 46, no. 1 (March 1994), 2.

65. Fishman, *Bourgeois Utopias*, pp. 200–205; Fishman "Beyond Suburbia," pp. 486–88 and 491; Garreau, *Edge City*; Paul Goldberger, "High-Tech Bibliophilia," *NY*, 24 May 2004, p. 90; LeGates and Stout, eds., *City Reader*, pp. 450–52 (editors' comments); John L. Thomas, "Holding the Middle Ground," in Fishman, *American Planning Tradition*, pp. 55–56; and Kunstler, *City in Mind*, pp. 60-75. For statistics on suburban poverty, taken from a U.S. Census Bureau report of August 2004, see Peter Dreier, "Poverty in the Suburbs," *The Nation*, 20 September 2004, p. 6.

66. Sharpe and Wallock, "Bold New City," pp. 1–30.

67. *Kirkus Reviews* for *Edge City*, posted on amazon.com; Peter Calthorpe and William Fulton, *The Regional City* (Washington, D.C.: Island Press, 2001), p. 5; and Corey Robin, "Grand Design," *WP*, 2 May 2004, p. B5.

68. John Cassidy, "Pump Dreams," *NY*, 11 October 2004, p. 47.

69. Robinson Jeffers, "Shine, Perishing Republic," in *Roan Stallion* (New York: Horace Liveright, 1925), p. 95.

8. The State of the Union

1. Fareed Zakaria, *The Future of Freedom* (New York: W.W. Norton, 2003), p. 24; and Nicholas von Hoffman, *Hoax* (New York: Nation Books, 2004), back cover and pp. 9, 36, 76, 107, 149, 154, and 190–91.

2. Todd Gitlin, introduction to *The Pursuit of Loneliness*, by Philip Slater (Boston: Beacon Press, 1990), pp. xiv–xv.

3. Daniel Jonah Goldhagen, *Hitler's Willing Executioners* (New York: Alfred A. Knopf, 1996). Critiques of this book are numerous and heavy, and the reader might wish to look at Clive James, "Blaming the Germans," *NY*, 22 April 1996, pp. 42–50, or Kristen R. Monroe,

"Comparative Politics—Hitler's Willing Executioners: Ordinary Germans and the Holocaust," *American Political Science Review* 91, no. 1 (March 1997), 212–13. Goldhagen provides a lengthy "reply to my critics" in *New Republic*, 23 December 1996, pp. 37–45.

4. Osama bin Laden's address of 29 October 2004 is posted at http://english.aljazeera .net/NR/exeres/79C62AF22=98FB=4A1C=B21F=2BC36E87F61F.htm. See also Patrick Buchanan, *Where the Right Went Wrong* (New York: St. Martin's, 2004), pp. 86–87.

5. Sharon Zukin, "Attention Shoppers: Your Dreams in Aisle 3," *CHE/Chronicle Review*, 19 December 2003, p. B5.

6. Murray quoted by Richard John Neuhaus in *The Naked Public Square*, 2d ed. (Grand Rapids Mich.: William B. Eerdmans, 1986), p. 85. Sonallah Ibrahim is quoted in David Remnick, "Going Nowhere," *NY*, 12–19 July 2004, p. 80.

7. Will Hutton, "The American Prosperity Myth," *The Nation*, 1–8 September 2003, p. 24; and April Witt, "Blog Interrupted," *WP Magazine*, 15 August 2004, pp. 12–17 and 25–30. Cutler's autobiographical novel is *The Washingtonienne* (New York: Hyperion, 2005).

8. David P. Barash, "Caught Between Choices: Personal Gain vs. Public Good," *CHE/Chronicle Review*, 16 April 2004, p. B13.

9. Rafael Ramos, "Edward Hopper: El pintor de la soledad americana," *La Vanguardia Magazine*, 11 July 2004, pp. 40–43; my translation.

10. For a case study of this phenomenon in Israel, see Tom Segev, *Elvis in Jerusalem* (New York: Metropolitan/Henry Holt, 2003); for the same in India, see Katherine Boo, "The Best Job in Town," *NY*, 5 July 2004, pp. 54–69.

11. Hutton, "American Prosperity Myth," p. 24; Stephen Carter, *Civility* (New York: Harper Perennial, 1998), *passim*.

12. Jeremy Rifkin, *The European Dream* (New York: Tarcher/Penguin, 2004), pp. 31–32.

13. Ibid., pp. 81-82. The number of homicides (instances of murder and nonnegligent manslaughter), however, dropped 33.7 percent in the United States from 1990 to 1999. It then rose 6.3 percent between 1999 and 2003. What caused the drop during the 1990s is not entirely clear, but likely factors include the huge growth in the prison system, and a general demographic shift to a somewhat older population. For specific data, see the FBI Web site, www.fbi.gov/ucr/ucr.htm, and also Brett Martel, "Murder Rate Up in U.S. Cities," posted on 22 June 2000 on the Associated Press Web site, www.ap.org.

14. Rifkin, *European Dream*, pp. 284–87; and *World Almanac 2005*.

15. Sidney Mintz, "You Are What You Eat," *TLS*, 14 September 2001, p. 7; and Dominique Moïsi, "I Was Wrong to Support the Iraq War," *IHT*, 25–26 September 2004, p. 6. In October 2004, I wrote an organization by the name of Mothers Opposed to Bush (MOB) about the appeal of the Iraqi mother, and asked whether they or any other women's organization had responded to me. I received no answer.

16. Richard Morin and Claudia Deane, "Most Want Rumsfeld to Stay, Poll Finds," *WP*, 7 May 2004; Steven Lee Myers and Eric Schmitt, "Questions Linger Over Prison Abuse Inquiries," *IHT*, 7 June 2004, p. 5; "Abu Ghraib Whitewash," *IHT*, 27 July 2004, p. 6; "Closer to the Truth," *WP*, 26 August 2004, p. A22; "A Failure of Accountability," *WP*, 29 August 2004, p. B6; "Learning Nothing from Abu Ghraib," *IHT*, 29 October 2004, p. 6; "Abu Ghraib, Caribbean Style," *IHT*, 2 December 2004, p. 8; "The System Endures," *WP*, 5 December 2004, p. B6.

17. David Remnick, "Hearts and Minds," *NY*, 17 May 2004, pp. 27 and 30; Hanna Rosin, "When Joseph Comes Marching Home," *WP*, 17 May 2004, p. C1; Wil S. Hylton, "The Conscience of Joe Darby," *GQ*, posted on 27 July 2004 at http://us.gq.com.

18. "Rumsfeld Says Terror Outweighs Jail Abuse," *WP*, 11 September 2004, p. A4. There is a large literature on Milgram and the meaning of his work. In addition to *Obedience to*

Authority (New York: Harper and Row, 1974) see, for example, Thomas Blass, *The Man Who Shocked the World* (Boulder, Colo.: Perseus, 2004). The quotation from the letter to the National Science Foundation is from John Darley's review of the latter in the *TLS*, 10 December 2004, p. 11. For Zimbardo, see the publications list posted on his Web site, www.zimbardo.com/zimbardo.html.

19. Mark Dow, *American Gulag* (Berkeley: University of California Press, 2004); Michael Isikoff, "Brooklyn's Version of Abu Ghraib?," *Newsweek*, 24 May 2004, p. 5; Vincent Schiraldi and Mark Soler, "Locked Up Too Tight," *WP*, 19 September 2004, p. B5; Alan Elsner, "Terror Cells," *WP*, 9 May 2004, p. D1; and Jonathan Cohn, "America's Abu Ghraibs," *New Republic*, 24 May 2004.

20. Katharine Q. Seelye, "Troubled Ohio Region Turns Deaf Ear to Kerry," *IHT*, 7 September 2004, p. 4.

21. Jennifer Lee, "Students with Gadgets a Hang-up for Teachers," *IHT*, 17–18 August 2002, p. 1 (from the *NYT*); and Matt Gouras, "Honor Roll Is Suspended in Nashville," *WP*, 25 January 2004, p. A13.

22. "$40,000 Library Mural Misspells Names," posted 7 October 2004 at http://story.news.yahoo.com

23. Louis Menand, "The Unpolitical Animal," *NY*, 30 August 2004, pp. 92 and 94; David Mindich, "Dude, Where's Your Newspaper?," *CHE/Chronicle Review*, 8 October 2004, p. B5 (citing a Roper survey); Tamar Lewin, "Writing in Schools Is Found Both Dismal and Neglected," *NYT*, 26 April 2003, p. A13; Carlin Romano, "Who Killed Literary Reading?," *CHE/Chronicle Review*, 23 July 2004, p. B13 (from the National Endowment for the Arts report "Reading at Risk"); Andrew Solomon, "The Closing of the American Book," *IHT*, 17–18 July 2004, p. 5. Data on number of senators and so on are from a 1997 survey conducted by the National Constitution Center in Philadelphia (www.constitutioncenter.org); Cicero quoted by Lewis Lapham in "The Simple Life," *Harper's*, December 2005, p. 9.

24. Stephen Kinzer, "America Yawns at Foreign Fiction," *NYT*, 26 July 2003.

25. Patricia Williams, "Wonderland," *The Nation*, 18 October 2004, p. 10.

26. Michael Mann, *Incoherent Empire* (London: Verso, 2003), p. 102.

27. Gerald Celente quoted by Mark Hertsgaard in *The Eagle's Shadow* (New York: Farrar, Straus and Giroux, 2002); review of McKibben by Timothy Hilliard, posted 22 July 2002 at www.amazon.com.

28. William J. Broad, "U.S. Is Losing Its Dominance in the Sciences," *NYT*, 3 May 2004, pp. A1 and 19; and Charles Murray, "Prole Models," *WSJ*, 6 February 2001.

29. Jonathan Yardley, review of *Sore Winners*, by John Powers, in *WP Book World*, 1 August 2004, p. 2; Peter Singer, *The President of Good and Evil* (New York: Dutton, 2004); and Justin A. Frank, *Bush on the Couch* (New York: Regan Books, 2004).

30. John Powers, *Sore Winners* (New York: Doubleday, 2004), p. 95. I discuss the issue of self-correcting cycles in American history in chapter 9.

31. Walter M. McDougall, *Freedom Just Around the Corner* (New York: HarperCollins, 2004), p. 15.

9. Empire Falls

1. I am omitting any discussion here of the "wishful thinking" type of argument because it is, and has been, so easily debunked. Perhaps the best example of this genre is the "communitarian" movement associated with the sociologist Amitai Etzioni (*The Spirit of Community, The New Golden Rule*), which does understand that there can be no real social change without dealing with what I have referred to as the "microcosm"—that is, the everyday values and behaviors of individual American citizens. So far, so good. But as

Etzioni's critics have pointed out, communitarian prescriptions for accomplishing this finally boil down to preaching: they are exhortatory, and as such don't have any political clout. They are, in other words, empty, not grounded in social or historical conditions as given in reality. Popular during the Reagan years and immediately thereafter, the movement seems to have petered out. For the most incisive critiques of the communitarian position, see Richard Sennett, "Drowning in Syrup," *TLS*, 7 February 1997, pp. 3–4; Otto Newman and Richard de Zoysa, "Communitarianism: The New Panacea?," *Sociological Perspectives* 40 (1997), 623–38; Steven Lukes, "The Responsive Community," *Dissent* 45, no. 2 (Spring 1998), 87–89; Robert S. Boynton, "The Everything Expert," *The Nation*, 14 July 2003; and "Communitarian Conceits," *The Economist*, 18 March 1995, pp. 16–17.

2. Anatol Lieven, *America Right or Wrong* (New York: Oxford University Press, 2004); and Geoffrey R. Stone, *Perilous Times* (New York: W. W. Norton, 2004). One could also argue that many of these pendulum swings were not so dramatic, basically contained within the orbit of American capitalism or American imperial policy. I have in many ways argued this, saying, for example, that the New Deal preserved basic economic arrangements rather than altering them, or that the Bush Jr. foreign policy program has a lot of continuity with that of President Clinton. In addition, my argument in chapter 7, that many of the tramlines of the nation's "personality" were laid down in the 1790s, would suggest that while changes can occur, they probably aren't going to be all that radical. What thus appears radical today—the decline of the United States—is really part of a process of gradual transformation, in many ways foreshadowed by structural problems that were present from the early days of the Republic.

3. Eric Foner, "Suspension of Disbelief," *The Nation*, 6 December 2004, pp. 36–38.

4. Immanuel Wallerstein, "Quo vadis America?," Commentary no. 141, 15 July 2004, Fernand Braudel Center, Binghamton University, posted at http://fbc/binghamton.edu/commentr .htm.

5. Tom Holland, *Rubicon* (London: Abacus, 2004), pp. 270–71.

6. Averil Cameron, *The Later Roman Empire* (Cambridge, Mass.: Harvard University Press, 1993), pp. 2–3; Chris Scarre, *Chronicle of the Roman Emperors* (London: Thames and Hudson, 1995), p. 221; Charles Freeman, *The Closing of the Western Mind* (London: William Heinemann, 2002), 322 (quotes from Augustine and Lactantius); Anthony Gottlieb, review of Freeman, *NYT Book Review*, 15 February 2004, p. 12.

7. Gore Vidal, *Julian* (New York: Signet, 1965), p. 431. Vidal wrote this work before and after the Kennedy assassination, and one can't help but wonder if that is whom he had in mind here.

8. Andrew J. Bacevich, *American Empire* (Cambridge, Mass.: Harvard University Press, 2002), pp. 95–96; and Chalmers Johnson, *The Sorrows of Empire* (New York: Metropolitan/ Henry Holt, 2004), pp. 255–56.

9. Alexander Cockburn, "Zombies for Kerry," *The Nation*, 13 September 2004, p. 18.

10. William Greider, "Questions for Kerry," *The Nation*, 23 February 2004, pp. 6–7; Jennifer Barrett, "Promoting the Patriot Act," *Newsweek*, 26 April 2004, posted at http://msnbc.msn.com; Jim VandeHei, "In Hindsight, Kerry Says He'd Still Vote for War," *WP*, 10 August 2004; Brian Knowlton, "Convention Opens in Shadow of 9/11," *IHT*, 31 August 2004, p. 1; Brian Knowlton, "Bush Now Vows to 'Win' War on Terror," *IHT*, 1 September 2004, p. 1; and Roger Cohen, "Bush's Momentary Shift on War Against Terror," *IHT*, 1 September 2004, p. 2.

11. Robert B. Reich, "W's Second Term," *American Prospect*, April 2004.

12. Barrett, "Promoting the Patriot Act."

13. Paul Krugman, "Ignorance Isn't Strength," *IHT*, 9–10 October 2004, p. 7; and Floyd Norris, "Kerry Failed to Connect on the Economy," *IHT*, 4 November 2004, p. 1. The lit-

erature on postmodern deception, Orwellian "newspeak," and the shift from thinking in terms of rational arguments to thinking in terms of slogans and images, is too vast for me to start citing here, but one essay the reader might find enlightening in this regard is Michael Lynch, "Who Cares About the Truth," *CHE/Chronicle Review*, 10 September 2004, pp. B6–8, which he subsequently elaborated in *True to Life: Why Truth Matters* (Cambridge, Mass.: MIT Press, 2004).

The University of Maryland survey referred to was conducted by the Program on International Policy Attitudes, in conjunction with Knowledge Networks, based in California. It also found that large percentages of Bush supporters believed he endorsed things he actually (strongly) opposed, such as the Comprehensive Nuclear Test Ban Treaty, the Kyoto Protocol, and the International Criminal Court. See Jim Lobe, "The World According to a Bush Voter," posted 21 October 2004 at www.alternet.org.

14. Todd Gitlin, *The Twilight of Common Dreams* (New York: Metropolitan/Henry Holt, 1995), p. 197; and "John Kerry for President," *The Nation*, 8 November 2004, p. 4.

15. "John Kerry for President," p. 8; Roger Cohen, "Parting Ways with Bush on the 'Character Issue,' " *IHT*, 20 October 2004, p. 2; Jane Mayer, "The Money Man," *NY*, 18 October 2004, pp. 176–89; and Louis Menand, "The Devil's Disciples," *NY*, 28 July 2003, p. 85. For more on Fritz Stern's analysis of our current situation, see also Chris Hedges, "Warning from a Student of Democracy's Collapse," posted 6 January 2005 at www .nytimes.com.

16. Simon Schama, "Onward Christian Soldiers," *GW*, 12–18 November 2004, p. 20.

17. The poll on American attitudes toward Muslims was conducted in 2004 by an independent firm at the request of the Council on American-Islamic Relations; see Omar Ahmad, "For America's Muslims, a Quest for Fairness," *IHT*, 19 November 2004, p. 8. Also relevant to this discussion is David Glenn, "On Death and Voting," *CHE*, 8 October 2004, pp. A14–16. For neocon literature, see, for example, Robert D. Kaplan, "Supremacy by Stealth," *Atlantic Monthly*, July–August 2003, pp. 66–79; and Norman Podhoretz, "World War IV: How It Started, What It Means, and Why We Have to Win," *Commentary*, September 2004.

18. The strip ran on 11 October 2004; see www.ucomics.com.

19. John Micklethwait and Adrian Wooldridge, *The Right Nation* (New York: Penguin, 2004).

20. Emmanuel Todd, *After the Empire*, trans. C. Jon Delogu (New York: Columbia University Press, 2003), pp. xxi–xxii, 14–15, 63–68, 98, and 197; Lester C. Thurow, *Fortune Favors the Bold* (New York: HarperBusiness, 2003); Neil Henderson, "Economists Warn of Dollar Slump as US Trade Gap Widens by $55 Billion," *GW*, 20–26 August 2004, p. 7; Gautam Adhikari, "The End of the Unipolar Myth," *IHT*, 27 September 2004, p. 6; William Greider, "The Serpent That Ate America's Lunch," *The Nation*, 10 May 2004, pp. 11–18; and Jeremy Rifkin, *The European Dream* (New York: Tarcher/Penguin, 2004), p. 64.

21. Will Hutton, "The American Prosperity Myth," *The Nation*, 1–8 September 2003, p. 22; "A Failed Presidency," *The Nation*, 13 September 2004, p. 3; Todd, *After the Empire*, p. 99; Rifkin, *European Dream*, pp. 64, 67, and 70; Parag Khanna, "The Metrosexual Superpower," *Foreign Policy*, July–August 2004; David J. Rothkopf, "Just As Scary As Terror," *WP*, 25 July 2004, pp. B1 and 3 (2003 investment data cited by Rothkopf came from a report from the Organization for Economic Cooperation and Development).

22. Johnson, *Sorrows*, p. 82; and Michael Lind, foreword to Todd, *After the Empire*, p. xi. Brzezinski is quoted in Adhikari, "End of the Unipolar Myth."

23. Jane Perlez, "Weary of U.S. Anxieties, Asia Warms to China's Vigor," *IHT*, 4 December 2003, pp. 1 and 4, and her "China's Political Strength Grows, Powered by Trade," *IHT*, 28–29 August 2004, p. 1 (both from *NYT*); Paul Keating, "The American Era Is Ending.

The Asian Century Is Dawning," *The Age* (Melbourne), 16 October 2003, p. 13; John Watts, "China Takes to the Capitalist Road," *GW*, 21–27 August 2003, p. 10; John Gittings, "China Joins Long March of Capitalism," *GW*, 14–20 November 2002, p. 4; Daniel Altman, "The China Question: Catch Up or Surpass?," *IHT*, 30–31 October 2004, p. 14; and Will Hutton, "Welcome to the Great Mall of China," *GW*, 13–19 May 2004, p. 12.

24. Ross Terrill, *The New Chinese Empire* (New York: Basic Books, 2004); Seth Kaplan, "China's Boom Leaves Many Behind," *IHT*, 26 March 2004, p. 7; Yilu Zhao, "Class Division Takes on New Form," *IHT*, 2 March 2004, p. 2; Jim Yardley, "An Explosion of Beggars in China," *IHT*, 8 April 2004, p. 1; Jonathan Watts, "China Admits First Rise in Poverty Since 1978," *GW*, 23–29 July 2004, p. 1; Philip J. Cunningham, "Man Versus Machine on Beijing's Streets," *IHT*, 3 August 2004, p. 7; and Joseph Kahn and Jim Yardley, "In China's Boom, $80 Debt Ends in a Student's Suicide," *IHT*, 2 August 2004, p. 1. Also relevant is Joseph Cohen, "China's Elite Learn to Flaunt It While the New Landless Weep," *NYT*, 25 December 2004, pp. A1 and C4; and the entire series entitled "The Great Divide," posted at www.nytimes.com/world.

25. Jianying Zha, *China Pop* (New York: New Press, 1996); Carl Goldstein, "Wal-Mart in China," *The Nation*, 8 December 2003, pp. 7 and 10; Gittings, "China Joins Long March of Capitalism"; Jim Yardley, "The Right to Beauty, Though Not a Birthright," *IHT*, 18 June 2004, p. 2; David Barboza, "China's Market Revolution," *IHT*, 7 March 2003, p. 1; Keating, "The American Era"; and Watts, "China Takes to the Capitalist Road."

26. Cunningham, "Man Versus Machine"; Peter James Froning, *Letter from China* (Bloomington Ind.: First Books, 2002), p. 181; and Isabel Hilton, "Long Way from a Global Power," *GW*, 19–25 November 2004, p. 6. For a discussion of Chinese attitudes toward public space, see Devan Sudjic, *The Edifice Complex: How the Rich and Powerful Shape the World* (New York: Penguin Press, 2005).

27. Rifkin, *European Dream*, pp. 45, 61, 66, and 68; Katrin Bennhold, "France-China Deals Awaken Europeans," *IHT*, 11 October 2004, p. 1; Richard Bernstein, "Chirac Bends to China, Keeping Gaullist Legacy," *IHT*, 15 October 2004, p. 2; and Khanna, "Metrosexual Superpower." For a detailed argument for European economic superiority, see T. R. Reid, *The United States of Europe* (New York: Penguin, 2004), and also the sharp critique of same by James Harding in "Both Sides Now," *WP Book World*, 9 January 2005, p. 4.

28. Khanna, "Metrosexual Superpower"; Craig S. Smith, "EU Military to Get a Home Base," *IHT*, 3 September 2003, p. 1; and Alan Riding, "A Call on Europe to Rearm," *IHT*, 19 July 2003, p. 22.

29. Khanna, "Metrosexual Superpower"; and Jennifer Joan Lee, "Europe Lures Students Once Bound for U.S.," *IHT*, 19 October 2004, p. 9.

30. Niall Ferguson, "A World Without Power," *Foreign Policy*, July–August 2004, p. 34; Richard Bernstein, "An Aging Europe May Find Itself on the Sidelines," *NYT*, 29 June 2003, p. 3; Carter Dougherty, "Sluggish Growth Projected for Germany," *IHT*, 20 October 2004, p. 11; and Katrin Bennhold, "France Headed for Stagnation, Report Warns," *IHT*, 20 October 2004, p. 14.

31. Robert Kagan, "Power and Weakness," *Policy Review*, June–July 2002, pp. 3–28; Robert Kagan, *Of Paradise and Power* (New York: Alfred A. Knopf, 2003); and Nicholas von Hoffman, *Hoax* (New York: Nation Books, 2004), p. 163.

32. Carl Honoré, *In Praise of Slowness* (San Francisco: HarperSanFrancisco, 2004), pp. 71–72, 75, and 88.

33. Ibid., pp. 159–60 and 164; Richard Bernstein, "Germans see Leisure as a Right," *IHT*, 3 July 2004, p. 4; and Craig S. Smith, "A Slacker's Manifesto Sells Briskly in France," *IHT*, 17 August 2004, p. 2 (quote from Maier in this article).

34. Peter Meiskins and Peter Whalley, "Should Europe Work More, or America Less?," *IHT*, 11 August 2004, p. 6; and Katrin Bennhold, "Continent Guards Its Right to Leisure," *IHT*, 19 July 2004, p. 1.

35. Joan McQueeney Mitric, "To Find a City's Soul, Take a Walk in its Parks," *IHT*, 24 September 2004, p. 7.

36. Rifkin, *European Dream*, pp. 59, 379, and *passim*; "Bowing to Bad Times, German Shopkeepers Extend Hours," *IHT*, 9 June 2003, p. 9; Mark Landler, "Schröder Speeds Up Sweeping Tax Cuts," *IHT*, 30 June 2003, p. 1; "Former Ally Faults Schröder," *IHT*, 9 August 2004, p. 3; "With Criticism Rising, Schröder Warns Against Party Division," *IHT*, 15 March 2004, p. 2; "Germans Rally to Protest Cuts in Welfare," *IHT*, 17 August 2004, p. 3; Eric Sylvers, "In Italy, a Way of Life Is Threatened," *IHT*, 20 August 2003, pp. 1 and 8; Elaine Sciolino, "French Approve Law to Delay Full Pensions," *IHT*, 25 July 2003, p. 5; "150,000 in Amsterdam Reject Plan to Cut Benefits," *IHT*, 4 October 2004, p. 3; Katrin Bennhold, "Shorter Workweek Gets a Second Look," *IHT*, 30 July 2004, pp. 1 and 5; and Thomas Fuller, "EU 'Opens the Door' to a Longer Workday," *IHT*, 23 September 2004, p. 1. The increase of the German workweek was also reported on the BBC World News, 24 August 2004.

37. Doug Saunders, "'European Dream' Relies on Immigrant Workers' Nightmares," posted at www.globeandmail.com on 4 September 2004.

38. Sophie Arie, "Italians Answer Call of Lonely Professor," *GW*, 24–30 September 2004, p. 11.

39. Alan Riding, "Thinkers Down and Out in Paris and London," *IHT*, 14 October 2004, p. 2.

40. Roger Cohen, "To Understand France, Look Around Its Villages," *IHT*, 14–15 August 2004, p. 2.

41. Benoît Duteurtre, *Le voyage en France* (Paris: Gallimard, 2001), especially pp. 53, 142, 206–9, 268, 277, and 285–89; my translation.

42. Ibid., p. 290.

43. Bob Herbert, "White House Echo Chamber," *IHT*, 20–21 November 2004, p. 7 (from *NYT*).

44. Michael J. Ybarra, *Washington Gone Crazy* (Hanover, N.H.: Steerforth Press, 2004), and the review by David Greenberg, "Nativist Son," *NYT Book Review*, 31 October 2004, pp. 8–9.

45. Thomas de Zengotita, "Common Ground," *Harper's Magazine*, January 2003, p. 44.

Index

About the Author

A CULTURAL HISTORIAN and social critic, Morris Berman has taught at a number of universities in Europe and North America, and has held visiting endowed chairs at Incarnate Word College (San Antonio), the University of New Mexico, and Weber State University. Between 1982 and 1988 he was the Lansdowne Professor in the History of Science at the University of Victoria, British Columbia. Berman won the Governor's Writers Award for Washington State in 1990, and was the first recipient of the annual Rollo May Center Grant for Humanistic Studies in 1992. He is the author of a trilogy on the evolution of human consciousness—*The Reenchantment of the World* (1981), *Coming to Our Senses* (1989), and *Wandering God: A Study in Nomadic Spirituality* (2000)—and in 2000 his *Twilight of American Culture* was named a Notable Book by the *New York Times Book Review*. Berman has done numerous radio and television interviews in Europe, the United States, and Asia, and in recent years has lectured in Australia, Colombia, Germany, Mexico, and New Zealand. Since 2003 he has been a Visiting Professor in Sociology at the Catholic University of America in Washington, D.C.